LIVING FOR THE CITY

The John Hope Franklin Series in
African American History and Culture

Waldo E. Martin Jr. and Patricia Sullivan, editors

LIVING FOR THE CITY

Migration, Education, and the Rise of the Black Panther Party in Oakland, California

DONNA JEAN MURCH

THE UNIVERSITY OF NORTH CAROLINA PRESS CHAPEL HILL

Set in Arno Pro
Manufactured in the United States of America

The paper in this book meets the guidelines for permanence
and durability of the Committee on Production Guidelines for
Book Longevity of the Council on Library Resources.

The University of North Carolina Press has been a member
of the Green Press Initiative since 2003.

LIBRARY OF CONGRESS CATALOGING-IN-PUBLICATION DATA

Murch, Donna Jean.
    Living for the city : migration, education, and the rise of the Black
    Panther Party in Oakland, California / Donna Jean Murch.
        p. cm. — (The John Hope Franklin series in African American history
    and culture)
    Includes bibliographical references and index.
    ISBN 978-0-8078-3376-6 (cloth : alk. paper)
    ISBN 978-0-8078-7113-3 (pbk. : alk. paper)
    1. African Americans—California—Oakland—Politics and govern-
ment—20th century. 2. African Americans—California—Oakland—
Social conditions—20th century. 3. African Americans—Southern States—
Migrations—History—20th century. 4. African Americans—Education
(Higher)—California—History—20th century. 5. Education, Higher—
California—History—20th century. 6. Black Panther Party—History.
7. Oakland (Calif.)—Social conditions—20th century. 8. Oakland
(Calif.)—Ethnic relations. I. Title.
    F869.02M87 2010
    322.4'20979466—dc22   2010013694

Portions of this work have appeared previously, in somewhat different form,
in "The Campus and the Street: Race, Migration, and the Origins of the Black
Panther Party in Oakland, CA," Souls 9, no.4 (October 2007): 333–45, and are
reprinted here with permission.

cloth   14 13 12 11 10   5 4 3 2 1
paper   14 13 12 11 10   5 4 3 2 1

For Betty Jean

CONTENTS

Acknowledgments xi

Abbreviations xiii

Introduction 3

PART I. CITY OF MIGRANTS, 1940–1960

1. Canaan Bound 15

2. Fortress California 41

PART II. THE CAMPUS AND THE STREET, 1961–1966

3. We Care Enough to Tell It 71

4. A Campus Where Black Power Won 97

PART III. BLACK POWER AND URBAN MOVEMENT, 1966–1982

5. Men with Guns 119

6. Survival Pending Revolution 169

7. A Chicken in Every Bag 191

Conclusion 229

Notes 237

Bibliography 277

Index 305

MAPS AND ILLUSTRATIONS

MAPS

African American Population Increase in Berkeley
and Oakland, 1940–1980 2

Oakland and Berkeley, 1940–1960 14

Oakland and Berkeley, 1960–1970 70

Oakland and Berkeley, 1966–1982 118

ILLUSTRATIONS

Walter Newton and Lee Edward Newton, 1941 21

Fraternal organization at DeFremery Park, 1950s 23

Anne Williams and Henry Dalton Williams, 1945 43

Girls learning the proper etiquette for drinking tea, 1950s 62

Oakland mayor Clifford Rischell and African American
assemblyman W. Byron Rumford greet black debutantes, 1950s 63

Donald Warden "street speaking," 1962 91

Merritt College 101

"Dignity Clothes" Afro-American Association
manufacturing facility 107

Anne Williams, 1963 110

Black Panther carrying books, 1968 114

Ten Point Program, 1966 128

"What Is A Pig?" by Emory Douglas, 1967 136

"Just Wait" by Emory Douglas, 1970 138

Black Panther guards at "Free Huey" rally, 1968 140

Black Panthers in Marin City, California, 1968 141

"Bootlickers Gallery," by Emory Douglas, ca. 1968 150

Kathleen Cleaver addresses the congregation at the
    Unitarian Church, San Rafael, California, 1968 152

"It's All the Same," by Douglas Emory, 1968 153

"Get out of the Ghetto," by Emory Douglas, 1970 154

"Hallelujah," by Emory Douglas, 1971 156

"Free Huey" rally, 1968 158

Audience listening to Eldridge Cleaver speak at the
    University of California, Berkeley, 1968 159

"Sure Glad You White Delegates Could Come,"
    COINTELPRO drawing, 1969 161

Black Panther feeding his son, "Free Huey" rally, 1968 170

Father Earl A. Neil, pastor of St. Augustine's Episcopal
    Church, 1968 173

Black Panthers from Sacramento, "Free Huey" rally, 1968 177

Children of Party members attending class in the
    Intercommunal Youth Institute, 1971 181

Women participating in the People's Free Food Program,
    Palo Alto, California, 1972 201

Bobby Seale's campaign car during the BPP mayoral
    campaign in Oakland, 1973 207

Bobby Seale campaigns on a city bus, Oakland, 1973 208

"Ants in My Pants Dance," electoral campaign flyer,
    Oakland, 1973 213

Bobby Seale speaks at the Black Community Survival
    Conference, Oakland, 1972 225

Huey P. Newton in the Alameda County Courthouse jail, 1968 231

ACKNOWLEDGMENTS

Living for the City is a history that could never have been written without the generosity of a whole community of people in Oakland and the East Bay. Their words and insights have informed every aspect of this study, and it is to both them and my parents that this work is dedicated. The love and support of many different groups of people made the completion of this book possible. The Department of History at Rutgers, the State University of New Jersey, the Department of History at the University of California at Berkeley, the Woodrow Wilson Foundation, the Mellon Mays Undergraduate Fellowship Program, and the American Institute for History Education provided invaluable financial and scholarly resources. The vibrant intellectual culture of Rutgers faculty and students has made writing not only possible, but pleasurable. Deborah Gray White has been a wonderful mentor, whose careful reading and commentary on multiple drafts of the manuscript have been nothing short of remarkable. Her brilliance as scholar and teacher provides a continuing source of inspiration. Similarly, Muhammad Ahmad, Mia Bay, Rudy Bell, Carolyn Brown, Natalie Byfield, Paul Clemens, Sue Cobble, Venus Green, James Gregory, Nancy Hewitt, Donald Hopkins, Hasan Jeffries, Peniel Joseph, Temma Kaplan, Steven Lawson, Khalid Mendani, Tony Platt, Beryl Satter, and Heather Thompson offered detailed and thoughtful feedback over the past five years. Ernest Allen's encyclopedic recall and wide-ranging knowledge of Black radicalism has shaped this project from its inception. I would also like to thank Rutgers history and political science librarian Thomas Glynn and research assistants Jason Gaylord, Chris Hayes, Melissa Hampton, Robin Mitchell, Keith Orejel, Stephanie Rogers, Ben Twagira, and Shannen Williams.

At the University of California, Berkeley, Professor Waldo Martin offered steady guidance and patience during the early stages of research, while Kerwin Klein has encouraged me to write about the things I cared about most. Robert Allen, Judith Butler, Kaja Silverman, Robert Chrisman, Robin Einhorn, Charles Henry, Percy Hintzen, Leon Litwack, Michael Rogin, and Ula Taylor contributed much to my intellectual development. Steven Lavoie,

Don Hausler, Kerry Taylor, and Nadine Wilmot kindly shared their insight and original research with me. Yohuru Williams and Komozi Woodard read the original manuscript for the University of North Carolina Press and offered advice that has made this a much better book. Chuck Grench has been a wonderful editor and a perfect fit.

A number of individuals, libraries, and repositories made crucial oral history, photographic, and archival materials available to me. I would like to thank Billy Jennings for opening his home and sharing his amazing archival collection on the Black Panther Party and other radical organizations of the period. Professor Clayborne Carson very generously granted access to his oral research interviews, which proved essential to the completion of this study. I thank as well the Bancroft Library's Regional Oral History Office, the Ford Foundation Archive, and the Oakland History Room of the Main Library. Polaris Images, the Estate of Pirkle Jones and Ruth Marion Branch, the African American Museum and Library in Oakland, the Dr. Huey P. Newton Foundation and the Green Library at Stanford University, the Artists Rights Society, Emory Douglas, Melvin Newton, Annie Williams, and Jamila and Khalid al-Mansour generously supplied images for the book.

Finally, my greatest debt is to my friends and family. The unconditional love and support of Donald Murch, Carla Tolson, William and Marlene Martin, and Khalid Mendani helped me to endure the many years it took to complete this project. Foremost, I would like to thank my mother. From an early age, her facility with people and ideas taught me to listen carefully and to value both the said and unsaid. Although she passed away nearly two decades ago, her keen sensitivity and powers of perception inform everything I do. Finally, Art Jones's amazing talent and personal generosity have made the past years some of my most interesting and productive.

ABBREVIATIONS

AA	Associated Agencies
AAA	Afro-American Association
AFL	American Federation of Labor
AFT	American Federation of Teachers
BPP	Black Panther Party
BPPNC	Black Panther Party of Northern California
BPPSD	Black Panther Party for Self Defense
BSA	Black Student Alliance
BSCP	Brotherhood of Sleeping Car Porters
BSU	Black Student Union
CAFEPC	California Fair Employment Practice Commission
CAP	community alert patrols
CBC	Congressional Black Caucus
COINTELPRO	Counter Intelligence Program
CORE	Congress of Racial Equality
CYA	California Youth Authority
DSC	Democratic Select Committee
FBI	Federal Bureau of Investigation
FEPC	Fair Employment Practices Commission
HBCUS	historically black colleges and universities
HUAC	House Un-American Activities Committee
IYI	Intercommunal Youth Institute
LAPD	Los Angeles Police Department
LCFO	Lowndes County Freedom Organization (Alabama)
NAACP	National Association for the Advancement of Colored People
NOI	Nation of Islam

OCS	Oakland Community School
ODAC	Oakland Direct Action Committee
OPD	Oakland Police Department
ORD	Oakland Recreation Department
PFP	Peace and Freedom Party
RAM	Revolutionary Action Movement
SAC	special agent in charge
SCLC	Southern Christian Leadership Conference
SCTC	Student Committee for Travel to Cuba
SNCC	Student Nonviolent Coordinating Committee
SSAC	Soul Students Advisory Council
UCLA	University of California at Los Angeles
UN	United Nations
WOPC	West Oakland Planning Committee

LIVING FOR THE CITY

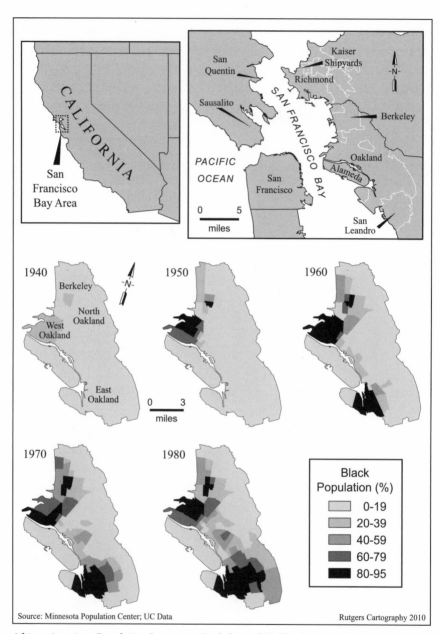

Source: Minnesota Population Center; UC Data

Rutgers Cartography 2010

African American Population Increase in Berkeley and Oakland, 1940–1980

INTRODUCTION

Stevie Wonder's urban anthem, "Living for the City," provides both the name and inspiration for my study of Black radicalism in Oakland. Released in 1973 during the twilight of the Black Power movement, the song is a profound allegory about African American migrants' ordeals in postwar cities. Like Sam Cooke's "A Change Is Gonna Come," written nearly a decade before, the narrative arc from the rural South to the northern city laments black people's recurrent battles with racial subordination despite movement across space and time. The song opens with a "young boy born in hard times Mississippi," who journeys north to escape his parents' life of incessant work and bare subsistence. He leaves behind the close-knit world of familial "love and affection" in search of opportunity, but the color line in jobs, threats by police, and horrors of prison all transform the city of hope into a place of sorrow. Caught between the fault lines of generation and region and the destructive effects of incarceration, the young protagonist descends into confusion and hopelessness. The rapid transformation of an innocent boy into a broken man dramatizes the precarious existence of urban migrants. Sung in a distorted and muffled voice that contrasts the joyful tone of the early verses, the song's conclusion expresses the frustration and anger of thwarted possibility: "This place is cruel, nowhere could be much colder. If we don't change, the world will soon be over."

Black popular music has long expressed the social and political crises confronting African American communities in periods of transition. Placed in its historical context, "Living for the City" can be seen as a meditation on the underlying anxieties, frustrations, and material circumstances that inspired the rise of Black Power and black consciousness in the postwar years. Through verse and metaphor, Wonder narrates a cautionary tale about the dangers confronting urban youth on the threshold to adulthood for whom neither economic survival, nor the political process, offered viable solutions. As this book will show, the song's themes of southern migration, black pride,

3

the promise and peril of increased educational access, and the destructive effects of the carceral state all contributed to their radicalization. The song's driving refrain, "Living for the city . . . living just enough for the city," spoke to how migrants changed the city and how the city changed them. Out of this historic encounter emerged a new and more militant strain of black activism.

Nowhere was the historical interplay between southern migration and Black radicalism more evident than in northern California at midcentury. Prior to World War II, Oakland and other Bay Area cities had relatively small black population settlements; however, in the era that coincided with the "long civil rights movement," black newcomers transformed the region with a far-reaching impact on labor, education, policing and incarceration, and electoral politics. In addition to sweeping demographic changes, the rapid influx of southern migrants altered the internal dynamics of local African American communities. With successive waves of chain migration, California's newcomers vitalized Bay Area political culture and increasingly challenged the leadership of an older generation of residents. In the 1940s, a resurgent labor movement gained unprecedented access to jobs, and in subsequent decades, migrant youth used unconventional tactics to challenge police violence and electoral exclusion.[1]

The coupling of "migrants and militants" was by no means unique to the Bay Area. Migration laid the foundations for many radical social movements in nineteenth- and twentieth-century cities.[2] Until recently, however, southern newcomers' contributions to the Black Power movement have been obscured by scholarly and popular memory that has artificially divided the larger black freedom struggle into discreet, binary terms set against one another by ideology and region. The tendency to understand Black Power as northern, urban, and violent in contrast to a southern movement of peaceful civil disobedience has rendered the political significance of California's migrant diaspora largely invisible.[3] Combined with the failure of recent historiography to disaggregate black urban populations by age, class, gender, and migration status, this narrow conceptual frame has eclipsed the foundational influence of southern newcomers.[4] *Living for the City* challenges this orthodoxy by excavating the submerged histories of East Bay migrant communities *and* exploring why they became so integral to the local and ultimately national history of Black Power and Black radicalism.[5]

Born in the South and raised in California cities, poor and working-class youth who came of age between the lynching of Emmett Till and the assassination of Malcolm X formed the core of the Bay Area "Black Power generation." Their emerging political consciousness reflected both their collective experience as migrants *and* their age.[6] With few exceptions, adolescents and young adults formed the overwhelming majority of the participants in Black radical groups in Oakland and Berkeley. In response to both the dangers and opportunities of metropolitan California, they led in an irreverent, popular movement that mobilized a young, newcomer population that remained marginal to the existing social infrastructure of civil rights and black uplift organizations.[7] Many faced a world that their parents did not understand and responded by creating political organizations that articulated not only their grievances but their vision for a different future.[8] In the East Bay of the 1960s, a litany of Black nationalist and radical groups competed for the attention of their peers. Between 1961 and 1966, the Afro-American Association (AAA), Black Panther Party of Northern California (BPPNC), Soul Students Advisory Council (SSAC), and the West Coast branch of the Revolutionary Action Movement (RAM) all sprung up on the urban campuses of the East Bay's public colleges and universities. Composed largely of southern migrants under twenty-five, including many students recruited from local high schools and community colleges, this dense matrix of youth activism embraced a broad range of personalities and ideological tendencies.[9] Although different factions engaged in debate and even bitter conflict, nearly all shared firm moorings in the East Bay's black community and California's system of higher education.

While these early stirrings of black consciousness laid the groundwork for the West Coast Black Power movement that received its fullest expression after the Watts rebellions, the founding of Oakland's Black Panther Party for Self Defense (BPPSD) in October 1966 marked an important milestone in Bay Area radicalism. More than any other local group or organization, the Oakland BPPSD embodied the aspirations and anger of migrant youth during a period of national and international upheaval. In his autobiography, *Revolutionary Suicide*, cofounder Huey Newton situated the genesis of the Oakland Panthers within the postwar history of flight, exile, and internal migration of millions of African Americans: "The great exodus of poor people out of the South during World War II sprang from the hope for a better life in the big cities of the North and West. In search of freedom, they left behind centuries of southern cruelty and repression. . . . The Black communities of Bedford-Stuyvesant, Newark, Brownsville, Watts, Detroit and many others stand as testament that racism is as oppressive in the North as in the South. Oakland is no different."[10]

The emergence of the Black Panther Party cannot be understood without recognizing the rich culture, historical memory, and expectations that Bay Area newcomers carried with them *and* the heartfelt disappointment they suffered in Oakland and other West Coast cities. The Panthers' core leadership, as well as their rank and file, consisted of recent migrants whose families traveled north and west to escape the southern racial regime, only to be confronted with new forms of segregation and repression. The BPPSD channeled this sentiment into focused action, interpreted through the transnational lens of decolonization and state socialism sweeping the globe.[11] At the national level, the Oakland Party drew its inspiration from a rural movement in Lowndes County, Alabama, while internationally it embraced the Cuban, Vietnamese, and Chinese revolutions as its own. The left turn to Maoism and Third Worldism was a larger global phenomenon; however, in the case of Bay Area radicalism, these allegiances also reflected the immediate past of northern California's black communities. With its overwhelming numbers of southern-born residents, black California was in many ways a coastal extension of the South. For West Coast migrants, less than a generation removed from southern agrarian struggles, Maoism and land-based insurgencies held a special appeal. The militant symbol of the Lowndes County panther signified not only the BPP's advocacy of armed self-defense but the continuities between migrants' southern, rural past and their urban present.[12]

Although *Living for the City* traces the Black Panther Party's rise and fall, internal development, and expansion beyond Oakland, its primary focus lies elsewhere.[13] Exploring the social origins of the BPP provides a window onto the radical intellectual and political movement that spanned black Oakland and the East Bay in the decades after World War II. By the spring of 1967, the Panthers' ability to draw press coverage with poignant spectacles like the March on Sacramento transformed the local group into a national sensation. From its inception, however, the BPP remained part of a larger culture of Black radicalism that included a variety of Bay Area activists and organizations. In the face of social crisis and police violence, the most disfranchised sectors of the African American community—young, poor, and migrant—challenged the legitimacy of state authorities and of the established black leadership. Through excavating this hidden history, *Living for the City* broadens the scholarship of the Black Power movement by moving beyond the celebrated and widely published national intellectuals to consider the contributions of black students and youth on the West Coast who created new forms of organization, grassroots mobilization, and political literacy.[14]

When looked at in hindsight, the accomplishments of the BPP and the

Bay Area Black Power generation were remarkable. Within less than a generation, migrant communities drawn to the Bay Area by federal defense industries gave birth to one of the most powerful antistatist movements of the postwar era. Study groups, street speaking, and police patrols became important means to disseminate ideas and to cultivate new registers of black consciousness. Youth groups worked to translate complex ideologies into popular forms with widespread appeal. Whether it was Afro-American Association cofounder Donald Warden's mastery of Pentecostal sermonizing or the Black Panther Party's symbolic invocation of the "pig," vernacular forms rooted in black southern idiom became essential to building popular support.[15] In his autobiography, BPP chief of staff David Hilliard, who had been born in Rockville, Alabama, and migrated to Oakland at age ten, recalled how the southern black diaspora inspired young Panthers' activism: "When I think about the influences that inspired the spirit and work of the Black Panther Party—many of which are still not understood—this culture figures large among them. Many of the most important members of the Party—people like John and Bobby Seale and Geronimo Pratt, Bobby Rush and Fred Hampton—were imbued with the moral and spiritual values of their parents; and the work that went into the Party, our dignity as an independent people, the communal ideal and practice that informed our programs, all stem in part from the civilization of which my mother and father were so representative a part."[16]

Bay Area Black radicalism was inextricably linked not only with the region's expansive southern diaspora but also with the thick network of public universities and colleges that crisscrossed the metropolitan area. Alienation from local schools, harassment by police, and growing incarceration prompted migrant youth to develop critiques of the existing order, and urban campuses became incubators of radical ideas. As first- and second-generation migrants came of age, many enrolled in community colleges and state universities and became active politically. The expanding reach of California's system of higher education helped make this possible. In the early 1960s, the state's Master Plan for Higher Education codified and extended the state's tripartite system of junior colleges, state universities, and elite "multiversities," by promising all residents with high school diplomas access to college or university tuition free. State efforts at liberal social engineering did not focus on African Americans, or even include them, in their policy calculus. Quite the contrary, social planners sought to realize California's own vision of growth liberalism that understood public education as essential to economic development and national defense. Nevertheless, the

California Master Plan and the new era of higher education it inaugurated had a profound if unintended effect on black residents.[17] The state's flagship system of public universities combined with the burgeoning black liberation movement led to unprecedented numbers of African American youth attending college for the first time. By 1969, the San Francisco Bay Area and Los Angeles had the highest rate of college attendance among youth of color in the United States' major metropolitan areas.[18]

More than any other college or university in northern California—including the much better known San Francisco State—Oakland City College (renamed Merritt in 1964) exemplified how the opening up of higher education nurtured a new generation of black activists and electoral politicians.[19] In addition to BPP founders Huey Newton and Bobby Seale, future Oakland city councilman Leo Bazille and Congressman Ronald Dellums attended Merritt and participated in its vibrant student culture.[20] With its proximity to U.C. Berkeley and its firm moorings in rapidly expanding black population settlements in northwest Oakland, Merritt laid the groundwork for the Black Power movement that emerged later in the decade. Agitation for Black Studies courses and debates about the "relevance" of education became essential to mobilizing African American youth. The decision to change rather than adapt to majority white institutions represented an important step in the development of antiassimilationism that undergirded Black Power ideology.[21] Student protest assumed a variety of forms, some of which intersected directly with campus-based struggles for inclusion, while others used California's three-tiered system of higher education as a base from which to enter urban politics. Campaigns to transform curriculum and hiring practices forged new social networks, a blending of Marxist and nationalist discourses, and ultimately a strategy of armed self-defense that later animated the Panthers and other tendencies of the local Black Power movement. As Leo Bazille explained, "All of this was sandbox politics, that prepared us for the larger sandbox called Oakland." This was true not only for personalities that became well-known in the late sixties but for the fluid group of East Bay youth who moved between the Afro-American Association, the Merritt Black Studies movement, and the handful of radical groups that coalesced in their wake.[22]

Louisiana migrant Anne Williams and her circle of friends from West Oakland's "Lower Bottom" were raised in the protected familiarity of the church and home. However, when she enrolled in Oakland City College in the early sixties, the school's thriving political culture came as a revelation. As Williams moved beyond the circumscribed world of her childhood, the meetings of the Afro-American Association and the stirrings of a loose set of ideas—that later crystallized under the heading "Black Power"—redefined the world she had known. In the same way that the Pentecostal church offered her parents a culture of affirmation in the face of Jim Crow, study groups and their debates about black consciousness addressed her generation's search for transcendent meaning. Attending Merritt and participating in the Afro-American Association and the Student Committee for Travel to Cuba (SCTC) fundamentally changed her self-concept by integrating her personal and familial history into transnational struggles for freedom, justice, and black liberation. Williams's experience was not an isolated one, and many of her contemporaries shared similar recollections.[23] Surprisingly, recent scholarship has largely overlooked this earlier period of black awakening on East Bay campuses. By reconstructing its history, *Living for the City* offers a new tale of origins for the Black Panther Party.[24] In the early sixties, campus activism at Merritt and U.C. Berkeley laid the foundations for the BPP by channeling the diffuse anger and entropy of young migrants into study groups and protests for curricular reform. In the aftermath of the Watts rebellions, these social networks—and the radical ideology they engendered—gave birth to the BPP and other tendencies in the California Black Power movement.[25]

The Panther Party's success in mobilizing large numbers of Bay Area youth reflected its ability to identify and redress their most immediate concerns. Paramount among these was the persistent threat of police violence. As white residents and municipal authorities reacted to the rapidly growing migrant population with hostility, black children and adolescents confronted an increasingly brutal state apparatus.[26] As for Stevie Wonder's anonymous protagonist, potential harassment, arrest, and unjust incarceration represented the most perilous aspect of urban life for many newcomers. In Oakland, "the police . . . were really the government," Newton remembered. "We had more contact with the police than we did the city council."[27] The Party responded by assembling armed patrols that challenged abuses by law enforcement. Its eclectic appeal combined youthful bravado, campus radicalism, and an irreverent use of the vernacular. Black nationalist and leftist ideology, blended with southern communities' long-standing faith in armed self-defense, education, and parallel institutions, inspired a range of strategies to confront the government violence and neglect migrant families suffered in the postwar era.[28]

Police patrols represented only the initial phase of the Party's activism, and by the close of the decade, the Bay Area BPP moved away from spectacular confrontations with law enforcement to more direct forms of grassroots organizing. While constant crisis marked the Party's first years, after 1968 the BPP revitalized its membership through setting up alternatives to state services. With the establishment of the Party's first breakfast programs, liberation schools, and regular publication of the *Black Panther* newspaper, the BPP expanded its base to include larger numbers of women, children, and older residents. Political education, which Huey Newton and Bobby Seale embraced from the beginning, provided a framework for the Panthers' wide-ranging efforts. By ministering to basic needs for food, shelter, education, and health care, the BPP highlighted the shortfalls of state welfare and its failure to remedy urban poverty. In a striking reversal from the Party's earlier militancy, during this later era of "survival pending revolution," the Panthers worked together with local churches and civil rights groups to launch a series of municipal campaigns that registered thousands of new black voters. In less than a decade after its founding, the revolutionary nationalist party traveled full circle from its youthful, migrant roots to become a power broker in local politics.

. . .

IN THE PAGES that follow, a complex and surprising tale unfolds that brings together recent newcomers from the South, the opportunities and constraints of postwar California, and a bold movement of black youth. This is a story of origins familiar and unfamiliar. Several generations of journalists, academics, and filmmakers have recounted the dramatic rise and fall of the Black Panther Party, but few have considered the importance of southern migration or public education to its genesis.[29] Differences of interpretation between this study and its predecessors lie not only in conception but also in sources. Without the words and insights of the participants, *Living for the City* could never have been written.

In contrast to earlier monographs on postwar black politics that take individual civil rights organizations or Great Society programs as their point of entry, *Living for the City* began with oral histories of Black Power activists themselves. From their accounts, I worked backward to unearth a largely forgotten history that has left behind few archival traces. Consequently, my study diverges from much of the governing wisdom of postwar scholarship that understands Black Power primarily as the product of liberal defeat. This history is not one I looked for, but rather one I found, not through telling, but through listening, and I am deeply indebted to the numerous people who shared both their stories and analysis.[30]

Although *Living for the City* does not spend extensive time in the rural

South, it draws on an exciting new body of literature revising that region's history. This scholarship has reoriented the story of Black radicalism—and, in the broadest sense, black modernism—from its largely northern, urban focus.[31] In many writings about the city, rural populations have long been associated with backwardness, poverty, ignorance, and especially in the North American case, social pathology. Dystopic images of overcrowded slums and broken families suffused portraits of black migration, with new-comers representing the antithesis of all that is forward looking, modern, and progressive.[32] *Living for the City* turns this image on its head by showing how African American migrants to northern California became the van-guard of a radical urban social movement that critiqued state violence, agi-tated for "relevant" education, and demanded the immediate redistribution of wealth. Drawing on long-standing strategies for survival, migrant youth mobilized large segments of Bay Area black communities by integrating the shared memory of a southern, rural past with the possibilities of the urban present.

PART ONE
CITY OF MIGRANTS, 1940–1960

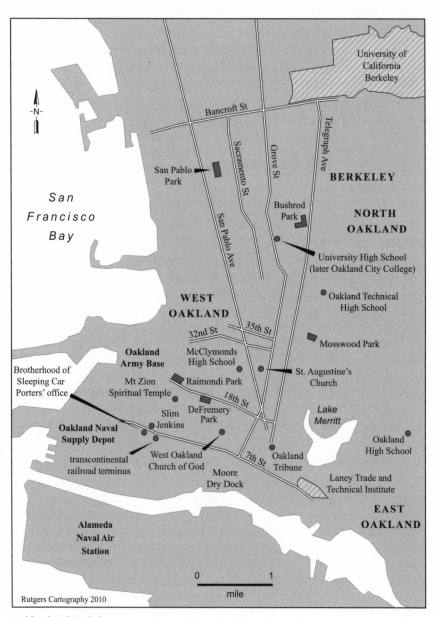

University of
California
Berkeley

Bancroft St

San Pablo
Park

Sacramento St

Grove St

Telegraph Ave

BERKELEY

San
Francisco
Bay

San Pablo Ave

Bushrod
Park

**NORTH
OAKLAND**

University High School
(later Oakland City College)

Oakland Technical
High School

**WEST
OAKLAND**

32nd St

35th St

Mosswood Park

**Oakland
Army Base**

McClymonds
High School

St. Augustine's
Church

Brotherhood of
Sleeping Car
Porters' office

Mt Zion
Spiritual Temple

Raimondi Park

18th St

*Lake
Merritt*

Slim
Jenkins

DeFremery
Park

**Oakland Naval
Supply Depot**

Oakland
High School

transcontinental
railroad terminus

West Oakland
Church of God

7th St

Oakland
Tribune

Moore
Dry Dock

Laney Trade and
Technical Institute

**Alameda
Naval Air
Station**

**EAST
OAKLAND**

0   1

mile

Rutgers Cartography 2010

Oakland and Berkeley, 1940–1960

1. CANAAN BOUND

In 1948, Harry Haywood wrote, "The Negro Question is agrarian in origin. . . . It presents the curious anomaly of a virtual serfdom in the very heart of the most highly industrialized country in the world."[1] World War II and the advent of the mechanical cotton picker resolved this contradiction by spurring the single largest black population movement in U.S. history. In the three decades following the economic collapse of the 1930s, African Americans who had been tethered to the land at near subsistence abandoned their rural moorings by relocating to cities. The 1950 census documented that in the past ten years "more persons moved from rural to urban areas than in any previous decade."[2] In an ever-expanding tide, migrants poured out of the South in pursuit of rising wages and living standards promised by major metropolitan areas. In 1940, 77 percent of the total black population lived in the South with over 49 percent in rural areas; two out of five worked as farmers, sharecroppers or farm laborers. In the next ten years over 1.6 million people migrated north and westward, to be followed by another 1.5 million in the subsequent decade.[3] Large-scale proletarianization accompanied this mass urbanization as migrants sought work in defense industries. The rate of socioeconomic change was remarkable. By 1970, more than half of the African American population settled outside the South with over 75 percent residing in cities. In less than a quarter century, urban became synonymous with "black."[4]

The repercussions of this internal migration extended throughout the United States leaving their deepest imprint on West Coast cities that historically possessed the smallest black populations. California boasted the largest increase of nineteen western states; a steady influx of newcomers poured into urban centers from San Diego to Marin City. During World War II, lucrative defense jobs made the "Golden State" a prime destination for southern migrants. Sociologist Charles Johnson explained, "To the romantic appeal of the west, has been added the real and actual opportunity for gainful employment, setting in motion a war-time migration of huge pro-portions."[5] Throughout the Pacific Coast, a syncretic relationship emerged between war industries and black migration; new settlements bloomed on the edges of military installations and defense plants. By 1943, the San Fran-cisco Chamber of Commerce declared the Bay Area "the largest shipbuild-ing center in the world."[6] With a dense ring of war industries surrounding the city, including Richmond's Kaiser shipyards to the north, Moore Dry Dock to the south, and an expansive new army base just east of the Bay Bridge, Oakland's black population mushroomed from 8,462 residents in 1940 (3 percent) to 47,562 in 1950 (12 percent). In less than a decade, the number of black residents increased over 500 percent.[7] A pattern of chain migration continued until by 1980 Oakland reached the racial tipping point with a black population of 157,484 (51 percent), over half of the city's total.[8] The resulting shift in demography secured its position as the largest black metropolis in northern California, second in the state only to Los Angeles in the numbers of African Americans.

In wartime and after, the East Bay's southern diaspora permeated every aspect of urban life. Industrial development, housing, police community re-lations, local government, and, especially, education became sites of conflict and contestation with long-standing residents. Scholars have amply docu-mented how black migration provoked white flight; however, this repre-sents only one part of the larger story of urban transformation. The influx of southern migrants profoundly altered the social organization of northern California's African American communities, ultimately laying the ground-work for their political mobilization in subsequent decades. Migrants, ini-tially branded as unwelcome "newcomers," quickly subsumed the small pre-war population into their quest for political access, a higher living standard, and in the case of the fortunate few, upward mobility. While Oakland's small black community fought for greater social and economic access prior to the war, these struggles vastly intensified in its wake. New social cleav-ages emerged based on the timing of arrival as well as between the groups able to realize the opportunity the San Francisco Bay Area afforded and those excluded from decent jobs, housing, and education.

Federal defense industries and the transformation of southern agricul-ture spurred the second wave of the Great Migration, resulting in black mi-grants' first of many fights for inclusion. While this mid-twentieth-century population exodus shared many similarities with its predecessor, it also had significant differences. One of the most important was the opening up of "a new migration geography" that connected Texas, Louisiana, and Arkansas to the Pacific Coast.[9] The increased role of the federal government in California's economy laid the foundation for this massive redistribution of population. West Coast cities first assumed their "metropolitan-military" character during the Progressive Era, but in the San Francisco Bay Area the strong link between defense and the local economy did not emerge until the late 1930s.[10] By the end of World War II, the federal government had become the largest public employer in the Bay Area, exceeding the number of jobs in California state and local government combined.[11] With the help of the National Association for the Advancement of Colored People (NAACP) and the West Coast branch of the Brotherhood of Sleeping Car Porters (BSCP), black migrants fought for and won access to highly paid wartime employment. In the process, their campaign highlighted the problem of racial discrimination and established key precedents for equal opportunity legislation and federal intervention to protect civil rights. Unfortunately, their victory proved short-lived. Postwar demobilization left Oakland with a sharply reduced industrial base. In sharp contrast to Los Angeles, which became a center for aerospace technology, the Bay Area's liberty ship industry had few peacetime applications. This hastened Oakland's deindustrialization as a steady stream of businesses began to flee to the East Bay's cheaper, more racially homogenous suburbs. By 1964, the federal government officially declared Oakland a "depressed area."[12]

Despite this economic retrenchment, waves of migrants displaced by agricultural mechanization continued to pour into the East Bay. Unemployment soared and many found themselves trapped in the familiar cycles of debt and subsistence that they had fled. Historian Gavin Wright has argued that "the oscillation from a decade of 'pull' to a decade of 'push' had profound effects on every aspect of human relations in the South."[13] In the postwar era, destruction of thousands of sharecroppers' homes transformed southern landscapes as mechanized "neo-plantations" replaced their faltering predecessors. African American migration took on the desperate quality of flight as people sought refuge in urban areas despite soaring unemployment rates. Chronic poverty was made worse by the frustrated expectations of new arrivals who vested western cities with special promise. Through challenging discrimination, migrants and their children confronted the established racial order. The older generation drew on churches, civil rights organizations, and the unions, while their children invented new forms of political expression forged in California cities. Ultimately, their combined aspiration produced a social movement that forever changed national understandings of the relationship between race and power, poverty and politics.[14]

. . .

THE INITIAL causes of mass exodus could be found first within the South itself. By the close of the Depression, the southern system of agriculture, which had formed the core of black subsistence since Reconstruction, was breaking apart. The Agricultural Adjustment Administration's policies had seriously damaged the system of tenancy through large-scale displacement of landless farmers. Attempts to raise cotton prices through restricting production combined with direct cash grants to owners with little federal oversight led to a sharp reduction in the land allotted for tenancy. Although black and white alike suffered, African Americans with no political recourse under segregation bore the brunt of this policy. While FDR bowed to the social order of the South by refusing to intervene more forcefully—"I know the South, and we've got to be patient"—a quiet economic revolution had been set in motion. Wage labor rapidly replaced tenancy, and agricultural workers' incomes dropped precipitously as industrial wages rose.[15] Death rates among African Americans, which had been steadily declining, suddenly spiked.[16] All these factors converged to drive rural populations first into nearby cites, and when employment opportunities opened up during the war, to the distant North and West.[17]

Wartime defense industries exacerbated the collapse of tenancy by stripping plantations of labor and providing a strong economic incentive for mechanization. The technology for preharvest cultivation had been available in the first decades of the century; however, it was rarely used in the South. It was not until a shortage of labor and an increase in wages ensued that it made economic sense for planters to implement change. In 1936, after Congress passed the Social Conservation and Domestic Allotment Act, which allowed for direct cash payments to tenants, owners' revenues declined, and they turned increasingly toward wage labor and its counterpart, mechanization.[18] Despite depressed conditions, plantation areas purchased large numbers of tractors in the 1930s, at a significantly higher rate than other regions. Tenant evictions accelerated in the second half of the decade, and the floundering southern industrial sector could not absorb the surplus population. According to historian Gavin Wright, "Five southern states had fewer industrial jobs in 1939 than they had in 1909, and the South as a whole enjoyed virtually zero net growth in industrial employment between 1929 and 1939."[19]

As employment opportunities opened up in federal defense industries, the mass out-migration of African Americans to northern cities left stretches of commodity agriculture in crisis. The population of farmers, composed primarily of sharecroppers and laborers, dropped by over 3 million people (22 percent) during the war.[20] Louisiana's cotton plantation parishes consistently hemorrhaged black population throughout the 1940s at a rate of between 4 and 31 percent. Sugar, grain, and truck subsistence parishes suffered more moderate losses. While many had chosen to relocate to larger parishes (cities of 10,000 or more), which experienced net gains, significant numbers fled the state altogether. In May 1943, a draft notice published in the *Madison Journal* noted that of the thirty-five black locals called up for selective service, only six remained; nineteen of the total had relocated to California or Nevada. In the resulting vacuum, women, children, and even prisoners of war were called upon to fill the labor shortage.[21] Farm wages nearly tripled, and a brief respite followed in the war's aftermath. However, black exodus spiked again in the late forties.

Initially, planters relented by trying to improve conditions at home. In hopes of retaining tenants, southern states responded to long-standing demands for "equalization" and increased funding to segregated schools. For a brief period between 1945 and 1950 this narrowed the racial education gap.[22] However, these efforts remained short-lived. In order to secure production, planters ultimately turned to mechanical cotton pickers which quickly made large numbers of sharecroppers and farmworkers extraneous. In the initial phases, the need for wage labor increased between 1945 and 1954. However, in the final stages of mechanization, obsolescence replaced the acute labor shortage almost immediately. By the midfifties, rural to urban migration had become a necessity rather than a choice.[23]

While people fled from regions throughout the South, and brought with them a diversity of experiences and backgrounds, Bay Area war migrants shared some particular characteristics. The majority came from Texas, Louisiana, and Oklahoma, with Arkansas and Mississippi supplying lesser numbers.[24] A slightly larger percentage of women had chosen to emigrate, and in the 19–24 age range, they outnumbered men by a ratio of two to one. The lure of lucrative defense jobs and the chance to abandon domestic work most certainly played a role. In the words of one female shipyard worker, "It took Hitler to get us out of the kitchens."[25] As a whole, the "newcomers" were significantly younger than the resident black population; the average age of men was 23.3 years, and of women, 22.9 years.[26]

In postwar Oakland, Louisiana held pride of place and exerted a constant influence on local politics and culture. Of the five states that East Bay migrants hailed from, Louisiana had the second largest black population, totaling 37 percent in 1930. It shared a number of similarities with its east-ern counterpart, Mississippi, including the rapid disfranchisement of African Americans in Reconstruction's aftermath and an entrenched system of separate and unequal schooling resulting in comparable illiteracy rates. However, there were also significant differences that became manifest in the transplanted African American community of the East Bay. Much larger percentages of Louisiana's black population lived in urban areas, and they had one of the highest rates of occupational mobility in the South. This resulted in significant numbers of black skilled and semi-skilled craftsmen who had a strong tradition of labor activism with roots stretching back to several unions and benevolent associations in the late nineteenth century. In New Orleans, for example, the building and transportation trades were completely dependent on African American skilled labor, with blacks constituting 28 percent of all carpenters and joiners, "62 percent of all coopers, 65 percent of all masons," and "75 percent of all longshoremen."[27] In sum, of the five states in question, Louisiana had the largest black professional class and the highest rates of income and property valuation. While suffering brutal segregation, black New Orleans possessed a strong infrastructure of businesses, universities, churches, and social organizations that made it possible to retreat from the hostile world of the white majority.[28]

The social profiles of wartime migrants refuted common stereotypes applied to them as a group. The secondary urban migration during the war served as an important contrast to the waves of newcomers that followed, who were composed largely of people displaced from rural areas.[29] Charles Johnson's extensive study, *The Negro War Worker*, revealed the image of the uncouth, if harmless, naïf set adrift in the industrial city as urban myth. In general, migrants were comparably educated to their California peers with little disparity, especially at the upper end. The average newcomers completed 8.64 years of schooling, and while larger numbers were concentrated in the lower grades, at the high school, college, and professional level, educational differences remained negligible. Johnson argued, in fact, that this polarization betrayed greater social ambition. "There is relatively less tendency for the old Negro residents to aspire toward higher education and professional careers than is found among newcomers, a large proportion of whom are bogged down at the lower grade levels."[30]

Similarly, migrants exhibited higher rates of matrimony and a greater likelihood to marry young; Johnson viewed both of these tendencies as strong indicators of social stability. All of these factors, especially migrants' relative youth combined with the ample numbers of skilled laborers among their ranks, made them more attractive to shipyard employers than their

Walter Newton (*right*) and Lee Edward Newton— father and older brother of BPP founder Huey P. Newton—in 1941, a year before the family's move from Monroe, Louisiana, to Oakland, California. Like thousands of southern newcomers, the Newton family migrated west during World War II to obtain work in the San Francisco Bay Area shipyards. Photograph courtesy of Melvin Newton.

local peers. Migrant families secured defense jobs at a much higher rate than locals, and their monthly gross reflected this: $329.32 for newcomers versus $294.40 for older residents. Not surprisingly, migrants favored industrial unions, voiced strong support for the Congress of Industrial Organizations and joined at higher rates. A very different picture began to emerge than that deployed against newcomers. As a group, migrants were relatively skilled, socially aspirant, and anxious to maximize the economic advantages denied them in the South.[31]

If Texas and Louisiana served as the ancestral homeland for many East Bay migrants, West Oakland represented the historical bridge to black California. This compact piece of land, bounded at its southern and western edge by Oakland's sloping harbors, served as the initial point of entry for African Americans. Its history was inseparable from its positioning as nexus between land transport and sea. In the late 1860s, the Central Pacific, the nation's first transcontinental railroad, chose West Oakland as its terminus, thereby making this small East Bay promontory the central transportation hub for San Francisco and other northern Californian towns. In order to maximize its use value and bypass San Francisco, Leland Stanford renovated the city's piers to extend the "iron horse" into deep-water shipping lanes. By April 1871, the Oakland Long Wharf reached 11,000 feet into the bay; the resulting effects were dramatic. Oakland quickly assumed its place as a major port with a hopeful industrial future.[32] With the transcontinental railroad as the largest employer in California, the possibilities seemed limitless.[33] As stevedores loaded and unloaded large cargoes of freight between the thickening networks of rail and ship lines, the pier became integral to urban growth. A community of white ethnics—Portuguese, Italian, Slovak, and Irish—together with a small sprinkling of black rail workers—settled the land surrounding the industrial port.[34] Immediate access to transportation also proved irresistible to business, and in the next half century a dense web of manufacturing and processing industries emerged in their shadow.[35]

By the early thirties, the Pullman Company, the Southern Pacific, and the Santa Fe had replaced their gargantuan ancestor. In the years spanning the railroad's evolution, black residents settled the land west of Lake Merritt.[36] Their numbers remained sparse and closely linked to the local transportation industry. In her 1931 column, "Activities Among Negroes," Delilah Beasley wrote that "the history of early black Oakland is largely the history of black railroad workers."[37] By the onset of the Depression, over one-third of the East Bay's African American labor force worked in this sector, which supplied over 60 percent of the local black community's income.[38] They served in a variety of capacities, as porters, cooks, waiters, and redcaps. The Pullman Company alone paid nearly $560,000 in annual wages, making it Oakland's single largest employer of blacks.[39] As an early pillar of the fragile middle class, Pullman porters held a special place of esteem for their comparatively "clean working conditions" and travel opportunities.[40]

Despite the domestic nature of their service, porters were known to be well-educated and cultured men who in another time and place would have formed a professional class. Two of the East Bay's most important political leaders, C. L. Dellums of the BSCP and NAACP and political boss D. G. Gibson, a former dining car waiter, emerged from their ranks.[41] This group served not only as a political elite, but also an economic one. Several of the city's most accomplished black real estate brokers also started out as porters.

Fraternal organization at DeFremery Park in West Oakland, 1950s. Photograph courtesy of the African American Museum and Library at Oakland.

They capitalized on their contact with whites to gain information about development prospects and translated these into small fortunes in property. In 1926, the formalization of restrictive covenants was, at least in part, a response to this entrepreneurial interest.[42] A network of lodges, social clubs, and fraternal societies flourished amidst the culture and economy of the rails. The city's two oldest black churches, the Beth Eden Baptist Church and Shiloh African Methodist Episcopal Church resided in the heart of West Oakland.[43]

Pullman porters also played a key role in disseminating information about the opportunities available to African Americans in northern California. The matrix of Pullman lines that crisscrossed the nation created a mythic "grapevine" that linked black communities throughout the United States.[44] African American migration streams shaped this network connecting southern and northern latitudes, rather than the traditional American settlement pattern of east to west. The San Francisco Bay Area held a special allure for black southerners. Segregation functioned like a palimpsest whose layers grew denser with the passage of time. The relative youth of the East Bay's black population meant that formal systems of racial control had not yet been consolidated. In California, rates of black property ownership numbered among the highest in the nation, and in contrast to the South, the sparseness of population allowed for greater individual freedom.[45] This dynamic was even reenacted inside the state itself. Large numbers of southern migrants who first settled in Los Angeles, which had a much older and larger African American community, later chose to move north in search of a less hostile environment with "fewer personal restrictions."[46] Geographic variation aside, African Americans throughout California suffered less physical repression, worked largely outside agriculture, and had greater access to integrated public services.[47] Most important, the state's promise of higher quality public education, at all levels, tapped a consistent motive for black migration throughout the twentieth century.[48]

Neighborhoods and Housing Segregation

Prior to World War II, the majority of Oakland's black residents lived in a small area close to the bay. The shoreline formed the western perimeter, with the Southern Pacific holdings to the south. Grove Street separated West Oakland from downtown and became a major thoroughfare for the community and a focal point of black public culture. In a literal push for upward mobility, African Americans steadily breached the contested northern boundary in the coming decades. During the interwar years, Eighteenth Street gave way to Thirty-Second, which Thirty-Fifth subsequently replaced. Ultimately, a handful of black homeowners—almost exclusively with the help of white proxies—quietly made their way above the numbered streets to Ashby Avenue in Berkeley, Oakland's neighbor to the north.[49] "Berkeley was always the first step up," remembered Norvel Smith. "You came into West Oakland, then North Oakland, and if you really made it, with a civil service job or something, you moved into South Berkeley."[50]

White residents fought this incremental progress at each juncture, and when the onslaught of war migrants flooded into Oakland, the noose of economic necessity and residential segregation tightened, forcing black new-

comers back toward the rail yards of the bay. One migrant worker who arrived in West Oakland in 1944 recalled that there was "such a small part of
the city that black folk could live in that they were sleeping on top of each
other."[51] Families, faced with the shortage of housing, often became homeless, forced to go door to door to see if there were garages, cellars or unused
space they could use.[52] Left to the vagaries of the private housing market
by discriminatory Federal Housing Authority programs, black newcomers
concentrated into a few contiguous census tracks in West Oakland on the
far side of Grove and San Pablo with the single largest concentration in the
area adjacent to the pier.[53] Older black residents responded with ambivalence, fearful that their relations with neighbors would suffer as these southern newcomers inundated the city.[54]

Changing racial demographics created a definite hardening of racial
lines. Black realtor Edith Hill, who later became instrumental in opening
up North and East Oakland real estate for purchase, described the kinds
of discriminatory practices faced by black homebuyers. "They'd use those
little picayunish excuses . . . they had two sets of standards, too. They had
double standards. Blacks or other minorities would have to earn more to
qualify, than whites. Few excuses—little infractions on their credit report—
where they would excuse some of those for whites, they'd make a big issue
for minorities. . . . Those were their ways of keeping you out of many of the
areas. And many of the areas they just wouldn't let you see them. And then
also, prior to the late '60s, minorities were not admitted to the Real Estate
Boards."[55]

Residential segregation exacerbated the severe housing crunch that Oakland faced in the 1940s. In the short span of seven years (1940–47), the city's
population grew by 100,000 people, but the number of available housing
units increased by only 14,000.[56] The Oakland Housing Authority made
some attempt to accommodate this need through building low-income
housing projects in West Oakland. Campbell Village opened in 1941 with
black residents occupying over half of the units. The following January,
Peralta Village opened its doors with a similar integrated policy. However,
segregated housing remained, and in May 1942 the newly constructed Lock-
wood Gardens admitted white residents only. A more common solution to
the pressing housing demand was building temporary housing shelters. An
array of buildings was put up quickly with their names drawn simply from
the streets that housed them: Bayview Villa, Cypress Village, Willow and
Magnolia Manor. The Maritime Commission and Moore Dry Dock Company also constructed some housing for war workers, including Chestnut

Court and Peralta Villa.[57] In 1945, West Oakland received a large boost in population when temporary war housing in Richmond, Berkeley, Albany, and Alameda was demolished. Pressure from these cities to export their surplus black labor force, now homeless, sent a stream of war refugees into the historically black district.[58] By 1950, roughly 85 percent of the city's black population lived in West Oakland, which served as the cultural and demographic pivot for the East Bay's larger community of color.[59]

Baby Harlem

Southern migrants expressed their social ambitions by establishing their own institutions and transforming many of the existing ones. Nothing reflected the urban promise of the city for African American migrants like Seventh Street, Oakland's historic black business district. Christened affectionately by residents as "Baby Harlem," this commercial strip in West Oakland became the center of black life in the East Bay well into the sixties.[60] The influx of newcomers provided a ready-made market for small retail, personal services, and especially entertainment. A teenage migrant from rural Arkansas later remembered, "Market Street and Seventh and San Pablo . . . was just bubbling over at the seams with black business after black business after black business."[61] Shipyard and military installations often ran around the clock with daytime work hours blurring into evening "swing shifts." Informal restaurants like "The Packhouse" and "The Garage" sprang up to tempt workers with plentiful and inexpensive southern-style food, while the twilight blues world of "juke joints," "honky-tonks," and "buckets of blood" offered a more ephemeral solace.[62] Margaret Starks, a migrant to the adjacent community of Richmond, California, remembered the significance of the blues club. "Those people didn't have too much, so they weren't about to let go of the music and the good times they were used to. It made them feel better. I remember one lady from Louisiana, had gold all in her mouth, told me that she loved to hear that music because . . . [it] made her forget all that stuff in the shipyards. She always felt better when she left."[63]

In the tradition of the western boomtown, some of Seventh Street's most powerful business people built small fortunes through liquor and gambling. While smaller in number than the Pullman elite, these colorful figures rivaled their visibility in West Oakland. Dance halls, blues clubs and poolrooms existed on a continuum with other more subterranean forms of vice industry that thrived during the war. Even the Brotherhood of Sleeping Car Porters was not above dabbling in entertainment. C. L. Dellums owned a large share in the Himes bowling alley just below the union's office. However, no one capitalized as effectively on the new opportunities availed by wartime than Harold "Slim" Jenkins. Immediately after the repeal of Prohibition in 1933, Jenkins opened the first liquor store in the city, which he soon expanded into a full service club and restaurant.

Slim Jenkins's Place was strategically located on Seventh Street, a stone's throw from the Southern Pacific rail yards. White linen tablecloths, cabaret-style singing, and a mixed white and black middle-class clientele set Slim Jenkins apart from the numerous "down home" blues clubs that lined "the strip."[64] Republican senator and *Oakland Tribune* publisher William Knowland was a regular customer, and in the subsequent decades, Jenkins's generous donations to civic and political causes, combined with his Republican Party affiliation, earned him the unofficial title of "Mayor of West Oakland."[65] Despite his yearning for respectability, many speculated that Jenkins's financing came from one of West Oakland's most celebrated "sporting life" figures, "Raincoat" Jones, a fixture of Seventh Street, who ran "his games before, during, and the war" with impunity from city hall.[66] Raincoat was also known to have influence with the police and other highly placed people, and in the early forties wild rumors circulated that his business activities extended into acting as a wildcat labor recruiter for Kaiser.[67]

Like future powerbrokers C. L. Dellums and Lionel Wilson, Slim Jenkins migrated to the Bay Area in the decades preceding the shipyard migrations. Born in Monroe, Louisiana, Jenkins arrived in California shortly after World War I.[68] The site he chose for his club was not only close to the rail yards but stood right next to the remains of the Creole Club, one of the West Coast's oldest jazz clubs. In 1922, the *California Voice* bemoaned its closing as a failure of black solidarity. However, the contrasting fates of the two jazz clubs reflected the historical changes wrought by the interwar years. Before the mass migrations of the early forties, the tiny community of West Oakland had neither the money nor the numbers to support a swanky black venue or the ample chain of businesses that lined Seventh Street during wartime and after. Women, as well as men, served as proprietors, and in the postwar era female entrepreneurs like Esther Mabry kept Seventh Street jumping. In 1959, Mabry opened Esther's Orbit Room, which became a West Oakland institution for nearly a half century. The successes of Slim Jenkins Place, Esther's Orbit Room, and the numerous bars, clubs, and restaurants that sprouted up wherever migrants put down roots symbolized how the southern diaspora vitalized and transformed black Oakland.[69]

Familiar styles of music and faith allowed southerners to recreate the social world they had left behind. Blues clubs competed not only with one another but also with the army of churches opening their doors to the swelling tide of southerners. Maya Angelou, a young migrant from Stamps, Arkansas, remembered Seventh Street as a place where "bars and smoke shops sat in the laps of storefront churches."[70] Although a sizeable portion of newcomers from southern Louisiana identified as Catholic, many from northern Louisiana, Texas, and other parts of the South embraced Evangelical Protestantism. Pentecostals and Southern Baptists predominated—especially among rural-urban migrants—and charismatic traditions deeply influenced styles of worship, even among black Catholics.[71] Prior to World War II, the small black communities of the Bay Area lacked the religious diversity and infrastructure to satisfy the religious thirsts of southern migrants. Rather than convert, many newcomers decided to start their own churches, and an array of sanctified and Pentecostal congregations emerged in the wake of wartime migration.

The founding of the West Oakland Church of God typified this process. In 1943, a group of shipyard migrants from Arkansas convinced Elton Pointer to relocate from Little Rock and come serve as their pastor. In the years to come, the minister's two youngest daughters made their family famous by choosing the stage name "The Pointer Sisters." Their older brother Fritz remembered the church raising as "a community event" with all kinds of people coming out to help.[72] For many, the West Oakland Church of God became an integral part of their daily lives. Anne Williams's family migrated from Mansfield, Louisiana, in 1944, and throughout her childhood they attended church events or meetings on an almost daily basis. Like the shipyards, services ran late into the night, along with regular trustee and board meetings and choir practice for all ages. Frequently, traveling evangelists passed through, sponsoring weekend revivals. Fritz Pointer remembered his membership in the church as "an incredibly dynamic life" that gave community members a status and visibility not available to them in the outside world.

Of all the congregation's many activities, foot-washing ceremonies stood out as the most vivid and tender of rituals.[73] The biblical story of Mary Magdalene and Jesus inspired this practice, but the psychic burdens of racial segregation endowed it with a deeper meaning. Men and women divided into separate groups, and within each circle, people of different status paired off. Frequently, elder and younger were chosen, but sometimes people of varying professions or levels within the church. As the minister read scripture aloud, one person knelt down and placed the other's foot in a shallow tub, sprinkled water over it and then carefully dried it with a towel. Then they reversed roles and repeated the ritual, thereby creating a mutual bond of humility and respect. Reflecting on its symbolism, Fritz Pointer noted, "The church is one of the few places that black men and women could get the kind of respect from one another that they couldn't get from the larger society. . . . I never knew the first name of many of the people in the church. The men of the church. I only knew them by their last names, by Brother Williams or Brother Stuart or Brother Hendricks or so. . . . But, I'm sure the larger society knew them probably as 'boy' or 'Johnny' or 'gal' or something like that."[74]

Churches also created alternate avenues of social mobility, and the "Harlem of the West Coast" would not have been complete without its own Father Divine. In 1945, a recent arrival from Louisiana, Louis H. Narcisse, founded the Mount Zion Spiritual Temple, which quickly became an Oakland institution. Mixing sanctified religion with elements of the Baptist and Catholic faiths, "King Narcisse"—as he became known—set up a vigorous organization that expanded to Richmond, Sacramento, and later Detroit. Within a couple of decades, church membership peaked at nearly 200,000 people, and Narcisse held weekly radio broadcasts for the faithful. The former shipyard worker preached a rousing social gospel summed up by the simple motto, "It's nice to be nice." Mt. Zion erected an elaborate church hierarchy of "saints," "princes and princesses," and a silk-robed "queen mother." Through contributions of money and time, ordinary people could ascend to the highest ranks of church leadership. Historian Shirley Ann Wilson Moore has argued that newcomer churches like Mt. Zion and the West Oakland Church of God played a foundational role in regulating "the degree, quality, and pace of assimilation into the urban environment."[75] They allowed migrants to recreate the world they had known while providing members with status and social recognition denied them elsewhere. Similarly, James Gregory has called religion "something of a synecdoche for the larger story of the Southern Diaspora," meaning that the forms of worship migrants carried with them became integral to the "southernization" of the northern cities.[76]

Although southern music and religious practices became essential to community formation for newcomers, they also created tensions with older black residents, who worried that migrants were not being sufficiently "acculturated" to living in California. Black old-timers feared that "newcomers were [so] busy bringing their own culture with them" that their presence would disrupt the long-established ties with white residents.[77] Within African American communities, the relationship of newcomers to older residents was a complex one, because their numbers created unprecedented economic opportunity. An unexpected consequence of urban concentration was the consolidation of the East Bay's black middle class. In addition to entrepreneurs like Slim Jenkins and Raincoat Jones, black professionals—lawyers, doctors, and dentists—also benefited from the vast increase in black population. Ultimately, this new market, combined with the opening up of government jobs made possible by a largely migrant-based union movement, enabled a new class of urban elite to supplant its railroad predecessors.[78]

Nevertheless, this reality was not always apparent to older residents, who often blamed newcomers for increasing racial conflict and de facto segregation. Royal Towns, who was the first African American hired by the Oakland Fire Department, complained that migrants "lacked the fellowship" that had once prevailed with white ethnic neighbors in West Oakland. Historically, all the local children had played together in the local estuary, but "when this influx of blacks came, they found a separate place . . . to go. They segregated themselves because of the way they were raised down south."[79] As the son of a Pullman porter born in 1899 on Fifth Street, Towns' ambivalence toward newcomers epitomized that of Oakland's black old-timers. Virginia Rose explained how mass migration unsettled this group and inspired resentment. "Well, there were lots of feelings. Some of the people that I know thought that the people who came from the South and West, like Oklahoma, were different and that their presence here might upset what they considered *a very delicate balance*. They didn't want the relationships between whites and black to change, even though there was a lot of racism here already"[80] (emphasis mine).

Ironically, Mrs. Rose had arrived in California in 1939, only a few years ahead of the shipyard migrants. As the wife of Joshua Rose, a YMCA official who had been transferred from Montclair, New Jersey, to Oakland, her story was an exceptional one. She was an outsider and one of the few newcomers from the Northeast. Her husband went on to become Oakland's first black city councilman, and their circle was part of a small group of self-designated black elites. But her comments spoke to a larger social truth. The comparatively recent arrival of so-called old-timers exacerbated their desire to set themselves apart from migrants. Social status often hinged on a few years' seniority in California and the careful unlearning of southern accents and patterns of speech. The vexed relationship with their recent southern past created long-lasting social cleavages that shaped African American class and community formation in the years to come. As will be evident in subsequent chapters, the tendency of city officials and social scientists to see migrants as pathological and culturally deprived reinforced this internal division within African American communities. This split was particularly destructive because it struck at the shared sense of southern culture and origin that animated Oakland's postwar communities, in matters not only of business but also of the spirit.

The Fight for Fair Employment

Of all the battles waged by migrants, the longest and most sustained was the struggle to obtain employment. Chester Himes's 1945 autobiographical novel, *If He Hollers Let Him Go*, poignantly illustrated the problems faced by black workers in California shipyards during World War II. In the course of only five days, the protagonist Robert Jones is demoted from his coveted position as the single Negro leaderman, beaten unconscious, accused of rape, and forced into the Jim Crow army. Racial violence so thoroughly saturated the industrial landscape of California defense industries that it filled the air itself. "It was that crazy, wild-eyed, unleashed hatred that the first Jap bomb on Pearl Harbor let loose in a flood," mused Jones. "All that crazy feeling of race as thick as gas fumes."[81] The novel ends bleakly as Robert Jones goes off to war, with death as the likely outcome.

"The entire West Coast area is characterized by problems which in newness and intensity distinguish it from the rest of the country," stated the *Final Report of the Fair Employment Practices Committee*.[82] Prior to the war, the black community of the San Francisco Bay Area was tiny. In the first quarter of the century, black residents, concerned about the lack of economic opportunity, actively discouraged migration. Historian Nathan I. Huggins, a San Francisco native, described the Bay Area's African American community prior to World War II as small and "self-satisfied . . . despite discrimination in almost every line of employment, pervasive restrictive covenants, and powerlessness in city politics."[83] Severe employment restrictions had retarded the development of a black industrial class. "I had been around here long enough then to realize that there wasn't very much work that Negroes could get," explained C. L. Dellums, a local business agent for the BSCP.[84]

National defense brought an unprecedented policy and capital investment in California, leading historian Gerald Nash to designate it as the transformative event of twentieth-century California history. The federal government invested over $40 billion in West Coast factories, military bases, and other capital improvements, and the resulting economic and demographic changes to the San Francisco Bay Area were immense.[85] Later C. L. Dellums, a Texas migrant himself, described how the stirrings of war transformed the face of the Bay Area economy. "Many of us felt strongly that the nation was really getting ready for war and not defense. Shipyards were being built all around the Bay and expanding."[86] Three years later the *San Francisco Chronicle* summed up this massive growth and diversification of the Bay Area economy by announcing that "the Second Gold Rush" had begun.[87]

The war catalyzed a massive expansion of army, navy, marine, and federal infrastructure with a subsequent explosion in the size of its industrial and white-collar workforce. Between 1937 and the end of the war, the navy alone completed construction of Treasure Island in the San Francisco Bay, the California Naval Station in Alameda, the Oakland Naval Supply Center and Naval Regional Medical Center, the Concord Naval Weapons Station, Crows Landing Naval Auxiliary Air Station, and Camp Park in Livermore.[88] Adding to the dense web of federal defense installations, a number of private corporations underwent wartime conversion. In 1936 the United States Marine Commission was established to administer the growth of the merchant fleet, and over the course of the war, the navy and the commission together allocated a total of $5 billion in contracts to the Bay Area shipbuilders. In the East Bay a chain of twelve shipyards, stretching from Alameda to Richmond, made the area the largest West Coast manufacturer of cargo ships. Shipbuilders included the gargantuan Kaiser complex in Richmond; Moore Dry Dock in Oakland; and General Engineering, Pacific Bridge, Bethlehem Steel, and Pacific Coast Engineering in Alameda.[89]

For African Americans the situation remained bleak. As revolutionary changes swept the Bay Area economy, migrant workers were initially shut out of this immense tide of opportunity almost entirely. Dellums explained, "Some months after the President's committee was in operation there wasn't an identifiable Negro working in any shipyard, and Kaiser alone had three or four [shipyards] in Richmond."[90] Using the political network of the BSCP, Dellums called his fellow union member Milton Webster in Washington. He asked Webster to send Clarence Johnson in order to "crack these shipyards."[91] At the time Johnson was working for the Public Housing Administration, but his career as an activist and civil rights leader had been forged in the California labor movement. Johnson had worked with the Dining Car Cooks and Waiters Union for the Bay Area Southern Pacific. Subsequently, he was appointed as the field representative of the Negro Employment and Training Branch of the War Production Board headed up by Robert Weaver, a member of Roosevelt's "Black Cabinet" who worked tirelessly to desegregate industry and establish a federal agency to prosecute job discrimination. These efforts ultimately culminated in the founding of the Fair Employment Practices Commission (FEPC).[92]

Johnson and Dellums struggled to desegregate the San Francisco Bay Area shipyards and other essential industries. While Dellums centered his activities in the BSCP, he worked with Johnson frequently and remained quite involved in "the whole FEPC set up." The trade-union leader was well acquainted with the role of employers in fostering discrimination. When challenged with the charge of discrimination, employers often responded that they did not hire blacks because they were afraid of retaliation by their white workforce. In the early years of the war, Dellums treated this claim skeptically. Rather than taking employers at their word, he worked with Clarence Johnson to check. Dellums described their tactics:

> So we went to work on the shipyards and we stayed on them until
> we opened up the gates. I recall we would go from Kaiser's to the
> union and back to Kaiser. The shipyards were blaming everything
> on the union but Clarence and I knew better. One day we got some
> union officials who knew us to let us have the written proof that it
> was the shipyard. When we went back and finally had the shipyard
> guy where we wanted him, Clarence pulled two referral cards out
> and placed them in front of that fellow and at the same time reached
> for the phone to call Washington. The man said, "That won't be
> necessary." He then took the phone and called one of the yards
> and gave these two names to the man he was talking to and said,
> "When they show up, put them to work even though they are
> Negroes."[93]

This structure remained a problem throughout the war. Frequently, employers sought to shield discriminatory hiring practices by blaming union referrals. Determining whether unions or employers were responsible for hiring discrimination against black workers remained a major dilemma for the San Francisco FEPC. Dellums's critical view of employers was typical of black trade unionists. In a survey of black war workers, Charles Johnson found high levels of support for industrial unions and even for the American Federation of Labor (AFL). They often viewed employers as the biggest obstacle to employment.[94]

C. L. Dellums was also active in trying to desegregate nonessential industries. He described how shifting labor patterns had created opportunities for black workers outside defense. White workers attracted by the higher wages of war industries had left their jobs as conductors in large numbers, leaving the Bay Area's streetcar line, the Key System, in turmoil. The extreme scarcity of workers opened up new possibilities for blacks who were refused employment before the war. Dellums and the local chapter of the NAACP seized the opportunity to "start the drive for Negro employment all over again."[95] During the thirties, a series of civil rights activists had emerged out of the black middle-class enclave of South Berkeley. Prominent figures included Tarea Pitman, William Byron Rumford, Walter Gordon, and Francis Albrier. The civil rights organization had been trying to open up the Key System for a long time. Limited time, resources, and personnel prevented them from having any real impact until World War II.[96]

The NAACP battle with the Bay Area's streetcar line demonstrated the kinds of employment barriers faced by black workers seeking to enter job classifications formerly occupied by white workers. The civil rights organization set up shop in downtown Oakland, renting an office on Broadway close to the bay. The local chapter recruited "qualified Negroes" to become motor-men and conductors, purposely choosing people they were certain would be able to pass the Key System's exam. Although the streetcar company now allowed blacks to take the exam, to date none had passed it. Management invoked special qualifications to block African Americans who were seeking employment. This pattern appeared repeatedly throughout different industries and work situations. When nonwhite subjects applied, the rules of the game changed arbitrarily. Employers expected black applicants to abide by time limits while taking the test, but waived these restrictions for whites.

To frustrate this strategy, NAACP organizers published the Key System questionnaire and set up classes to drill people for the timed test. Many black applicants virtually memorized the answers, and subsequently passed their exams. As activist pressure destroyed one barrier, the Key System erected a new one in its place. Upon successfully passing the exam, these applicants were required to take a physical. The company doctor found all twelve physically unfit. To contest this finding, the NAACP sponsored a second opinion. Not surprisingly, the medical team determined that the men were perfectly healthy. With this evidence in hand, Dellums wrote to the doctor providing the other medical statements and threatened to report him to the County Medical Association. Miraculously, the doctor declared all of the African American candidates had undergone a complete recovery and were in good condition.

Faced with the prospect of hiring black people, the Key System Company held up a new and even more formidable barrier—the closed-shop agreement. Like Kaiser, the Oakland transport company shielded itself by charging the union with racial discrimination. This accusation initiated a "vicious cycle which the NAACP had been fighting almost all of its existence." Dellums explained,

> The Negro went to the employer for a job and if he passed all these hurdles that I've just outlined with the Key System, then the company would tell him, "Well I'd like to hire you. You're okay. I want to hire you. . . . I'm anxious to hire you. But I've got an agreement with the union that I can only hire union members. So you can go to the union and if they take you in, you come on back. I want you!" So they'd act like they wanted to hire him. Well, of course they were lying. Then the Negro went to the union. The union said, "Well, we don't take in unemployed people. We only take in members who are working. If the company will give you a job, we'll be proud to take you into the union." So, you see the Negro was fighting that cycle.[97]

The vicious cycle of mutually reinforcing discrimination between organized labor and employers shut blacks out of whole industries. Unions would not accept black workers unless they were employed, and they could not be employed unless they were members of the unions. Although the level of discrimination of each union varied, this pattern formed the keystone of hiring discrimination for skilled industries with craft organization.

Dellums noted that it was during this period that the national Carmen's Union—later renamed the Amalgamated Streetcar Union—became the first AFL union to pass a positive antidiscrimination clause in its constitution. It contained provisions to discipline members who discriminated against workers because of race, creed, or color. Dellums attempted to intervene by contacting A. Philip Randolph, who in turn notified the head of the Carmen's Union. The national president contacted the local, but it refused to comply. The rank and file lined up behind its leadership, thereby insulating them from the orders of the president and constitution.[98] The national union's failure to force local compliance paralleled the FEPC's inability to sanction employers. Both institutions lacked real powers of enforcement at the local level. The FEPC could try to shame companies into compliance through holding public hearings, but it lacked the power to withhold defense contracts from discriminatory employers. Authority to revoke local charters or deny federal contracts would have vastly accelerated adoption of antidiscriminatory policies. Direct regulation and negative incentives were needed. But neither the national leadership of the Carmen's Union nor the FEPC possessed such powers of enforcement.[99]

Despite this particular defeat, activist pressure had far reaching effects. Black labor achieved both real and symbolic advances during the war. Defense industries had produced more than 600,000 jobs for African Americans and drawn a million black southerners to northern and western industrial centers. In the Bay Area over 70 percent of black newcomers found work in the shipyards, and black female employment trebled.[100] "The shift from farm to the factory, therefore, is by far the most outstanding change that took place in the male labor force during the war," declared the *Monthly Labor Review* in 1945. "Between 1940 and 1944, the number of Negroes employed as skilled craftsmen and foremen doubled, as did the number engaged as operatives. . . . Altogether, the number in both categories rose from about 500,000 to 1,000,000."[101]

By 1943, important shifts in local industrial policy toward black workers could be seen. Shipyards christened a number of Liberty ships with black monikers. This public relations campaign created incredible public spectacles acknowledging black accomplishment unimaginable a few years before. Such events lent the war a revolutionary quality on the domestic front. A 1945 article in the *Journal of Educational Sociology* proclaimed the West Coast "the new frontier of race relations."[102] C. L. Dellums described the launching of the George Washington Carver from the Kaiser shipyards:

> Fate plays a funny trick on these white people sometimes, because
> two years after they removed the barriers and allowed Negroes to
> go to work in the shipyards, one of the Kaiser shipyards in Richmond
> launched a ship named for a Negro—the George Washington Carver.
> . . . Miss Lena Horne was the guest of honor and she was going to
> swing the champagne bottle to launch the ship. . . . I thought it was
> an odd trick, that we had spent three days out there at that shipyard
> alone trying to get Negroes in there and then in about two years here
> they are launching a ship named for a Negro. It was estimated that
> there were about 10,000 Negroes working in the four shipyards by
> then.[103]

In spite of company propaganda campaigns like this one, the full utilization of Bay Area black workers remained a problem throughout the war. While total black employment had grown by leaps and bounds, hiring and placement discrimination was common. Complaints against shipyards, army and navy installations, and private defense agencies poured into the San Francisco FEPC between 1943 and 1945. Throughout this period, Dellums also organized a variety of nonindustrial workers, including clerks, stenographers, and telephone operators. Such dazzling spectacles as the launching of the George Washington Carver by Lena Horne did not dissolve institutional obstacles erected against black integration into the Bay Area workforce.[104]

Deindustrialization

The tide of economic opportunity unleashed by federal defense money drew migrants to the Bay Area, but this phenomenal growth rate proved fleeting. In Oakland and for much of the black population in Richmond, Hunters Point, and South Berkeley, five short years of boom developed into several long decades of bust. Soon after the war ended, the East Bay sank into a period of industrial decline, and structural unemployment became a permanent feature of the local economy.[105] By 1952, Oakland's industrial investment accounted for a mere 28 percent of Alameda County's total, and by 1964 the federal government officially classified the city as "depressed."[106] Oakland faced the two-pronged problem of a local business exodus exacerbated by an inability to attract new industry. After major employers Cal Pak, Marchant Calculators, and Nordstrom Valve relocated, over 7,000 people lost their jobs.[107] Businesses expressed four primary reasons for not locating in Oakland: crime, high rates of unionization, failure to attract growth industries like aerospace, and stiff resistance by older local firms.[108]

Despite the thriving Cold War economy of the 1950s, Oakland limped along. Deindustrialization had a devastating social impact on Oakland's black population. In 1959, 25 percent of the city's total population lived under the poverty line and roughly 10 percent earned less than $2,000 per year.[109] For black workers, the situation proved particularly acute. Union discrimination, concentration in temporary wartime industries like shipyards, and entrenched patterns of employer discrimination relegated much of the growing black population to secondary labor markets. As a result, an enduring class of the black unemployed and underemployed began to emerge. The decline of the Pullman porters represented one of the most poignant examples of how economic restructuring affected African American residents. As air travel replaced rail as the primary mode of cross-country transportation, a major pillar of black organized labor dissolved. Once the spine of the African American elite, the porters were furloughed in 1960. In a matter of months, a whole job classification became obsolete. The Department of Labor later listed their nonunionized counterparts in the service industry as one of the thirty lowest paid occupations. Annual salaries averaged under $2,800 per year.[110] The elimination of the porters and the loss of well-paid industrial jobs transformed the social landscape of the black community in the San Francisco Bay Area. The growing ranks of the jobless and working poor became a displaced population that was alienated from the traditional means of labor organization and civil rights protest. As black labor's remarkable gains rapidly receded in the war's aftermath—local authorities estimated that the ship industry's workforce shrank from 250,000 at the war's height to 12,000 people in 1946—African American newcomers found themselves vulnerable not only to economic decline but also to police violence.[111]

Even before the social crisis engendered by deindustrialization, law enforcement greeted the mass migration of African Americans into the Bay Area with hostility.[112] During the war, police routinely conducted wholesale sweeps of West Oakland. Brutal harassment of interracial couples—especially black men and white women—reflected the literal enforcement of the color line. This problem was so extensive that black couples of mixed hue complained repeatedly of police misconduct.[113] In the subsequent decade, treatment of the African American community worsened. During the early 1940s, the region's booming defense economy and desperate need for black labor served as a mediating force in community-police relations.[114] But in the lean years that followed, law enforcement blamed high crime rates on migrants and sought new methods to not only reduce but also prevent crime. As the "second gold rush" gave way to mass black unemployment, regional law enforcement viewed the Bay Area's surplus labor force with rising enmity. In response, the Oakland Police Department (OPD) implemented a core restructuring and expansion that led to rampant incursions into African American communities. While the first wave of migrants in the 1940s suffered targeted harassment and incarceration, by the midfifties, the OPD began to systematically surveil and criminalize black migrants.[115]

Police and social service agencies repeatedly identified "newcomers" as the fountainhead of crime and social disorder. "It is very possible that the trouble comes from immigrant Negroes . . . who are held well under control in the South," reported the *Oakland Observer*. "But coming North, [they] have found themselves thrilled with a new 'freedom.'"[116] In 1950, complaints against police brutality had gotten so bad that Vernon L. Kilpatrick, a Democratic assemblyman from Los Angeles, presided over a legislative inquiry.

Thirty-three residents testified about physical attacks, insults, and one murder committed by the department. The communist-led East Bay Civil Rights Congress played an important role in bringing these issues to the public's attention. Examples included Anna Lee Harris, a young housewife who had been jailed by the police arbitrarily and subjected to three days of venereal tests that later proved negative; Stanley Wilson, a black musician, who came to the police station to pay a traffic fine and was beaten severely when police saw his spouse was white; and the tragic case of Andrew L. Hines, who was fatally shot in custody after police picked him up on "suspicion of loitering." Ultimately, the Kilpatrick Committee censored the Oakland Police Department for its failure to discipline misconduct and establish "high standards of in-service training." Legislators expressed particular concern about the effect of police mistreatment on young migrants. Committee members worried about the future effects of alienating the youth from local government, noting that the "value of fair treatment of these persons and consequent benefits . . . to all society cannot be overemphasized."[117]

In addition to the reforms suggested by the Kilpatrick Committee, civil rights activists fought to desegregate the all-white ranks of the OPD. During the war, law enforcement relented and hired the first patrolmen of color. This change largely reflected an attempt to maintain the bounds of segregation, as the department immediately assigned black candidates to patrol recently settled migrant neighborhoods. In 1943, two African Americans, Adrien C. Bridges and Leon S. Daniels, received appointments as duration officers. Despite the temporary nature of their employment, their presence marked an important shift in hiring practices.[118] In subsequent years, the OPD hired a handful of new people of color, including Oakland's first black civil service policeman, Hadwick Thompson. Throughout the 1950s and 1960s, he recruited for the OPD through local churches, the ministerial alliance, and in southern black colleges. His efforts, however, remained largely in vain. A perverse logic led police departments to refuse well-qualified black candidates who scored well on their entrance exams. Instead, they selected less-educated men who were easier to control. Despite small gains in hiring, the combination of hiring discrimination and tokenism ensured a segregated and hostile police force. The department remained only nominally integrated well into the postwar era, in spite of the NAACP's and other organizations' constant pressure for reform.[119] By 1970, there were only 36 black officers out of a total police force of 711 in Oakland.[120] In Richmond, the total never exceeded 7 out of a police force of over 100.[121]

. . .

IN THE TWO decades after World War II, a popular myth circulated throughout Oakland that the federal government and Maritime Commission had
transported "boxcar loads of migrants from the U.S. South, dumped them
in Oakland, then left them stranded."[122] While no concrete evidence of systematic labor recruitment existed, this rumor gave voice to the racist backlash that typified local government's response to black migration. In 1961,
city manager Wayne Thompson identified the settlement of "large numbers
of minority or deprived groups" and the ensuing flight by older residents
as Oakland's biggest problem. Officials complained that the municipality
faced the changing population, and the high unemployment and increased
need for state services that accompanied it, in fiscal isolation. From their
viewpoint, challenges in the "human sphere" far exceeded those of industrial decline and an aging physical infrastructure.[123] Anxiety about Oakland's deepening "urban crisis" prompted Thompson and his allies to search
for outside money, first from the Ford Foundation and later from President
Lyndon B. Johnson's Office of Economic Opportunity.[124] While these measures represented liberal solutions to the dilemma of urban poverty, the resulting integration of municipal agencies governing schools, recreation, and
police paved the way for a new and more repressive postwar racial order.
Local authorities characterized migrant communities as the sources rather
than the victims of economic decline. In the years to come, the southern
diaspora that animated Seventh Street, the army of storefront churches, and
gutbucket blues clubs became redefined as a problem to be managed.

2. FORTRESS CALIFORNIA

World War II migrants entered the Bay Area in a time of abundance; by contrast their children and successors faced a declining local economy, an increasingly hostile state and local government, and an uncertain future. In the two decades that followed, jobs and opportunity receded, while barriers in housing, education, and employment became more deeply entrenched. City officials often identified migrant youth as the font of social disorganization and sought to contain the effects of "cultural deprivation."[1] Like the impermeable wall in *Native Son* that separated the black environs of Chicago from the city beyond, an increasingly disciplinary school and penal system obscured their parents' dream of possibility. This had serious consequences for young African American migrants, who hoped that they, too, could realize the Golden State's promise of prosperity and social access. Although a segment of this group proved successful, many more did not. With successive generations of black Californians, class disparities grew rather than abated. While their parents faced housing and employment discrimination, young people confronted a new regime of repressive social-service agencies, segregated schooling, and police and penal authorities.

The story of southern migrants and their "rising expectations" was not unique to the city of Oakland or the state of California. In the era spanning the Great Migrations, southern newcomers repeatedly expressed their frustration with northern cities by referring to them as "Up South." However, each city and region contained its peculiar disappointments.[2] For many West Coast migrants, the Bay Area's initial promise made the subsequent era particularly devastating. The bounty created by federal subsidy for wartime defense created an artificial world that proved unsustainable in the peace that followed. The migrant workforce remained, but their shipyard jobs and fair employment protections had vanished. At the same time, black newcomers floundered in a rapidly growing metropolitan and state economy that largely denied them entry.[3] The proximity of wealth made the problems of poverty and unemployment all the more acute.

To make matters worse, young migrants faced the growing ire of the state. White anxieties about the changing demographics of Oakland focused on black children and teenagers. In the winter of 1962, *Time* interviewed city officials about their efforts to contain the effects of black migration. "Since 1950 the number of Negroes in the city has leaped from 48,000 to 84,000— or from 12% to 23% of the total population. The swelling Negro segment aggravated Oakland's *fever chart*. The schools got worse, crime and juvenile delinquency rose, slums spread" (emphasis mine). Evelio Grillo, Oakland's newly appointed "juvenile control coordinator," explained how these social problems became manifest with the young. "We've got one housing project in Oakland, a fine one that is all by itself and all Negro. I'll guarantee that if you put your son there he'll be a delinquent in six months—if he's normal. If I took my son there, I'd give him a switchblade."[4]

The tendency to view black migration to northern cities as a national crisis fueled a retrenchment of municipal services and an increasingly disciplinary stance of schools and law enforcement toward black youth.[5] Municipal officials and school administrators often invoked the disease metaphor of fever to express their discomfort with the changing composition of the city's schools and streets.[6] Cold War rhetoric of contagion and containment justified local government's repressive attitude. At midcentury, California led the nation in the modernization of policing, and it embarked on the construction of the nation's most comprehensive system of youth incarceration. The California Youth Authority (CYA) combined forces with other state and local agencies to extend its reach into all domains of young people's lives from education to recreation, from school to street.

Born in the South

Like their parents, many of the black children who came of age in the early sixties were born in the South. However, in contrast to the older generation, they remained too far removed from their previous lives to have them serve as templates for the new. Many came as small children and had only the faintest recollection of their places of birth. In 1942, Anne Williams was born in Alexandria, Louisiana, where her father worked off and on as an itinerant singer in a small gospel quartet that traveled from town to town throughout rural Louisiana and Mississippi. When his daughter turned two, Mr. Williams brought the family to California, and they settled in West Oakland's

Anne Williams, age three, and her brother Henry Dalton Williams, age five, shortly after their arrival in West Oakland from Winnfield, Louisiana, in 1945. Photograph courtesy of Anne Williams.

"Lower Bottom."[7] Anne later remembered nothing more of her early childhood than a dirt road, chickens, and pecans on the ground.[8] However, she described how her parents' past lives shaped her own. They were "fearful of just about everything" and hesitant to allow her to participate in activities outside the home or church. Williams noted that the sense of imminent danger and unpredictability that suffused her parents' experience under segregation often influenced how they viewed the city, causing them to lead relatively insular, proscribed lives. She explained, "I think it was a carryover, some vestige from the South . . . [about] how bad things happen, and people aren't seen again. They didn't go far beyond our immediate neighborhood. We had a car, but there wasn't a lot of going back and forth from North Oakland to West Oakland or to San Francisco or to Alameda. We stayed pretty much within a radius, a small, small radius."[9]

The dynamics of chain migration meant that in the two decades following World War II, many children and teenagers followed their parents and older relatives west. Parents worked long hours and invested precious leisure time in recreating the world of the southern familiar through churches and benevolent associations. Whereas older people often viewed the city with fear, their children glimpsed new possibilities. Theirs was not a singular attitude, and of this generation born in the South, young people responded to the city in different ways. Age and the timing of arrival shaped their experiences. As the migration progressed, youth left from poorer and more rural parts of the South.[10] For these newcomers, rural-urban migration converged with the movement west. Many faced not only the distinct culture and expectations of a new region but also the customs of urban living. The density of the city itself represented something unprecedented. Freddie Boone, who had been raised in Wewoka, Oklahoma, and who had not relocated to Oakland until he was twelve years old, explained, "So now I got all of these people around, I mean a whole lot of people, I was like in Disneyland in a way, because everything was new, and it was a whole lot newness. Even the way I talked, because I talked 'flat' with somewhat Oklahoma . . . flatness to it. And so in other words. . . . Rice would be like riiice. 'Mama give me some of that riiiice.'"[11] Boone contrasted his own words with those of California natives, who sounded "crispier" and more insistent.[12]

A "flat tongue" was not the only legacy of a rural childhood spent in the South. Some young people raised on farms derived a strong sense of confidence and self-sufficiency from the variety of skills they developed from working at a young age. Freddie Boone prided himself on his ability to "do everything on the farm," including trap, hunt, and harvest crops. At age five, he learned how to shoot a gun. When faced with the unfamiliar ways of the city and the challenges of language, Boone reminded himself that he could use a rifle and run a whole farm if need be, and these abilities helped counter his sense of uncertainty.[13]

Although he came of age in Berkeley, Robert Seale also prided himself on his early experience with guns "down South." He and his extended family moved to California at the end of World War II. After his birth in 1936, the family shuttled between Dallas, San Antonio, and Port Arthur, Texas, trying to earn enough money for the cross-country journey to the West Coast. Like many wartime migrants, his father, George Seale, was a skilled carpenter who hoped to find work in California's booming defense industry. He moved to Berkeley, and before the war's end, his wife and children followed. While the family dreamed of living in a beautiful "private house," they settled into a four-room barracks-style apartment in Berkeley's Cordonices Village, one of the many temporary housing shelters hastily erected for defense migrants in the East Bay. Throughout his childhood, Bobby returned to visit relatives in Jasper, Texas, and other remote areas. Like Boone, he learned how to hunt and fish at a young age, later bragging that he owned his first rifle at twelve. His early knowledge of firearms became an important source of pride and informed his future activism.[14]

Bobby Seale's and Freddie Boone's experiences reflected those of their peers, but they also showed how gender as well as migration status profoundly influenced young people's impressions of city living. Many southern families remained deeply religious and socially conservative. Parents expected girls to remain close to home, and many young women could not venture easily into the public world of the street. Anne Williams attended church almost every night and, as she grew older, eschewed lipstick, fancy dress, and other vanities her parents deemed sinful. Others turned increasingly to their peers and to the parks and streets of West Oakland for leisure and adventure. Although a few girls succeeded, this type of rebellion was much more accessible to boys. The church represented the most enduring institution of the world older migrants had known, and the struggle to maintain its primacy was often waged with their children. This dynamic was strongest with newcomers from rural areas who viewed the city not only as dangerous but also profane. Pentecostalism's strict rules and list of prohibitions often created conflict within migrant families. In contrast to their parents who responded to the foreign world of urban California by trying to recreate the familiar, young people sought out new points of reference. Unlike their parents, they recognized California as their future and the South as their past.[15]

Both Huey Newton and Fritz Pointer were ministers' sons, and in distinct ways their differences with their fathers' generation shaped Oakland's history. Walter Newton moved to Louisiana in the mid-1930s, where he worked a series of jobs and preached nights at Bethel Baptist. His son Huey was born in Monroe, Louisiana, in 1942. His parents named their youngest of seven after Huey Pierce Long, the state's notorious right-wing populist governor. Walter Sr. admired Long's "ability to talk one philosophy" while implementing another.[16] In 1945, the Newton family migrated west to Oakland at the tail end of the wartime boom. The family was deeply religious and attended church every day; their father moonlighted as the associate pastor for Antioch Baptist Church, where Huey belonged to the Baptist Young People's Union, the Young Deacons, and the junior choir.[17] He later described his childhood as typical of the generation burdened by the disappointments of southern exodus. For many years, the young Newton contemplated joining the ministry, but he gave up the idea once he began studying philosophy at Oakland City College.[18] The church offered a viable strategy for surviving the wages of the city. As Huey grew older, the enticements of "the sporting life" and the monastic world of books and college represented others.

Like Newton, Fritz Pointer was also a war baby. Born in Little Rock, Arkansas, in 1943, he relocated with his parents to Oakland in 1944. His father immediately established the West Oakland Church of God at the corner of Tenth and Myrtle, and it quickly became a focal point for the migrant neighborhood near DeFremery Park. By the time Pointer turned fifteen, he began to contest his father's rules. The young teenager chafed under the relentless prohibitions against smoking, drinking, movies, records, and even dances. "I thought there was something dishonest about him having lived the life he had lived, of a young man, doing the things that he had done which included gambling and bootlegging and all those things, and then coming to an epiphany or religious salvation. I resented that," explained Fritz. Reaction against perceived hypocrisy led him to challenge his father's authority. "Trying to find a life outside of it of course, I went to the extremely [sic] other way. Because there was no real balance, it was either one way or the other."[19] Pointer became involved in petty crime in West Oakland and, like Newton, ultimately ended up serving a term in a CYA juvenile prison. While his rebellion was intensely personal in nature, it also revealed some of the generational tensions engendered by the experience of migration. It was difficult to recreate the self-contained worlds of black southern communities in California's "bad cities," and parents struggled to insulate their children from potential dangers and temptations.[20]

Black Youth Culture and the Perils of the City

In the face of an unfamiliar world, migrant youths sought their own grounds for self-realization and assertion. Like Mexican Americans before them, black children and adolescents often turned to one another for companionship and protection.[21] As an industrial garden of single-family homes punctuated with plush green parks, Oakland's public spaces became central to an emerging black youth culture. Groups of teenagers banded together into informal neighborhood clubs and "gangs" that reflected black settlement patterns. The "Aves," "Junction," and "Brookfield Boys" announced their proximity to Thirty-Fifth Avenue, the rail yards, and the newly built housing project Brookfield Village respectively. DeFremery Park in West Oakland and Arroyo Park in East Oakland became the meeting points for youth from Oakland's two largest black enclaves. Other recreation sites included Bushrod Park near Kaiser Hospital in North Oakland and the infamous mazelike Sobrante Park. Throughout the late forties and fifties, groups of teenagers and preteens gathered, socialized, and vied for control of these public spaces.[22] An adolescent Huey Newton briefly joined a West Oakland street gang called "The Brotherhood."[23] These loose confederations of young people should not be confused with the complex organizations that emerged later. Bounded by geographic markers, small groups of children and adolescents formed quasi-social clubs. In contrast to their successors, they had no ties to the highly structured underground economy in "the numbers" or illicit drugs.[24]

In 1945, Raymond Johnson and his mother arrived in Oakland from Pine Bluff, Arkansas. After the war, they struggled to survive in the city on her single income. The family initially settled in West Oakland near Seventh and Wood and then later relocated to the East Side. As a young teen, the urban world that Raymond and his peers moved through was a highly segmented one, divided into several block-long territories, carefully defended by local groups. Historic West Oakland splintered into a series of smaller enclaves with colorful names like the "Lower Bottom," "Dog Town," and after the construction of the Acorn Housing Project, the "Cornfield."[25] The physical contrast between public housing and single-family homes erected fault lines in the built environment that exacerbated social divisions among youth. Raymond Johnson explained, "We were communities and so when the word went out, [we] would all come to defend the community."[26]

Gender and masculine pride strongly influenced this dynamic. Dating friends or relatives from other neighborhoods could be risky business. As young boys moved through the city, they were always attentive to whose neighborhood they might be passing through. A walk to school might mean crossing the territory of several different clubs, and for protection, teenagers traveled in groups. These early Bay Area gangs differed significantly from their counterparts on the East Coast and in southern California. Composed largely of black southern migrants, social clubs did not cleave sharply along racial or ethnic lines. Rapid white flight to San Leandro, Castro Valley, and other East Bay suburbs meant fewer battles with white youth. In select cases, the white families who stayed in Oakland, either by choice or economic necessity, mixed or assimilated with their black neighbors. Similarly, although several Mexican youth gangs existed in Oakland, there was little conflict with African American peers. The physical geography of the city, not class or origin, set the groups apart.[27]

Although they rarely fought with white youth, police harassment was common. Raymond Johnson later attended the majority white Fremont

High School at Forty-Sixth Avenue and Foothill Boulevard, and as he walked home from school, police frequently stopped him. One night after playing basketball in the school gym, a police cruiser picked him up and placed him in a lineup. The teenager ended up spending the night in jail and missing the following day of school. Arrest and detention could unleash a cascade of problems that left individuals enmeshed within the penal system of the California Youth Authority. Johnson later fought with Fremont's star running back—who happened to be a "Junction boy" from a rival gang. As a result, authorities sentenced him to a two-year term in the CYA's notorious Preston School of Industry that forever altered the course of his life.[28]

Anxieties over the rapid influx of black migrants made local government and the Oakland school system hypervigilant about conflict and behavior problems with students. Racial fear focused acutely on black male youth branded as delinquent. Johnson's case was not atypical. Conflict in school often resulted in authorities designating a select group of migrant youth as "troublemakers." Many boys, and a smaller number of girls, shared this experience. City schools and agencies' disciplinary stance toward young migrants helped provoke the youth movements of the subsequent decade. By the midsixties, the same parks and recreation areas dominated by social clubs and early gangs became meeting grounds for young people to organize politically. Not surprisingly, their shared experience of repression led them to contemplate new forms of resistance.[29] Johnson explained how his sense of powerless affected him and fed his desire to become politically active: "I was harassed all the time and everyday, being by yourself when the cops jammed you [up]. . . . I mean they knock you around, carry on, and there's nothing you can do or say."[30]

In addition to his very personal conflict with his father, Fritz Pointer understood the origins of "delinquency" in migrants' antagonistic relationship with the school system that deteriorated as children grew older. When young people entered junior high school on the cusp of adolescence, the numbers of black teachers receded and the gaps in the curriculum became more obvious. Pointer explained, "I think it began to develop as a lack of identification with the education system, [it] became foreign to me about that time. The material, the teachers—became whiter and whiter. And the real sense of identity with the institution began to fade. We really felt alienated. From junior high on . . . I was like, 'What am I doing here!'"[31] This sentiment was not uncommon. Huey Newton later wrote, "We went to school and we got kicked out. We drifted into patterns of petty delinquency. We were not necessarily criminally inclined, but we were angry."[32]

Jimmy Garrett, a young migrant from Dallas, Texas, who arrived in Los Angeles described a similar problem. As he entered public school in California at age twelve, he became increasingly self-conscious. Both peers and teachers ridiculed his southern-inflected speech. Garrett soon found himself trapped in an elaborate tracking system that separated students into five different levels. The school's organizational structure functioned like a social pyramid with a small elite group termed "X" at the top, and children placed into descending tracks from A to D. The migrant majority ended up in the two lowest levels; their families' relative poverty and recent arrival from the South guaranteed them a place at the bottom. Garrett remembered these classes as dead ends. "School gets paid for you to sit. You sit 'til you get sixteen, then you get out. Or you get pregnant if you're a girl, and you're [put] out." Unwittingly, tracking systems reinforced behaviors they branded as delinquency. With classes that amounted to little more than holding tanks for youth, Garrett recognized that being assigned to D group meant joining the local street gang, the "Roaming Twenties."[33]

Ultimately, tracking stratified students on the basis of class and migration status in ways that affected not only their future opportunities but their self-conceptions. Even if they resisted, young people often believed their teachers. Diminished expectations meant diminished performance. Track A students did A work, while track D students did D work. Garrett described how this hierarchy affected him: "First I went to L.A., and there were white people everywhere in L.A. And this was, to me, just really strange. . . . I came out of a segregated situation. I was considered to be smart in my elementary school and dumb [here], and that's a heavy thing. [First], I had to face the culture shock of dealing with whites. The second thing, I had to face the shock of being dumb."[34]

California and the Battle against De Facto Segregation

Throughout California, black parents witnessed the travails of their children and fought to improve the schools by confronting de facto segregation and the lowered set of expectations that accompanied it. In the years after the passage of *Brown v. Board of Education*, the Oakland NAACP campaigned to elect black members to the Oakland school board, to eliminate the gerrymandering of school districts, and to prevent the closing of Oakland's historic McClymonds High School.

The West Coast presented a complex scenario for civil rights activists. With its distinct multiracial and multiethnic history, California had a "crazy-quilt system of de jure discrimination" that diverged in important ways from other parts of the country. In the words of historian Mark Brilliant, a series of color lines cleaved the state, rather than a single biracial divide.[35] For the first half of the twentieth century, the most organized system of school segregation targeted Mexican Americans rather than African Americans, and it differed in significant ways from southern racial practices. California statutes did not explicitly name Mexicans or Negroes in the list of segregated groups that included "Indians, Mongolians, and Orientals," and local school districts applied the laws selectively. They diverted children into "Mexican schools" only if they were available, and local officials made distinctions of color and class, allowing some children of Mexican descent access to white schools. Perhaps most important, these statutory restrictions focused only on primary education, and in all cases ended with high school.[36] In April 1947, the Ninth Circuit Court of Appeals' decision in *Mendez v. Westminster School District of Orange County* brought this era of ad hoc school segregation to a close, and by June, Governor Earl Warren struck down the last of the discriminatory school statutes.[37]

For black Californians, these judicial decisions had marginal effects. With a population of less than 1 percent of the state's total on the eve of World War II, African Americans—particularly in northern California—inhabited an ambiguous racial status.[38] While they suffered legal employment and housing discrimination, there was no statutory exclusion from public schools and other facilities. It was not until the large-scale migration of the 1940s that black residents became the sustained focus of racial anxieties. During and after the war, white backlash against the growing migrant presence inaugurated a new racial order marked by de facto segregation, restriction of municipal services, and an increasingly invasive criminal justice system. Much of this rancor focused on the young. In a growing chorus, local newspapers and city officials expressed concern over the changing composition of the schools and the rise in juvenile delinquency. Class cleavages in the African American community itself, reinforced by the continuing waves of migration, also exacerbated the marginalization of southern newcomers. Social scientist Charles Johnson noted that almost half of older black residents held migrants responsible for "augment[ing] racial difficulties in the city." Given its tenuous origins, the black middle class was eager to distance itself from more recent arrivals. Historian Marilynn Johnson noted, "Some black residents resented the southern migrants, holding them responsible for resurgent racism."[39]

While intraracial differences of geography, class, and migration status divided the East Bay's black residents, all could agree on the dangers of increasing school segregation in the postwar era. For civil rights activists, the passage of *Brown vs. Board of Education* in 1954 raised the question of whether the Supreme Court's declaration of "separate as inherently unequal" applied to de facto as well as de jure segregation. Like its neighbor to the south, Los Angeles, school segregation in Oakland actually grew worse in the wake of the Supreme Court's landmark decision.[40] But the measures taken to confront this problem varied greatly across the state. Los Angeles, San Francisco, and Richmond faced court-ordered desegregation, while Berkeley and Riverside implemented voluntary busing programs. Oakland represented a third alternative, as the NAACP and other activist groups waged the battle over race and schooling in the political rather than the judicial arena. In attempting to do so, they confronted the same structures and policies that barred much of Oakland's newly settled African American community from electoral representation.[41]

Like the rest of the city government, the Oakland school system originated in the Progressive Era and was "as such naturally resistant to the newcomers' goals."[42] A charter system of governance reinforced corporate interests by placing much of the power of decision making in the hands of nonelected officials. Large defense corporations Bechtel and Kaiser dominated local politics along with the Republican bulwark of the Knowland machine.[43] In the name of progressive ideals of efficiency and expertise, Oakland adopted citywide council and mayoral elections early in the century, thereby eliminating the ward-based system that favored minority constituencies. Questions of procedure superseded concern with the effective delivery of city services. True power flowed from the city manager's office through the network of planners, government professionals, and heads of local agencies.[44] Although a broad-based labor coalition attempted to challenge the antidemocratic structure of local government, it fell to defeat in the aftermath of the Oakland General Strike of 1946.[45]

Historically, school politics in Oakland had been a rather sleepy and indifferent affair. Not until southern migration expanded the black population over fivefold in a single decade did public education became politicized.[46] Although voters elected Oakland's seven-member school board, several institutional practices created a self-reproducing body that remained impervious to the rapidly changing demographics of the city. Upon retirement, school board members appointed successors and supported them as incumbents in the general election. As a result, in forty-eight campaigns over a four-decade span, only five nonincumbents attained electoral office. Not surprisingly, the class and racial composition of the board reflected this insularity. It remained nearly all male, white, and Republican, until a local African American lawyer, Barney Hilburn, ran in 1958. In the coming years, voters would not elect a second black candidate for another decade. Significantly, both African American officials were Republicans.[47]

Despite these long-standing obstacles to democratic participation, black parents and civil rights organizations fought to roll back the advancing tide of de facto segregation. This was no small task. In confronting the Oakland school system, black families faced a complicated and unwieldy set of problems that ranged from persistent patterns of hiring discrimination to the racialized culture of the schools themselves. When California's Fair Employment Practices Commission (CAFEPC) conducted a study of institutional racism in the Oakland district in 1964, even black community institutions like West Oakland's McClymonds High School revealed persistent inequalities in curriculum, administration, and treatment of students.[48]

Oakland Unified consistently allocated resources to segregated white schools in wealthy areas of the city while neglecting overcrowded schools in the "flatlands." In the early sixties, this issue came to a head with the building of Skyline High School in the Oakland hills. Black parents and civil rights leaders charged the school board with "gerrymandering" the district and draining resources from the rapidly integrating schools in the low-lying areas of the city.[49] In the spring of 1966, they formed the Ad Hoc Committee for Quality Education to protest the board's unfair use of resources and its miseducation of their children.[50]

McClymonds High School

"Africa with a few missionaries" was how Freddie Boone described the atmosphere of McClymonds High School in the late fifties. He matriculated there from 1959 to 1963.[51] Although McClymonds's principal was white, African Americans made up the majority of the staff, and the student body was nearly all black and heavily migrant. From Boone's perspective, this lent the school a familiar and protective quality, reinforced by its rich sports and arts curriculum that overlapped with programming at the nearby DeFremery Park Recreation Center. McClymonds's basketball courts became legendary for producing Bill Russell and other NBA stars. The Bay Area pianist Edwin Kelly headed the school's musical program, and he exposed students to the rich Bay Area jazz scene at an early age. Boone, an aspiring drummer, remembered his experiences in the music classes, band, and "Rec Center" as the best part of high school.[52]

Many generations of black Oaklanders shared Boone's affectionate memories of McClymonds. The novelty of attending high school reinforced pride in this West Oakland institution. For many young migrants, this experience was a new one, largely denied their parents and grandparents. As sociologist Charles Johnson noted, the majority of shipyard migrants attended school for a mere eight years for women and seven years for men.[53] Historically, Jim Crow school districts refused to build or staff black high schools. It was not until the 1920s that southern youth of color gained widespread access to secondary education. This advance occurred mainly through the efforts of individual African American communities that sponsored the construction and maintenance of black high schools themselves. Despite these efforts, by the mid-1930s less than 20 percent of black youth attended secondary schools, and in some states the average was half that.[54] In Louisiana, for example, southern whites attended high school at a rate nearly five times that of their black peers. Given their historic denial, access to public education was a particularly meaningful and urgent concern for southern migrant families.[55]

While West Oakland embraced McClymonds as a community institution, in the decade after World War II, black parents expressed concern about its academic rigor and treatment of students. In 1957, a group of about twenty parents organized a meeting with McClymonds's principal and staff to protest the school's "record of low expectations and achievement."[56] They cited poor rates of college attendance among "Mack" graduates, and a recurring pattern of school counselors and officials discouraging students from continuing their education. Administrators responded defensively by emphasizing the students' insufficient preparation for high school. A representative from the University of California at Berkeley added that McClymonds graduates who did continue on to college rarely made it through their first year. These opposing views encapsulated the painful divide between black families and the leadership of the Oakland schools, culminating in widespread school boycotts and community activism of the following decade. Parents focused on substandard curriculum, teaching methods, and treatment of students, while school administrators emphasized the "cultural deprivation" and educational deficiency of the migrant youth they purported to serve.[57]

Black parents may not have been privy to the data at the time, but ample evidence supported their contention. In 1952, the Oakland school district's assistant superintendent and director of architecture published an article describing how the physical design for the new McClymonds facility reflected the special "needs of the pupils of this area." The large percentage of "Negro" students and other "nationalities," high rates of transiency, and disparate levels of academic preparation necessitated a "modified" curriculum. School officials explained, for example, how the science program differed from other local high schools: "Biology is required as in other schools, but with a somewhat different content and objectives. As an illustration, a good deal of attention is given to the care of the hair, skin, and feet. . . . In addition, attitudes and habits that will be useful throughout life can be given the proper emphasis. The care of the feet has proved to be an unusually interesting and worthwhile unit." Similarly, disturbing themes of industrial education echoed throughout the physical design of the school, which featured an extensive "homemaking suite" with "almost every type of modern equipment, including . . . automatic washers and dryers" and "all necessary facilities for ironing and personal grooming."[58]

California FEPC findings exposed the set of assumptions that justified this limited course of instruction.[59] Upon interviewing principals and teachers in majority black schools like McClymonds, investigators noted the consistent emphasis on discipline, comportment, and hygiene over academic achievement. In response, a progressive white member of the school board proposed closing down the historic high school, because it personified the problems associated with de facto segregation—black concentration, white flight, and substandard academics. Despite their frustration, Oakland's African American community rallied to McClymonds's defense.[60] In many respects, the school symbolized the most deeply cherished culture and history of West Oakland. Parents did not want to eliminate McClymonds but rather to raise the overall quality of its curriculum and instruction to levels comparable with the best schools in the city.

Although conditions in McClymonds and its feeder schools were far from ideal, institutions in other parts of the city exhibited even more striking racial inequality. As black settlement expanded north and east, neighborhood schools proved more resistant to black newcomers. Castlemont and Oakland Technical High School employed much smaller numbers of black teachers and lacked the community infrastructure of McClymonds. By the early sixties, these two high schools became flashpoints of racial conflict, as the once majority white student bodies receded. In the face of rapid change, school administrators failed to adapt to the new group of young people that filled their corridors. In contrast to Freddie Boone's fond recollections of McClymonds, Huey Newton, who attended primary and secondary schools in North Oakland, remembered with bitterness that "during those long years in the Oakland public schools, I did not have one teacher who taught me anything relevant to my own life or experience."[61]

Hiring discrimination proved one of the biggest obstacles to making the Oakland Unified School District receptive to its growing black student body. In 1964, C. L. Dellums and the California Fair Employment Practices Commission published "A Report on Oakland Schools" that provided a window into the structural problems within the district. In the 1962–63 school year, the administration hired 318 teachers for positions in elementary, secondary, special fields, and community college instruction. While decisive racial breakdowns of new teachers were not available, the FEPC identified clear patterns that marginalized black applicants. The district recruited applicants from twenty-two colleges in California and from "preferred schools" outside the state in every major region except the South. The school system's failure to establish "personal contact" with southern schools disadvantaged black teachers, who trained in large numbers in historically black colleges and universities (HBCUs). Despite their exclusion, black institutions from five southern states, including Texas, Louisiana, and Oklahoma, took the initiative to send job applicants.[62]

Although prospective black teachers faced barriers, entering the ranks of school administration and nonteaching personnel proved nearly impossible for African Americans. This category included principals, vice principals, guidance counselors, health, and special education personnel. Only three of the city's eighty-three elementary school principals and two out of thirty-four junior high principals were of African descent. Of the city's seventeen high schools, including the majority black McClymonds, not a single one had a black principal.[63] In order to correct this inequity, C. L. Dellums proposed that the school district employ "a color consciousness" in hiring to ensure that teachers "from all racial and national groups would be selected when qualified and for any position at any school."[64]

In addition to hiring, school placement showed clear patterns of racial discrimination. Oakland Unified assigned the vast majority of African American teachers to elementary, junior high, and high schools with majority black student bodies.[65] Across the district, nearly 70 percent of African American teachers taught in "Negro schools," leading the FEPC to conclude that "Negro teachers have primarily been hired to teach Negro students and that the non-Negro teachers, especially the Caucasian ones, have been hired on the basis of merit to fill vacancies wherever they exist." Black instructors also appeared disproportionately in the ranks of substitute teachers. Despite composing roughly 10 percent of Oakland's teaching faculty in the early sixties, African Americans, according to an FEPC estimate, made up nearly half of substitutes.[66] Interviews with black teachers and their advocates revealed that most applicants of color "were relegated to substitute work and must prove their classroom ability in this manner" to become eligible for regular employment. Many of these placement disparities, like hiring, could be traced back to ranking procedures that marginalized HBCUs and their graduates.[67]

In exploring the process of teacher selection in greater detail, the FEPC found that larger numbers of black instructors failed the subjective evaluation by other teachers. When the district interviewed candidates, "voice and speech qualities" appeared to be essential criteria, leading investigators to conclude that simply attending a "predominantly Negro school in the southern part of the United States . . . and . . . speak[ing] with a strong and noticeable regional accent was enough to disqualify them."[68] Theoretically, the same issue also applied to white southern migrants, but they constituted a small proportion of the applicant pool. Bias against southern speech and idiom served as one of the most enduring social barriers to migrant youth and teacher alike. One principal in a majority black school declared that they would not allow a drama department because the "Negro students have a special accent and are not suited for stage work."[69] This devaluation of southern language and culture created a steep terrain of class differentiation within the African American community; policing speech and cleansing it of the obvious signs of southern origins became essential to professional success.

Community dissatisfaction with the Oakland school system extended beyond its failure to hire African American teachers and administrators in sufficient numbers. Parents expressed anger over the authoritarian teaching methods used on their children. This concern extended to black teachers as well as their white peers, thereby raising more fundamental concerns about how the Oakland school system responded to its changing student body. In addition to revealing discrimination in hiring and promotion of school personnel, the CAFEPC also identified differential standards and treatment of black students as pervasive problems throughout the Oakland Unified School District. Faculty often viewed academic achievement in racial terms, identifying "Oriental students" as the highest achievers, followed by "Caucasian" students, with "Negroes" and "Spanish speakers" at the bottom. They reserved their harshest judgments and the lowest expectations for black and Latino boys.[70] While these attitudes recurred time and again, the report also showed variation based on the racial makeup of the schools. These patterns repeated themselves with such frequency that the CAFEPC divided its report into sections examining "racially mixed, predominantly Negro, and predominantly Caucasian" institutions separately.

According to observers, a culture of discipline and control reigned in majority-black high schools. Principals were "almost completely discipline oriented," and the school established student patrols to keep order in the hallways. Administration and staff focused on the dress of and behavior of students, noting with pride that their institution had fewer broken windows and "less outlandish" student apparel than at other high schools. The concern with discipline and control was so extreme that one principal actually related to the FEPC staff that "we cannot have the students meet very often in assembly where all of the students are present, and we must limit the number of school activities that would require a large attendance by the student body, such as theatrical productions." He attributed this to the fact that "Negro students" easily get "the fever."[71]

Many of these issues came to a head in the case of Irene Sawyer, an African American teacher who graduated from Mills College with a bachelor's degree in art before being hired by Oakland Unified in 1952. A decade later, the district removed her from a junior high school in East Oakland after parents and staff complained repeatedly that she had abused students by using racial epithets and referring to their children as "niggers" and "black bastards." Sawyer allegedly told one little girl in the seventh grade, "You are a Negro you know, you are nothing but little ignorant fools."[72] Initially, the *San Francisco Chronicle* championed her case, attracting the attention of Roy Wilkins, who subsequently wrote a national column defending her "high standards." After Dellums and the California FEPC carefully investigated the case, Wilkins publicly retracted his statements and declared that they had not been issued on behalf of the NAACP but rather as part of his personal newspaper column.[73] The Sawyer case highlighted a disturbing pattern that the FEPC observed repeatedly in majority black schools:

> At each predominantly Negro school that was visited, the investigator asked the principal to introduce him to any Negro teacher that the principal felt was doing a very good job. Almost invariably, this Negro teacher turns out to be a strict and harsh disciplinarian. Several Negro teachers in this category had such strong feelings about Negro

students that their feelings amounted to hostility. In each instance, when asked, they would reply that keeping order in school was the prime job of the school. These were teachers who were very critical of the Negro students and took it upon themselves to criticize dress and behavior as their prime role as faculty members.[74]

Juvenile Delinquency and the California Youth Authority

The increasingly disciplinary culture of black schools did not take place in a vacuum. As racial change began to transform many of Oakland's neighborhoods, schools became essential to city politics. Government officials feared that racial conflict would accelerate white flight and therefore sought to shape school policy. City officials and the growing phalanx of social workers employed to manage the changes facing the city carefully watched the "newcomer population," whom they often deemed "culturally deprived." Conflicts in schools and generational tensions within migrant communities were of particular concern.[75]

Like many state institutions in California, the corrections industry vastly expanded during and after World War II. In 1941 the state established the California Youth Authority and, in 1944, the Adult Authority. Based on the older model of individualized treatment, these two institutions had full discretionary powers to determine parole release dates. While this system represented a triumph of the progressive ideas of therapeutic rehabilitation based on the ideal of individualized treatment, the ultimate effect was to make prison sentences completely indeterminate. The infusion of federal defense money and newfound prosperity enabled the state to build five medium security adult facilities between 1944 and 1950.[76] This new state capacity dovetailed with the increasing concern over juvenile delinquency at the state and federal level. In 1953, J. Edgar Hoover, the head of the Federal Bureau of Investigation (FBI) issued a special report to "all law enforcement officials," warning about the dangerous effects of California's baby boom: "The first wave in this flood tide of new citizens born between 1940 and 1950 has just this year reached the 'teen age,' the period in which some of them will inevitably incline toward juvenile delinquency and, later, a full-fledged criminal career."[77]

In the 1950s, neighborhood change in Oakland took place at a breakneck pace. The nonwhite population in West Oakland grew from 50 percent in 1950 to 70 percent in 1960. North and East Oakland had even more radical shifts in composition. In the same decade, their minority populations increased from 15 percent to 61 percent and 8 percent to 51 percent, respectively. From the viewpoint of older residents, significant differences in age exacerbated racial change. In the northern and western sections of the city adjacent to Oakland City College, "an increasingly youthful black population dwelt beside an increasingly elderly white population."[78]

Local government responded to the waves of black migration and white flight by focusing on "juvenile delinquency." Public service agencies fielded the cascade of disputes that followed from changing demographics. An array of white parents, merchants, and residents filed complaints, while school grounds and recreation areas became flash points of racial conflict. Neighborhoods undergoing swift racial transition sought to obtain funds from the city council for reorganizing social service agencies. When city government refused to allocate money for specific areas, groups banded together to form the neighborhood-based Associated Agencies (AA) and District Community Councils.[79] In its final form, the Associated Agencies of Oakland encompassed three tiers of government responsible for youth and family services. At the local level, the AA integrated the Oakland public school system, recreation, and police departments with the county's probation, welfare, and health agencies. Finally, these two divisions began to work closely with the California Youth Authority, one of the state's largest penal institutions.[80] Evelio Grillo, a Cuban-born migrant, who had relocated to the San Francisco Bay Area from Tampa via New Orleans, became instrumental in this municipal reorganization.[81] He helped set up section committees, composed of line workers and low-level supervisors, in each neighborhood throughout Oakland. The timing of their establishment reflected the greatest areas of black population influx, thereby underlining their true purpose—managing racial transition. The areas that experienced the least demographic change were slowest to set up local programs. By contrast, neighborhood agencies in target areas with large numbers of newcomers became hypervigilant about potential "control problems." Meetings with multiple family service and juvenile agencies allowed older residents to work together to identify and track "troublemakers."[82]

The City of Oakland and the Oakland School District provided funds and hired Grillo as the city's first "juvenile control coordinator."[83] He became responsible for overseeing the integration of schools, recreation facilities, and municipal authorities. Participants shared information about individual youths who had come to the attention of more than one agency. Their greatest fear focused on the "rumble." Increasingly, the category of black youth itself became defined as a social problem at best and as a criminal presence at worst. Judith May, a U.C. Berkeley researcher who worked closely with Oakland city government, explained, "Since World War II, low-income blacks and other minorities have largely fallen within the purview of care-taking professionals: they have been the subjects of local government rather than citizens. The care rendered them has been stingy and repressive."[84]

Officials often used Cold War metaphors of contagion and containment to describe black residents, with the greatest threat emanating from black children and adolescents. Oakland city manager Wayne Thompson, known for his liberal goodwill, explained the logic behind the Associated Agencies. Elementary, junior high, and secondary schools were the font of "social disorganization," and if left unchecked they would degenerate into a state of gang warfare and destroy the social fabric of the city.

> Soon, the adults become involved and develop animosities among
> themselves.... If you didn't stop it, it would spread into the business
> sections and even infect the industrial community.... We had eyes
> and ears in those areas to alert us in advance.... Before the Associ-
> ated Agencies program, it was an admission of weakness on the part
> of the school official, or an admission of failure if he even let a police-
> man in the door. He might have had a riotous condition existing in
> the school, but he'd refuse to let an "outsider" in. What a change now!
> The first man they call is the policeman.[85]

One of the most disturbing aspects of this integration of schools with police was the tracking of youths identified as delinquent. In some cases, police surveilled and even arrested individuals that had been identified by school and recreational staff, despite the fact that they had no prior records. City officials hoped to use preventive policing to stop the advancing tide of "social disorganization." This meant forging strong alliances between the Alameda County Probation Department, California Youth Authority, and the Oakland Recreation Department (ORD) to expand the reach of police into the everyday life of black youth through, among other avenues, the unlikely guise of recreational programs. It soon became common practice for parole officers to attend OPD-sponsored dances, and by agreement the police controlled the lighting.[86] Through careful observance of section committee meetings, Judith May observed, "The Associated Agencies was essentially a neighborhood-based deployment operation utilizing intelligence supplied by its members to coordinate the application of police power and administrative sanctions to juveniles so as to maintain control over a territory."[87] In the fifties city officials joined forces with black reformers and the Urban

League to penetrate deeper into migrant communities and to identify so-called "maladjusted children."[88]

DeFremery Park and Black Uplift

Black social workers and middle-class elites played an important role in the postwar racial order. Since the late 1940s, black reformers focused their attention on DeFremery and other public parks. They expressed concern about large numbers of migrant youth with working parents and little support from their far-flung extended families. By providing "supportive nurturing in a structured setting right in their own community," they sought to counter the "lure of the street" and its companion, juvenile delinquency.[89] In 1947, the ORD hired Dorothy Pitts and established the DeFremery Park Recreation Center. Pitts had previously worked for the Urban League, and she hoped to build character and elevate the self-esteem of West Oakland youth through a program of constructive leisure. Organized recreation served as a means to "socialize" young people to "integrate [them] into an urban society."[90]

By the early 1960s, DeFremery became part of a larger campaign to manage migrants and combat juvenile delinquency. The long hand of uplift ideology extended into DeFremery's programming for youth, and class socialization was a recurrent theme. Activities ranged from personal and familial improvement to dance lessons. Self-help manifested itself in gendered ways that sought to shore up the two-parent family, to reinforce traditional ideas of chastity and femininity for young women, and to initiate young men into the masculine world of fraternal orders and organized sports. DeFremery offered charm and etiquette classes for preteens and young adults, a "Mother of the Year" award, and a yearly Sadie Hawkins dance. It also featured its own ad hoc "Duke and Duchess Club" along with the "the Gay Ladies and the Bold Bachelors," modeled on the elite black social club, "Jack and Jill."[91]

Local government strongly supported this agenda, and in the fifties the Republican mayor of Oakland, Clifford Rischell, attended the DeFremery Recreation Center's debutante ball, along with California's first black assemblyman, Byron Rumford. A photograph taken in the late 1950s showed a stream of young women descending the staircase of DeFremery's Victorian mansion with Rischell and Rumford waiting at the base.[92] Behind the recreation center's flurry of activities and programs lay a larger anxiety about the rapidly changing demographics of the East Bay. The social ambitions of black reformers converged with the increasing wariness of Oakland's

Girls learning the proper etiquette for drinking tea in a charm school class at the DeFremery Recreation Center, 1950s. Founded by city officials in 1947, the center became integral to the cultural and social life of West Oakland in the postwar years. Photograph by E. F. Joseph, courtesy of the African American Museum and Library at Oakland.

Republican city government about the rapid influx of black migrants and the resulting changes to neighborhoods and schools. Director Pitts claimed that their success in "recreating youth" culminated in a substantial drop in "juvenile delinquency" between 1947 and 1955.[93] With its central location in West Oakland, DeFremery competed with other service organizations—including the Nation of Islam, the YMCA/YWCA, and the church—for the "hearts and minds" of migrant youth.[94]

A significant portion of the new black leadership class that entered Oakland politics in the sixties emerged from the ranks of social workers and administrators. Municipal agencies and poverty programs created a direct conduit to electoral politics. The trajectory of future congressman Ronald Dellums was one of the best examples. While a graduate student in social welfare at U.C. Berkeley, Dellums worked for the Oakland Recreation Department, first as the after-school recreation director at Lafayette Elementary School and later as playground director at DeFremery Park. After receiving his M.A., Dellums headed up the Bayview Community Center, Hunters Point Youth Opportunity Center, and the employment division of the San Francisco Economic Opportunity Council.[95] He later became an important force for social change in the Bay Area, using far-flung networks that bridged the youth vote of northern California's public campuses with its rapidly expanding migrant presence. Nevertheless, Dellums's candidacy revealed a shift in black political power in the East Bay. In a 1974 doctoral thesis from U.C. Berkeley, sociologist Will Tate argued that increased "black

Oakland mayor Clifford Rischell (*right*) and African American assemblyman W. Byron Rumford greet black debutantes at the DeFremery Recreation Center, 1950s. In addition to sponsoring self-improvement classes, the center staged lavish coming-out balls such as this. Photograph by E. F. Joseph, courtesy of the African American Museum and Library at Oakland.

visibility" in postwar Oakland gave birth to a "new urban elite." By managing the rapidly expanding African American population, this group played an essential role in postwar city politics. With its moorings firmly in the public sector, this new elite superseded their older Pullman predecessors, whose status depended on secret societies and a segregated economy.[96]

Modernization of Policing

While the pageantry of DeFremery Park hinted at the growing class polarization of the local African American community, law enforcement's push for modernization represented the single most important factor in the criminalization of black youth. Changes in East Bay law enforcement reflected a national trend toward "legalistic policing," characterized by modern equipment, formalized systems, and greater emphasis on juvenile detention. Ironically, while this new wisdom officially downplayed overt targeting of poor, minority, and other marginal groups—through vigorous enforcement of misdemeanors, including traffic tickets, loitering, and curfew violations—it vastly increased charges of police "harassment." In addition, Oakland's new police chief dissolved local precincts, concentrated the OPD into a single headquarters, and overhauled hiring practices in favor of better-educated, more affluent candidates.[97]

In practice, these policies created an almost exclusively white middle-class force that resided outside the city and had little understanding or connection to the populations they served. Disconnection from the community severely handicapped intelligence capabilities, making law enforcement dependent on neighborhood-based youth services for information. The line between service and surveillance soon collapsed. The police department ceded territory to the recreations department by abandoning its own "group guidance" and recreation programs. Interestingly, in contrast to other cities, Oakland did not establish new agencies to deal with the growing number of youth gangs. Instead, police worked in tandem with the school system and the ORD, which provided regular reports about participants in its programs.[98]

Oakland's reinvigorated police force became a constant and intrusive presence in people's lives. Systematic arrests of young offenders linked them into the web of professional services, including probation officers, judges, and child guidance clinics, thereby further blurring the line between "authoritative" police functions and family services. Given the pervasive hostility toward black migrants, this framework laid the basis for the simultaneous criminalization of black youth and the long-term neglect of black families. The Associated Agencies' focus on organizational cooperation and control meant that social services paid little attention to their effectiveness in meeting the needs of the public. Disciplinary concerns eclipsed their relationship with clients and created a vacuum that would later be addressed first by the Ford Foundation, then by Great Society agencies, and ultimately by Panther survival programs.[99]

The postwar focus on preventive policing put a certain type of young person at risk. While all black children and adolescents faced potential harassment and exposure to the California Youth Authority, the heaviest burden lay on a carefully watched group of "newcomer" youth, whom police, recreation, and school officials designated as "socially maladjusted." Ever vigilant about gangs and juvenile delinquency, city officials sought to isolate and contain these young people apart from the rest of the black population.[100] As a poor migrant from a single-parent home, Raymond Johnson was exactly the kind of young person that the state both feared and demonized. After repeated run-ins with authorities, he described the feeling of always "being in the eye of the police." Johnson understood all too well that attracting too much attention could be dangerous. The California Youth Authority was filled with "the guys that were the most visible," who also tended to be "the ones [who] were the least afraid." When released, they sauntered "down the street, [as if to say] heck with some cops." Foreshadowing the organized conflict with law enforcement that later emerged in Oakland, Johnson remembered, "Before you were visible because you were in the street out there all the time making your hustle, . . . and then you became more visible because you were politicized."[101]

Youth Authority facilities could be brutal places, and many children and adolescents had experiences that marked them for life.[102] After cycling in and out of "juvy," Raymond Johnson ended up in the Preston School of Industry, one of the CYA's most notorious juvenile prisons. Originally constructed in 1893, this neo-Gothic edifice, with its dark tower and ornate architecture, resembled a "medieval dungeon." To many, it simply became known as "the Castle."[103] The brutality of its treatment regime reinforced its sinister appearance. Preston was California's "largest and toughest" reformatory, and law enforcement often identified its inmates as the state's "worst young criminal offenders and delinquents." Originally touted as a model institution, Preston was rocked by a series of scandals during World War II, and its reputation only grew worse in the decades to come. Critics described the facility as "the San Quentin of the California Youth Authority."[104] The youth prison employed a military system structuring inmates' days with a regimented program with few educational or recreational programs. Officials used peer monitors and silent marches to subdue the inmates, and physical abuse was common. Not surprisingly, Preston failed miserably in achieving the CYA's stated goal of rehabilitation.[105] Raymond Johnson served a two-year term there from 1962 to 1964, and he remembered it as a profoundly "racist institution." For discipline infractions, guards took him down into the lower recesses of the building and beat him. He remembered being chained to a wall and locked overnight in a little room filled with rats and other vermin.[106]

Emory Douglas suffered a similar regime of abuse in the California Youth

Authority. Like Johnson, Douglas was a migrant from a single-parent household. Born in Grand Rapids, Michigan, Emory moved to San Francisco with his mother in 1951, after his parents divorced.[107] Like many of his peers, Douglas cycled in and out of the CYA, where he endured the virulent racism of guards, who commonly used the "n" word and told him to "go back to Africa." With much sadness, his mother, Lorraine Douglas—who worked at a handicapped concession stand for the city's state and federal offices—watched not only her son but multiple generations of young people pass through "juvy" and other state services. She observed up close how these encounters left many families with deep grievances.[108]

While Newton, Pointer, Johnson, and Douglas all faced detention as juveniles, the young Eldridge Cleaver experienced the CYA as a direct conduit to the adult prison system. His sojourn through California's network of correctional institutions started with his parents' relocation to Los Angeles in 1947. When Eldridge turned eleven, the Cleaver family migrated to the West Coast from Wabbasekka, Arkansas. They lived for a time in Watts, and like other rural-urban migrants, the young Eldridge Cleaver was often embarrassed by his southern origins. He later remembered that for black Angelinos "Watts was a place of shame." Young people used "Watts as an epithet in much the same way as city boys used 'country" as a terms of derision."[109] Trapped at the economic and social margins of the city, Cleaver found his own means of survival and escape. Less than a year after the family's arrival in California, police charged Eldridge with vandalism and theft. After subsequent arrests, Cleaver spent nearly two decades in California's youth and adult prisons.[110] He later explained the impact of his time at CYA on the future direction of his life:

> When you focus on the adult penitentiaries, you're looking at the end
> of the line, trying to see where the process begins. But if you really
> want to understand and see what's behind the prison system, you have
> to look at Juvenile Hall. . . . That's where I started my career. . . . They
> took me to Juvenile Hall, and it took me about six months to get out
> again. . . . Then I moved up the ladder from Juvenile Hall to Whittier
> Reform School for youngsters. I graduated from there with honors
> and went to another one a little higher, Preston School of Industries.
> I graduate[d] from that one and they jumped me up to the big leagues
> to the adult penitentiary system.[111]

As these personal histories indicate, racial profiling, culture of poverty ideology, deindustrialization, and the postwar expansion in penal infrastructure all contributed to California's incarceration of significant numbers of black male children and adolescents. The largest inmate population came from Los Angeles County, but Bay Area youth were also well represented.[112] Raymond Johnson remembered meeting Huey Newton and other future Panthers regularly on the streets of Oakland and in the halls of the California Youth Authority.[113] For this group of young migrants, the experience became so commonplace that they developed their own euphemisms to explain their prolonged periods of absence. Many parolees described their stints in the CYA as "Going to Europe."[114]

. . .

CALIFORNIA'S CAMPAIGNS against juvenile delinquency had far-reaching effects. One of the compelling questions is to what extent state and local government produced exactly the social problem they feared most. By harassing and arresting large numbers of young people, and by creating a revolving door between juvenile prisons and society at large, authorities criminalized a segment of black youth that the Black Panther Party later embraced as "the lumpen." The combined effects of employment discrimination, school segregation, and postwar deindustrialization meant widespread poverty and joblessness for many of Oakland's southern migrants. While all African Americans suffered unemployment rates two to three times those of whites, the job prospects for black youth proved particularly dire. For some, petty crime offered recourse to the informal economy, supplementing life at the social and economic margins. Initially, this group was fluid, without clear divisions from the larger community or the traditional black working class; however, as growing numbers of young people became enmeshed in the criminal justice system, this began to change. To explain the destructive effects of the carceral state on a vulnerable cross section of black youth, Eldridge Cleaver used the perverse metaphor of a cradle-to-grave school system:

> I noticed that every time I went back to jail, the same guys were in
> Juvenile Hall with me there were also there again. They arrived there
> soon after I got there, or a little bit before I left. They always seemed
> to make the scene. In the California prison system, they carry you
> from Juvenile Hall to the old folks' colony down in San Luis Obispo,
> and wait for you to die. Then they bury you there. . . . You will find
> graduating classes moving up from Juvenile Hall, all the way up.
> . . . It occurred to me that this was a social failure, one that cannot be
> justified. . . . Not by any stretch of the imagination can the children

in Juvenile Halls be condemned, because they're innocent, and they're processed by an environment that they have no control over.[115]

Given their age, race, and class, migrant youth had little power to counter abuses by police and penal authorities through established channels. Instead, in the years to come, they invented new modes of resistance. From 1955 to 1966, a shift occurred from the organized efforts of parents associations and civil rights activists to a broader and more spontaneous protest movement of young people themselves. The places in which they encountered state power—schools, police, youth authorities, and even parks and recreation—became essential to their growing racial and class consciousness. They did not accept their fate passively, and in less than a generation, the defense migration of World War II gave birth to a sustained and militant opposition to the state, centered in radical black youth culture. First- and second-generation migrants developed new forms of politics and speech to counter the hostility that greeted them in West Coast cities. And in the 1960s, organizations like the Afro-American Association and the Black Panther Party for Self Defense channeled both their anger and their pain into a concrete program of consciousness-raising and action.

PART TWO.
THE CAMPUS AND THE STREET, 1961–1966

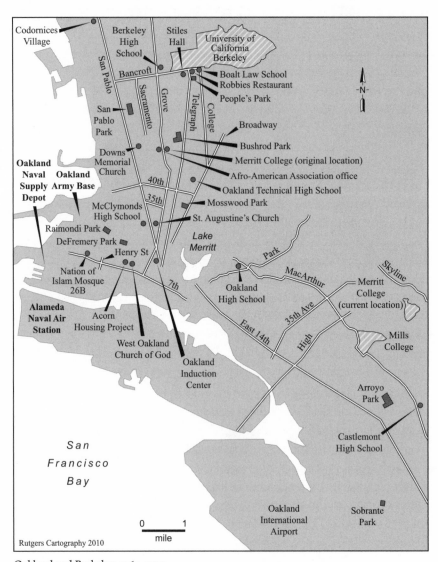

Codornices
Village

Berkeley
High
School

Stiles
Hall

University of
California
Berkeley

San Pablo

Bancroft

Sacramento

Grove

Telegraph

College

-N-

Boalt Law School
Robbies Restaurant

People's Park

San
Pablo
Park

Broadway

Downs
Memorial
Church

Bushrod Park

Merritt College (original location)

Oakland
Naval
Supply
Depot

Oakland
Army Base

40th

Afro-American Association office

Oakland Technical High School

35th

Mosswood Park

McClymonds
High School

St. Augustine's Church

Raimondi Park

DeFremery Park

Henry St

Lake
Merritt

Park

MacArthur

Skyline

Merritt
College
(current location)

Nation of
Islam Mosque
26B

7th

Oakland
High School

35th Ave

Alameda
Naval Air
Station

Acorn
Housing Project

East 14th

High

Mills
College

West Oakland
Church of God

Oakland
Induction
Center

Arroyo
Park

Castlemont
High School

San
Francisco
Bay

0   1
mile

Oakland
International
Airport

Sobrante
Park

Oakland and Berkeley, 1960–1970

3. WE CARE ENOUGH TO TELL IT

Throughout the spring of 1961, black college students waged a campaign to have Malcolm X speak at the University of California, Berkeley. Initially the university administration granted permission but then abruptly withdrew its approval. Vice Chancellor Edward W. Strong explained that having the minister speak violated Article Nine, Section Nine of the California State Constitution, mandating that the university remain "independent of all political or sectarian influence."[1] In response, a small but determined group of black students encompassing a range of backgrounds, political orientations, and fields of study came together to confront the university's administration. They barraged the campus newspapers with angry letters and met repeatedly with school officials, but their efforts had little effect. The youth chapter of the NAACP had no choice but to move the event off campus to Stiles Hall on Bancroft Avenue—the southern boundary of the university.[2]

In early May, Malcolm X addressed his talk, "Elijah Muhammad: Messenger to the American Negro," to a multiracial crowd composed largely of Berkeley students and young people from the surrounding community. With characteristic wit, the minister joked playfully with the audience that U.C. Berkeley had prevented him from speaking because he *was* a religious figure, while San Quentin had done so because he *was not*.[3] Although no written records of the speech remain, the fight to have Malcolm X speak proved as important as his presence. Within less than a year after his visit, the core group of students that struggled to bring him to campus formed an all-black organization called the Afro-American Association. In a few short years, the association expanded from a campus study group into an important force in Bay Area black politics. Led initially by powerful and charismatic law students Donald Warden, Henry Ramsey, and Donald Hopkins, the association would help to ignite a broad-based youth movement that drew on the resources of Bay Area colleges and universities to address the problems facing the East Bay's migrant majority. While its earliest membership came from

71

Berkeley students from all over the United States, the association soon attracted young people from local high schools and community colleges.[4]

Many personal memoirs and formal histories have remarked on the stealthy advance of the 1964 Free Speech Movement. At first glance, the relatively placid world of Berkeley in the early sixties appeared to have more in common with the staid timbre of the preceding decade.[5] And yet, there were distinct signs often at the literal margins of the campus that revealed the upheaval to come. Lesser known and more poorly understood was how black students' growing presence on the Berkeley campus and at other Bay Area schools fed the development of the West Coast's Black Power movement after 1965. While the Watts rebellions signaled a turning point, inaugurating a new militant and anti-integrationist strain of black politics, many of the social networks and ideas that formed the core of California's Black Power movement had their roots on the campuses of public colleges and universities. In the years bounded by the victory of Nkrumah's Convention People's Party in Ghana and the Birmingham riots in Alabama, a small group of black students—largely invisible to Berkeley's wider community—began meeting in an informal study group to debate the meaning of color and nation.[6] Over the next decade, their conversations expanded in ever-widening circles to Merritt College, San Francisco State, and the East Bay's southern diaspora.

As California's first indigenous Black nationalist organization, the Afro-American Association laid the intellectual foundations for the West Coast Black Power Movement that exploded out of Los Angeles and Oakland in the aftermath of the Watts rebellions. Its loose membership included figures who went on to prominence across a spectrum of black politics, ranging from future Oakland mayor Elihu Harris to Ronald Everett (later known as Maulana Karenga) of the US organization and Huey Newton of the Black Panther Party. The association was a crucial link in explaining why Black nationalism and Black Power developed such firm moorings in California, despite the comparatively small percentage of the black population and the recentness of their migration.[7] Berkeley graduate students Donald Warden, Henry Ramsey, and Donald Hopkins founded the organization and received an official charter from Berkeley's Associated Students of the University of California in March 1962. However, their ambitions extended beyond the "sandbox politics" of university life, and they expanded their base into the rapidly growing black population centers of the Bay Area. Using "street speaking" and Harlem-style rallies, association members recruited in San Francisco's Fillmore District, West Oakland's Seventh Street, and black

Richmond. Despite attempts to mobilize ordinary residents, the AAA had its greatest impact on black students at local community colleges and secondary schools.

In the early sixties, African decolonization, the teachings of Malcolm X and the Nation of Islam, and the militant internationalism of Robert F. Williams raised a compelling set of concerns that intertwined with and helped revitalize students' approaches to local struggles. Many of the ideas generated in the association, including their debates about the nature of identity, African retention, and the integrationist sins of the black middle class, anticipated cultural nationalist thought of subsequent years. Although historians have largely overlooked this early black student movement in the East Bay, it was a crucial prelude to the better known tale of Black Power after Watts.[8] This chapter considers the events leading up to the Afro-American Association's founding at Berkeley in the spring of 1961 and documents its efforts at recruitment and expansion into the East Bay's migrant diaspora. Chapter four continues this story and considers how the AAA helped to catalyze a radical Black Studies movement at Merritt College that preceded the establishment of the Black Panther Party for Self Defense.

• • •

THE EMERGENCE of the Afro-American Association was intimately tied to the cultural and structural changes overtaking U.C. Berkeley in the late fifties and early sixties. While black students faced particular obstacles, their growing politicization overlapped with that of the larger student body. Malcolm X's speech at Stiles Hall was one of a litany of events in spring 1961 that brought the distant events of the Cold War and the civil rights movement to the immediate campus community. The year before, Bay Area college students—over half of whom came from U.C. Berkeley—successfully disrupted the House Un-American Activities Committee's (HUAC) proceedings in San Francisco. Armed with petitions containing 1,000 signatures from fellow students and 300 from faculty members, they staged a sit-in in the rotunda of city hall, where U.C. Berkeley student Douglas Wachter had been summoned to testify. Both the intensity of the opposition and the $250,000 cost to the city convinced San Francisco mayor George Christopher to deny HUAC future access. Although the expanding tide of campus radicalization in California remained largely invisible to the general public until 1964, HUAC's defeat emboldened students and hinted at the upheaval to come.[9]

Berkeley president Clark Kerr embodied many of the contradictions of the postwar University of California, which sought to maintain a precarious balance between the demands of popular education with a unique role among American universities as the leading military contractor of the Cold War.[10] As president of the United States' largest and arguably most prominent public university, Clark Kerr became a self-designated emissary of higher education, delivering a series of lectures on the subject at Harvard in the early sixties.[11] An expert in economics and labor relations, Kerr invented the idea of the "multiversity," which made the increasingly specialized and anomic world of higher education fully accessible to the American public. Using Berkeley as a model, he assailed the historical image of the university as a disinterested "community of masters and students." The postwar multiversity was the quintessential pluralist institution, serving the many rather than the few.[12] It could fulfill even the most personal and profane wants of its major constituencies, including parking for faculty, sports for alumni, and sex for students.[13] Kerr's role as the public university's kindly statesman sometimes conflicted with his authorship of California's Master Plan for Higher Education. In this capacity, he fought ruthlessly with the California state system to consolidate the University of California's elite status as the exclusive graduate research institution strategically positioned to maximize federal research dollars released in the wake of Sputnik.[14]

While conflicts over free speech fueled Berkeley's growing student movement, larger structural problems contributed equally, if not more, to student discontent. In 1962, California surpassed New York as America's most populous state. Regional increase combined with the postwar baby boom created explosive growth in the student population. In the years spanning the 1950 and 1960 censuses, the state's population increased by half, while its school enrollment doubled.[15] The spike in college-age youth alone, however, could not explain swelling college enrollments. The changing labor market and increased rate of high school graduation also accelerated demand for higher education. In the Golden State, residents increasingly viewed a university degree as a right rather than a privilege.[16] This had major repercussions for U.C. Berkeley, whose student body expanded from 18,728 to 25,454 between 1960 and 1964.[17] Taught primarily by overworked and underpaid teaching assistants, the burgeoning undergraduate population became chronically neglected.[18]

Along with this increased scale of California's public universities came a qualitative change in student profiles. Groups who historically had limited access to higher education entered in ever greater numbers. Lower middle-class and working-class students formed a larger percentage of the student body with a sizeable number from southern California.[19] Beginning in the late fifties, the representation of students of color also increased. External factors, including southern migration, extensive media coverage of student activism at HBCUs, and state scholarship programs for foreign students helped generate momentum. African American students formed a small but growing percentage of Berkeley's rapidly expanding student body.

Until the late fifties, the African American presence on California campuses was too small and diffuse to be called a community. Although the University of California did not collect statistics on the racial breakdown of the Berkeley student population until 1966, anecdotal evidence revealed that there were fewer than 100 black students out of nearly 20,000 by 1960. As the civil rights movement progressed, their numbers gradually increased, until by 1966, black students, including both native-born and African, breached the 1 percent barrier with 226 undergraduate and graduate students enrolled at Berkeley.[20] For this select group, the experience of attending the University of California proved deeply alienating. Mary Lewis, an underclassman who attended Howard before coming to Berkeley, described a profound sense of displacement. She explained, "One of the experiences that . . . all of us black folks who were here during that period experienced was . . . all of the alienation of invisibility, and for most of us it was a first-time experience."[21] White students confirmed Lewis's perception. Activist Jo Freeman described a benevolent racial liberalism among progressive students who opposed Jim Crow, South African apartheid, and southern school desegregation. The homogeneous campus, however, made racism and even the presence of black people themselves seem distant and abstract. Freeman explained, "Racial discrimination, where it existed, was challenged, but since racial minorities were less than 2 percent of the student body, and most of those were foreign students, such challenges had little real-world impact. Racial segregation was automatically assumed to be evil, but it was also seen as something *other* people did. . . . Racism as something other than racial segregation or discrimination was not part of our vocabulary. Conceptually, it did not exist."[22]

Berkeley's first real generation of black students experienced intense social isolation that encouraged them to look to the world beyond campus.[23] In spring 1961, a succession of events created a powerful convergence between the southern civil rights movement and struggles for independence in Africa and the Caribbean. Patrice Lumumba's murder in January, followed in a few short months by Robert F. Williams's exile to Cuba, prompted students to rethink their approach to domestic racial politics. On March 1, 1961, Donald Warden, a third-year law student, wrote an angry editorial to the *Daily Cali-*

fornian accusing the U.C. Berkeley chapter of the NAACP of failing "in its philosophical and intellectual duty to the campus."[24] He argued that it had ignored the most pressing issues for the black community: the emerging African states, Harlem's vivid support for Castro and Lumumba, the destructive effects of Christianity, and "color discrimination in the Negro World."[25] The organization that Langston Hughes dubbed "the world's biggest law firm" had become obsolete.[26]

Warden's attack on the youth chapter of the NAACP reflected frustration with the national leadership for its failure to support African liberation struggles.[27] Several weeks before, word had reached the United States that Katangan forces had murdered the democratically elected leader of Congo, Patrice Lumumba. As rumors proliferated about Central Intelligence Agency involvement and United Nations (UN) collusion, protests shook New York, Chicago, and Washington.[28] Not since Italy's invasion of Ethiopia had African Americans demonstrated such fervent anticolonialism.[29] Ever fearful of Black radicalism, the NAACP's executive secretary Roy Wilkins claimed these UN demonstrations did not "represent either the sentiment or the tactics of American Negroes," and he criticized the press for providing misleading images.[30] In 1961, the NAACP represented a formidable opponent. With more than 500,000 members nationwide, it was the United States' oldest and largest civil rights organization.[31] Unfortunately, Warden's choice of local agon was misplaced. Overworked students ran the campus chapter, and with its meager budget and resources, it bore little, if any, resemblance to the national NAACP.[32] The young membership channeled most of their energy into supporting Bishop Roy Nichols's campaign to become the first black member of the Berkeley school board, while protesting the campus career center's sponsorship of discriminatory employers, like United Airlines, who refused to hire African Americans for flight service.[33] Moreover, students aligned themselves not with Roy Wilkins, but rather with Robert F. Williams and Malcolm X, both of whom they helped bring to Berkeley in the spring of 1961.[34]

In mid-April, a debate took place between Donald Warden and the head of the student chapter of the NAACP, J. Herman Blake, in Berkeley's Wheeler Auditorium. Warden condemned the organization in an almost comic fashion. As he put it, the association was a white man's organization so retrograde that the United States would have a black president long before the civil rights organization. Its strategy of eliminating legal barriers had created a black middle class that was psychologically displaced. The "black bourgeoisie was black to the white folk and white to the black folk."[35] American mass media and Christianity promoted this cultural alienation by instilling the notion that "good and God are white and black is bad." To resolve this dilemma of identity, Warden argued, separation of the races was necessary. Only then could the black community turn inward to heal its own divisions and achieve dignity.[36]

J. Herman Blake's demeanor contrasted sharply with Warden's charismatic, oppositional style. The president of the local chapter was an older student with square shoulders, a heavy beard, and a decided earnestness. In his first year of graduate school, the Woodrow Wilson fellow had thrown himself into politics and had become the real force behind the youth chapter. As a long-time member, his decision to join the campus chapter represented a continuation of earlier activism in Mount Vernon.[37] Blake argued quietly that his Harlem childhood had well acquainted him with all the problems that flowed from segregation. And in response to Warden's charge that the NAACP had failed to represent the black majority's true interests, Blake countered that the organization's purpose had remained the same since its founding: "We shall not be satisfied with anything less than our full manhood rights."[38] Although each had certain personal idiosyncrasies, the division between Warden and Blake foreshadowed an increasing emphasis on issues of culture, identity, and internationalism in black politics that grew stronger as the decade progressed.

Donald Warden was an unconventional charismatic figure with a natural talent for organization building. His sometimes grandiose sense of personal style contained elements of contradiction that stemmed from an unusual personal history. His politics had been shaped at an early age by his father's ambition to establish a Garveyite-style settlement in a rural area near Pittsburgh. In the 1920s, George J. Warden purchased a large tract of land located seven miles from the city and tried to convince his colleagues in the post office to help him establish an all-black town. Although they refused, he decided to build a family home in a heavily wooded area on the edge of the city. In the process, a thriving white ethnic community sprung up around the Warden homestead. Through an ironic twist of fate, George Warden's nationalism landed his twelve children in an all-white suburb, later christened Brighton Heights. Before the age of integration, the Warden children became well acquainted with the problems befalling black children in all-white schools and neighborhoods. Donald, the second youngest child, later wrote, "In short, I was privy on a first-hand basis to the precious 'benefits' of integration. My growing up experiences in Brighton Heights summarized all the battles of the civil rights strategies for more than seventy years, i.e., the opportunity to live, eat, sleep, be entertained and be educated right next to White people."[39] The conclusions he drew from this experience were rather bleak. As he left to attend college at Howard University in Washington, D.C., he mused, "Integration was a myth, a hoax, a deception, and besides, it would never work."[40]

For Warden, Howard proved to be a mixed blessing. The excellence of the faculty impressed Warden immediately, as did the range and diversity of black students, many of whom came from Africa and the Caribbean. In the late fifties Howard was a thriving institution, with E. Franklin Frazier in the sociology department, John Hope Franklin in history, and Arthur P. Davis in literature.[41] Racial segregation fostered a concentration of extraordinary postwar black intellectuals, who were soon dispersed as discriminatory colleges and universities removed hiring barriers. In this era, Howard also drew black people from all over the world. The academic achievement of African students, in particular, impressed Warden, and he later argued that they should serve as models for their American counterparts. While the exposure to a historically black institution offered a welcome change from western Pennsylvania, the campus culture showed that the problems of color and caste remained present even when whites were not. Warden later expressed frustration with the stifling "country club flavor of Howard life" in which students used bleaching creams, changed three times a day, and conducted brown paper bag tests on their peers.[42] Howard confirmed E. Franklin Frazier's pessimistic view of an isolated and fragile black elite that attempted to shore itself up through accumulation and conspicuous consumption. In *Black Bourgeoisie* Frazier wrote, "In escaping into a world of make believe, middle-class Negroes have rejected both identification with the Negro and his traditional culture. Through delusions of wealth and power they have sought identification with the white America which continues to reject them."[43] Frazier's themes haunted Warden throughout his life and dominated his recollections of the period. *Black Bourgeoisie* remained a major impetus behind his desire to create new forms of African American political and cultural expression.[44]

After graduating from Howard, Donald Warden enrolled in U.C. Berkeley's School of Law. Throughout his tenure as a law student, Warden maintained a high profile on campus. In small groups, he was known to preach and not just talk, and he enjoyed considerable attention from the larger Berkeley community. Some accused him of creating a public mystique among white students, while carefully cultivating an organized following among blacks.

One of his favorite tricks at parties was to pretend he had never seen electric lights and to attempt to blow them out.[45]

In the early sixties, Robbies, a Chinese restaurant on Telegraph Avenue near Durant, served as a regular meeting place for Donald Warden and a small circle of fellow students.[46] Robbies brought together an eclectic mix of marginal groups, including aspiring artists, black and white radicals, Trotskyites, Marxist-Leninists, beatniks and assorted campus "free spirits."[47] The crowd was disproportionately male; single women attended with less frequency and more formality. Women usually accompanied partners or attended organizational meetings rather than socializing casually. Robbies also represented the gray world of student life where black and white students met, socialized, and dated. While the reverse was seen occasionally, more often than not black men accompanied white women. Given the relative social segregation of the rest of campus culture, the mere fact of interracial association became significant.[48]

Sometime during 1960 or 1961, a dozen or so black students began meeting regularly at the house of Mary Lewis and Anne Cook several blocks south of campus. Lewis came originally from Detroit, and her family had close ties to the black leadership of the United Auto Workers.[49] Early members established a pattern that persisted throughout the life of the Afro-American Association. Students met, socialized, and talked politics incessantly. Donald Hopkins later remembered that their "social life revolved around the Afro-American Association . . . politics and social life were almost inextricable."[50] This intensity of engagement mirrored that of other movement organizations, and explained the group's depth of influence on its membership.[51]

While the handful of black students integrating U.C. Berkeley shared the alienating experience of social invisibility, California's elite "multiversity" also provided unique opportunities. One of the most important was its capacity to enable far-flung social networks that would have been impossible in the world beyond campus. In contrast to Berkeley's general student body, many of the black students came from outside of California. Intraracial class and regional diversity fostered nationalist inclinations. The variety in their backgrounds contributed to an increasing self-consciousness about shared elements of black culture and identity. Donald Hopkins, a graduate student in political science, grew up in Kansas City where his mother had worked as a maid, while Donald Warden was a postman's son from Pittsburgh. Other members hailed from cities and states spanning the country: Henry Ramsey from North Carolina, Mary Lewis from the Motor City, and Maurice Dawson from Chicago's Hyde Park.[52] One early association member explained, "We were all here in California, in effect alone. With just our minds and our hearts. . . . [We] came from all over the United States not only with diversity in terms of regional location, but also in terms of background."[53]

Several different factors contributed to a change in self-definition among Negro students in Berkeley of the early sixties. National and international events interlaced with local conditions. The most immediate influence was the presence of African students in relatively large numbers on campus. African students formed a significant portion of Berkeley's black population, and they also contributed to a growing awareness of continental independence movements. While the University did not keep separate statistics on African versus native-born black students, many people reported that the numbers of foreign students far exceeded those of their domestic counterparts.[54] As part of Cold War negotiations, Eisenhower agreed to educate a certain number of Ghanaians in technical professions. He signed agreements in 1958, and the students arrived at U.C. Berkeley in the early 1960s. Students from Kenya and later Nigeria soon followed. In 1960, "the Year of Africa," the total population of students in American universities from sub-Saharan Africa exceeded 1,600. This figure later tripled in the course of the decade.[55]

U.C. Berkeley's growing number of African students was intricately linked with the process of decolonization itself. In 1960, seventeen African nations claimed their independence, and in the subsequent years of Kennedy's presidency, eight more followed.[56] Many independence leaders attended American universities, and, as in the case of Kenya, foreign institutions provided skills and status crucial for the "Africanization" of the civil-service class.[57] Donald Warden himself had been deeply influenced by his extensive contact with Africans students at Howard prior to attending Berkeley. In the early 1960s, Howard had the single largest population of African exchange students, totaling nearly 300 per year.[58] The interest in Africa was not limited to Warden's immediate circle but extended to all segments of Berkeley's black community. In 1961 the Berkeley chapter of the NAACP sponsored several events bringing together African and Afro-American students, including a social at a parent's home. Margot Dashiell remembered the afternoon as a watershed event; "Now we knew Africans."[59] Students forged important friendships, and it became commonplace for Africans and black Americans to socialize together. In the midsixties, a Berkeley chapter of Crossroads Africa was set up and it, too, helped raise awareness of African liberation struggles.[60]

The increasing prominence of the Nation of Islam (NOI) also influenced students' changing self-conceptions. Through documentaries and press coverage like Malcolm X's appearance in "The Hate that Hate Produced," the Nation had effectively used negative publicity to strengthen its visibility. Malcolm X's telegenic appeal and his remarkable gifts of language and organizing ability helped the Nation to expand its number of temples tenfold in less than a decade.[61] The popularity of C. Eric Lincoln's *Black Muslims in America* in 1961 also helped to increase the NOI's notoriety.[62] For years, this new religious group had been using the spelling "Muslim" rather than the traditional "Moslem" to set themselves apart.[63] Lincoln acknowledged the significance and coined the term "Black Muslim" to differentiate the race-conscious ideology of the sect from the more universalist doctrines of orthodox Islam. The name stuck and soon came into common parlance, much to Malcolm X's and other Nation members' dismay.[64] James Baldwin's publication of *The Fire Next Time* the following year sought to interpret the deeper meaning of this ascendant movement for liberal critics. He linked the Nation's rise to E. Franklin Frazier's "cities of destruction" fed by the wages of segregation and the northern exodus of black southern migrants.[65] Most important, Malcolm X's founding of *Mr. Muhammad Speaks* in 1960 made direct inroads into urban black communities. With a circulation exceeding 600,000 copies a week, it soon became the most widely read black weekly. In the early sixties, thanks to a combination of Malcolm X's innovative organizing techniques and national press attention, the Nation's ideas had been widely disseminated. The organization's radical ideology extended much further than its own institutions and helped forge a new cultural black militancy.[66]

Inspired by Malcolm X's example, several early members of the Afro-American Association actually began to attend Nation of Islam meetings in West Oakland. Elijah Muhammad had set up two mosques in the Bay Area with Temple 26 A located in San Francisco and Temple 26 B in West Oakland. Maurice Dawson remembered the services as eclectic events mixing numerology, facts, history, and political commentary. Men and women took their places in gender-segregated spaces on either side of the mosque. Lessons emphasized contemporary events to help participants assimilate new information. Ministers contrasted the strategies of civil rights leaders with their own. "We don't turn cheeks—that is only going to get you two broken jaws" was a common refrain. The encounter with the NOI left a lasting impression on the fledgling student organization, and the association later adapted some of its institutional strategies.[67]

The core ideological overlap between the Afro-American Association and the Nation of Islam was the cultivation of an enduring black tradition of self-help, racial pride, and economic enterprise. Warden cited E. Franklin Frazier's claim that Marcus Garvey was the twentieth century's only true mass black leader.[68] The Nation of Islam proved useful as a contemporary bridge to broader themes of black culture and consciousness, remaining most compelling when it resonated directly with Garveyism. Diverging views of Africa and territorial nationalism set the NOI apart from the increasingly radicalized black students on the Berkeley campus. Territorial separation seemed largely irrelevant, as did the Nation's racial theosophy. The role of Africa had been transformed in the students' minds. African liberation movements made the continent not a potential place of return or colonization, but rather a constant source of inspiration for domestic racial struggles.[69]

The pressure for racial redefinition had important secular influences independent from Malcolm X and the Nation of Islam. Tensions emerged from within the civil rights movement itself. The advocacy of love in the face of relentless violence became harder and harder to justify. As members of Berkeley's NAACP chapter watched the events unfolding in the South, they became increasingly uneasy. Many held King responsible for the large numbers of deaths and injuries that had occurred. Students had become even more suspicious of Roy Wilkins and the national leadership of the NAACP. Cedric Robinson explained, "We wanted a different kind of analysis, a politics that emerged from an analysis of race in America and race in the globe. That was the reason for the natural organic relationship . . . moving from the African students that we knew on campus to an interest in their countries . . . the sense that these were global as well as international dynamics at the time."[70]

The Fair Play for Cuba Committee and the student NAACP invited Robert F. Williams to speak at the Berkeley Little Theater in March 1961. Williams, a World War II veteran who headed up the Monroe, North Carolina, chapter of the NAACP, had garnered international attention for "armed self-reliance" and for directly confronting the Ku Klux Klan. In 1959, after Roy Wilkins expelled him from his post, Williams began publishing the *Crusader*. His writings were among the first to explicitly link North American black freedom struggles with those of the Third World, especially in Africa. In spring 1961, Williams had been forced into exile after having been falsely accused of kidnapping a white couple.[71] Members of Berkeley's NAACP found his activist vision of civil rights deeply appealing. They saw themselves as "a group of young angry folks who didn't like the way that things were going." Frustrated by what they saw as a quiescent and accommodating older generation, the students "wanted the University to know that there was this New Negro."[72] A similar impulse lead the NAACP to invite the local pastor Bishop Roy Nichols to come and speak on the topic several months later, but its members became sorely disappointed.[73] J. Herman Blake remembered, "the more he [Nichols] talked, the more that the New Negro sounded like the old colored folks."[74] In contrast to the bishop's anemic speech, Robert F. Williams provided a refreshing example of a militant international black politics. At Berkeley, he expressed support for Castro and his government's humanitarian, antiracist policies, which contrasted vividly with life behind the "cotton curtain" in the southern United States.

While the presence of African students, the high visibility of the Nation of Islam, and Robert F. Williams all were key factors in 1961, by far the most important event for the formation of the Afro-American Association was Malcolm X's visit in May. Future members of both the Afro-American Association and the campus NAACP expressed deep admiration for him. Even J. Herman Blake, who vehemently opposed the separatist politics of the Nation, praised the young minister. After the speech, he formed a close relationship with the imam from the West Oakland Temple and Malcolm X himself. Watching "an eighth-grade dropout lecturing essentially a whole group of graduate students and faculty, and meeting them on their terms and besting them" thrilled Blake.[75] Although Malcolm X is best known for his anger, what most impressed the students was his eloquence. Shortly after the minister's visit, the campus NAACP dissolved. Blake and the others had stretched themselves too thin and retreated from campus activism. The president of the youth chapter soon left the Bay Area, and did not return until nearly a decade later to help write Huey Newton's autobiography, *Revolutionary Suicide*. Lack of resources and manpower provided only half of the explanation. Much of the membership became active elsewhere and ultimately shifted allegiances.[76] While Warden had drawn strict divisions between the philosophy of the NAACP and his own, most black students did not see such serious fault lines. In hindsight, Cedric Robinson remembered the two organizations as synonymous.[77] Black writer Leslie Alexander Lacy described Malcolm X's effect on expatriate Afro-Americans at the University of Ghana-Legon as providing them with "a new sense of cultural euphoria." The same could be said of African American students at U.C. Berkeley in the early sixties.[78]

An emergent Black nationalist consciousness sought to reach into the

most intimate domains of life, including the realms of worship, self-definition, and desire. Donald Warden's youthful exuberance represented one
expression of a larger shift in sensibility. This new fusion mixed an older
tradition represented by Marcus Garvey and Elijah Muhammad with contemporary elements that were unique to postwar America. The politics of
sex and sexuality played an overt role for the first time in Black nationalist discourse. In its wake, some established pillars of black community life
came under fire, including the integrity of the black church and family. One
of the most bitterly contested points from the debate was Warden's assertion
that Negro character had collapsed so profoundly that Marilyn Monroe had
become the true object of black male desire. He returned again and again
to this theme and mentioned it in an article published in *Root and Branch*
the following year: "Veterans on the Korean battlefield joyfully glimpsed
their Marilyn Monroe 'pinup' for inspiration and shamefully concealed the
pictures of their mother or sisters or even wives. . . . Seldom do these white
Americans stop to realize that all Americans desire white women, and for
better or worse, the Negro has been made an American."[79] When Warden
made a similar point during the debate, black women in the audience became quite upset. A number of people interpreted his attempt at denounc-
ing internalized white supremacy as a denial of black men's true affection
for black women. As in Malcolm X's autobiography published several years
later, the confession and repudiation of desire for white women became an
important proving ground for Black nationalist identity. Revelation was precarious business, however, because admitting the desire implied a tenuous-
ness of black family ties. Traditionalists like Blake became disgusted even at
its mention.[80]

Given the history of miscegenation discourse as a justification for racial
violence, it is hardly surprising that interracial involvement became taboo.
But the real issue was more subtle. Warden also stressed "color discrimination within the Negro World" meaning the bias for the light skinned over
the dark. The tendency to dwell on these issues rather than deny their existence served a purpose. In the tradition of the jeremiad, nationalism offered
the chance to remake oneself, to throw off centuries of oppression. Expos-
ing white supremacy's influence on the most private of domains revealed the
extent of its power. Focusing on the politics of desire shifted the focus of
racial struggle to the more diffuse battleground of the psychological. This
early view of black masculinity and interracial sexuality was later amplified
in Eldridge Cleaver's 1968 bestseller, *Soul on Ice*. Warden's writings over six

years before showed the deep resonance these ideas had with social groups his own age.[81]

Black nationalism on the Berkeley campus always had an ironic flavor. The numbers of black students were so small and the constant contact with white students, teachers, and institutions so extensive that the ideal of separatism functioned more as a discourse than as an ideology. This quality reached caricature proportion in the case of Richard Thorne, who started his political career championing separatism and ended it founding an interracial sex cult, the Sexual Freedom League. Certainly, the Bay Area's liberal culture of race relations was in sharp contrast to the hypersegregated cities in which the Nation of Islam flourished: Chicago, New York, and Detroit. Black students at Berkeley did experience a great deal of isolation and alienation, but their only possible retreat into an all-black world was one of their own construction. Integration and its discontents provided the impetus to form study groups and, ultimately, Black Studies programs.

In the early sixties, the term "black" itself had not yet come into common parlance, and the Nation of Islam had taken only tentative steps toward changing self-representation through the use of the term "so-called Negro."[82] Accomplishments of the civil rights movement and the expanding influence of the NOI helped to make "Negro" obsolete, but what should replace it was uncertain. In *The Fire Next Time*, James Baldwin argued that this crisis of naming reflected a peculiar sense of historical isolation. In contrast to Africans, who formed a majority in their own countries and "sought to reclaim their land and break the colonial yoke ... [t]he American Negro is a unique creation; he has no counterpart anywhere, and no predecessors."[83] Rather than a rearticulation of the Du Boisian dilemma, this period witnessed a decisive break as black students sought new forms of self-conception.[84] How could African Americans assume the subjectivity of a transnational majority while retaining their historical identity as an oppressed minority? Blackness and its inherent promise of diaspora provided not only the linguistic but the conceptual bridge. Donald Warden explained that the term "black" undercut the divisive effects of color consciousness associated with New World trauma: "That's why we used the term black to describe African Americans. We were not using black to describe the complexion of skin, we were using black to describe the continent of Africa, the black continent."[85] He went on to argue, somewhat self-servingly, that the West Coast lay at the forefront of this linguistic movement.[86]

Warden understood the adoption of "black" or "Afro-American" in vanguardist terms. The association worked actively toward the dissemination of these names, and popularizing their use became one of its most pressing concerns. However, embracing the term "black" met with a history of entrenched resistance by Oakland's Negro community. Policeman Hadwick Thompson recalled an infamous case from the late forties in which residents sued the *Oakland Tribune* for referring to them as "black." Instead, they demanded that the newspaper use the "more polite terms" of "colored" or "Negro." Thompson explained their rationale: "We are not a color, we are a race. Black does not describe us." In hindsight, this incident betrayed the intense generational change of the early sixties. According to Thompson, "young Negroes" understood their identities in ways radically different and unimaginable a decade before.[87] Association members stripped the word "black" of its debased connotations and redefined it through insurgent political struggles on the African continent. One of the first activities Berkeley students organized for the larger East Bay community was an Oakland rally and screening of the South African documentary *Come Back Africa*, featuring Miriam Makeba and Hugh Maskela.[88]

Constant discussion and debate motivated students to choose readings in common. A loose study group evolved. U.C. Berkeley graduate students from a variety of disciplines and a sprinkling of undergraduates from Berkeley and San Francisco State began to informally read books of immediate political relevance. Initially discussion focused on classic black history texts. W. E. B. Du Bois's *The Souls of Black Folk*, Carter G. Woodson's *The Miseducation of the Negro*, and Ralph Ellison's *Invisible Man* numbered among group selections.[89] However, E. David Cronon's *Black Moses: The Story of Marcus Garvey*, Melville J. Herskovits's *The Myth of the Negro Past*, and E. Franklin Frazier's *Black Bourgeoisie* elicited the most debate. Together, these volumes and the controversy they engendered had the greatest impact on the association's evolving ideology. Discussion of Frazier and Herskovits revealed how social science scholarship on race and culture directly influenced Black nationalist self-conception in the early 1960s.[90]

The strange "intellectual" career of African retention showed how African Americans' views on racial identity had been transformed over the past two decades. Melville Herskovits published *The Myth of the Negro Past* in 1941 as the first volume of Gunnar Myrdal's Carnegie Corporation study of the American Negro. Like his fellow anthropologist Franz Boas, Herskovits stressed the therapeutic power of culture for African Americans.[91] His work emphasized the deep continuities of West African practices and those of the New World. Contrary to the notion that "the Negro is thus a man without a past," Herskovits argued that deep and enduring streams of culture connected the two continents, most obviously through religious practice. If these links were unclear, it was not because they did not exist but because they remained invisible to social science.[92]

In the first two decades following *Myth*'s publication, black sociologists emerged as Herskovits's most strident critics. While acknowledging the glories of antiquity, University of Chicago–trained E. Franklin Frazier and fellow Carnegie researcher Charles Johnson adamantly rejected the idea of African survivals.[93] Both chose to stress the effects of damage and loss as central to the process of becoming American. Frazier's scorched-earth view of the African past justified his adamant support for integration in the present. He saw his book, *Black Bourgeoisie*, as an assault on reactionary segments of black society that benefited from segregation. It was not until several years after *Black Bourgeoisie*'s publication in 1957 that Frazier even ventured to question the wisdom of integration.[94]

Although Herskovits's work received a cold reception initially, *Myth* became very influential during the social upheaval of the early civil rights movement and after. As Berkeley students struggled for a language to articulate their new sense of identity in spring 1961, the turn toward a separate cultural past made sense. The anthropologist helped to provide a historical logic for a reinvigorated, anticolonial Black nationalism.[95] His documentation of African retention provided raw material for a new racial paradigm that justified the establishment of Black Studies programs and strategic opposition to assimilation. In fact, Herskovits's pioneering study has now been canonized as one of the original "historiographical roots" of African Diaspora studies.[96]

Ultimately, the Afro-American Association successfully fused the opposing views of Herskovits and Frazier to fashion its own antiassimilationist ideology. The fact that the group chose such conflicting views revealed the different and sometimes contradictory elements in their evolving conception of black identity. Warden and the Afro-American Association reserved its greatest rancor not for the dominant white society so much as the compliant black middle class. At times Warden's rhetoric came close to resembling that of white opponents of civil rights. He emphasized the obsessive need of "integrationists" to be with whites—to marry them, attend school with them, and to live with them. His attack drew its force from images of racial amalgamation. Integration meant assimilation and assimilation meant erasing all vestiges of African descent. Both Frazier and Warden demonized the "black bourgeoisie," but for opposite reasons. Frazier blamed them for their collusion with segregation, while Warden blamed them for their collusion with integration.[97]

In an article entitled "The Black Negro," published in *Root and Branch* during the winter of 1962, Warden quoted *Black Bourgeoisie*'s indictment of the middle class at length:

> Their emotional and mental conflicts arise partly from their constant striving for status within the Negro world as well as in the estimation of whites. In fact, they have tended to over-emphasize their conformity to white ideals and this rejection has created considerable self-hatred, since it is attributed to their Negro characteristics. Since they do not truly identify with Negroes, the hollowness of the black bourgeoisie's pretended "racial pride" is revealed in the value in which it places upon a white or light complexion. Because of their social isolation and lack of cultural tradition, the members of the black bourgeoisie in the United States seem to be in the process of becoming nobody.[98]

In the early 1960s, people rarely used the word "integration," and "assimilation" even less so. Many African American preferred "desegregation," a legal term associated with social, economic, and political rights. After the civil rights movement achieved a number of legal victories, implementation replaced litigation as the primary strategy. Warden and others in the association argued that, while civil rights leaders spoke of desegregation and compliance with Brown, what they truly advocated was assimilation.[99] For AAA members, Frazier's *Black Bourgeoisie* served as a cautionary tale of assimilation's pitfalls. An enervated black middle class highlighted the potential dangers of social aspiration.[100]

As the study group grew, its membership expanded beyond the Berkeley campus. The initial dozen or so members grew over fourfold, and the meetings moved to Donald Hopkins's apartment off of Shattuck. Larger numbers of San Francisco State and Cal State Hayward students began to attend.[101] In order to create continuity, the association established some basic ground rules. New initiates needed a reference from an AAA member, and they had to purchase chosen readings before the meetings. For the first week they were not allowed to speak. Older participants successfully undercut potential sectarianism and grandstanding by formalizing these practices. Maurice Dawson explained, "You cannot out mau mau Jomo Kenyatta," meaning "Shut up brother and listen."[102]

Several early conflicts emerged in the study group. The proposed name of the organization was the first. Donald Hopkins recalled that students debated whether or not it should be called the Afro-American Association or the African American Association. After much disagreement, they chose the former as a compromise.[103] The second issue was whether or not people of other races or ethnicities could attend the meetings. A young woman named Tony who was recently married and pregnant wanted to bring her partner who was Jewish. The group agreed that while the child would be allowed to attend, membership remained open only to people of African descent.[104] The rationale for this was not racial exclusivity, but rather the recognition that the group represented one of the only places where black students could spend time together for a few hours each week. In every other public aspect of their lives, this was impossible. The final conflict was the most serious for the evolving structure of the association: should the AAA remain a study group or turn more directly to community action? Warden favored the status quo but was in the minority. He soon acquiesced to demands for more direct social engagement.[105]

As the AAA searched for ways to reach out to the Bay Area's black population, the group's opposition to integration became a driving force behind its attempts at mass recruitment. Participants searched for different forms of activism and finally turned to Harlem-style street rallies.[106] Although street speaking had long been a staple of Black nationalist political culture, the Afro-American Association adapted it to the particularities of the East Bay. In contrast to New York's political geography, college campuses became an important focal point.[107] As a spontaneous response to national events, informal street speaking started nearly a year before the Afro-American Association received its official charter. Looking back, Maurice Dawson remembered the uproar over Robert F. Williams's expulsion from the NAACP as a turning point. His name was poised on everyone's lips. Not only was the local president justified in his response; he was a decorated veteran with broad-based support in his hometown. "They ain't scared of nothing or nobody," Dawson explained. "This was the talk of the Bay Area. . . . It was the genesis of the growth and evolution, frankly, of racial pride in the East Bay."[108]

Frustrated by inaccuracies in the mainstream press, association members traveled to downtown Oakland to address the public directly. As they stood outside Swan's Meat Market near Seventh Street early one Saturday morning, they held up copies of the *Oakland Tribune* and the *San Francisco Chronicle*. They proclaimed support for Robert F. Williams and explained why he had been forced to arm himself. The choice of Swan's was not random. In the early sixties, Seventh Street still retained some of its grandeur as Oakland's black business district. Although the strip would soon crumble like its more famous San Francisco counterpart, the Fillmore, the thoroughfare remained the closest equivalent Oakland had to a black public sphere.[109]

Outreach "to the masses" became an important aspect of the Afro-American Association's philosophy. Following the Robert F. Williams rally, the AAA staged "street speakings" at high-traffic areas in San Francisco and the East Bay. A pattern soon evolved where regular gatherings met at Fillmore and Ellis in San Francisco's Western Addition, Tenth and Bissell in Richmond, and Seventh and Henry Street in West Oakland.[110] Speakers engaged with the crowd and discussed a variety of issues, including child rearing, black-on-black crime, and maintaining families. In keeping with the nationalist focus of the group, themes did not focus exclusively on traditional politics but also targeted internal dynamics in the black community. Family and nation building remained persistent themes.[111]

It is difficult to obtain exact figures about the Afro-American Association's membership, because no official records were kept and the group was always decentralized. However, a consistent pattern emerged in how the association defined its outreach efforts, which paralleled those of the Nation of Islam. The masses were not defined in terms of a traditional working class. Warden insisted on bringing people in from the community, but the people he focused on were at the edges of the economy. Ernest Allen explained, "What happened is that when Warden and others inside the Association talked about who the masses were, it was the pimps, the prostitutes, the black domestics and so forth and so on, you don't get any sense at all of any industrial workers, or people who work at the Naval Supply."[112] The black "masses" became synonymous with the economically marginal, who were designated as the real people. This tendency was not insignificant, because several years later the Panthers took up the same idea. The ideological inflection was different of course. The Panthers designated this class as a revolutionary vanguard, while Warden saw them as raw material for reform.[113]

A core group of students emerged, all male, who organized and staffed regular Saturday street rallies. Donald Warden likened their awakening racial consciousness to religious conversion and later referred to this group affectionately as "born again."[114] A San Francisco State student, Welton Smith, was among the most prominent, but others emerged including Robert Ward, Henry Ramsey, Hal Perry, Maurice Dawson, and Warden himself. Max Roach later memorialized their dynamism by writing *Speak, Brother,*

Donald Warden "street speaking" in San Francisco's Fillmore district, 1962. Photograph courtesy of Khalid al-Mansour and Jamila al-Mansour.

Speak.[115] A pattern developed in which they held rallies in San Francisco until early afternoon before moving on to Oakland and to Richmond. The "born again" derided drug and alcohol use while stressing racial solidarity over class division, sharing and collectivity over material interest, African pride, and above all else, the transformative power of education. They spoke most often at Merritt College, where they consistently attracted the largest crowds. Warden explained, "In a very real sense, the philosophy of the Afro-American Association was born out of the street meetings. It was here that we heard, firsthand, the anger, fears, hopes, aspirations, contradictions, and class divisions within Black America."[116]

Street speaking had a playful quality that used a combination of ridicule and entertainment to draw people in. As a regular described it, "It is like playing the dozens, but not playing the dozens."[117] The point was not simply to win but to convince. Accessible language, direct eye contact, and an ability to improvise rather than read went a long way. Speakers teased hecklers rather than confronting them directly and drew on a colorful array of facts to impress their audience. One of the regular speakers described a trick that he had learned from Malcolm X. Using three-by-five note cards, he wrote down contemporary and historical facts; when paused at a light or walking around, he referred to them constantly until they were permanently committed to memory. He hoped this might help him assume Malcolm's characteristic air of authority.[118]

Maurice Dawson observed how "rapping" evolved out of regular street speaking. This new style of oratory represented a departure from previous forms and incorporated elements from contemporary popular culture. Activists with no access to public halls searched for methods of reaching the people that were free and accessible. Conventions of popular music were a natural medium to draw a crowd. With its roots in doo-wop, rapping was a language of persuasion. Spoken over the bridge in a song, the background music receded into a quiet harmony, and the speaker mouthed the words over the instrumental. According to Dawson, rapping was "pretty, sounded good, believable for the moment and could be effective." The Afro-American Association took this form and replaced romantic appeals with political sermons. Donald Warden's *Burn Baby Burn* created shortly after the Watts riot is one of the best examples of this genre.[119]

The strategy of street speaking reflected a larger shift of sensibility, besides the practical issue of recruitment. The invocation of the street remained important throughout the sixties and was tied to the simultaneous dynamics of urbanization and the expanding horizon of black political activity. Many later remarked on how Malcolm X and Huey Newton bridged the two worlds of the street and the university. Given E. Franklin Frazier's assertion of a black class structure built more on social capital than income, this designation was especially meaningful. The street and the university had cultural as well as economic dimensions. The street promised a special knowledge born of conflict and deprivation that connected one to the deepest resonance of black urban life. It functioned as a trusted measure of experience that contrasted the remote culture of academic learning. Immediate, visceral, and mired in the most intractable aspects of segregation and the poverty it engendered, the street addressed problems that the discourse of civil rights and equality never could.

A dialogue developed between the study group and street rallies that provided direct access to ordinary people outside the university. Material from rallies began to directly inform on-going discussions about the nature of black identity. In order to maintain momentum and broaden the membership base, the AAA began to hold meetings at a popular restaurant called Bosun's Locker on Monday evenings.[120] During this period, Huey Newton and other Merritt students became increasingly active in the association.[121]

When Bosun's could no longer accommodate all those interested in attending meetings, the group moved to Downs Memorial Church. Pastor Bishop Roy Nichols, who was sometimes called the "Martin Luther King of the East Bay," furnished the student group with space. Downs, a United Methodist church located in North Oakland, was renowned for its affluent congregation. Some of the East Bay's more cynical residents called it "the black silk-stocking church," although its reputation for social and political activism tempered resentments.[122] In the 1950s, Nichols ran for Oakland city council, and he was later elected as the first black school board member in Berkeley. Ronald Dellums also had long-standing ties to Downs. When the Berkeley councilman considered a bid for national office, he consulted with the church's membership. Ironically, Downs also actively recruited new membership for the NAACP. In short, it was a bulwark of the kind of racial liberalism that the Afro-American Association inveighed against. The willingness of the church leadership to make facilities available to Warden revealed how different sectors of the black community, while theoretically opposed, offered aid and assistance to the fledgling youth organization. While the AAA defined itself publicly against traditional elders—Christian and middle class—they welcomed their support.[123] This fact underlined the generational nature of this new form of politics that spoke the language of ideology but reflected less clearly defined differences of age and sensibility. Downs's congregation also expressed strong support for the association's emphasis on black history and economic uplift.[124]

Throughout the summer, the AAA organized marches from one library to another to popularize themes of education in Oakland's black neighborhoods, which Warden affectionately referred to as "Soulville."[125] In fall 1962, the association started an ad hoc campaign among black celebrities to promote "educational themes." At times, the founder of the AAA could be shameless in his attempts to enlist support. Without any prior contact, he simply accosted entertainers at local concerts and invited them to join the group. In this way, he met Marvin Gaye, Miriam Makeba, Aretha Franklin, and James Brown. In fact, Warden later alleged that the AAA's efforts inspired the Godfather of Soul's 1966 single "Don't Be a Dropout."[126] All of these innovative methods of outreach focused on a single goal—encouraging local black youth to value education itself, independently from the legalistic framework of racial integration.[127]

During the same period, the association established a weekly program on Oakland's KDIA radio station. At a cost of $65 per week, the Sonderling network broadcast "We Care Enough to Tell It Just Like It Is" every Saturday morning.[128] Soon after the show debuted, local chapters of the Congress of Racial Equality (CORE), the NAACP, and the Urban League protested its content and demanded equal airtime. The station finally agreed to sponsor all four groups for free. For several years, the NAACP, represented by Ray Taliaferro, and the Afro-American Association merged their two broadcasts and presented a weekly debate. Ultimately, the show became very popular and served as an important medium for publicizing the Bay Area black freedom movement. Over the next several years, "We Care Enough" gave rise to other black programming on radio and television. In the coming years, Donald Warden hosted his own radio talk show, "Matchline," which promised to "match problems with solutions." After the Watts rebellions, ABC developed a new television show called "Black Dignity" for Channel 7. The pilot proved quite successful, and the network later expanded its model to other cities.[129]

While the Afro-American Association never achieved the full media savvy of the Black Panther Party, its consistent efforts to directly utilize popular culture and stage public events strongly influenced its successors. The line between entertainment and politics grew ever more blurred as activists reached out through electronic media. Warden's strategies predated the Panthers by several years but showed clearly how a service oriented organization could be built with minimal financial resources, if it developed innovative modes of recruitment. Garvey's street parades served as an important precedent, but their scale was unachievable in the diffuse industrial suburbs of California. So activists turned to the young audiences on high school and college campuses.

The staging of the Mind of the Ghetto Conference at McClymonds's high school proved one of the association's most successful outreach attempts. The idea was to create a public forum where "blacks could talk out loud with each other about problems and solutions." A spectrum of activists from integrationist to radical attended the conference, including Maulana Karenga, Malcolm X, Bishop Roy Nichols, attorney Cecil Moore of Philadelphia, and Muhammad Ali. Warden later explained that "the title of the conference was carefully selected to underscore the mental component of the black ghetto."[130]

Complex reasoning lay behind the choice of McClymonds. Warden argued that the high school's mixed legacy epitomized that of West Oakland.

A number of prominent African Americans had graduated from the historic black high school, but it was surrounded by run-down buildings, public housing, and many of the problems that typified concentrated urban poverty. The neighborhood provided just the cross section of the black community that the association targeted: aspirant working-class people, the hard-core unemployed, and those who had turned to more informal means of support. Workshops ran throughout the day with speakers at night. One workshop entitled "Pride, Pimps, and Prostitutes" featured interviews with "cosmopolites" and sought to explain why young women turned to prostitution. Family breakdown and lack of support impelled the depressed and alienated into this unfortunate life choice. Dramatizing their plight by having participants themselves speak, rather than simply condemning them outright, attracted the attentions of the neighborhood and helped spark interest in the association's activities.[131]

. . .

BY THE EVE of 1963, the Afro-American Association had reached the height of its powers of influence. In its first two years, the student membership moved from participating in a study group to developing new ways of engaging the black populations beyond the Berkeley campus. The enthusiastic support the AAA received from different segments of the African American community reflected its widespread appeal. Strikingly, many in its ranks went on to distinguish themselves in electoral or radical politics: Ronald Dellums briefly attended meetings, as did Otho Green, Elihu Harris, Donald Hopkins, Ernest Allen, Cedric Robinson, Henry Ramsey, Huey Newton, Bobby Seale, and Maulana Karenga.[132] As is clear from the list of participants, the AAA represented a watershed moment in Black nationalist politics that influenced many of the social movement groups, and even electoral campaigns, that followed in its wake.

The association's importance extended far beyond the particulars of its organizational life. By nurturing a new expression of Black cultural nationalism, the study group played a crucial role in the unfolding history of Black Power thought. In contrast to earlier articulations, the association's philosophy brought together two central concerns of the postwar era: decolonization and popular media. The group celebrated a deep and heart-felt identification with the African continent forged on the cusp of Third World Liberation. Rather than understanding themselves as part of a domestic minority, the AAA was emboldened by the victories of Nasser, Nkrumah, and Kenyatta to identify with broader diasporic and international struggles for black self-determination. While the AAA shared in a long tradition of Pan-

Africanist thought, its ideology was inseparable from the period in which it emerged. The very presence of African students at American universities made the politics of decolonization immediate and concrete to its young membership. The AAA showed how African liberation movements transformed black Americans' self-conception. Contained within the very words "black" and "Afro-American" was a history of anticolonial victory. The association actively promoted the use of these terms, while also trying to cultivate the historical consciousness that inspired them. Through a wide and varied reading list that brought together cultural anthropology, critical black sociology, and classic works in African American history, the AAA politicized a whole generation of black students who passed through Bay Area colleges and universities in the late fifties and early sixties. In addition to creating a legacy of radical black internationalism, the Afro-American Association influenced subsequent activism through its innovative use of media. Donald Warden and the "born again" recognized the importance of black culture to black consciousness and embraced a variety of popular forms. Pentecostal preaching, doo-wop, and stump speaking all became tools used to recruit and proselytize. Inspired by Marcus Garvey's public performances, the association incorporated and adapted contemporary popular culture to promote its nationalist agenda. Sponsoring radio and television programs as well as Harlem-style street rallies enabled the AAA to mobilize the African American populations beyond the campus boundaries. Ultimately, the group brought together a compelling mixture of people and ideas that set the stage for many of the developments later in the decade. Perhaps most significant, the Afro-American Association improvised a language and aesthetic that spoke to the ethos of Black Power well before the term was ever used.[133]

4. A CAMPUS WHERE BLACK POWER WON

While the Afro-American Association recruited throughout Oakland, its largest following emerged at Merritt College, affectionately known to black residents as "Grove Street." With California's restructuring of public education under the Master Plan as backdrop, the rapidly expanding black student population vastly extended the organization's reach and brought comparatively privileged U.C. Berkeley students into dialogue with the East Bay's vibrant southern diaspora. By regularly staging street rallies and locating their headquarters adjacent to the school, the association helped catalyze a militant working-class student movement that culminated in the founding of the Black Panther Party for Self Defense. The common ground of "Afro-Americanism," and the redefinition of identity it promised, attracted groups that would later fracture into a variety of political tendencies from reformist to revolutionary. The first members of the AAA represented an inchoate black elite from across the country that was being groomed for middle-class lives of integration and influence. By contrast, their more numerous counterparts at "Grove Street" had a much more uncertain trajectory. The student body came largely from poor migrant families that were educationally underserved and subject to the volatile economic fortunes of postwar Oakland. Nevertheless, both populations viewed public education as an important avenue for self-realization and social mobility. Ultimately, the intellectual union of these two groups set the stage for the East Bay's Black Power movement.[1]

As the first real generation of black college students entered Bay Area colleges and universities, California's educational system was undergoing a complete restructuring. In the early sixties, the Master Plan for Higher Education revolutionized the state's dense network of public institutions. Policymakers developed the plan in response to a series of long-term pressures that the Golden State had faced since World War II. In the subsequent decades, these issues came to a head. Recurrent waves of in-migration combined with immense economic growth necessitated a much more comprehensive education policy. Officials expected California's student population to double in fifteen years. In fact, it actually quadrupled. In 1960, 227,000 students enrolled in the state's institutions of higher education; by 1975 the total reached 1 million.[2] Given this unprecedented demand, a way had to be found to accommodate the huge increase. Sixty different resolutions restructured governance, organization, and finance of the state's educational system. The Master Plan also established a decentralized method of administration that increased local control over public institutions. No single board ruled over the entire system; instead, the state erected separate structures of governance for each tier.[3]

This new era in higher education institutionalized the tripartite system of education that had developed on an ad hoc basis in California since the Progressive Era, consisting of the University of California, California State, and Junior College systems. It allowed for official methods of transfer between tiers so that, in theory, all students could gain access to the University of California. New opportunity shaped some of the more practical concerns of the Black Studies movement at the community college level. Moreover, it also vastly extended the number and size of junior colleges. Partial state funding for local initiatives provided for twenty-two new campuses that were required to admit all students with high school diplomas. This new capacity expanded working-class college enrollment and provided the institutional base for Merritt's influx of black students. In this sense it was democratizing. More schools and more funding meant more access. On the other hand, by clearly delineating the funding and degree-granting powers of each level—university (doctoral), state (master's and bachelor's), and community college (associate), the plan exacerbated long-standing divisions of race and class between tiers.[4]

As large numbers of black southern migrants poured into California during and after World War II, they immediately recognized low-cost, accessible higher education as one of the state's most important resources. Starting in the late fifties, community institutions like Oakland City College witnessed a steady increase in the population of African American students that quickly outstripped their numbers in the comparatively elite University of California system. While architects of the Master Plan gave little thought to how their attempts at social engineering would affect African American migrant communities, the expansion of California's system of higher education had far-reaching effects on local black youth. Increased enrollment meant not only better economic opportunities, but also participation in the increasingly militant campus culture of the early sixties. Study groups, black student unions, and protests for a Black Studies curriculum became important means of consciousness-raising. As a result, many of the radical groups that emerged later in the decade stemmed from this earlier period of black student activism.

Historian William O'Neill has argued that the democratization of higher education inaugurated a basic shift in youth culture from secondary schools to colleges and universities: "When the sixties began, youth culture meant the way adolescents lived. Its central institutions were the high school and the mass media. Its principal activities were consuming goods and enacting courtship rituals. . . . As time went on, college enrollments increased to the point where colleges were nearly as influential as high schools in the shaping the young."[5] On the West Coast, this structural shift contributed to the spread of Black nationalism and later Black Power among African American youth. Starting in the early twentieth century, California boasted the largest university enrollment in the country.[6] While black youth lacked equal access to many of the Golden State's abundant resources, they clearly benefited from California's unprecedented investment in public higher education. By 1969, the San Francisco Bay Area had the highest rate of college completion for people of color nationally. Over 13 percent of nonwhite residents age twenty-five or older had completed four years or more of college. This remarkable figure was nearly double the percentage for New York City and six times that for St. Louis, Missouri. At 11 percent, Los Angeles alone remotely approached levels of minority college completion comparable to those in the Bay Area.[7] These numbers had a political as well as socioeconomic significance. The early infrastructure for Black Power organizing in California centered in study groups at public universities. A mutually reinforcing dynamic took hold in which the increase in black students fed political organizing, and political organizing, in turn, attracted people who would never have considered attending college. The resulting synergy between the expansion of higher education and the politicization of African American youth is a crucial, and understudied, aspect of postwar Black radicalism.[8]

The tendency in an older Black Power historiography to overemphasize issues of violence versus nonviolence and white expulsion from civil rights organizations has obscured the internal changes inside northern and western black communities produced by migration, rapid urbanization, and newfound educational access. In California, black college students appeared consistently at the forefront of radicalism; however, few studies have explored why. Ironically, more attention to this phenomenon has come from the right than from the left. In his notorious Trilateral Commission Report, *Crisis of Democracy*, Samuel Huntington argued that the democratic surge of the 1960s, expressed most profoundly in the "higher levels of self consciousness" among blacks, Chicanos, and other marginal groups, stemmed from the "transitory *process* of change rather than the . . . lasting *results* of change." Steeped in anticommunist modernization theory, Huntington pointed to the rapid increase in college enrollments by previously excluded groups as a major factor in the explosion of university protest. Both the speed and scale of minorities' entry into higher education explained the intensity of campus upheaval. However, this development proved temporary. As the opening up of American universities to new groups became institutionalized, student activism slowly declined over time. While elite bias led many journalists and academics to overlook the developments at Merritt in favor of those at U.C. Berkeley and San Francisco State, this little-known community college exemplified how the democratization of higher education inaugurated a new era of black protest. In less than a decade, as African American enrollment increased nearly fourfold, Merritt produced one of the nation's most important black student movements. As home to an early black student union, Black Studies program, and the internationally known Black Panther Party for Self Defense, Merritt clearly demonstrated how the integration of black youth into "historically white" institutions inspired new and influential expressions of racial militancy.[9]

. . .

THE SCHOOL THAT came to be known as Merritt College went through many different transformations. Its origins were elite. In 1923 the Oakland school board commissioned Charles Dickey to build a secondary school. University High School was to serve the sons and daughters of academic faculty and expose them to the most modern pedagogy that Berkeley of the twenties could offer. Expansive courtyards, wide hallways, and arched windows were meant to draw students toward "higher thoughts."[10] University High's design and curriculum represented a triumph of Progressive ideals. At the head of the auditorium a hand-carved sign proclaimed "The Progress of All Through All: Under the Leadership of the Wisest and Best."[11]

Amidst the disruptions of war, University High School closed its doors in 1946. The Merritt Business School moved into the building soon after to provide veterans and working-class people with practical education.[12] Several miles away in downtown Oakland sat its sister school, the Laney Trade and Technical Institute. As the class and age composition of the student body shifted, vocational training and private enterprise replaced the lofty

Merritt College. Originally known as Oakland City College, its name was changed in 1964. This urban campus nurtured an early Black Studies movement that ultimately gave birth to the Black Panther Party. Despite its foundational influence on the BPP and other radical groups, Merritt has been overshadowed by U.C. Berkeley and San Francisco State in histories of the sixties. Nevertheless, student and faculty activism at this North Oakland community college was crucial to the emergence of Bay Area Black radicalism. Still photograph from the film *Merritt College: Home of the Black Panthers*, courtesy of Richard Heymann and Peralta TV.

ideals of Merritt's Progressive ancestor.[13] The Oakland Unified School District presided over both schools until local officials established the Oakland Junior College system in 1953.

In the early fifties, Merritt and Laney developed a clear division of intellectual labor. Merritt specialized in the liberal arts and came to be known as the "queen of the humanities," while Laney continued to be a vocational school with extensive apprenticeship programs.[14] The types of curriculum taught at each junior college shaped their student body profile and their long-term development. At Laney segregated plumbing and carpentry unions barred students of color from training programs, thereby keeping the trade school "lily white" prior to the district's restructuring in 1964.[15] Conditions at Laney were so bad that, when faced with consent decrees, the unions chose to move their programs off campus rather than desegregate.[16] As a result, it was probably easier for African American youth to attend U.C. Berkeley than to enter a unionized building trade in the East Bay in the early sixties. While Laney boasted a large and well-organized black student body by the end of the decade, it lacked the density and continuity of political culture of Merritt, which had begun the process of integration nearly a decade before.[17]

Life at Oakland City College for students of color proved only marginally better. Their numbers languished in the single or double digits, and conservative Greek life pervaded campus culture. Male students sported short hair and university aspirations; among "girls," girdles and gloves were common. Instructor Harriet Polt summed up the mood: "In classes we talked about 'conformity,' which we teachers condemned. Students found this puzzling."[18] Apathy ruled and political organizing, of even the most parochial type, was rare. Despite their power on campus, fraternities and sororities often scrambled to recruit new pledges and officers. Several alumni joked that during the late fifties and early sixties elections on the campus could best be described as "sandbox" rather than student government.[19] Although the school remained well funded and staffed, the Merritt campus lacked vitality.

Huey Newton's brother Melvin graduated in 1959 and remembered the campus as a fifties nightmare replete with theme days and dunking booths. Once a year, the school sponsored frontier days, and people dressed up in "western outfits."[20] Nearly all chose cowboy or miner costumes. Staff erected mock cages around campus to jail those who refused to participate. The whole scene reeked of fifties naiveté with an underlying racial edge more absurd than threatening. "It was basically a white thing," Newton explained.[21] In a few short years, this all changed radically with the influx of a heavily migrant black student body from the surrounding neighborhood.

There were places of reprieve. A handful of black students gathered at a single table on the far side of the cafeteria. Despite their tiny numbers, some remarkable people passed through Oakland City College in the late fifties. Melvin Newton shared classes with future congressman Ronald Dellums and *Oakland Post* publisher Tom Berkeley. For a few years Newton's life paralleled Dellums's; they both transferred from the junior college to state schools and later completed M.A. degrees in social work at U.C. Berkeley's Haviland Hall.[22] Each year a larger group of African American students entered, but their numbers rapidly dwindled as the semester progressed. A split emerged in their cohort; a small group made steady progress toward their degrees and stuck close together. For many more, however, classification exams and academic probation turned the school into a revolving door. The dropout rate spiked during the first six months. High attrition rates and placement tests became the most formidable obstacles to progress.[23] Former student Bill Love explained, "Everybody had to take an exam to go there, and your score on the exam determined whether you were allowed to enter regularly or on probation. . . . You would have a big population the first day and then we [were] gone. Much of the initial motivation for Black Studies and Black Power was in opposition to that."[24]

As the decade progressed, a portrait of a new type of Merritt student emerged. The signs appeared everywhere. A memo prepared by the Peralta administration in 1965 noted that the "Negro" student body comprised between 8 and 10 percent of the college's enrollment, even though the primary school population was less than half white. In less than two years, these figures doubled and tripled. By 1966, African Americans constituted nearly a quarter of Merritt's student body, and by 1967, over 30 percent.[25]

The shifting composition of Oakland City College attracted the attention of researchers in U.C. Berkeley's criminology department who were anxious to document the urbanization of southern newcomers and their children. Their report identified higher education as a major factor shaping the urbanization of migrant youth: "The young Negro population is relying heavily on accessible community colleges for advanced education. These colleges are acutely aware of the special problems they are encountering with this growing new group. . . . Their roots are in the South, but geographical and social mobility has brought them to the west coast."[26] The report went on to describe the junior college as the primary instrument of socialization *and* as the gateway between migrant populations and upward mobility. Black youth represented only one stage in a much longer process of new groups entering the city and seeking out the "educational ladder to social advancement."[27]

Personal testimony and autobiographical writings from Merritt students supported these observations. Not only were many the first members of their families to attend college, they were also relatively recent arrivals from the South who still retained strong cultural ties to their parents' places of origin. Their intermediary status as migrants led them to look "backwards as much as forwards" and helped to provide additional motivation for seizing opportunity unimaginable a decade before.[28] While Huey Newton was exceptional in many ways, his background typified that of the growing black student population at Merritt College. He was the child of Louisiana migrants, raised in poverty in Oakland by parents who had come to California in search of better jobs and more educational opportunity. The family shuttled back and forth between California and Louisiana, and Newton's older siblings often spent summers in Monroe. Sharecropping, racial violence, and segregated schools transformed western cities into havens of promise. "We were children of migrants that came here for social opportunity," explained Newton's older brother Melvyn. "I don't know if they [his parents] necessarily knew what schools were like out here, but they knew what the conditions were like out *there*."[29] The memory of the South remained ever present, evoking a none-too-distant past of rural poverty.

Community colleges became particularly important for this aspirant generation, whose hopes had been dashed by Oakland's faltering public education system. In his autobiography Huey Newton described how his experience in Oakland schools had left him functionally illiterate. This produced in him a profound shame, made worse by his older brother's achievements in school. Melvin was the first to attend Merritt and later went on to complete degrees at San Jose State and U.C. Berkeley.[30] Huey Newton explained, "It seems to me that nothing is more painful than a sense of shame that overwhelms you and afflicts the soul. . . . I had been hurt many times in fights, but nothing equaled the pain I felt at not being able to read."[31] His hunger for education mixed with and inflamed his hunger for a clear and definable sense of self.

Years before Merritt engendered an organized student movement, U.C. Berkeley researchers recognized its importance as a nexus point between migrants' rural, southern past and their urban present. The school exemplified national trends, including the blackening of American cities through white flight and internal migration, increased college attendance among working-class people and youth of color, and the rising expectations and political mobilization that accompanied this change in social status. A report compiled in 1964 examined how young newcomers attempted to reconcile the two radically different worlds they traversed: "The new Negro group that emerged in the course of our research consists of vigorous young people who have a distinct subculture, partially composed of certain vestiges of their southern rural tradition learned by actual rearing in the South, or passed by their parents who themselves grew up there. At the same time they aspire to education to equip themselves better for success in today's world. They want and are demanding a free and open voice in determining their future, unbounded by the limitations of race."[32]

The contradictory roles of the junior college as both socializing instrument and means of social access created an ambiguity in how black student organizing expressed itself on campus. Student activists worked to remake Merritt in their image by institutionalizing Black Studies, on the one hand, while simultaneously targeting transfer rules so that they could gain greater access to California's prestigious state college and university system, on the other. A more diffuse impulse for community control mixed with very specific personal and collective ambitions.[33]

In response to the changing demographics of the student body and the California Master Plan, Merritt's administration vastly increased its vocational and training programs. At the time of accreditation in 1962, the college offered only four major fields in occupational training; by 1966 this had been expanded to forty-four. The Peralta system established a separate Trade and Technical Division in this period, and the first graduates received their degrees in 1967. Given the exclusionary nature of many union apprenticeship programs, vocational education filled a core need, and large numbers of African Americans and Native Americans enrolled in these courses. Over time, Merritt developed a bifurcated approach to minority student demands. First, the school focused on using federal antipoverty funds to expand the practical nature of job training and career development. Second, it responded directly to protest by increasing humanities and social science courses in Black and Africana Studies. These seemingly divergent responses reflected different aspects of the student movement. The school administration sought to undercut the root causes of political mobilization by targeting poverty and skills disparity, while also making direct concessions to a growing racial and internationalist consciousness among its students.[34]

In the short but crucial five years spanning 1964 to 1969, the Merritt College campus underwent a demographic revolution that foreshadowed changes that would sweep the East Bay in the decade to come. The black population had grown from less than 10 percent to 40 percent of the total student body, and with numbers came a demand for representation both in curriculum and hiring practices. *Newsweek* and other national publications expressed alarm at these events. "What is happening at this two-year junior college has perhaps more importance to the black community than the more publicized events at San Francisco State, Brandeis, Berkeley, or Harvard," wrote *Newsweek* in February 1969. As a "turn around place" for low-income black students, Merritt represented a social truth much closer to the immediate realities of growing black urban populations of the 1960s.[35]

Merritt College and the Afro-American Association

Afro-American Association member Ernest Allen described himself and his friends as "upwardly mobile, working class, ambivalent and nervous."[36] His story was common to many politically active students at Merritt. Allen's father owned a grocery store and had some college; however, Ernest was the first to complete a degree. Largely insulated by the all-black world of East Oakland, he hoped to use his training in a technical field to become an engineer and work in a big corporation like IBM. This ambition filled him with contradictory emotions. Allen later reflected, "I saw my trajectory. . . . And there was a certain amount of apprehension. In other words, I certainly expected that life was going to be different. There was this vast unknown."[37] Ernest and his fellow students hoped that their education would propel them forward into a more affluent white world. However, guilt about leaving others behind created ambivalence. Some refused to understand their education in purely functionalist terms and began organizing to integrate Black and Africana Studies into Merritt's humanities and social science offerings. For others, like first-generation migrant Bobby Seale the process of politicization was less direct. In the late fifties, Seale started attending Merritt College part time to earn a degree in engineering.[38] Initially, he enrolled in classes to improve his job prospects; however, once he became immersed in the campus political culture, he began to understand education in broader terms.[39] After attending Merritt intermittently for several years, his interest in "American Black History" grew, and he shifted his emphasis from technical training to the humanities.[40]

As is clear from the personal histories of many Merritt students, much of the education at the college took place outside the classroom. In the mid-sixties, the campus boasted a thriving political culture that embraced many different tendencies in radical politics, from revolutionary nationalism to orthodox Marxism. While a variety of political groups vied for the hearts and minds of Merritt students, the Nation of Islam and the Afro-American Association made the deepest inroads into Merritt's rapidly growing black student body. These two "militant nationalist" groups received the most support, while integrationist organizations like the NAACP and CORE inspired little, if any, positive response.[41] A number of Merritt students attended Malcolm X's 1963 speech at U.C. Berkeley and viewed it as a life-changing event. However, their enthusiasm aggravated a growing generational gap between the young students, many of whom were not yet of voting age, and their parents. Older migrants remained wary of the NOI because of its anti-Christian rhetoric and its direct confrontational tactics with whites. A few students argued that the Nation's boldness secretly resonated with their families, but they remained too afraid of backlash to support Malcolm X openly.[42] For the East Bay's older generation of southern newcomers, in contrast to their children, the memory of southern repression still loomed large.

The AAA's deep imprint on "Grove College" reflected the effectiveness of street speaking and the power of proximity. From Downs Memorial Church, the association moved its offices to 422 Grove Street, just across the street

"Dignity Clothes" Afro-American Association manufacturing facility at Fifty-fifth and Grove Streets in North Oakland. Starting in 1964, Donald Warden and other members of the association set up a headquarters for the AAA several blocks from Merritt College. For a brief period, they manufactured African-inspired garments for sale locally. Photograph by Walter Taylor, courtesy of Khalid al-Mansour and Jamila al-Mansour.

from Merritt. This was the largest facility yet, and it could accommodate up to 150 people. The AAA also set up a clothing factory with a dozen or so machines and started manufacturing "Dignity Clothes," including a West African–inspired garment called a "Simba." Association meetings took on a modified format, and Monday gatherings sponsored events and lectures that reached up to 200 in attendance. Fridays remained devoted to small book discussion groups with little more than twenty to twenty-five people. After months of meetings, sources on African and African American history were exhausted, and the group turned to a broader reading list, including the Bible and the Koran. Donald Warden's abiding interest in religion no doubt played a role in this choice. During this period, the class composition of the group changed somewhat; older people formed a larger presence, with a mixture of professional and blue-collar members.[43]

Upon setting up permanent headquarters on Grove Street, the Afro-American Association established an informal employment office. Academic advising was a major concern of Donald Warden and other members who felt that black students' failure to major in practical disciplines impeded their future career prospects and hurt the development of the larger black community. He later explained, "Economically we stressed converting education opportunity for free technical training into permanent employment positions. Vocational training and working with one's hands was always praised."[44] Warden expressed concern that over half of black college graduates ended up employed in the civil service—a safe but poorly paid alternative to the private sector.[45]

Sometimes Warden's more conservative plan for economic uplift overshadowed his emphasis on racial pride and African history. In hindsight, he criticized the institutionalization of Black Studies programs because he feared that they had encouraged the preexisting tendency of students to major in impractical social science and humanities fields. African and African American history could be mastered in the summer or evening but should not impinge on "those subjects that were critical to nation building and . . . to prosperity for the group."[46] The hard sciences of chemistry, physics, biology, and especially medicine, had to be given primacy. Warden pointed to the strategies of Africans and other foreign nationals as examples that should be emulated by native-born black students.[47] While focusing on strategies of nation building, Warden's emphasis on a technocratic elite reflected an older tradition of uplift ideology that placed an almost religious faith in the liberating power of education and racial solidarity. This long-standing political tradition celebrated education as the key to liberation while emphasizing the racial union of "Black elites and the masses."[48] Warden remembered that he felt the most intense sense of accomplishment "looking out over the audience and seeing black professionals, blue and white collar workers, the underclass and unemployed completely integrated around a platform of constructive activity."[49]

The greatest significance of the Afro-American Association could be found not in the writings of Donald Warden, but in the ways that he and other senior members of the AAA exposed black youth throughout the Bay Area to broader debates about the meaning of black identity. Street speaking and study group meetings enabled young migrants to connect their lived experience to the revolutionary developments of decolonization, independence, and state socialism sweeping the globe in the early sixties. This was nowhere more evident than in the life of Anne Williams. She enrolled in Oakland City College in fall 1961 and planned to complete an accelerated training program to become a registered nurse. Williams entered with a very specific focus but soon became immersed in the community college's vibrant political culture. Despite growing up in a deeply religious and socially conservative household, the sheltered young woman soon found herself drawn into the forbidden world of radical politics. Her first exposure to the AAA started in a corner of the cafeteria where all the black students met, debated, and played bid whist. Through friends, Williams became involved in the Afro-American Association and started participating in study group sessions.

The weekly meetings inspired passionate exchanges about a range of topics from the importance of armed self-defense to the relevance of Marxism and sexual liberation for black people. Williams listened intently but often remained quiet, deferring to the "senior intellectuals" in the group. Nevertheless, the AAA's exploration of black consciousness made her reexamine many of her trusted assumptions and beliefs. Much to the dismay of her family, she stopped straightening her hair and adopted the short natural worn by many women in the group. Over time, the vibrant culture of the Afro-American Association came to occupy the same social and transcendental space as the Pentecostal church of her childhood. She began to reflect on the social distance that she had traveled from rural Louisiana to West Oakland's "Lower Bottom," and from there to the campus of Oakland City College. Drawing on her own experience, she questioned the best way forward for all black people. "I think from my involvement [with the Afro-American Association] I was able to gather the strength," Williams later explained. "People started reading existential materials—Albert Camus and people like that and Nietzsche. We're talking about them while at the same time we're talking about [whether or not] we should go with what our parents [wanted]. Our parents are linked to Martin Luther King and that's just too passive given the violence, and the horrific things that we were seeing happening all at once. . . . Turn the other cheek? This is what we had been told, and it just didn't feel right for so many of us."[50]

For Williams and her peers, the intellectual culture and social networks of the AAA became a bridge to other political tendencies. Through Afro-American Association member Ken Simmons, Williams met Fred Jerome from the Student Committee for Travel to Cuba during a reception in the South Bay. Jerome later came to Oakland City College to recruit students to join the SCTC's solidarity efforts with Cuba. In the months after the Bay of Pigs invasion, Jerome and Lavey Laub began organizing student trips to the island in order to protest the U.S. government's travel ban. During the spring semester of 1962, Anne Williams and fellow AAA member Jim Lacy traveled to Cuba with the SCTC, along with fifty-nine other university students from across the country. Huey Newton signed up to go as well, but canceled at the last minute. The SCTC trip proved to be life-changing. Anne had never traveled outside the country, so she obtained a passport for the

Anne Williams in her passport photograph taken in the spring of 1963, before her trip to Cuba with the Student Committee for Travel to Cuba. Photograph courtesy of Anne Williams.

first time. Shortly after their arrival, the group attended the island's 26th of July celebration commemorating the start of the Cuban Revolution with Fidel Castro's attack on the Moncada Barracks in 1953. Williams and Lacy listened to long, impassioned speeches by the president and climbed the Sierra Madres in a Russian tank truck to retrace the revolutionaries' retreat into the mountains. Most important, she and some of the other black students met with Robert F. Williams and his wife Mabel. The couple invited them to dinner and the students witnessed the Williamses' exile firsthand. "I could see in his eyes and his wife's eyes that they were totally separated from their families and their community and probably could not go back," Anne later remebered.[51] Although she had always described herself as apolitical, the trip to Cuba became a turning point in her life. Backlash against the SCTC action prevented the students from returning home, and what was supposed to be a short trip dragged on through most of the summer. Williams began to wonder if she, too, faced exile. No country would allow the group to fly into one of its airports for fear of creating an international incident. Finally, after six weeks of waiting, Spain relented; the students flew to there and then back to the United States.[52] Upon her return, Anne faced the worry and recriminations of her family, who could not understand why she had participated in such an action. But for Williams, the Cuban experience initiated her into a much larger world in which the rights of citizenship, freedom, and liberty became immediate and personal.[53]

The Fight for Black Studies

The recruitment efforts of the Afro-American Association, combined with the unfolding events of the southern civil rights movement, inspired a militant movement for Black Studies at Merritt College in the mid-sixties. In contrast to Warden's more conservative vision of economic nationalism, curricular battles at the community college directly tapped the aspirations of working-class black youth in a time of political flux. Many of the new black students were first-generation college students motivated by a variety of aspirations: to gain training for semiskilled jobs, to earn credits for transfer to four-year universities, and a more fundamental desire to see themselves reflected in the curriculum. Ernest Allen explained, "The fact that it [Merritt College] was located right in the middle of a community was a historical accident, but what people made of it was something else."[54] The boundary between Merritt and North Oakland was completely porous. People passed on and off the campus, and many residents from the surrounding area hung out in the cafeteria, a major hub for debate.[55]

Under student pressure Merritt College established its first Black Studies course in 1964. Although the class was scheduled in the evenings and taught as part of an experimental program, it became extremely popular. The students attending sharply contrasted with the homogeneous Merritt student body of the late fifties. By all accounts, the class was all black, working class, and older. A significant number of students were in their mid- to late twenties. Others, like future Panther leader Bobby Seale and city council member Leo Bazille, were former military. As the enrollment of people of color and working-class youth grew, veterans formed an increasingly visible presence at Merritt. Soon students began to demand that rather than only offering the class in the evenings, it should also be available as a full-credit course in the daytime. Leo Bazille said it best: "Malcolm was a big influence. Black nationalism and Black Africa reinforced the idea that Warden had planted. Black history at night ought to be brought into the day."[56]

Most of the students at Merritt had very little knowledge of African American history in general and of Black nationalism in particular. Marcus Garvey's *Philosophy and Opinions* had long since disappeared from local bookstores, and mass reprinting did not take place until later in the decade.[57] The Afro-American Association's study group and street speaking attracted a core group of Merritt students who went on to prominence in various Black radical organizations. This group included Huey Newton, Bobby Seale, Ernest Allen, Richard Thorne, and Marvin Jackman. Pressuring Merritt's administration to institute a Black Studies course became their initial foray into radical politics. This movement gathered strength and went on to broaden its demands, first to create a full-fledged Black Studies program, then a department, and finally the appointment of a black president.[58]

Between 1964 and 1966, African American students formed the Soul Students Advisory Council, which became a prototype for student organizing. They fought for more "biologically black" faculty and the expansion of a Black Studies curriculum based on an interdisciplinary model. Leo Bazille who became president of Soul Students in 1966 described the organization as a place where youth met and devised political involvements. The same year they changed their name to "Black Student Union," which at that time was a new term. One of Soul Students' most decisive accomplishments was prompting the administration to hire Sidney Walton as a student advisor. Black students considered issues of placement and transfer to the California State and University systems to be of paramount importance. Poor counseling had been a major obstruction in the past. In 1965, SSAC pushed for the recruitment of a person of color who would be sensitive to their needs. Bobby Seale threatened that they would shut the school down if someone was not hired immediately.[59] The president of Merritt called Walton and offered him the position, and he accepted that same year.[60]

In many ways Sidney Walton was uniquely suited for the position, both in terms of professional experience and personality. He had taught for several years in Fremont, and later became the principal of the city's continuation high school. Walton was actually the first black teacher hired in the district, which was predominantly Anglo, Portuguese, and Latino. Significant numbers of African Americans did not move to the distant suburb until the General Motors plant opened in 1960. While working there, Walton became active in San Francisco's American Federation of Teachers (AFT) and the Fremont California Teachers Association. He later complained bitterly that the latter amounted to little more than a company union. Walton used his experience as a labor organizer for the AFT to set up another teachers union in Fremont.[61] In terms of personality, Sidney Walton could best be described in one word—"dogged." He worked tirelessly at projects to see them to completion. Some complained he was power hungry, controlling, and even hostile. But whatever the assessment, it is clear that he became a driving force behind the push for the institutionalization of black faculty and Black Studies at Merritt. In order to document his campaign, Walton self-published a book called *The Black Curriculum: Developing a Program in Afro-American Studies* that was intended as a blueprint for establishing Black Studies programs at other campuses. By sharing resources and correspondence with the Merritt administration, he hoped to help other schools recreate his successes.[62]

The central issues that the Black Student Union lobbied for were the right to have Afro-American Studies classes count for transfer to University of California schools; the hiring of a "biologically black" president and teaching staff; and a full-fledged Afro-American Studies program. However, activists faced a structural obstacle—the number of credentialed instructors available was limited. As a result, they proposed changing the accreditation system so that people with associate degrees could be appointed as Afro-American Studies instructors. Walton and his supporters wanted a faculty that more closely resembled the student body. As he explained, "The Black community is aware of the apparent relationship existing in the ghetto wherein the higher the degree of the teacher the less relevant the person is to the contemporary student in terms of Black awareness."[63]

Challenging the district's hiring practices became the first step in establishing Merritt's Black Studies program. Walton, in fact, entitled an entire chapter of his book "Tricknology—The Role of Credentialing in the Perpetuation of White Racism."[64] He ridiculed the current system of hiring and promotion as the "white man's welfare system" that enabled older faculty to stonewall black instructors. Walton and his fellow activists attacked tenure as "one of the greatest enemies of relevant education for Black youngsters," a surprising position for a former AFT organizer.[65] He felt the only way to change higher education was for the African American community to immediately seize control over hiring from white-dominated administrators. Invoking the language of Great Society activism, Walton declared that this meant demanding "maximum feasible participation and shared power in the educational decision-making process."[66]

Bay Area Black Educators, an organization with a membership of nearly 400 drawn from all educational levels, partnered with Walton and the Black Student Union to introduce two resolutions to the California State Board of Education in early June 1968.[67] The first asked the board to create a new credential major in Afro-American Studies that would be applicable at all education levels. The second introduced the controversial proposal of allowing community college students to become instructors shortly after graduation. The resolution demanded that, given the exceptional nature of Mer-

Black Panther carrying books, August 25, 1968. Photograph © Pirkle Jones Foundation.

ritt's flagship Afro-American Studies program and its overwhelming need for certified instructors in this field, the State Board of Education should issue partial credentials to interested students upon completion of their associate degrees. Changing the system of certification would enable them to teach under the supervision of a master teacher or a department chairman until they completed all requirements. More extensive internship programs would also be set up to foster professional development for this new pool of faculty.[68]

Bay Area Black Educators justified this unprecedented change in policy by citing dismal statistics about the tiny numbers of black teacher candidates enrolled in California's public and private systems of higher education. On many University of California campuses, black students formed less than 1 percent of total undergraduate populations.[69] Given financial constraints and the relatively low pay of teaching professions, only a handful of this already extremely limited group chose to major in education. The numbers were startling. An informal survey from the 1966–67 school year revealed only six black graduates from the School of Education at Berkeley, and fifteen from San Francisco State for both elementary and secondary credentials. Given settlement patterns and more equitable hiring practices of metropolitan areas, urban campuses had the highest rates of minority attendance in the whole state. Many rural and suburban schools had no candidates at all. Local school districts anxious to hire more minority teachers had, like Kaiser before them, turned to the South for labor recruitment. In the 1960s, after substantial pressure by black activists, schools in Richmond, Stockton, Palo Alto, and Oakland all organized regular trips to HBCUs for this purpose. They consistently visited Atlanta University, Southern University, and Tuskegee Institute.[70]

The proposed changes to the credentialing system created a local firestorm among the faculty of Merritt. In early May 1968, 86 out of 138 polled said that they supported "the idea of a partial credential, but *only if based on the BA degree.*" One hundred and eight rejected the proposal to allow the associate degree as a sufficient qualification, and Merritt's faculty senate moved to immediately rescind the proposed amendment for the State Board of Education.[71] After several months of negotiation and modification, the State Board of Education passed a revised version of the resolutions in mid-October 1968, nearly a month before the uprisings at San Francisco State.[72]

The new guidelines defined Afro-American Studies broadly as "the study of the Afro-American community, its people, politics, culture, philosophy, art, music, literature, economics, history, and social development."[73] The board placed strict time limits on this temporary program meant to remedy the immediate crisis at Merritt. Partial credentials based on associate degrees in Afro-American Studies could only be obtained before July 1, 1970, and then only under special circumstances. The Committee of Credentials had to establish that a "qualified person holding a regular teaching credential" was unavailable, and the district or county superintendent or agency seeking to hire had to complete a special statement of need.[74]

As the battle over faculty hiring and Black Studies escalated, students moved from staging regular strikes and boycotts to direct confrontations with Merritt's administration. In a letter to a senior official, President Ed Redford complained that Walton and the Black Student Union used strong-arm tactics; no demand was made without an accompanying threat. Redford charged that protestors frequently disrupted faculty meetings by packing them with students or by reading elaborate statements that ignored the business at hand. Most serious of all, Redford claimed that Walton spearheaded this campaign of intimidation by making direct threats of physical violence against him and other members of the Merritt faculty and staff. Allegedly, Walton used the common refrain that if the administration did not accede to his demands, he could no longer prevent black students from burning the college down. In fact, there would never be a new college in the hills, because "it [would] be burned down as fast as it [was] constructed."[75]

. . .

ULTIMATELY, BY THE close of 1968 Merritt students had succeeded in having all of their demands met, including a Black Studies department with substantial numbers of African American instructors, the appointment of a black president, and the right to use Afro-American Studies classes for transfer to the University of California. The Black Student Union's final demand was a symbolic one: the establishment of February 21 as Malcolm X Day. The price for these victories was a virulent backlash. Within three years, the district administration moved Merritt College from its firm moorings in a historically black neighborhood in the flats to an isolated hill campus. While the relocation had been in the planning stages for over a decade, many speculated that campus militancy had hastened the move.[76]

Despite the rifts that would emerge soon after, fighting for Black Studies helped to create a united front for groups and personalities that easily veered into partisan conflict. As Huey Newton explained, "Everyone—from Warden and the Afro-American Association to Malcolm X and the Muslims to all the other groups active in the Bay Area at that time—believed strongly that the failure to include Black history in the college curriculum was a scandal. We all set out to do something about it."[77] Merritt's successes and the national obsession with the Panthers attracted the attentions of the *Wall Street Journal* the following year. In the November 18, 1969, issue, the newspaper asked facetiously, "What happens when Black militants gain the upper-hand on a college campus?" Although the nation's educators feared such an outcome, "nowhere does it appear more of a reality than at Merritt College, a little-known two year junior college located in one of this city's sprawling Black slums." The anxiety created was palpable; Merritt represented a campus in which Black Studies had been institutionalized and a black social movement had found its base. In essence, Merritt was "A Campus Where Black Power Won."[78]

PART THREE.
BLACK POWER AND URBAN MOVEMENT, 1966–1982

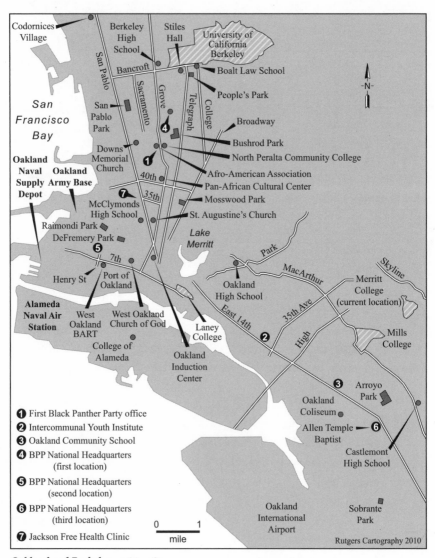

Codornices Village

Berkeley High School

Stiles Hall

University of California Berkeley

Boalt Law School

People's Park

San Pablo

San Francisco Bay

Bancroft

Sacramento

Grove

Telegraph

College

San Pablo Park

Broadway

Downs Memorial Church

❹

❶

Bushrod Park

North Peralta Community College

Oakland Naval Supply Depot

Oakland Army Base

Afro-American Association

Pan-African Cultural Center

40th

❼

35th

Mosswood Park

McClymonds High School

St. Augustine's Church

Raimondi Park

DeFremery Park

❺

Lake Merritt

Park

7th

Henry St

Port of Oakland

Oakland High School

MacArthur

Skyline

Merritt College (current location)

Alameda Naval Air Station

West Oakland BART

West Oakland Church of God

Laney College

East 14th

35th Ave

High

Mills College

College of Alameda

Oakland Induction Center

❷

❸

Arroyo Park

Oakland Coliseum

Allen Temple Baptist

❻

Castlemont High School

❶ First Black Panther Party office
❷ Intercommunal Youth Institute
❸ Oakland Community School
❹ BPP National Headquarters (first location)
❺ BPP National Headquarters (second location)
❻ BPP National Headquarters (third location)
❼ Jackson Free Health Clinic

Oakland International Airport

Sobrante Park

0 — 1
mile

Rutgers Cartography 2010

-N-

Oakland and Berkeley, 1966–1982

5. MEN WITH GUNS

In the aftermath of the Watts rebellions, the failure of community programs to remedy chronic unemployment and police brutality prompted a
core group of black activists to leave campuses and engage in direct action
in the streets.[1] The spontaneous uprisings in Watts called attention to the
problems faced by California's migrant communities and created a sense of
urgency about police violence and the suffocating conditions of West Coast
cities. Increasingly, the tactics of nonviolent passive resistance seemed irrelevant, and the radicalization of the southern civil rights movement provided a new language and conception for black struggle across the country.[2]
Stokely Carmichael's ascendance to the chairmanship of the Student Nonviolent Coordinating Committee (SNCC) in June 1966, combined with the
events of the Meredith March, demonstrated the growing appeal of "Black
Power." His speech on the U.C. Berkeley campus in late October encapsulated these developments and brought them directly to the East Bay.[3] Local
activists soon met his call for independent black organizing and institution
building in ways that he could not have predicted.

In October 1966 several weeks before the Black Power Conference,
Bobby Seale and Huey Newton began meeting to formalize the political
platform for a new organization they called the Black Panther Party for Self
Defense. Their earlier participation in Merritt College's Black Studies movement forged networks of allies, as well as opponents, that shaped the local
Black Power movement for years to come. After founding the BPPSD, Newton and Seale downplayed their student origins and ongoing campus support in favor of "brothers off the block," who they celebrated as their base.
This choice reflected their desire to not only include but also foreground the
young people most excluded from traditional uplift and civil rights politics.

At first glimpse, these two seemed unlikely candidates for leading a nationwide social movement. In 1966, Huey Newton was twenty-five, marginally employed, and a parolee.[4] Bobby Seale was several years older, cycling

between day jobs, and working intermittently as a stand-up comic at a local nightspot.[5] While their backgrounds precluded involvement in more traditional avenues of black politics, they became an essential asset in organizing the most disfranchised sectors of Oakland's migrant community. Drawing on his own experience, Huey Newton developed an expansive critique of the state that spoke to the disappointment and grievances of Bay Area youth. A whole generation found itself displaced and burdened by the false hopes of southern exodus. They traveled to California with their parents to escape the poverty and brutality of the Jim Crow South only to find that the bountiful supply of industrial jobs that drew their families had disappeared. A segregated and hostile school system combined with law enforcement's systematic campaign of harassment and containment relegated many to life at the social and economic margins.[6] The Black Panther Party channeled migrant youths' alienation into an organized program of self-defense and community service.

The emergence of the Oakland-based BPPSD reflected both the particular conjuncture of Bay Area migrant communities and the changing nature of the southern civil rights movement in mid-decade. In the face of the federal government's failure to enforce the Civil Rights Act of 1964, southern activists developed new strategies for asserting black political rights.[7] In Jonesboro, Louisiana, the Deacons for Defense tapped into a long-standing tradition of armed self-defense to prevent the Ku Klux Klan and other white paramilitary groups from intimidating black citizens. Similarly, in Lowndes County, Alabama, SNCC workers organized a new political party to run black candidates for public office. Although Lowndes was simply an extension of SNCC's voting rights campaign, the choice of a crouching black panther as their party symbol betrayed a new spirit of militancy. Lowndes workers broke with the earlier wisdom of nonviolent passive resistance by working with the Deacons for Defense, the Nation of Islam, and other volunteers to protect black activists and voters.[8] In a fundraising tour in Los Angeles, organizer John Hulett explained that African Americans "never had any protection and today we aren't looking for anyone to protect us. We are going to protect ourselves."[9]

Significantly, both the Deacons and the Lowndes County Freedom Organization (LCFO) had deep roots in black rural communities, not unlike those that many Bay Area migrants had so recently left. Their vision for black liberation resonated strongly with Huey Newton, Bobby Seale, and other California activists. The midsixties witnessed a proliferation of Panther parties throughout the West Coast, including the Black Panther Party of Northern California, the Black Panther Political Party of Watts, and the Oakland-based Black Panther Party for Self Defense. These organizations emerged independently, linked only through the shared inspiration of the LCFO. The appeal of panther iconography was inseparable from the existential struggle of migrant youth against police brutality and the new technologies of incarceration that the Golden State pioneered.[10] California led the nation in the scale and infrastructure of youth detention as well as the militarization of domestic policing. This tendency reached a crisis point in the aftermath of the Watts rebellions when the Los Angeles Police Department (LAPD) arrested over 5,000 people, many of whom were juveniles. The state response to Watts as much as the popular uprising itself did much to radicalize California's urban communities in its wake.[11] In this moment of crisis, black migrants looked to the South. In the East Bay, black political culture, like churches, music, and almost every dimension of postwar African American life, retained binding ties to a recent southern past.[12] The East Bay's Black Panther Party adapted the Deacons and Lowndes County's model of armed self-defense to address the peculiar forms of racial violence and segregation of West Coast cities. Given the parallel migration of white southerners and their heavy representation in the ranks of the LAPD and the OPD, this leap was not a difficult one.[13]

Oakland—the Next Watts?

Washington policymakers closely watched Oakland in the months after Watts. Following their lead, the *Wall Street Journal* published a series of articles on the city's social and political life. To readers, it must have seemed surprising to see such a comparatively small city—only the fifth largest in California—receive such extensive coverage. However, it quickly became clear why this industrial suburb of San Francisco had attracted so much national attention. After Watts, federal policymakers drafted a confidential report examining conditions in cities across the country to see if the urban uprisings would spread. Oakland appeared at the top of the list, and the *Wall Street Journal* proclaimed the city a "racial tinderbox" on the verge of a social explosion. The question was whether the federal government could provide much needed relief while also financing the growing expenditures on defense. "It reaches to the heart of the 'guns or butter' problem that finds President Johnson striving to scale down his costly Great Society plans, many of them designed to aid poor Negroes."[14]

Perhaps more than any other metropolitan region, the San Francisco

Bay Area experienced the deep contradiction that underlay Johnson's waning War on Poverty and the military escalation in Vietnam. Northern California's postwar "Arsenal of Democracy" with its extensive military and defense infrastructure had been reinvigorated in the 1960s as a major point of disembarkation for the Vietnam War.[15] The Oakland Naval Supply Center, Alameda Air Station, and nearby Concord Naval Weapons Station processed seemingly endless supplies of military hardware, weapons, and men. As hundreds of thousands of soldiers passed through the Oakland Army Base and Airport, the vast expenditures on defense became a visible part of daily life.[16] Awash in federal research and development dollars, U.C. Berkeley and Stanford provided the intellectual superstructure. In the San Francisco Bay Area, raw martial power and university expertise converged.[17] Through regular demonstrations, Berkeley antiwar activists called attention to the military-industrial complex in their midst. Starting in October 1965, the Vietnam Day Committee sponsored marches from the Berkeley campus to the Oakland Induction Center to publicize its essential role in the Vietnam War effort.[18]

Within less than a few miles of this military edifice lay ravaged West Oakland, where nearly half of all families lived below the poverty line and a third relied on welfare for their survival.[19] The *Wall Street Journal* claimed that the unemployment rate among black residents was five times that of the national average.[20] In response, local activists demanded federal work relief to meet these "Depression-like" conditions. "What we need here is jobs, jobs, jobs, not training for *no* jobs," explained one resident. Instead, they were told the money simply was not there.[21]

In conjunction with the vigorous black and white student movements sweeping Bay Area campuses, this situation represented potential social dynamite, and Oakland city leaders were acutely aware of their vulnerability. In February 1966, *Ramparts* journalist Warren Hinckle enumerated their fears of "outsiders," "intellectuals," and "agitators," all framed by the larger fear of Oakland as the next Watts. "Oakland's leaders see a twofold spectre haunting their grimy city: the fear of an explosion from the ghetto within, and an invasion of 'outside agitators' from the sprawling, adjacent Berkeley campus of the University of California."[22] Despite these anxieties, Oakland never erupted in spontaneous rebellions, or at least not in the way that was expected. Poverty officials gladly took credit, but the truth lay elsewhere.[23] As a more cohesive migrant community than Watts with a vibrant tradition of radicalism, Oakland instead gave birth to an expansive social movement that permanently transformed not only the East Bay but the larger world beyond. It drew its slogans and symbols from the vanguard of the southern civil rights movement and its urgency from the looming social crisis in California cities.[24]

Lowndes County

In the summer of 1965, Stokely Carmichael joined together with grassroots activists in Alabama to form a third party, the Lowndes County Freedom Organization, with the emblem of a large, crouching black cat. Local ballots displayed symbols as well as names of political parties, because of the high rate of illiteracy among voters. Lowndes County represented one of the most daunting citadels of white supremacist rule in the Deep South. Situated between the Edmund Pettus Bridge and Montgomery, the Lowndes establishment faced no organized opposition since the end of Reconstruction. "One of the poorest counties in the nation, it was feudal. About eighty families owned 90 percent of the land," Carmichael explained. "Of a population of fifteen thousand, twelve thousand were African, not a one of whom could vote."[25] The omnipresence of the Klan and white control of the local Democratic Party made voter registration impossible.

Initially, the title of "Black Panther Party" had not been chosen by SNCC but by the white-dominated local media. In a widely circulated article published by the *New Yorker* in October 1966, Carmichael complained about the racial logic that underlay the media's designation of the LCFO as the "Black Panther Party." He pointed out that local newspapers never referred to the Alabama Democratic Party as the "White Cock Party," despite their choice of the racialized symbol and slogan, "White Supremacy for the Right." "No one ever talked about 'white power' because power in this country is white," Carmichael wrote. "The furor over that black panther reveals the problems that white America has with color and sex; the furor over 'Black Power' reveals how deeply racism runs and the great fear which is attached to it."[26]

Despite its complex origins or perhaps because of them, the idea of a "black panther party" proved compelling to many in northern and western cities. It embodied a graphic image of resistance that resonated far beyond the LCFO's stated aim of black electoral representation. Cofounder John Hulett explained its message: "The black panther is an animal that when it is pressured it moves back until it is cornered, then it comes out fighting for life or death. We felt we had been pushed back long enough and that it was time for the Negroes to come out and take over."[27] Although the LCFO's goal was to elect black officials in a county that was over 83 percent African American, the political symbolism of the panther took on a life of its own. Across the country, activists appropriated the idea and adapted it to the specific needs of their local black freedom struggles.

Word of the Lowndes County Panthers spread to Oakland through a number of different channels.[28] Prior to the Students for a Democratic Society–sponsored Black Power conference at U.C. Berkeley in early November, a local SNCC support group circulated flyers throughout the Bay Area with the panther logo. Both Newton and Seale claimed one of these pamphlets as their initial inspiration.[29] However, an even more direct link was through Mark Comfort, a fellow activist who traveled to Lowndes in spring 1966 to set up security and self-defense forces for the LCFO. Comfort was a military veteran with a long history of community organizing in Oakland. Like many of his peers, he was also a southern migrant, born in Oklahoma in 1934.[30] A tall and commanding figure arrayed in a black beret and gold earring, Comfort had become a central figure in Oakland grassroots politics by 1966. For several years, he had worked with Youth Corps and the Ad Hoc Committee to End Discrimination, an interracial civil rights group composed largely of university students and members of the Bay Area branches of CORE. In spring 1964, the Ad Hoc Committee took on the *Oakland Tribune*, charging the newspaper with discriminatory hiring practices.[31] In December, the group staged a large demonstration blocking access to the Tribune Building (the "Tower of Power"), and police arrested eighteen demonstrators. For his part in this action, Mark Comfort was sentenced by the court to six months in jail for "maintaining himself as a public nuisance and refusing to disperse at the scene of a riot." In a pattern that proved prophetic, the criminal justice system forced the civil rights group to redirect its efforts from direct action protests to defending its members in court.[32]

After the Ad Hoc Committee dissolved, Comfort founded his own organization, the Oakland Direct Action Committee (ODAC). Drawing on his earlier experience, he set up a headquarters in East Oakland to launch a sustained organizing campaign among local youth. In a 1965 interview with Berkeley's *Spider Magazine*, Comfort described how ODAC sought to immerse itself in the lives of residents. "We went into the community—some people came down from campus for a couple of days and did block work, but no one has been back because it's hard, going from door to door talking to people, and a lot of people don't like to do it because it's a long, drawn out process. But it's very important, because how are we going to know exactly what is happening in the black community unless you talk to the people to find out exactly what they would like to see done."[33] Instead of relying on student volunteers or paid staff, Comfort brought in young people from the surrounding area. The neighborhood was in the same district as Castlemont, where Ford Foundation–sponsored programs focused their efforts a few years earlier. With input from local youth, ODAC established clubs with colorful names like the Alm Boy Dukes and the Enchanted Maffions to rival the lure of local streets gangs.[34]

Comfort's work with East Oakland teenagers attracted the attention of the federal Economic Development Administration representative Amory Bradford, who solicited his assistance in establishing more effective job-training programs.[35] Although Comfort was well-respected by federal officials, he had a number of powerful enemies, including Oakland mayor John Houlihan and publisher William Knowland. Picketing the *Tribune* and giving interviews to *Wall Street Journal* reporters earned him substantial enmity, and Comfort became well-acquainted with the problem of police intimidation. Law enforcement regularly surveilled the ODAC office and harassed its members. Comfort remained convinced that if action was not taken immediately Oakland would erupt in violence.[36]

In May 1966, Mark Comfort led a California delegation to Lowndes County to protect voters and civil rights workers during the first county election since the passage of the Voting Rights Act. He was not alone. Across the United States, a spectrum of radical groups expressed interest in adapting the concept of the "black panther party" to their own local communities.[37] Along with activists from New York, Philadelphia, and Detroit, Comfort approached Carmichael about starting their own regional panther parties. Without hesitation the chairman of SNCC responded, "We ain't got a patent. Feel free. If local conditions indicate, go for it."[38] Comfort took the idea back to the West Coast, and over the coming months, it spread like wildfire. Nearly a dozen new parties emerged across California, all with similar names.[39] In the San Francisco Bay Area, two groups competed for recognition. Both of them had their origins—and antagonisms—in campus struggles.

In Defense of Self-Defense

The year 1966 had been difficult for Huey Newton. He had recently been released from the California Youth Authority after serving a six-month sentence for stabbing fellow black teen Odell Lee.[40] Although Newton had renewed his friendship with former Merritt classmate Bobby Seale, he struggled with a sense of malaise that plagued him through much of his teenage years and young adulthood, later describing the years prior to the founding of the BPPSD as difficult ones of great "inner turmoil."[41] In March, police arrested Newton again after an altercation with a Berkeley police officer. While hanging out with a group of friends in a café along Telegraph, Bobby Seale climbed on a chair to recite Ronald Stone's poem, "Uncle Sammy Call Me Fulla Lucifer." "You school my naïve heart to sing red-white-and-blue-stars-and-stripes songs and to pledge eternal to all things blue, true-blue-eyed blond, blond-haired, white chalk white skin with U.S.A. tattooed all over."[42] When officer Eugene Sabatini attempted to take Seale into custody for disturbing the peace, Huey Newton hit him in the face and fled. The City of Berkeley later charged Newton with felonious assault, which he subsequently plea-bargained to a misdemeanor with a promise never to return to Telegraph.[43]

In the coming months, Huey Newton worked intermittently with Merritt student activists, but a confrontation with the Soul Students Advisory Council soon led him to abandon the black student movement altogether. Newton and Seale both expressed frustration with RAM, SSAC, and the Afro-American Association over their chronic unwillingness, or inability, to translate ideas into action. In the words of Bobby Seale, "Huey was one for implementing things."[44] They continually harangued their enemies as "cultural nationalists," their pseudonym for those who fetishized African language and custom, refused alliances with all whites, and failed to make distinctions of class.[45] Although they stressed cultural nationalism as the core ideological divide, in reality their most poignant source of conflict with other Black radicals was their peers' resistance to carrying loaded guns. In his autobiography, Newton described how he and Bobby searched for a program to mobilize the community. Ultimately, they found this through addressing police violence and advocating the right to bear arms.[46]

In early 1966, an opportunity presented itself to make this vision concrete. Soul Students' negotiations with Merritt College's administration had bogged down. Newton proposed sponsoring a rally in support of the Afro-American Studies program in which SSAC members would strap on guns and march outside the campus on May 19, Malcolm X's birthday. In keeping with the minister's philosophy of self-defense, Soul Students' first priority should be recruiting and broadening support from the "lumpen proletariat"—the hustlers, unemployed, and "the downtrodden" populations surrounding the school.[47] According to Newton, this action would politicize the broader community, call attention to police brutality, and intimidate the administrators into taking the activists' demands more seriously.[48] His fellow students refused, and Newton's relationship with the organization quickly soured. It deteriorated even further when the SSAC's membership accused him of stealing after discovering that he and Bobby Seale used money from the SSAC's treasury for bail and legal costs for the Sabatini case.[49] After breaking with the Merritt student organization, Newton approached the skeleton branch of the West Cost Revolutionary Action Movement with a program of armed self-defense. To the earlier idea of carrying weapons, Newton added a new one—patrolling the police. RAM also rebuffed him, dismissing his plan as "suicidal."[50] Bobby and Huey interpreted their cowardice as a fatal flaw that would make it impossible for these "intellectual" groups to ever garner a mass following.[51]

Newton and Seale lambasted the Merritt activists for their self-satisfaction and failure to effectively reach out and organize those with the greatest potential for social change. "We just went to the streets, where we should have been in the first place—those four or five years that preceded this showed us that," Seale later wrote. "Before Huey decided to leave college, he wanted to implement things there, and educate those on the college level to the necessity of bringing the brothers off the block to the college level."[52] Now, he turned this strategy on its head. Whereas before he tried to bring "the streets" into the school—as in his proposal to have an armed march outside Merritt—he now sought to bring the school into "the streets." Like Prometheus's gift of fire, Newton brought new skills and knowledge from the university with him into grassroots struggles.

The Black Panther Party for Self Defense

As Newton searched for a medium to "capture the imagination" of Oakland's black community, he turned to the law library at the North Oakland Service Center, a poverty program that employed Bobby Seale. Drawing on his training from law school, Newton poured over the California penal code and soon discovered an old statute that legalized carrying unconcealed weapons. After spending the summer discussing the right to bear arms with "brothers on the street," Newton and Seale decided that they needed a concrete program to present to people before starting police patrols. On October 15, 1966, in less than twenty minutes, Seale and Newton drafted the "Black Panther Party and Program" in the center.[53]

The Ten Point Program took its form from the Nation of Islam, its content from the Constitution and Bill of Rights, and its collectivist ideology from the East Bay left.[54] The program consisted of ten insistent demands, followed

OCTOBER 1966 BLACK PANTHER PARTY PLATFORM AND PROGRAM

What We Want
What We Believe

1. **We want freedom. We want power to determine the destiny of our Black Community.**

   We believe that black people will not be free until we are able to determine our destiny.

2. **We want full employment for our people.**

   We believe that the federal government is responsible and obligated to give every man employment or a guaranteed income. We believe that if the white American businessmen will not give full employment, then the means of production should be taken from the businessmen and placed in the community so that the people of the community can organize and employ all of its people and give a high standard of living.

3. **We want an end to the robbery by the white man of our Black Community.**

   We believe that this racist government has robbed us and now we are demanding the overdue debt of forty acres and two mules. Forty acres and two mules was promised 100 years ago as restitution for slave labor and mass murder of black people. We will accept the payment in currency which will be distributed to our many communities. The Germans are now aiding the Jews in Israel for the genocide of the Jewish people. The Germans murdered six million Jews. The American racist has taken part in the slaughter of over fifty million black people; therefore, we feel that this is a modest demand that we make.

4. **We want decent housing, fit for shelter of human beings.**

   We believe that if the white landlords will not give decent housing to our black community, then the housing and the land should be made into cooperatives so that our community, with government aid, can build and make decent housing for its people.

5. **We want education for our people that exposes the true nature of this decadent American society. We want education that teaches us our true history and our role in the present-day society.**

   We believe in an educational system that will give to our people a knowledge of self. If a man does not have knowledge of himself and his position in society and the world, then he has little chance to relate to anything else.

6. **We want all black men to be exempt from military service.**

   We believe that Black people should not be forced to fight in the military service to defend a racist government that does not protect us. We will not fight and kill other people of color in the world who, like black people, are being victimized by the white racist government of America. We will protect ourselves from the force and violence of the racist police and the racist military, by whatever means necessary.

Ten Point Program, drafted by Huey P. Newton and Bobby Seale in October 1966

7. We want an immediate end to POLICE BRUTALITY and MURDER of black people.

We believe we can end police brutality in our black community by organizing black self-defense groups that are dedicated to defending our black community from racist police oppression and brutality. The Second Amendment to the Constitution of the United States gives a right to bear arms. We therefore believe that all black people should arm themselves for self-defense.

8. We want freedom for all black men held in federal, state, county and city prisons and jails.

We believe that all black people should be released from the many jails and prisons because they have not received a fair and impartial trial.

9. We want all black people when brought to trial to be tried in court by a jury of their peer group or people from their black communities, as defined by the Constitution of the United States.

We believe that the courts should follow the United States Constitution so that black people will receive fair trials. The 14th Amendment of the U.S. Constitution gives a man a right to be tried by his peer group. A peer is a person from a similar economic, social, religious, geographical, environmental, historical and racial background. To do this the court will be forced to select a jury from the black community from which the black defendant came. We have been, and are being tried by all-white juries that have no understanding of the "average reasoning man" of the black community.

10. We want land, bread, housing, education, clothing, justice and peace. And as our major political objective, a United Nations–supervised plebiscite to be held throughout the black colony in which only black colonial subjects will be allowed to participate, for the purpose of determining the will of black people as to their national destiny.

When, in the course of human events, it becomes necessary for one people to dissolve the political bands which have connected them with another, and to assume, among the powers of the earth, the separate and equal station to which the laws of nature and nature's God entitle them, a decent respect to the opinions of mankind requires that they should declare the causes which impel them to the separation.

We hold these truths to be self-evident, that all men are created equal; that they are endowed by their Creator with certain unalienable rights; that among these are life, liberty, and the pursuit of happiness. *That, to secure these rights, governments are instituted among men, deriving their just powers from the consent of the governed; that, whenever any form of government becomes destructive of these ends, it is the right of the people to alter or to abolish it, and to institute a new government, laying its foundation on such principles, and organizing its powers in such form, as to them shall seem most likely to effect their safety and happiness.* Prudence, indeed, will dictate that governments long established should not be changed for light and transient causes; and, accordingly, all experience hath shown, that mankind are more disposed to suffer, while evils are sufferable, than to right themselves by abolishing the forms to which they are accustomed. *But, when a long train of abuses and usurpations, pursuing invariably the same object, evinces a design to reduce them under absolute despotism, it is their right, it is their duty, to throw off such government, and to provide new guards for their future security.*

by firm explanations of belief. Newton and Seale appropriated the structure from the "Muslim Program," a statement published weekly in *Muhammad Speaks* in two parts: "What Muslims Want" and "What Muslims Believe." The semblance of form and the difference of ideology were instructive. The first point was the same—"We want freedom"—but the Panther leaders replaced Elijah Muhammad's "We want a full and complete freedom" with "We want power to determine the destiny of our black community."[55] This statement placed the new party firmly within a Black nationalist tradition, but like the Afro-American Association's public rhetoric, it also revealed the transnational influence of decolonization. Points Six and Eight, which demanded that all African American men be exempted from military service and freed from "federal, state, county, and city prisons and jails," closely paralleled the Nation's demand for tax exemption and release of "all believers of Islam now held in federal prisons."[56] While Newton and Seale drew on the Nation's manifesto, they replaced its separatist pronouncements on racial mixing, religious orthodoxy, and territorial partitioning with the Party's humanistic appeals for decent housing, employment, and education. The single point that remained identical was Point Seven, "We want an immediate end to POLICE BRUTALITY and MURDER of black people."[57] Along with this platform, Huey and Bobby established a basic structure for the Party with Newton serving as the "Minister of Defense" and Seale as the "Chairman of the Black Panther Party."[58]

The connections between the "Muslim Program" and the Ten Points revealed the wide reach of the Nation and the diffusion of its ideas and political strategies. Its connection to the Panthers was not hard to trace. Like Donald Warden and other AAA members, Newton briefly attended the local mosque in West Oakland. The writings of Malcolm X and C. Eric Lincoln's *Black Muslims in America* also strongly influenced him.[59] As the largest and oldest Black nationalist organization, the NOI provided a shared language and political culture that informed a broad range of Black Power activism in California, from early student groups like the Afro-American Association and Soul Students Advisory Council through the BPPSD. Although the Panthers adamantly opposed the racial and religious nationalism of the Nation, the Party still bore the imprint of its organizing and rhetorical strategies.

Moreover, the Ten Point Program expressed the grievances of the East Bay's migrant community by identifying the barriers they faced to full citizenship and human self-realization. Bobby Seale described the gritty materialism that underlay what appeared to be a reformist program: "Huey understood that you answer the momentary desires and needs of the people, that you try to instruct them and politically educate them . . . and . . . the people themselves will [wage] a revolution to make sure that they have these basic desires and needs fulfilled."[60] This strategy could be seen clearly in their program's focus on material essentials. Point Two, calling for full employment, for example, addressed rapid deindustrialization following World War II that had dashed the rising expectations of southern newcomers. For the younger generation who came of age in the early 1960s, unemployment was particularly brutal and had led to a near subsistence living standard that exacerbated constant conflict with the police.[61] The Panthers continual rhetoric of "survival" spoke directly to these primary needs, and laid the groundwork for the Party's mass appeal. Although the BPP's Ten Point Program fell squarely within reformist and rights-based political tradition, its aims were much more ambitious.[62]

Historian Paul Alkebulan christened Malcolm X "the ideological patron saint of the Black Panther Party."[63] While the former minister had tremendous impact on every member of California's Black Power generation, the BPP set about translating his legacy into concrete action. Panther Landon Williams explained, "We felt ourselves to be the heirs of Malcolm and I remember Malcolm saying we demand to be treated as a man and a human being in this society right now, and we will have it by any means necessary."[64] Malcolm X's secular nationalism, which emerged fully after his split from the NOI, reoriented Black radical politics toward urban ills faced by migrants pouring into northern cities.[65] Police brutality, substandard housing, and gerrymandering called for immediate intervention, rather than abstract promises of future territorial separation.[66] His urgency inspired the early BPP and led them to search for new means of building a mass movement. Huey Newton pointed to the unfulfilled thrust of Malcolm X's Organization of Afro-American Unity combined with his insistence on the right to bear arms as an ever-present influence on the Black Panther Party for Self Defense.[67]

Police Patrols

Several months before drafting the Ten Point Program, Newton started his police patrols informally by purchasing a police radio and tailing dispatches to West Oakland. He carefully observed the proceedings, and if he noted a violation of the law, Newton informed the victim of his rights and recited sections of the penal code from memory.[68] Panther police patrols grew out of a larger movement against police brutality in California's major cities. In the aftermath of Watts, a variety of groups emerged. In southern California, Lennair Eggleston, known as "Brother Lennie," assembled community alert patrols (CAP) to monitor the LAPD. Rather than guns, CAP members carried notebooks and tape recorders to document police misconduct.[69] Closer to home, Marc Comfort and ODAC extended their efforts from youth organizing into setting up street patrols in the summer of 1966.[70] Significantly, Brother Lennie, Danny Grey, Chester Wright, and Marc Comfort all spoke about police and community issues at U.C. Berkeley's Black Power Conference within a few weeks of the BPPSD's founding.[71]

While Newton's concept was not entirely original, his armed patrols broke decisively with the existing wisdom of both liberals and nationalists concerning police brutality. He criticized the failure of many cities to establish successful civilian review boards and the ineffectual nature of the Watts patrols that relied on police authorities themselves as the ultimate arbiters of conduct. Instead, by encouraging African Americans to arm themselves, Newton hoped to raise "encounters to a higher level" and to enforce a change in behavior.[72] Through resurrecting an old statute from the California penal code that legalized carrying unconcealed weapons, Newton made the community alert patrol into an active form of resistance. Significantly, he argued that the primary purpose of the patrols was not organizing but recruitment. Blunting police violence would impress the public and attract people to the Party.[73]

In order to make their platform of self-defense a reality, Bobby Seale and Huey Newton needed to obtain guns and recruit their peers. David Hilliard remembered being approached by Newton to join the Party. "We're gonna defend ourselves," Huey told him, "Malcolm talked about the right to defend ourselves by any means necessary. We're gonna be the personification of Malcolm X's dreams."[74] Newton then showed him the small arsenal they had assembled: "a shotgun, revolver, a .45, one or two smaller pistols [and] an M1 [carbine.]"[75] Richard Aoki, a Japanese American activist affiliated with Merritt College, made the first donation.[76] This small collection grew substantially as they channeled money from the sales of Mao's *Little Red Book* and later from their newspaper into acquiring more weaponry.[77] From their talks with people, they quickly realized that in order to attract a following, they needed to instruct through example.

As the Party grew, patrolling became a regular activity. "As our forces built up, we doubled the patrols, then tripled them," explained Newton, "We began to patrol everywhere—Oakland, Richmond, and Berkeley."[78] Their characteristic uniform—black leather jacket, beret, and black boots—increased their visibility in the community. Newton, Seale, and their new recruits drove around Oakland carefully observing police activity. Upon witnessing the questioning of black subjects, they would approach, stand at the allotted legal distance, and ask whether or not the detainee was being mistreated. In cases of obvious harassment, they loudly recited the penal code to educate both the victims and the bystanders of their rights. If police chose to arrest the individual, the BPPSD sometimes donated bail. Panther vehicles even tailed the police with loaded weapons, thereby inverting relations of power and reminding law enforcement of their duty to serve, rather than occupy, African American neighborhoods.[79]

The Party justified these actions by defining the black community as a colony within the mother country that was regularly subjected to violence by a foreign occupying army. The Panthers did not create this idea—the internal colonization thesis spanned a number of Black Power and Black nationalist organizations. However, their police patrols translated the concept into a concrete form of politics. They appropriated paramilitary structure and imagery in service of community-based organizing. Enforcing Point Seven was simply the first step in liberating the San Francisco Bay Area's black population. The media's negative reduction of the Panthers to thugs decontextualized their use of guns and stripped it of its social meaning. Journalist Gene Marine explained how this type of representation ignored the political program that accompanied their display of armed self-defense. "The Black Panthers, even as people began to be aware of them, meant to white observers only Black Americans with guns. Although they were conceived and have been shaped as a revolutionary political party, they continue to be seen by white observers as merely militant and probably nihilistic revolutionaries-without-a-revolution."[80]

Contrary to their simplistic portrayal in the press, Newton and Seale worked hard to adapt Frantz Fanon's revolutionary ideology to the particularities of Oakland. Originally born in Martinique and educated in France, Fanon had joined the anticolonial struggle for Algerian independence. His most famous work, *Wretched of the Earth*, argued that violence was a necessary part of decolonization. The peasant and lumpen classes played a central role in the brutal process of purging colonial oppression. This idea intrigued Newton, because like Donald Warden and the Nation of Islam, he saw the "brothers on the block" as the key constituency for organizing. He and Bobby Seale hoped to unite this group with the expanding black student body on the state and community college campuses. From his training in the Afro-American Association, Huey had mastered the art of street speaking, which he and Bobby called "shooting everybody down." In his public performances Newton frequently invoked the anticolonial philosopher: "Fanon explicitly pointed out that if you didn't organize the lumpen proletariat and give a base for organizing the brother who's pimping, the brother who's hustling, the unemployed, the downtrodden, the brother's who's robbing the banks, who's not politically conscious—that's what lumpen proletariat means—that if you didn't relate to these cats, the power structure would organize these cats against you."[81] Although Newton later referred to himself at various points as a socialist, "dialectical materialist," or Marxist-Leninist, his celebration of the lumpen proletariat broke with classical Marxist principles. In conventional Marxism, the lumpen constituted an epiphenomenal class of little political significance who lacked any material relation to the means of production. In fact, their practice of larceny, property crime, and other forms of vice reenacted the larger capitalist ethos. Need and instability made them susceptible to the forces of power and difficult to organize.[82]

Through focusing on the issue of police brutality, Huey Newton tapped an immense reserve of anger, especially among teenagers and young adults. By the mid-1960s, black youth suffered frequent police harassment and physical assault. Traffic stops had become dangerous flash points, and a range of real and imagined offenses from minor violations—failure to use tail lights or jaywalking—to parking meter expirations often escalated into confrontations with law enforcement. In San Francisco, constant surveillance of youth inside their own neighborhoods was so bad that police forced many to wear identification necklaces with their names and ages for easy apprehension. Like soldiers before them, kids referred to these medallions as their "dog tags."[83] The Panthers' idea for police patrols fed not only on historic resentments of black youths against police harassment but also on their repeated arrests and exposure to the brutal whims of the California Youth Authority. Collective anger over police violence, incarceration, and the criminalization of black youth contributed to a growing distrust of all local government among African Americans. The president of the Oakland Police Department Welfare Association, Mark Mullins, explained that the numerous demands for police review boards "indicate[d] a deep suspicion of our entire system of government since the advocates, by asking for a review board, are saying that they are unable to obtain justice through normal established democratic processes."[84]

As Huey Newton struggled to articulate his epistemology of action, the use of language and symbol became an essential part of his program. He waged the battle for armed self-defense first through a change of consciousness. At Merritt, he developed an interest in A. J. Ayers's logical positivism: "Nothing can be real if it cannot be conceptualized, articulated, and shared." This framework stayed with the young revolutionary throughout his life, and he later adapted it to the "ideological method of dialectical materialism."[85] Newton had always been eclectic in his tastes, merging sometimes wildly different theorists and intellectual traditions to the needs of the moment. This antagonized more dogmatic leftists to whom he responded, "Well we're not Marxists. We are dialectical materialists, and if that means that we come up with different answers than Marx, we're alright with that, because Marx wasn't a Marxist either—he was a dialectical materialist too."[86]

Ultimately, Newton mixed his interest in positivism and scientific Marxism to create a new definition of power, which defined intellectual work as the first step toward actualization. "True Power is the ability to define phenomenon and make it act in a desired manner," he explained, "That's what none of the brothers have. None of us have it. And we have to band together to create it."[87] Although Newton railed against other Bay Area Black Power groups for chasing abstractions, to a large extent, this was disingenuous. Like the Afro-American Association, Soul Students, and RAM before them, the Panthers were firmly rooted in an organic intellectual movement, and at Newton's insistence the BPP consistently emphasized political education and theory as essential to their program.

Newton used dialectical thinking to craft a political symbolism to mobilize the East Bay's migrant community. In this respect the BPP embodied precisely what Oakland's city government most feared, a convergence between campus radicalism and a grassroots movement of the urban poor. This coupling produced one of the most profound expressions of the crisis of state legitimacy—the idea of the policemen as pig. The choice of the term, which became so popular that in a few years it was ridiculed as a movement cliché, was the product of careful thought. The BPPSD sought to introduce the term into everyday language to spur a change first of consciousness and then of action. Newton explained, "I knew that images had to be changed. I know sociologically that words, the power of the word, words stigmatize people and we felt that the police needed the label, a label other than that fear image that they carried in the community."[88] He also understood that Panther recruits consisted largely of recent migrants from the South and therefore crafted a political language and system of symbols that were meaningful to them. "The Black community can relate to the true characteristics of the pig because most of us come from rural backgrounds and have observed the nature of pigs. Many of the police, too, are hired right out of the South and are

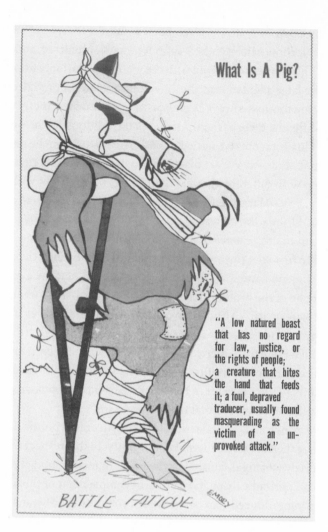

What Is A Pig?

"A low natured beast that has no regard for law, justice, or the rights of people; a creature that bites the hand that feeds it; a foul, depraved traducer, usually found masquerading as the victim of an unprovoked attack."

BATTLE FATIGUE

"What Is A Pig?" Political cartoon from the *Black Panther*, December 20, 1967. © 2009 Emory Douglas / Artists Rights Society (ARS), New York.

familiar with the behavior of pigs. They know exactly what the word implies. To call a policeman a pig conveys the idea of someone who is brutal, gross and uncaring."[89] In addition to addressing migrants, the Party purposely chose an animal that was racially neutral. Given the crackdown of Oakland police on student protestors during the free speech and antiwar demonstrations, Newton wanted to include progressive white youth as well.[90]

Recruitment

The BPPSD's public demonstrations attracted crowds filled with potential recruits. The improvised paramilitary style—part revolutionary, part hipster—punctuated by the open display of weapons, created powerful images of black masculine self-realization that mesmerized onlookers.[91] Like the use of the pig, the symbolism of men with guns also spoke to the migrant experience. Many of the young people who joined the Party had learned to hunt, fish, and shoot at an early age, and they took great pride in their knowledge of firearms. Civil rights historians have long made distinctions between organizers and mobilizers as pursuing separate strategies for grassroots outreach.[92] From the first, Newton very consciously planned actions that would attract the maximum amount of attention from the press and public.

The Panthers' willingness to directly confront police spoke to a whole generation of black youth in California cities who had been told in myriad ways that they were not welcome. Nearly all of the early recruits, were young, male, and southern born, like Huey and Bobby themselves.[93] While they boldly proclaimed to organize the lumpen proletariat, prior to the March on Sacramento most members were long-time friends, neighbors, and schoolmates from North Oakland. Fifteen-year-old Robert Hutton became the first official member of the Party. Originally born in Arkansas, his family relocated to Oakland when he was three. Seale met the young teenager through his work with the North Oakland poverty center and affectionately nicknamed him "Lil' Bobby." Hutton faced problems shared by many of his peers. After having been "pushed out" by the Oakland public school system, he was left largely illiterate. At the center, Bobby Seale took a special interest in Lil' Bobby, regularly tutoring him and teaching him to read. When the Party was formalized, Hutton received the title of treasurer.[94]

Through pooling their resources, Seale, Newton, and Hutton opened an office at 5624 Grove Street on January 1, 1967, a stone's throw from Merritt College and the Afro-American Association headquarters. They painted a sign in the office's front window—BLACK PANTHER PARTY FOR SELF DEFENSE.[95] The BPPSD strengthened its ties to the surrounding community by setting up an advisory board drawn principally from the North Oakland poverty program. Board member Ruth Beckford became closely involved with the Party and even made curtains for the office and brought over supplies. As members began to filter in, admission remained relatively informal. A recruit explained, "In the early days, if you came in and wanted to be a Party member, you could be one. If you were willing to do the work, it was like ok, you are a Party member."[96]

The BPPSD also represented an important step in postintegrationist black politics that repudiated assimilation and separatism while seeking new methods for the assumption of power. The BPPSD did not accept whites di-

JUST WAIT UNTIL I GET A LITTLE BIGGER
SO THAT I CAN WEAR MY DADDY'S HAT
AND SHOOT MY DADDY'S GUN

"Just Wait." This drawing originally appeared on the back of the *Black Panther*, November 14, 1970. © 2009 Emory Douglas / Artists Rights Society (ARS), New York.

rectly into its organization but instead actively cultivated allies outside.[97] In contrast to cultural nationalists' separatism, the Party declared, "We're not Black separatists, we don't believe in abstract notions of integration and abstract notions of separation."[98] Instead, the Panthers strongly encouraged financial and political support from other groups, progressive whites included; however, coalition rather than integration inspired this alliance.

One of the Panthers' first community actions took place on Fifty-fifth and Market near the antipoverty program where Newton and Seale worked. Several pedestrians had been killed at the intersection, which had no stoplight. They attempted to get the city to put up a stop sign and made little progress with the local bureaucracy. So Newton and Seale went out and started directing traffic, and very soon a signal was installed. This strategy of forcing the hand of local government through assuming some of its powers was repeated a number of times throughout the Party's history. Policing the police, food giveaways, and public service actions like the one on Market highlighted the delinquent role of government inside of Oakland's black neighborhoods. The implicit message was clear—either improve state services or face an angry movement of local youth.[99]

Veterans appeared prominently among the Panthers' early ranks and their military experience provided much needed knowledge of and access to firearms. "A number of people who I knew had just come from Vietnam and they helped to train us in weaponry," explained Newton.[100] Rather than fostering a sense of patriotism, military service radicalized a core group of soldiers and even paved the way for their participation in social movements. The GI Bill reinforced this tendency by providing large numbers of working-class youth unprecedented access to colleges and universities. Numerous examples existed among the Panthers' leadership and its rank and file. Before attending Merritt College, Bobby Seale enlisted in the air force in the late fifties, where he served for several years before being dishonorably discharged after a dispute with his commanding officer.[101] Similarly, Japanese American Richard Aoki, who supplied the Party with much of its arsenal, joined the military before graduating from U.C. Berkeley in the early sixties. During World War II, the federal government forced the Aoki family out of their home in West Oakland and relocated them to the infamous Japanese internment camp Tanforan. Young Richard's stint in the army heightened his distrust of and anger at the American government, while simultaneously training him in the skills to oppose it.[102] Another of the BPPSD's first six, Elbert "Big Man" Howard, served in the military for four years, before requesting a transfer to Travis Air Force Base in 1960. Howard, a southern migrant from Chattanooga, Tennessee, chose the service "to be around airplanes," but a discriminatory placement system denied him a position as an aircraft mechanic.[103] After completing his tour in northern California, Howard used his GI Bill benefits to enroll in Merritt College where he joined the Soul Students Advisory Council. Through his student activism, he befriended Newton and Seale, later entering the inner circle of Oakland's Panther leadership.[104]

In addition to veterans, the BPP also attracted the children of military families. Andre Russell moved to Oakland to work with the Party in 1969. He grew up in Tar Heel, North Carolina, near Fort Bragg, where his mother, father, aunts, and uncles all served in the armed forces. At age eleven, Russell watched his father die of pulmonary distress from an ailment caused by asbestos exposure in the service. At the time, the family lived in Washington,

Black Panther guards at "Free Huey" rally, Bobby Hutton Memorial Park, August 25, 1968. The park was originally known as DeFremery Park, but after the Oakland Police Department shot the Panthers' youngest member in April 1968, the BPP and its supporters renamed it "Bobby Hutton Memorial Park." For the decade and a half of the Party's existence, the park was the Panthers' central location for community organizing and public gatherings. Photograph by Ruth-Marion Baruch, no. 21 from the series "Black Panthers 1968." © Pirkle Jones Foundation, estate of Ruth-Marion Baruch.

D.C., and segregated hospitals and ambulance services often refused to assist black patients. Garfield, the closest "colored" hospital, had closed years before. When Andre discovered that his father had collapsed one morning, he waited hours for help to arrive, but it never did. That evening, the elder Russell died at home in excruciating pain. Witnessing his father's suffering politicized the young boy and changed the future course of his life. Andre later explained, "That's when I started to really understand racism. . . . You can go and put your life on the line for this country. And then you come home and you can't even get medical treatment." Many shared his disillusionment, and in the coming years, a number of other veterans participated in formal and informal capacities with the BPP, including John Sloane, Raymond Hewitt, Robert Webb, June Hilliard, John Seale, George Edwards, Randy and Landon Williams, Geronimo Pratt, Mojo Powell, and Raymond Johnson. Their experiences in the military, like those of Robert F. Williams, became a gateway into the world of radical politics.[105]

Black Panthers in Marin City, California, August 31, 1968. Photograph by Pirkle Jones, no. 58 from the series "Black Panthers 1968." © Pirkle Jones Foundation.

As is clear from the significant presence of ex-military, the social composition of the Black Panther Party was always more varied than its self-representation, which celebrated the lumpen proletariat as vanguard. Despite the leadership's protestation to the contrary, from its inception, the BPP had strong ties to Black Studies and black student organizing on local state and community college campuses (especially at Laney College, San Francisco State, and Merritt). Like the armed forces, higher education provided a funnel for highly skilled party members, and in later years its activist infrastructure supported the Panthers' electoral campaigns. Elendar Barnes, an early member of the Party, described the range of people who where drawn into the party. The convergence of students and the "street" was inseparable from the vast increase in educational access among poor youth.

> Oakland City College brought a lot of different people together. It
> [the party] was community driven, you know, out of the community,
> but it was also involved in Oakland City College. So you had those
> people who were in school, and then you had the people who were
> street and some of those people were one and the same. They were
> going to school because you could get financial aid. . . . They became

Panthers and recruited because of their experience with the police or because it was "cool." And then they had a mind change as a result of being involved. And the whole thing of packing guns to protect yourself was real for a lot of Black males. Although it was grassroots, there was a cross section of people involved, from low income to working class to middle class.[106]

While the Black Panther Party had its origins firmly in early organizing efforts at Berkeley and Merritt College, Seale and Newton quickly distanced themselves from their campus roots and cultivated their image as "brothers on the block." Newton viewed the gun as a powerful "recruiting device" that would attract youth from the broader community, thereby bridging the gap between students and the grass roots. This duality, merging different strata from "college and community," remained a hallmark of the Black Panther Party throughout its history. Given the sharp spike in local college attendance, this dynamic was strongest in Oakland, but it was true for other chapters as well. In describing the Chicago chapter, David Hilliard likened its strategy to Bunchy Carter's efforts in Los Angeles: "They [tried] to forge an alliance between the two largest concentrations of black youth—the campus and the streets."[107]

. . .

FEBRUARY 1967 MARKED another important turning point for the BPPSD both in terms of new members and their profile in the Bay Area. A coalition of Black Power activists headed up by the Black Panther Party of Northern California came together to plan a conference on Malcolm X's legacy. They invited Malcolm X's widow, Betty Shabazz, to speak on the anniversary of her husband's assassination and chose the fledgling "Oakland Panthers" to head security.[108] Tension remained high during Shabazz's visit, because earlier in the week the LAPD forced Shabazz's escorts, the US organization, into retreat, leaving her alone and vulnerable on the street. Newton was determined that this would not happen in Oakland. The Panthers proceeded to the airport with openly displayed shotguns, met Shabazz on the plane, and escorted her through the terminal. Afterward, a nasty conflict ensued with Roy Ballard, Kenneth Freeman, and several other BPPNC members, when it became clear that Jon George, their lawyer, had advised them not to load their guns.[109] Newton was furious that they had placed both Shabazz and other Party members at risk. David Hilliard ridiculed their breach by adapting a phrase from Mao's *Little Red Book*: "They're not Panthers. They're paper Panthers."[110]

The conflict with the BPPNC marked a continuation of the ongoing dispute in campus politics at Merritt College. Former participants in Soul Students Advisory Council and West Coast RAM composed the core of the Black Panther Party of Northern California. In addition to the history of personal conflict between the two Panther parties, the ideological split remained. As with the proposed march outside Merritt, BPPNC continued to oppose the open display of weapons and the provocation of the police. By contrast, Huey Newton and Bobby Seale embraced the dialectic of repression and resistance as essential to building a mass movement.

Partisan struggle between the different Panther parties had not only local but national repercussions. Stokely Carmichael traveled to the Bay Area to resolve the dispute between the two factions with the hope of integrating them into a larger umbrella organization. However, after meeting with both groups, he realized this was impossible. "We sat and we discussed and discussed. Discussed with them collectively. With them in groups and individually," Carmichael remembered. "It became clear quick that no one coming in from outside could hope to solve these contradictions. . . . Histories went back years between these groups. Members once of the same group had split into factions and these were competitive, if not openly hostile."[111] When the chairman of SNCC returned to the Bay Area months later, the issue had been resolved. It was later widely rumored that Newton forced the BPPNC to relinquish their title and disband within several months of the incident.[112]

While state subversion and ideological differences played a crucial role, they were not the only explanation of intergroup strife. Precisely the system of organization that made the Panthers phenomenally successful in extending their reach into national politics led to tensions with local black political groups. Their remarkable ability to commandeer resources, draw energy and focus toward the Party, and mobilize toward a desired goal meant that the BPP was not always tolerant of political differences. Guns could be used not only in recruiting members and confronting police but also in challenging potential rivals. The US organization, while best known, was not the only Black Power/Nationalist group that clashed with the Panthers. Other activists in Oakland faced "strong-arm tactics" when they resisted efforts to be incorporated into the BPP's orbit.[113] In subsequent years, the Panthers' frequent public denunciation of these groups as "reactionaries," "armchair revolutionaries," and, most cutting of all given the widespread influence of the Nation of Islam, "pork chop nationalists," undermined opportunities for Black nationalist unity.[114]

Shortly after the Shabazz visit, the Black Panther Party of Northern California dissolved under pressure from the BPPSD. However, in other parts of the country, revolutionary nationalists continued to share their skepticism. RAM cofounder, Max Stanford, alternately referred to the BPPSD's strategy of police patrols as "adventurous" or "romantic." RAM, which modeled itself on the teachings of Robert F. Williams, also set up armed self-defense wings, but they functioned clandestinely. Local cells of RAM established rifle clubs and quietly prepared contingency plans.[115] In contrast to the gun laws in California, those in northeastern states were much more restrictive, and marching through the streets of crowded cities like New York or Philadelphia with loaded rifles seemed outlandish.[116] Stanford also worried that the BPPSD's direct confrontation with law enforcement would antagonize California's virulent right wing and unleash a wave of backlash against a whole spectrum of Black radical organizations. After witnessing the events in the Bay Area, he immediately began to demobilize RAM, but it was already too late. In June 1967, the FBI staged a full-scale raid on his home in Philadelphia and a series of other locations, arresting a total of fourteen "alleged" members of RAM. The scale and brutality of state repression foreshadowed the fate of Oakland's Black Panther Party for Self Defense in the coming years.[117]

Despite the tensions with other groups, the BPPSD continued to grow. The Shabazz visit attracted a new wave of recruits, including Emory Douglas and Eldridge Cleaver, both of whom profoundly influenced the Party's development. The BPPSD's vision immediately impressed the young graphic artist, who initially affiliated with the "San Francisco Panthers." At the time, Douglas was twenty-four years old and majoring in commercial design at City College of San Francisco. He later described how Newton's program addressed his most immediate concerns, noting, "When I heard Huey and seen them come over, it just kind of spoke to my desire . . . frustrations and everything else. Because across the country, you had a lot of young blacks who was in the riots being shot and killed and you wanted to do something."[118]

In December 1966, Soledad Prison released Eldridge Cleaver.[119] Through his relationship with lawyer Beverly Axelrod, he forged strong ties with the San Francisco left and became something of a celebrity in activist circles. For several years, *Ramparts* published excerpts of his prison correspondence, and after he settled in San Francisco, he became a regular staff writer for the magazine. With a few failed attempts, the Panthers tried to recruit Cleaver into their organization. Initially he rebuffed them, but after watching Huey Newton confront the police with loaded weapons outside *Ramparts'* offices, he changed his mind.[120] Prior to joining the Panther Party, Cleaver attempted to revive Malcolm X's Organization of Afro-American Unity in the Bay Area. He had not been successful and realized that in many respects he was an "outsider" and "interloper unfolding a program to organize *their* community."[121]

While Eldridge Cleaver shared many similarities with his fellow Bay Area activists, he also had some significant differences. In contrast to Newton, Seale, and other Black radicals, he had not come out of the local student movement. He was significantly older, from southern California, and nearly all of his formative years had been spent in prison. Among the rank and file, his penchant for violent and exaggerated speech soon earned him the nickname "Papa Rage." Although Huey and Bobby played with the idea of being lumpen, proclaiming their short stints in CYA as proof, Cleaver was the real thing. The man who went on to serve as the Panther's minister of information went from CYA to San Quentin Prison in 1954, before receiving a twelve-year conviction on rape charges. His path to the Panthers passed through Black Muslim organizing in California's prison system. Particularities of Cleaver's personal history combined with the conservative forms of racial Islam practiced by inmates left a strong imprint on his emerging consciousness. As demonstrated by his infamous formulation of "rape as revolution" in *Soul on Ice*, long before his acquaintance with Oakland's BPP, his template for black liberation relied explicitly on assertions of masculine dominance. It was the display of arms and force that drew Cleaver into the Party, and his propensity toward violence that ultimately propelled him to leave it. Throughout his tenure in the Oakland-based party, his ideas on gender and violence shaped the Panthers' evolution in significant ways.[122]

Denzil Dowell and the March on Sacramento

On April 1, 1967, the Martinez Sheriff's Department murdered a black teen named Denzil Dowell in North Richmond. It was a particularly gruesome killing. Police fired a rapid succession of shotgun blasts at the unarmed youth and then left the scene without calling an ambulance. Several hours later, family members discovered his battered body.[123] Oakland activist Mark Comfort got involved and recommended that the Dowell family approach the BPPSD for assistance. Seale and Newton worked closely with the family and pressured the city of Richmond to investigate. Despite a series of discrepancies, Contra Costa County declared the Dowell shooting "a justifiable homicide." In the subsequent weeks, the BPPSD sponsored rallies in support of the family that attracted large crowds in North Richmond. They later claimed over 300 new applicants for Party membership in Richmond alone.[124] As part of an unincorporated area that received minimal social services, this all-black community proved ripe for organizing. Like West Oakland, its population was largely migrant, young and poor.[125] The Panthers' demonstrations gave residents a medium to express their anger about not only the Dowell murder but also the series of police shootings and beatings that had taken place in the past year. In December, authorities shot two men and later savagely beat a woman and young teenager.[126]

North Richmond residents turned out in large numbers for Panther demonstrations and raised a variety of grievances, including complaints about the use of corporal punishment in local schools. In the weeks after the Dowell shooting, an armed Panther patrol escorted a group of mothers to Richmond's Helms Junior High School and waited outside as they confronted the principal. Angered by the constant mistreatment of the students, the parents reportedly told the school administration, "We're concerned citizens, and we'll whip your ass and anyone else's that we hear of slapping our children around."[127] The Dowell case represented the first instance of Panther organizing outside Oakland. The publicity increased their visibility throughout the San Francisco Bay Area and helped them to establish new chapters, including one in Richmond headed up by George Dowell, Denzil's older brother.[128] Like Donald Warden before them, the Panthers traveled to black population centers in the Fillmore, South Berkeley, and Richmond to hold rallies and recruit members.[129] The Dowell murder also prompted the publication of the first edition of the Party's newspaper. The April 25 issue of the *Black Panther Community News Service*, which contained a detailed account of the shooting, affirmed, "We believe that we can end police brutality in our black community by organizing black self-defense groups that are dedicated to defending our black community from racist police oppression and brutality."[130]

As the Party's notoriety increased, so, too, did the backlash from local, county, and state law enforcement and government officials. Police carried detailed lists of Party members and began to tail and harass them regularly. The local press, which provided the most extensive coverage of the BPPSD, fanned the flames. In an article dated April 20, 1967, the *San Francisco Examiner* asked why the Black Panthers had not been arrested for their "self-defense forays with their weapons," only to answer rhetorically, "Because under California law . . . it's legal." In response, Don Mulford, a Republican assemblyman representing the city of Piedmont, drafted an antigun bill that "prohibited the carrying of firearms on one's person in a vehicle, in any public place or any public street." It also banned regular citizens from possessing loaded weapons in or near the capitol or other government buildings.[131]

On May 2, a group of thirty Panthers converged on the state capitol in Sacramento to protest the Mulford Bill. Bobby Seale led the armed delegation, which included rank-and-file panthers Warren Tucker, Emory Douglas, Sherwin Forte, and Lil' Bobby Hutton. What became know as the "March on Sacramento" contained a diverse group of activists. Community organizer Mark Comfort and members of the Dowell family accompanied the group along with six female Party members. Eldridge Cleaver covered the event for *Ramparts* magazine, rather than participating directly. Wearing a .45 holstered to his hip, Bobby Seale led the way into the capitol. As the Panthers marched inside with M1 rifles pointing skyward, they passed within thirty feet of Governor Ronald Reagan, who was addressing a crowd of children outside.[132] Flanked by television and wire-service reporters, they entered the assembly chambers and proceeded to read Executive Mandate Number One. Although Huey Newton did not attend the march because of parole considerations, he drafted a fiery statement: "The Black Panther Party for Self-Defense calls upon the American People in general and the Black People in particular to take careful note of the racist California Legislature now considering legislation aimed at keeping Black People disarmed and powerless at the very time that racist police agencies throughout the country intensify the terror, brutality, murder and repression of Black People."[133] Newton placed this current crisis within a long history of American racial violence spanning Native American genocide, African slavery, and the atomic holocausts of Hiroshima and Nagasaki. The struggle against police repression at home was inseparable from the expanding war in Vietnam. "As the aggression of the racist American Government escalates in Vietnam, the police agencies of America escalate the repression of Black people throughout the ghettos of America. Vicious police dogs, cattle prods, and increased patrols have become familiar sights in Black communities. . . . The Black Panther Party for Self-Defense believes that the time has come for Black people to arm themselves against this terror before it is too late."[134]

After the March on Sacramento, the police arrested the group and charged Bobby Seale with possessing a concealed weapon. Law enforcement detained the others under an obscure California law that made it illegal to disrupt proceedings of the state assembly.[135] Although the cost of bail and legal support caused the BPPSD hardship in the short run, Sacramento created a "colossal" media spectacle that transformed the small local organization into a national phenomenon. All over the country people expressed interest in joining the Party and starting local chapters. Initially elated by their success in using the press to mobilize and expand the base of the organization, Huey Newton later viewed the Sacramento march with ambivalence. The free publicity came with an enduring cost. The event provoked "a turning point in police perception" in which for the first time authorities arrested Panthers in large numbers and began to actively disarm them.[136]

In July 1967, the California assembly passed the Mulford Act, thereby forcing the BPPSD to disband its police patrols. In the coming months and years, armed self-defense receded increasingly into the background as the Party stressed survival programs, political education, and electoral representation. However, the die had been cast, and the Party spent much of the next decade and a half of its existence reckoning with these sensational images of black men and women with loaded guns.[137] David Hilliard remembered how prurient interest drove the coverage: "Militancy, not ideology was what they wanted."[138] As another Party member described its ultimate effect, "White people at the mercy of news media believed that black men were beginning to march armed on their policymakers—a belief sure to spread a wave of panic in white suburbia."[139]

A systematic campaign of repression ensued that shaped the future direction of the BPPSD and its young membership.[140] Initially, local law enforcement and city officials greeted the Panther Party with shock and incredulousness, but the sense of surprise quickly cohered into an organized effort to eliminate the fledgling group. Over the summer, law enforcement's surveillance and harassment of Party members escalated to such an extent that many "felt they could not go out in public without being stopped by a police car."[141] Although spectacular confrontations with the police received the most attention from the press, the OPD and courts waged a quiet war of attrition that steadily eroded the Party's resources, not only in terms of money, but also public opinion. Sensational press coverage and police harassment worked in tandem; newspapers denounced the Panthers as hoodlums and thugs, and the steady stream of arrests created proof.[142]

Patrolmen carrying lists of Panthers' license plates regularly tailed their vehicles. Often they were threatened with moving violations or the amorphous charge of disturbing the peace. Ultimately, this tactic depleted the Party's scant financial resources and fed a steady stream of negative publicity.[143] Moreover, traffic stops provoked a level of tension between police and the Party members that made direct conflict inevitable. In the early morning hours of October 28, 1967, Officer John Frey pulled over Huey Newton and Gene McKinney on Seventh Street in West Oakland. Frey called for back up, and almost immediately, a second police cruiser arrived on the scene. The subsequent events later became the subject of much debate; however, the immediate outcome was clear. John Frey lay dead, while his fellow patrolman Herbert Heanes was seriously wounded.[144] Huey Newton fled the scene, and later collapsed in the emergency room at Kaiser Hospital. A photograph taken the next day showed Newton prone in agonizing pain manacled to a hospital gurney. Policemen placed the handcuffs in such a way that forced him to arch his back and extend his hands upward. With his face distorted with pain from a large abdominal wound, the image conveyed the disturbing impression of torture.[145] In his autobiography, *Revolutionary Suicide*, Newton described how he envisioned his last moments: "I wanted my death to be something the people could relate to, a basis for further mobilization of the community."[146]

Although Newton did not die—shortly after his hospitalization at Kaiser he was transferred to Highland Hospital and then to the medical ward at San Quentin—he faced three felony charges and the death penalty. His wounding, incarceration, and subsequent trial catalyzed a new phase in the history of the BPPSD. Through the Party's effective deployment of a counter-media strategy and political coalition building, the "Free Huey" movement vastly expanded its visibility and reach. The representation of the Panthers as victims of violence rather than its perpetrators made them sympathetic to a much larger segment of the public.[147] For African Americans in particular, Newton's perceived mistreatment spoke to an ongoing history of police brutality and unjust incarceration. Precisely what the Kilpatrick Committee most feared had come to pass; a generation of young African Americans had become deeply alienated from law enforcement and from city and state government. Throughout the Bay Area, rumors circulated about police guards mistreating Newton in Kaiser Hospital by repeatedly kicking his bed so hard as to tear loose his sutured abdominal wounds.[148] A broad spectrum of black political activists, including local civil rights and cultural nationalist groups like the Pan-African Cultural Center came together to express their solidarity.[149]

While many white Americans responded to the BPPSD with a mixture of fear and derision, the Party inspired a range of emotions in African American communities. The Bay Area had a rich tradition of its own black press, and their coverage of the BPPSD differed significantly from the mainstream media. Founded in 1947, the *Sun Reporter* served as the region's largest black newspaper, claiming a readership of over 100,000.[150] The editor, Carleton Goodlett, was a colorful figure, who had migrated to San Francisco from

bootlickers gallery

Her back faces to Harlem.

"Bootlickers Gallery." Political cartoon, ca. 1968. © 2009 Emory Douglas / Artists Rights Society (ARS), New York.

Oklahoma in the 1930s. He was rumored to have ties to the local Communist Party as well as the NAACP, and his paper contained an eclectic mix of society events, civil rights coverage, and local news.[151] Although the *Sun Reporter* did not endorse the Sacramento march—an editorial called the action "a bit too audacious," arguing that this "truly astonishing caper probably did more harm than good for the Negro's cause"—the newspaper nevertheless provided a more nuanced portrait.[152] In contrast to the white media's singular focus on men with guns, the *Sun Reporter* highlighted the Panthers' political program and considered its relevance to earlier civil rights campaigns. Columnist Thomas Fleming interviewed Mark Comfort and argued that grassroots activists joined the Panthers "because of the failure of picket lines in the last thirteen years to bring about any meaningful changes in the social position of American-born Negroes."[153] The decade long struggle to establish civilian review boards for local police forces, combined with the long shadow of the California Youth Authority, created the conditions for a home-grown armed self-defense movement that claimed not only impulsive youth but seasoned activists like Comfort.

Although the black press provided a glimpse of elite perception of the Panthers, gauging the opinions of ordinary African Americans is a more difficult historical proposition. The sharp increase in the Party's membership showed that large numbers of urban youth across the country supported the Panthers' program of armed self-defense. In the first years after the BPP's founding, youth from Kansas City, Missouri, to Winston-Salem, North Carolina, and from Portland, Oregon, to New Orleans, Louisiana, all expressed interest in starting local chapters.[154] Throughout different regions, the character and composition of the individual chapters reflected the social geography of the communities from which they emerged. In the Oakland metropolitan area, the Party exploded in size and made deeper inroads into different geographic parts of the city. At the outset, much of the earlier membership came from North and West Oakland, but by the summer of 1967, chapters in Richmond, San Francisco, and East Oakland had been formed.[155]

"Free Huey or the Sky Is the Limit"

Less than six months after the triumphant March on Sacramento, the Black Panther Party reached a crossroads. By the close of 1967, founder Huey Newton languished in jail, and despite the Party's immense visibility in the media and its growing national popularity, the BPP's actual membership in the city of its birth dwindled to a mere seventy-five active participants.[156] The ongoing campaign of state repression steadily eroded the Party's gains and damaged its efforts at local recruitment. In November 1967, activist Kathleen Neal moved to Oakland from Atlanta, where she had worked in SNCC's national office as the campus program secretary.[157] Given the media blitz of the past year, she was surprised to find the Party in a "total state of collapse," without an office, meetings, or newspaper. "The arrests of Bobby and the other members after Sacramento had reduced the BPP to just a handful of people. . . . For all practical purposes it was defunct, not the idea but the actual structure."[158] While the press projected the Panther image around the world, the Party staggered under the weight of multiple legal cases, depleting the BPP of both funds and leadership. "Huey was in jail, Bobby was in jail, everybody that could speak and organize [was] in jail," remembered Kathleen.[159] Handicapped by the constant threat of parole violations, Eldridge Cleaver remained reluctant to fully engage in advocacy. Ultimately,

Kathleen Cleaver addresses the congregation at the Unitarian Church, San Rafael, California, October 6, 1968. Photograph by Ruth-Marion Baruch, no. 120 from the series "Black Panthers 1968." © Pirkle Jones Foundation, estate of Ruth-Marion Baruch.

the role of spokesperson was thrust upon him, and Cleaver decided "staying out of jail [was] not as important as Huey Newton staying out of the gas chamber."[160]

As Neal puzzled over the Party's disarray, the possibilities excited her.[161] Frustrated by SNCC's decline and its inability to lay down roots in northern cities, she relished the Black Panther Party's potential. "I came out of Atlanta and came to California, and I was *very* excited by what I saw happening in Oakland," she later explained. "It was virgin territory. No one had—no black organization had—done anything in Oakland. I mean you didn't have to come *behind* the SCLC [Southern Christian Leadership Conference] or *behind* the NAACP . . . it was a completely unorganized community *ripe* to do something."[162] By late December, Neal married Eldridge Cleaver and joined the Party's leadership as the first woman appointed to the Central Committee. She assumed the title of communication secretary and became the female face of the Party in 1968.[163]

Within months of Kathleen's arrival, the Cleavers and Panther artist Emory Douglas launched the "Free Huey" campaign. By design, they cultivated a broad spectrum of alliances, seeking out coalition partners to gain

IT'S ALL THE SAME

"It's All the Same." Political cartoon from the *Black Panther*, September 28, 1968. © 2009 Emory Douglas / Artists Rights Society (ARS), New York.

support and access to resources.[164] Playing on widespread anxiety about the urban rebellions sweeping across American cities, Eldridge coined the slogan, "Free Huey or the Sky Is the Limit." In contrast to liberal appeals, "Free Huey" evoked the spirit of global liberation movements sweeping the world in 1968. Its most striking claim was not that Newton was innocent but that a fair trial was impossible. Radical journalist Gene Marine explained, "It's a long way from freeing Tom Mooney . . . Sacco and Vanzetti, or the Rosenbergs. For the cry was not that injustice had been done; it was that justice was impossible."[165]

During this period, the Black Panther Party shifted from its earlier focus on police harassment and brutality to the larger issues of incarceration and punishment.[166] The "Free Huey" campaign transformed Newton's case into a powerful symbol of state-sponsored violence against people of color. For their supporters, the Panthers inverted Newton's prosecution into a trial of the carceral state itself. The Cleavers skillfully used his ordeal to dramatize the inherent violence of the American government. Appealing to black migrants and white radicals alike, Eldridge Cleaver used the term "pig" to condemn racial violence at home and U.S. aggression abroad. His formulation capitalized on the fury over the Vietnam War and created a bridge between the Black Panther Party and the radical wing of the peace movement. In an address on the Michigan State campus, Cleaver linked black liberation, campus radicalism, and anger over the war: "We would like to say that

"Get out of the Ghetto." Political cartoon from the *Black Panther*, January 3, 1970.
© 2009 Emory Douglas / Artists Rights Society (ARS), New York.

the Democrats and Republicans will never hold another convention in this country. . . . We're never going to allow another pig to take national office in this country. We're going to close the book on the entire history of Babylon up to this point. This history of the pig by the pig and for the pig. Its lies and blueprints for international criminal activities. You're all ashamed of it now because your heroes are all revealed to be villains."[167]

Like the Bay Area black student movement before them, the BPP used "political education" as a strategic tool. In the same speech, Eldridge Cleaver stressed the importance of educating "the people of California so that they can see through the prosecution."[168] Given their limited financial resources and relentless vilification in the press, the BPP resorted to producing its own media. During the "Free Huey" campaign, the *Black Panther* became the Party's most effective means of countering negative publicity and mobilizing support. After its first issue in April 1967, the Party managed to publish only a handful of papers between July and January of the following year. In early 1968, the Cleavers not only revived the paper, but transformed the *Black Panther* from a monthly into a weekly. Expanded distribution made it possible to give regular updates on Panther legal cases, to coordinate chapters across city and region, and to inform supporters of upcoming events.[169]

Starting with the third edition of the paper, Emory Douglas supervised the *Black Panther*'s layout and graphics until its demise in October 1980.

His contributions as artist and organic intellectual played a crucial role in making the newspaper into an effective organizing tool. Douglas's powerful images rendered political ideas in graphic form, dramatizing the fate of ordinary people at the mercy of an unjust state. Ranging in style from Cuban revolutionary art to German expressionist woodcuts, the images that punctuated every issue of the *Black Panther* placed the Party's persecution and the ongoing oppression of African Americans on a global stage. In a 1972 speech at Fisk University, Douglas called for a "revolutionary art" that would engage, rather than repudiate, popular media:

> If we take this structure of commercial art and add a brand-new content to it, then we will begin to analyze Black people and our situation for the purpose of raising our consciousness to the oppression we are subjected to. . . . The artist has to be on the ground; he has to hear the sounds of the people, the cries of the people, the suffering of the people, the laughter of the people—the dark side and the bright side of our lives. The dark side is the oppression, the suffering, the decadent living, which we always expose. But the bright side is that which we praise; beautiful Black people who are rising up and resisting.[170]

The *Black Panther*'s innovative design, broad coverage of local chapters, and radical internationalism made the paper extremely popular. To maintain its distribution, the BPP required that the rank and file sell a fixed quota of newspapers. At a cost of 25¢ per issue, circulation estimates ranged as high as 139,000 issues weekly.[171] Once institutionalized, the *Black Panther* became a major source of income and recruitment until the late 1970s.[172] Sam Napier, who became the BPP's tireless circulation manager after joining the San Francisco chapter in 1968, traveled all over the country establishing new circulation routes.[173] With the help of Douglas and others, Napier erected an elaborate network that required printing and transportation of the paper to central distribution in San Francisco once a week. From there, the bundles shipped to cities across the United States and abroad. Getting out the weekly paper proved an enormous task that forced many to work into the early morning hours of the next day. Looking back, Party members joked that if you wanted to test whether someone had truly been a Bay Area Panther, ask them what they did every Wednesday night.[174] They remained extremely proud of this accomplishment, because as Emory Douglas explained, "The paper gave black, poor, and dispossessed people a grassroots point of view on the news that they never had before."[175]

On February 17, 1968, the BPP staged a massive rally at the Oakland Audi-

HALLELUJAH! THE MIGHT AND THE POWER OF THE PEOPLE IS BEGINNING TO SHOW.

"Hallelujah." *Black Panther*,
May 29, 1971. © 2009 Emory
Douglas / Artists Rights
Society (ARS), New York.

torium in support of Huey Newton. While this event coincided with Newton's birthday, it was one of many large demonstrations organized by the
Cleavers that spring.[176] As over 5,000 bystanders looked on, SNCC leaders
James Foreman, H. Rap Brown, and Stokely Carmichael joined peace activist Bob Avakian and Berkeley city councilman Ronald Dellums on stage.
A triumphant Eldridge Cleaver introduced Stokely Carmichael as the Panthers' "Prime Minister of Afro-America" and H. Rap Brown as the "Minister
of Justice."[177] To the surprise of SNCC's foremost advocates of Black Power,
the BPP also used the "Free Huey" rally to celebrate its recent coalition
with white radicals. Only two days before, KPFA—Berkeley's local grassroots radio station—broadcast a discussion of the Panthers' alliance with
the Peace and Freedom Party (PFP).[178] Founded in fall 1967, this California
antiwar electoral party registered over 100,000 new members and qualified
for the state ballot in January 1968.[179] In the magazine *Commonweal*, Cleaver

later described the historic significance of bringing these two groups together: "The Black Panther Party, through its coalition with the Peace and Freedom Party and its merger with SNCC, has [become] the vector of communication between the most important vortexes of black and white radicalism in America."[180]

What followed was a long and somewhat convoluted speech by Carmichael, punctuated by the explosive remarks of Brown. To mobilize support for Huey's defense, SNCC's former chairman called for unity among black people across divides of geography and nation. In a rising cadence, he declared, "We must develop an undying love as is personified in Brother Huey P. Newton. . . . The major enemy is not your brother, flesh of your flesh and blood of your blood. The major enemy is the honky and institutions of racism."[181] On the question of the left, Carmichael was even more emphatic: socialism and communism were "ideolog[ies] not suited for black people."[182] With mischievous irony, Rap Brown asked the racially mixed audience, "How many white folks you kill today?"[183]

While the rally was well attended, the political dissonance between SNCC and the BPP was hard to ignore. Although everyone involved placed great faith in their alliance, the working relationship between the two groups proved short-lived.[184] Carmichael bristled at Cleaver's embrace of white radicals and his unexpected announcement of a SNCC/BPP "merger."[185] Although the SNCC leadership accepted symbolic titles in the Panther hierarchy, the BPP had not formally approached the organization's Central Committee to secure their support.[186] The Panthers' primary interest lay in drawing Black Power's representative, Stokely Carmichael, into the Party's inner circle. However, the former chairman's influence in SNCC declined as his national popularity increased, and there was little reason to believe that the rest of the organization would follow.[187]

For their part, the Cleavers questioned SNCC's ability to move "from its southern Christian movement structure into a cadre-disciplined, urban organization." While SNCC's political experience, national recognition, and international solidarity networks offered important resources to the fledgling organization, Carmichael's professed anti-Marxism and opposition to working with whites represented serious obstacles.[188] Ultimately, the conflict between the two groups stemmed from differences in history, organizing philosophy, and geography. The historic strength of the Bay Area left combined with the dynamics of southern migrant communities created a unique political culture that the SNCC leadership failed to grasp.[189] In a 1980 interview, Kathleen Cleaver argued that the Panthers' origins on the West

"Free Huey" rally, Bobby Hutton Memorial Park, July 14, 1968. The DeFremery Recreation Center is visible at the left. Within less than a decade, the center shifted from being the home of city-sponsored, organized recreation to being the site of BPP mass gatherings. Photograph by Ruth-Marion Baruch, no. 86 from the series "Black Panthers 1968." © Pirkle Jones Foundation, estate of Ruth-Marion Baruch.

Coast and their comparative newness made them more receptive to inter-racial coalition. Whereas SNCC started out as "a beloved community" with white and black working together, and then went through a period of disillusionment, the Panthers lacked this divisive past. The BPP looked to progressive whites not as "brothers" but as strategic allies. In her words, "The Black Panther Party . . . was not a carry-over from a mass movement in the least. . . . SNCC had a long history and . . . was supposed to show a model of what a genuine American society, a democracy, would really be like. . . . The Black Panther Party had *nothing* similar at all. It was started [with] the Ten Point Program." The BPP's Black nationalist/Marxist orientation, democratic centralist structure, and recent origins in California's migrant communities meant that "for the Black Panther Party, there was no break in its history."[190]

Despite its hopeful beginning, by July, the alliance with SNCC was largely defunct; however, the Panthers continued to work with the Peace and Freedom Party for a few more months by running Kathleen Cleaver and Bobby Seale for the California State Assembly, Huey P. Newton for Congress, and Eldridge Cleaver for president.[191] While BPP/PFP candidates garnered

Audience listening to Eldridge Cleaver speak at the University of California, Berkeley, October 3, 1968. Photograph by Pirkle Jones, no. 111 from the series "Black Panthers 1968." © Pirkle Jones Foundation.

small numbers of votes, these electoral campaigns raised money for Huey's defense and forged ties with antiwar activists that proved important in the years to come.[192] Of all the Panther leadership, Eldridge was the closest to the counterculture and New Left, which he embraced as "white mother country radicals."[193] By 1969, Cleaver even reformulated the BPP's advocacy of lumpen struggle to include campus activists: "Those of us who are not in [an] advantaged position, black people, Mexican-Americans, Puerto Ricans ... and also middle-class college students, all find ourselves in the position wherein our lives are manipulated and controlled."[194]

The Panthers' outreach to PFP and subsequent conflict with SNCC highlighted both the evolution of the BPP's ideology over time and the distinct contours of Bay Area political geography.[195] While African American communities across the United States shared political aspirations and confronted similar impediments after 1965, local particulars created diverse regional expressions of Black Power.[196] One of the outstanding features of the San Francisco Bay Area was the cross-fertilization between university-based protest and urban political struggles. Although campus activism has often been studied in isolation, in the postwar Bay Area these arenas were thoroughly intertwined. The historical strength of student movements and the institutional left, combined with the racial and ethnic diversity of California, explained the Panthers' embrace of class analysis and interracial coalition. From the formation of the Afro-American Association in 1961 to the Oakland Black Panther Party in 1966, black students worked to mobilize the migrant populations surrounding their urban campuses.[197] However, their political awakening also emerged in tandem with the free speech and antiwar movements sweeping the Bay Area. With characteristic force, Eldridge Cleaver identified the pivotal role of the university in broader struggles for social transformation: "In the compartmentalized thinking of the traditional American society, the college community and the college campus is viewed as something separate and distinct from the rest of the community. . . . But nothing could be further from the truth. . . . A connection needs to be made between the college campus and the community so that the repression and the tactics of the ruling class can be defeated by the total community being involved."[198]

Repression Breeds Resistance

Although the formal coalitions with SNCC and PFP ultimately lasted less than a year, the growing support of "Free Huey" infuriated local and federal law enforcement. While there were many growing fissures in the Panther solidarity networks, these were not visible to outsiders who witnessed an unprecedented degree of unity. From the announcement of the Peace and Freedom coalition through Martin Luther King's assassination in April, the Party endured a steady escalation of police harassment. Immediately following the February 17 rally, law enforcement arrested a number of Panthers from the San Francisco and Oakland chapters. Bail and legal costs quickly depleted the funds that Stokely Carmichael and SNCC helped raise.[199] While much of the Party conflict took place with local police, the FBI orchestrated a coordinated national effort to infiltrate and destroy the BPP. On March 4, 1968, J. Edgar Hoover issued an FBI memo urging law enforcement to "prevent . . . coalition . . . [and] the rise of a black 'MESSIAH' who would unify and electrify the black nationalist movement."[200]

By using Newton's political persecution to mobilize a broad spectrum of black support—ranging from separatist advocates of Black Power to liberal electoral politicians like Berkeley city councilman Ron Dellums—the "Free Huey" campaign did precisely what the FBI feared most. Indeed, the Panthers went a step further. Cosponsoring candidates with the Peace and Free-

"Sure Glad You White Delegates Could Come," COINTELPRO drawing, enclosed with memo to FBI director from Special Agent in Charge, San Diego, Calif., July 14, 1969. Freedom of Information Act Reading Room, FBI, Washington, D.C.

dom Party demonstrated the BPP's significant inroads into largely white anti-war and New Left circles. The Panthers' ability to build not only black unity but cross-racial solidarity inspired particular alarm. In the years since the Church Committee in 1976, Freedom of Information Act requests revealed a deeply disturbing pattern of FBI manipulation of racial and sexual anxieties. One of the most egregious examples was J. Edgar Hoover's memo to San Diego's special agent in charge (SAC) suggesting his office raise the specter of interracial sex to sabotage the Panther's United Front Against Fascism conference. The FBI Director requested a series of cartoons that would "point out the intentions of the BPP to use white female members and even wives of members of New Left groups."[201] In response, the San Diego office drafted a series of racist images—reminiscent of *Birth of a Nation*—portraying exaggerated black characters' lewd pursuit of white women. Although Hoover ultimately decided against their dissemination, this exchange revealed the extent of law enforcement tactics, which included surveillance, harassment, and selective prosecutions, as well as active infiltration, the manufacture of false documents, and the use of agent provocateurs.[202] In letters to local law enforcement, Hoover repeatedly stressed, "No opportunity should be missed to exploit through counterintelligence techniques the organization and personal conflicts of the leaderships of the groups."[203]

While activists at the time remained unaware of the full extent of cooperation between federal and local law enforcement, Kathleen Cleaver observed a qualitatively different scale of harassment starting in the spring of 1968. "Huey Newton's trial was set for about April 15. It was the second week in April . . . the culmination [of] all these rallies to 'Free Huey.' . . . It was a lot of tension [and] a lot of organizing."[204] As rank-and-file Panthers traveled across the Bay Area putting up posters and handing out campaign literature for BPP/PFP candidates, police immediately tore them down. Search and seizure of Panther automobiles became a daily ritual.[205] Similarly, the FBI employed some of its most vicious tactics to prevent distribution of the *Black Panther*, including spraying it with the foul-smelling organic compound skatole, coordinating with the Internal Revenue Service's Activist Organizations Committee, and encouraging local unions to boycott freight shipments.[206] Law enforcement's relentless targeting of the leadership was even more vicious. On February 25, the Berkeley police raided Bobby Seale's home and charged him and his wife "with conspiracy to commit murder." The *Black Panther* recounted how uniformed police and "several other white men in plainclothes, bearing an assortment of shotguns, rifles and service revolvers" entered the house without a warrant and knocked Artie Seale "against the wall," leveling weapons at the family's "faces and midsections."[207] Black superior court judge Lionel Wilson subsequently threw out the charges against Seale because of insufficient evidence.[208]

Backlash extended far beyond Oakland and was even worse in cities like Los Angeles and Chicago that were notorious for police brutality and corruption. In March, the federal agents and the LAPD shot and killed Glen Carter, brother of Alprentice "Bunchy" Carter who founded the southern California chapter of the BPP. Glen Carter was the first member of the Party killed by law enforcement, and in the coming years, nearly two dozen others met a similar fate.[209] From prison, Huey Newton responded to this onslaught by issuing Executive Mandate Number Three, one of the Party's most strident statements on self-defense to date.[210] "We draw the line," it asserted, "at the threshold of our doors. . . . It is therefore mandated . . . that all members must acquire the technical equipment to defend their homes and their dependents. . . . Any member of the Party having such technical equipment who fails to defend his threshold shall be expelled from the Party for Life."[211]

"A Terrible and Bloody Chapter"

With each police action and Panther response, the level of violence escalated. Even churches affiliated with the BPP came under attack. On the evening of

April 3, 1968, six squadrons of police officers attempted to storm St. Augustine's Episcopal Church in West Oakland to search for Party members who had been holding weekly meetings inside. Law enforcement's overwhelming show of force included officers with loaded shotguns trying to force their way into the inner sanctuary. The pastor, Father Earl A. Neil, a veteran of the southern civil rights movement, met the Oakland police at the door and refused them entry. In an interview with a local reporter several days later, the minister explained his deep distress at the conduct of the Oakland police. "If a community organization, which is trying to work for the betterment of the black community, cannot meet in the sanctity and sanctuary of a church building, where can they meet?" he asked. "If this incident is allowed to go unchallenged, then no church building is safe. I think that we will be entering into a new phase of the black liberation movement, namely the persecution of the Black Church."[212]

The next day, the assassination of the Reverend Martin Luther King Jr. provided the spark that ignited this tinderbox. As cities across America burned, East Bay youth took to the streets. Three hundred students from Oakland High walked out of their classes and held an impromptu discussion of racial issues on the campus lawn. In East Palo Alto, young people overturned and set fire to a car outside Ravenswood High, forcing the administration to close a few hours after opening. Later in the day, witnesses reported youths throwing bottles onto the Bayshore Freeway from Berkeley's University Avenue overpass.[213] Demonstrations also broke out at Castlemont and Oakland Technical High School, with groups of community college students from the Peralta System participating. In response, many secondary schools shut their doors and released over 65,000 young people from classes. While the East Bay experienced minor upheavals compared to Detroit and Washington, D.C., throughout the night several small fires erupted in East Oakland.[214]

As Eldridge Cleaver watched the mounting violence, he started planning an offensive attack on the Oakland police.[215] Many BPP members refused to participate. Cleaver's plan not only exceeded the scope of previous Panther self-defense efforts; it flew directly in the face of Party doctrine. Since November 1966, the Oakland public schools faced periodic student uprisings. During these demonstrations, the BPP always counseled against random violence, preferring instead to channel black discontent into the structured regimen of the Party.[216] Moreover, Newton had officially suspended street patrolling the year before, after the ratification of the Mulford Bill. Despite fellow Panthers' objections to his scheme as "spontaneous, irrational, and unorganized," Cleaver remained adamant.[217] If the BPP did not respond with the same visceral force as the urban rebellions sweeping the country, the Party would loose its status as vanguard.[218] Before the Panthers could achieve a consensus, an unexpected encounter with the police presented Cleaver with an opportunity for confrontation. Hours before, he wrote, "The death of Dr. King signals the end of an era and the beginning of a terrible and bloody chapter that may remain unwritten, because there may be no scribe left to capture on paper the holocaust to come."[219]

While older, more experienced BPP members followed Eldridge Cleaver reluctantly, the BPP's youngest officer, Treasurer Lil' Bobby Hutton, wanted to demonstrate his commitment. The seventeen-year-old, who was the BPP's first recruit, particularly admired senior male leaders, like Eldridge and Bunchy, who had served time in prison and returned to help the community.[220] They also shared a loose kinship. Although their families did not know one another, Cleaver and Hutton came from the same Arkansas county. Lil' Bobby's fate symbolized both the appeal of the Black Panther Party to young migrant teenagers and its potential dangers. Although accounts varied about who fired first, on April 6, police stopped a vehicle carrying Eldridge Cleaver and a small group of Panthers. A forty-five-minute shootout ensued that left one officer seriously injured.[221] Police called for backup, and as fellow Panthers scattered, Cleaver and Hutton took refuge in a small house on Twenty-eighth Street. After being doused with tear gas, they agreed to come out with their hands up. To preempt any accusation that he was armed, Cleaver walked out without his clothes, but Hutton was too modest. As they emerged, police fired on the teenager, and he was killed instantly. Sources later revealed that between six and seventeen rounds perforated his body.[222]

Like so many of the Party's encounters with law enforcement, this incident remains shrouded in mystery and contradictory accounts. The precise timing and circumstances of the police shooting became the biggest points of contention. Exit wounds clearly demonstrated that Hutton had been shot in the back. Officers on the scene explained this by arguing that after initial capture, the teenager tried to run away. In contrast to the authorities' testimony at trial, the Panthers and a large segment of the local black community viewed the Oakland Police Department's action as the cold-blooded execution of a much beloved Panther youth. Federal and local law enforcement's concerted campaign to destroy the Black Panther Party, combined with the long history of police violence against ordinary African Americans, explained the outpouring of anger and sorrow over Hutton's murder. His name became enshrined in black community remembrance, and starting in the summer of 1968, West Oakland's DeFremery Park—the cultural and recreational center for black newcomers since World War II—became popularly known as "Bobby Hutton Memorial Park."[223]

While Cleaver's rhetoric and deed have been understood as representative of the nihilistic tendency of the Black Panther Party, it is important to consider the particulars of the man himself. The BPP's ad hoc leadership structure combined with its rapid development, constant crisis of repression, and top-down organization meant that at different times, single individuals dominated the Party's ideology. Despite his remarkable gifts of language and political charisma, Cleaver's tenure as the de facto head of the BPP through much of 1968 proved disastrous. His support for guerrilla warfare, anarchist influence, and misogyny all served to damage the Party internally and to bring down repression from without. In November 1968, he fled into exile to avoid serving his remaining prison sentence for a rape conviction from the previous decade. In the coming years, his continued advocacy of armed struggle helped initiate a crippling ideological split within the Black Panther Party that resulted in the needless incarcerations and deaths of its young membership.[224]

In the person of Eldridge Cleaver, the accumulated impact of the carceral state, the California Youth Authority, the California Adult Authority, local police, and parole intertwined most directly with the origins and aspirations of the Black Panther Party.[225] To understand why the BPP leadership sought out Cleaver, one must consider its recent past. The experience of police harassment, juvenile detention, and incarceration represented the Janus-faced nature of southern newcomers' odyssey in northern cities. As the younger generation of black migrants came of age, ever-larger numbers became enmeshed in the juvenile justice system.[226] Black male children and adolescents suffered harassment and detention in the largest numbers, and their experiences profoundly influenced their ideas of gender and resistance, in some instances leading them to embrace the "convict" or "outlaw" as emblems of masculine rebellion.[227] Huey Newton's early writings typified this romantic tendency. His youth and traumatic stints in the California Youth Authority left him particularly impressionable. Before meeting Cleaver in person or reading *Soul on Ice*, Newton praised him as a living symbol of resistance to the carceral state.[228] In his autobiography, he wrote with naive enthusiasm, "Because of Eldridge's past experience and his deep involvement in the movement, I was particularly eager to meet him. No ex-convict could be all bad."[229] Reinforced by the traumatic loss of Malcolm X, this sentiment appeared throughout the writings of the Panther youth. In his autobiography, David Hilliard remembered, "Eldridge inspire[d] me on a personal level. . . . He was left to destroy himself in a prison cage. Instead he has mastered language and made the entire society listen to him."[230]

While Huey Newton, Emory Douglas, and many of the early Party members spent time in juvenile facilities, the experience of incarceration was not singular to their political formation.[231] Their work with the Afro-American Association and the vital black student culture of Merritt and other Bay Area community colleges inspired their direct entree into Black radicalism. By contrast, nearly all of Cleaver's adolescence and young adulthood was spent behind bars. His ideological embrace of the Nation of Islam and Bakuninist-style anarchism grew out of inmate study groups and the largely unwritten history of Black Power behind prison walls.[232] Upon release, Cleaver carried these ideas into the Black Panther Party, along with his peculiar views on gender, rape, and revolution.[233] Ironically, Cleaver recognized the destructive impact of his incarceration. In a remarkably candid reflection from *Ramparts* in December 1968, Eldridge described its legacy: "I didn't leave anything in that penitentiary except half of my mind and half of my soul, and that's dead there. I have no use for it. It's theirs."[234]

In contrast to the early civil rights movement's emphasis on uplift and respectability, the Black Panther Party not only confronted police and penal issues, but actively recruited and organized those most affected by state efforts to contain the urban poor. In doing so, they also imported into their organization the complex set of problems associated with crime and punishment, sometimes with unforeseen consequences. Eldridge Cleaver's actions had grave consequences for Bobby Hutton, the Party's national headquarters, and all of its regional chapters. His support for offensive attack on law enforcement went far beyond earlier Panther police patrols and provided a justification for new levels of state repression. Perversely, Cleaver's vision of syndicalist revolt reinforced FBI director J. Edgar Hoover's systematic campaign against the BPP, leading to a snowballing effect of violence. Hutton's murder dramatized the dangers of adventurism, with the youngest among the Panthers' ranks the most vulnerable.[235]

In the aftermath of the April 6 shootout, the organized assault by law enforcement intensified with increasing FBI penetration into the fabric of the Oakland community. After David Hilliard's six-year-old son, Darryl, set a fire at school, an FBI agent came to the family's door and threatened to charge the child with a serious offense.[236] In June 1968, Alameda County convicted Bobby Seale on a weapons charge and sentenced him to three years of probation.[237] The following year, a Chicago judge ordered him "bound and gagged" while on trial for "conspiracy" for his involvement in demonstrations at the Democratic National Convention.[238] Ultimately, the wave of repression culminated in the Chicago Police Department's murder of Fred Hampton and Mark Clark on December 4, 1969. Nearly a decade later, the Church Committee concluded that the organized campaign against the Panthers represented one of the most vicious examples of domestic repression in history. Their report criticized the FBI for engaging "in lawless tactics and respond[ing] to deep-seated social problems by fomenting violence and unrest."[239]

. . .

THERE IS AN OLD SAYING that there are only three ways a black man can get an education: college, prison, and the military. Strikingly, in their first years the Panthers drew both their ideology of armed self-defense and their predominantly male membership from all three channels. The idea of using loaded weapons as a form of protest started with Huey Newton proposing an armed demonstration on the Merritt campus. Although this action never took place, his plan to force the college's administration into adopting a Black Studies program ultimately gave birth to the police patrol. Similarly, when Eldridge Cleaver joined the BPP shortly after its founding, he carried into the Party his social networks and a vision of syndicalist revolt forged inside the walls of the California Youth and Adult Authorities. Finally, Panthers like Bobby Seale and Elbert Howard brought weapons training and martial tactics from the armed forces. Their status as ex-military instilled a sense of pride, as did their early knowledge of firearms.[240] Brought together by the shared experience of police violence, authoritarian schools, and all too frequent stints of juvenile incarceration, activists in the Party's first two years drew from this well of anger and pain. Of all the barriers migrants faced, the carceral state of police, prisons, and intrusive municipal authorities proved the most daunting, and the Panthers capitalized on black youths' feelings of subjection and powerlessness.

By appealing to their peers through bold symbolic actions like the March on Sacramento, the BPPSD transformed itself from a small regional group of activists into a national phenomenon. In less than five years, the Oakland-based Party blossomed into an expansive social movement with branches in over sixty-one U.S. cities and twenty-six states. As the urban rebellions swept cities from Watts to Detroit, the Panthers provided a concrete alternative to more traditional civil rights protest and government-sponsored community action programs, on the one hand, and the outpouring of frustration and anger of the "long hot summers", on the other. The BPPSD sought to redirect the social energy of these spontaneous uprisings into an organized political program advocating full employment and an end to police and penal incursions into African American communities.[241]

But the Panthers' popularity came with a price. Through special FBI directives and the Counter Intelligence Program (COINTELPRO), Hoover and other police agencies sought to cripple the Party through mass incarcerations, harassment, and infiltration.[242] Law enforcement's campaign culminated in a shootout between Officer Frey and Huey Newton that resulted in his imprisonment and trial for capital murder. In many respects, the BPPSD was completely unprepared for the enormity of what it faced. Both founders of the Party were under thirty-five, and many of the rank and file were in their late teens. With Huey Newton and Bobby Seale either jailed or on trial through much of 1968, Eldridge Cleaver became the default head of the Party. His influence on the Panthers was complex and contradictory. He and Kathleen orchestrated a remarkable defense campaign that created a broad set of alliances and an effective media strategy to "Free Huey." The greater visibility expanded the Party and strengthened its solidarity networks; however, Cleaver simultaneously advocated guerrilla warfare, first in rhetoric and later in deed, that resulted in a direct confrontation with the police, the shooting of Bobby Hutton, and a whole new round of incarceration and prosecution. Ultimately his short tenure as head of the BPP exacerbated the ever-worsening onslaught of repression, ending in his exile and a near destruction of the Party.[243] In order to survive, the Black Panther Party was forced to reconstitute itself by developing new organizing strategies that would draw it closer to the everyday needs and aspirations of the East Bay's migrant communities.

6. SURVIVAL PENDING REVOLUTION

With the Cleavers in exile, the Black Panther Party embarked on a new phase in its history in late 1968.[1] At a local church in the East Bay, the BPP sponsored a free breakfast program to feed hungry children before school. A larger initiative to build popular support for the Party inspired its turn to community service.[2] In dramatic fashion, the Panthers moved beyond their youth base in "the campus and the street" to forge broader networks across intraracial divides of generation, class, and migration status. In order to achieve this, the spectacular confrontation with the carceral state that launched the Black Panther Party—symbolized by their paramilitary uniforms, guns, and police patrols—gave way to a broader definition of state violence.[3] While the BPP's Ten Point Program embraced grassroots socialism, commitment to political education, and self-determination from its inception, the phase from 1968 to 1972 turned these "wants" into a concrete organizing practice.[4] Strikingly, the organization's new focus not only changed the image of the Party; it also transformed the organization internally. Much larger numbers of women joined, and they played an essential role in extending the network of Panther solidarity and support into broader segments of the African American population.[5]

Scholars continue to debate the significance of this phase in the Black Panther Party's history, and whether or not community programs represented continuity or a break from the Party's earlier advocacy of police patrols and armed self-defense. In keeping with the press coverage of the period, many popular accounts have understood the Panthers' new focus as a conservative shift from revolution to reform.[6] However, a more useful framework for understanding this new development was the Panthers' attempt to create a long-term organizing strategy to ensure the Party's survival in the face of massive state repression.[7] What is most striking is how the BPP expanded their base by returning to the core survival strategies of southern migrants. For their parents' generation, churches, sororal/fraternal groups, mutual-aid

Black Panther feeding his son, "Free Huey" rally, Bobby Hutton Memorial Park, Oakland, July 28, 1968. Photograph by Ruth-Marion Baruch, no. 29 from the series "Black Panthers 1968." © Pirkle Jones Foundation, estate of Ruth-Marion Baruch.

societies, "welfare rights" organizing, and electoral representation served as weapons in black migrants' everyday war against urban poverty.[8] As the Panthers struggled to counter the law enforcement and media onslaught that accompanied the rise of COINTELPRO and the United States' larger shift right after 1968, they incorporated many of these same strategies. Ultimately, the BPP mobilized large numbers of African Americans by establishing parallel institutions to address shortcomings in public welfare and education. As historian Paul Alkebulan has shown, these programs were as important for the Party's survival as for the communities they purported to serve.[9]

. . .

THE POLICE MURDERS of Bobby Hutton and Deputy Chairman Fred Hampton, combined with the spectacle of Bobby Seale's prosecution in Chicago, prompted civil rights leaders to come to the Panthers' defense. In a striking reversal of fate, personalities and institutions the Panthers previously ridiculed became strategic allies against state repression. In November 1969,

Percy Steele of the Bay Area Urban League warned of the "national and international consequences" of Bobby Seale's federal trial in Chicago. Drawing on the rhetoric of Cold War civil rights, Steele argued, "The direct denial of Mr. Seale's rights—especially being bound and gagged in an American courtroom—is a sham to justice and lays bare this country's claim to being a land of equal opportunity and of democracy."[10] Similarly, the Northern Area Conference of the NAACP went even further and drafted a letter to President Richard Nixon demanding that the attorney general investigate "the persecution, harassment, and killings of persons in the Black Panther Party."[11]

In response to this chorus of outrage, the executive director of the NAACP felt compelled to act. Immediately following the shootings of Fred Hampton and Mark Clark in Chicago, Roy Wilkins worked with former Supreme Court justice Arthur J. Goldberg to set up the Commission of Inquiry into the Black Panthers and Law Enforcement. Given the harsh rhetoric that the BPP directed at the civil rights leader in its early years, Wilkins's advocacy was surprising. Between 1967 and 1970, the Black Panther regularly denounced the NAACP's executive director as an Uncle Tom and printed unflattering caricatures of him in their "Bootlickers' Gallery."[12] Nevertheless, the intensity of state violence against the BPP brought even the most conservative figures to the Party's defense. The twenty-five-member body Wilkins put together with the help of Judge Goldberg and former U.S. attorney general Ramsey Clark immediately launched a formal investigation into the role of the FBI and local law enforcement in the deaths of Mark Clark and Fred Hampton. Theirs was not an isolated effort. The NAACP Legal Defense Fund offered its services, and Kenneth Clarke's Applied Research Center drafted a preliminary report criticizing police and FBI tactics. In May, the NAACP donated $50,000 to sustain the commission after the Ford Foundation and other liberal donors refused funding.[13] Released several years later, the commission's final report heavily criticized authorities, concluding, "Of all the violence, official violence is the most destructive."[14]

In addition to concern over police killings and the roll back of civil liberties, the closer ties between civil rights organizations and the Panthers could be traced to the social programs the BPP implemented in early 1969. Through advocating community control of police, free breakfast programs, health clinics, and "black liberation schools," the Black Panther Party reached out to older, and more conservative, segments of the African American community. In the November 16, 1968, issue of the Black Panther, Bobby Seale explained, "The Black Panther Party has the youth throughout the San Francisco, Oakland, Bay Area. . . . But the older people, we would like to say to you . . . we're very concerned about community problems and we're going to relate more to community problems" and to "the election process." To mobilize this group, Seale proposed introducing a ballot initiative for the decentralization of the police in Berkeley and Richmond, as well as running a Party slate for local elections in April 1969. He also announced plans to feed "welfare children" in the morning before school by using the facilities of local churches.[15]

In order to make these ideas a reality, the Party leadership looked increasingly to outside support. In its first year, the BPP set up an advisory board composed of older people, many of whom had ties with the North Oakland poverty center where Seale worked. During this new phase, the BPP relied on these allies to help implement their community initiatives. The organization also started actively recruiting women for the first time. An advertisement in the newspaper declared, "The Black Panther Party is calling on all mothers, and others who want to work with this revolutionary program of making sure that our young . . . ha[ve] full stomach[s] before going to school in the morning. The schools and the Board of Education should have had this program going on a long time ago . . . mothers, Welfare recipients, grandmothers, guardians and others who are trying to raise children. . . . LET'S DO IT NOW! Support this part of the Black Panther Party Program."[16]

After working initially with Concord Baptist and the historic Downs Memorial Church, the Black Panther Party sponsored its first free breakfast program at Saint Augustine's Episcopal in West Oakland.[17] The church rector, Father Earl A. Neil, had a long-standing relationship with the Party. When Huey Newton faced the death penalty for shooting Officer Frey, the Episcopal priest served as spiritual advisor. Father Neil also brought much needed expertise as a civil rights worker and community organizer. After serving in several urban ministries in the early sixties, he volunteered in the voter education and registration drive in McComb, Mississippi, in the summer of 1964 and in Selma the following year. Before moving to Oakland, Neil also worked with Dr. King and the Southern Christian Leadership Conference's open housing drive in Chicago while serving as the co-vicar of the Christ Church in Woodlawn. Like his parishioner Ruth Beckford, who served on the Panther's advisory board, Neil played a key role in the planning and running of the Panthers' community programs.[18]

While St. Augustine's social ministry was exceptional, Neil's alliance with the Panther Party revealed a larger truth. In the Bay Area and many cities throughout the United States, Panther community programs would have been impossible without the support of local churches. The Panther

Father Earl A. Neil, pastor of St. Augustine's Episcopal Church, September 22, 1968. Photograph by Ruth-Marion Baruch. © Pirkle Jones Foundation, estate of Ruth-Marion Baruch.

leadership recognized this fact and actively cultivated the black clergy. On May 19, 1971, Huey Newton addressed the Center for Black Urban Studies at the Graduate Theological Union in Berkeley. He used his talk, "On the Relevance of the Black Church," as an opportunity to reach out to black ministers across the country. After acknowledging the Party's earlier mistakes in alienating itself from this foundational institution of black people, Newton proposed a new partnership: "We will work with the church to establish a community which will satisfy most of our needs so that we can live and operate as a group."[19] The Panthers' reconciliation with the black church marked a return to the same survival strategies for living in the city as their parents' generation. Like the Afro-American Association's reliance on Downs Memorial, the BPP's embrace of voluntarism and community service depended on the spiritual infrastructure that E. Franklin Frazier celebrated as "a nation within a nation."[20] Local congregations helped set up breakfast programs, food and clothing giveaways, and health services. They also provided a much-needed anchor in the face of increasing conflict from within the Panther organization and state repression from without.

While the Party leadership used survival programs to reconnect with the broader African American community, their efforts also strengthened the Party internally. According to Landon Williams, the idea for a breakfast program arose spontaneously as Bobby Seale and the Panthers' advisory board discussed the problem of rank-and-file discipline. Public drinking, incidents of harassment against white "hippies," and a series of robberies demonstrated the need for a structured regimen that would instill Party discipline while improving relations with the larger black population. One Party member joked that the best way to keep the young membership busy would be to supply meals to hungry school children. A discussion ensued about the impact of hunger and poverty on young people's ability to learn. Seale later declared that if the BPP was not able to "put a chicken in every basket, they could put a breakfast in every hungry kid's stomach."[21] As part of a national rectification campaign, the Party expanded these efforts throughout 1969. The idea spread rapidly across the country with insider estimates claiming that, by November 1969, twenty-nine branches served over 22,000 children regularly.[22] Breakfast programs ultimately became a conduit to the larger social problems facing the African American community and fostered more ambitious outreach efforts. In retrospect, food giveaways established an important precedent, if not a prompt, for the expansion of state and federal lunch programs.[23]

Nixon, Reagan, and the Attack on Welfare

Placed in its broader historical context, the Panthers' work with churches and other grassroots institutions must also be understood as a response to political backlash and state retrenchment in the late sixties. The BPP emerged on the cusp of "maximum feasible participation"; by 1969, however, community action programs were in rapid retreat. Although many historians have stressed the BPP's vexed relationship with the Great Society, the Panthers' survival programs reached their height not under Johnson but during the ascendance of President Richard Nixon and California governor Ronald Reagan. Decades before his attack on "welfare queens" as president, the Republican politician threatened to roll back California's social safety net by purging state rolls of "welfare cheats" and restricting access to Medi-Cal. "Welfare has proliferated and grown into a leviathan of unsupportable dimensions," declared the governor at the beginning of his second term in 1971. "Here in California nearly a million children are growing up in the stultifying atmosphere of programs that reward people for not working." Although his plans for draconian "welfare reform" were never implemented, his rhetoric fostered deep anxieties about the state's ongoing commitment to the urban poor.[24]

In the late sixties, the dismantling of the Great Society, Reagan's assault on California's welfare system, and the ongoing use of means testing resulted in widespread black dissatisfaction with government assistance. At its most ambitious, the Black Panther Party sought to provide an alternative to the disciplinary and restrictive nature of state welfare. During a visit to Philadelphia for the People's Revolutionary Constitutional Convention in September 1970, Huey Newton expressed the hope that the BPP would "lay a new foundation for the welfare of the poor people in this country."[25] High levels of black urban poverty, exacerbated by state and federal retrenchment, explained the overwhelming response to the Panthers' food and clothing programs.[26] Drawing on this well of discontent in cities across the country, the Black Panther reported frequently on issues of housing and welfare rights and courted activists from this burgeoning movement.[27] While several Black Power organizations sponsored breakfast programs, including Newark's Congress of African People, the crucial difference between them and the Panthers was the BPP's high-quality newspaper with widespread distribution. The Black Panther politicized welfare rights by showing a coordinated national effort that highlighted the Party's successes and the government's failures.[28]

Deborah Johnson (later known as Akua Njeri), widow of slain Panther leader Fred Hampton, explained how the Panthers' programs addressed the pitfalls of state assistance: "We started feeding the children in the community without asking how many children you got and how many different daddies of children you got or if you're getting an aid check. Those things were not important to us and we did not say we had to wait for federal funds. As a matter of fact we could not accept any federal funds at all because we felt that an enemy that was trying to destroy us would not give federal funds to a group that had no vested interest in that enemy's survival."[29] Although her observations were drawn from Chicago's survival programs, Johnson's analysis was relevant for BPP chapters in the Bay Area. Food programs provided a concrete vision of community control that undermined deeply engrained anticommunism and fear of militancy. "We know that people didn't have an understanding of socialism or communism and that they might say they're against that," explained Johnson. "But people basically thought that children had a right to be fed and learn on a full stomach."[30]

Comrade Sister

Deborah Johnson's activism exemplified the central role of female Panthers in this new phase of the Party's history. As law enforcement imprisoned or murdered male Party members, women stepped to the fore. According to Bobby Seale, young women made up over 60 percent of the rank and file by 1969.[31] For the first time, they also entered the ranks of Panther officers, first with Kathleen Cleaver as communications secretary and subsequently with Elaine Brown's appointment as minister of information in 1971.[32] Their entree into the national headquarters of the Party was part of a larger influx that helped expand and strengthen the Bay Area BPP. As chapters spread rapidly across the country, a steady stream of skilled and educated Party members flowed back to the San Francisco Bay Area. Many, if not the majority, were well-educated and experienced women activists. While this relocation was a trickle compared to California's expansive southern diaspora, this "political migration" shaped the Bay Area chapters of the Party in significant ways.[33] Female activists played an essential role in the Party's transformation and development of survival programs in its "Base of Operations."[34]

The activist career of Ericka Huggins typified this new group of Panther women. Originally from Washington, D.C., she first became active in politics after attending the March on Washington in 1963 as a high school student. In 1965, she graduated and enrolled in the historically black Cheyney State University. Soon after, she transferred to Lincoln University, where the radical black student culture nurtured her growing politicization and interest "in serving the community." After reading an article about Newton's trial in *Ramparts*, she and her husband, John Huggins, left school to join the "Huey Newton Defense Committee" in November 1967. The couple relocated to Los Angeles to stay with family in hopes of eventually moving up to Oakland. In the interim, they joined the southern California chapter of the BPP. Huggins later described the Party's allure: "young black people who were willing to do more than wait for the government to come up with a plan to end poverty and oppressive conditions of people of color."[35] For the young activist, the West Coast also represented new expansive possibilities that brought together the most urgent political struggles of the late sixties. "Everything was happening in California—every movement you can imagine. . . . There were all kinds of organizations for African Americans that

Black Panthers from Sacramento, "Free Huey" rally, Bobby Hutton Memorial Park, Oakland, August 25, 1968. Photograph by Pirkle Jones, no. 62 from the series "Black Panthers 1968." © Pirkle Jones Foundation.

had sprung up all over the place. . . . The alternative schools and associations were blossoming everywhere. Student movements on every campus. And then there was a lot of *collaborative* activity that went on . . . between the groups of students and the groups of color. . . . It was continual *movement*."[36]

In January 1969, members of the US organization murdered John Huggins and Bunchy Carter in a shootout on the University of California at Los Angeles (UCLA) campus, unleashing a tide of violence between the two groups.[37] With her infant daughter, Mai, Ericka fled southern California to her in-laws in New Haven, Connecticut, where she subsequently established a breakfast program and liberation school.[38] As founder and "Acting Deputy Chairman" of the New Haven BPP, Huggins became the first woman to head up a local chapter. Her pioneering status as female leader was also greeted with an unprecedented scale of government repression. In May, the federal authorities arrested her and Bobby Seale on conspiracy charges. Despite a national campaign to "Free Bobby and Ericka," Huggins spent nearly two years in jail awaiting trial before all charges were dropped for lack of evidence.[39] Huggins's case became a turning point for women in the Party, because her incarceration and physical abuse at the hands of authorities showed that female Panthers faced the same brutal state repression as their male counterparts. In response, Eldridge Cleaver reversed his earlier public stance on "pussy power," which limited Panther women's activism to their sexual capacity to influence men. In a letter to the *Black Panther* newspaper from exile, Cleaver declared, "The incarceration and the suffering of Sister Ericka should be a stinging rebuke to all manifestations of male chauvinism within our ranks. That we must purge our ranks and our hearts, and our minds and our understanding of any chauvinism . . . we must too recognize that a woman can be just as revolutionary as a man and that she has equal stature."[40]

Upon release from prison, Ericka Huggins immediately moved to Oakland in 1971.[41] Initially she worked on the *Black Panther*, before becoming a teacher in the Intercommunal Youth Institute (IYI) under Brenda Bay. In early 1974, Huggins became director of the school, which she headed up until its closure in 1982. Her support for progressive pedagogy left a lasting imprint on the institute that melded with earlier forms of political education. She later explained how this new phase in the Party's history linked to its origins: "I think that the school's principles came from the socialist principles we tried to live in the Black Panther Party. One of them being critical thinking—that children should learn not *what* to think but *how* to think . . . the school was an expression of the collective wisdom of the people who envisioned it. And it was . . . a living thing [that] changed every year." Huggins' comments revealed that the same spirit of political improvisation that animated the Panther police patrols and food giveaways became manifest in its educational programs.[42]

Liberation Schools

Although the Panther schools have been the least studied of the survival programs, the Intercommunal Youth Institute—later renamed Oakland Community School (OCS)—represented the longest-running institution of the Black Panther Party in the Bay Area. Largely staffed and run by women, the liberation schools, the IYI, and larger campaign of "political education" became arguably the Black Panther Party's most important organizing legacy.[43] From its earliest iteration, the Party defined education both as a human right and as an essential stage in politicization. Originally drafted in October 1966, the Ten Point Program called for a transformation of public schooling: "We want education for our people that exposes the true nature of this decadent American society. We want education that teaches us our true history and our role in the present-day society. We believe in an educational system that will give to our people a knowledge of self."[44] The Panther platform clearly drew on its roots in the Bay Area Black Studies movement most recently, and further back, to the founders' status as migrant children and adolescents in Bay Area public schools. The BPP expressed the alienation of a larger segment of southern-born youth who experienced the public school system as disciplinary and stultifying. While antagonism often centered on white teachers and administrators, there were also tensions with black staff. In fact, Huey Newton argued that it was conflicts in the Berkeley and Oakland school systems that prompted his earliest stirrings of racial and class consciousness.[45]

As the Party evolved, its conception of education moved from a critique of existing institutions to an attempt to establish its own. In different stages of the BPP's history, the Party employed different forms of political education for its membership and the larger community.[46] Up until the founding of the IYI in 1971, educational efforts varied and were somewhat ad hoc. In the early years, the BPP used adult political education classes to recruit and socialize new rank-and-file members.[47] In 1968, national headquarters established the "Huey Newton Ideological Institute" for training Central Committee members and regional leadership from chapters across the country. Representatives from Chicago and the southern California BPP, for example, traveled to the Bay Area to participate. The Ideological Institute became part of a larger effort to standardize Party doctrine and to disseminate Huey Newton's "dialectical method" and organizing strategies.[48]

After 1968, political education moved from being a tool for developing internal cohesion to a centerpiece for Party expansion and institution building. Given the BPP's concern with fighting hunger in order to cultivate learning, developing schools was, in a sense, the next logical step. Ericka Huggins later explained that free breakfast programs, and the other attempts of the Party to meet the material needs of black people living in the city, became part of a broader movement to expand the political consciousness and self-concept of African American youth: "Real change occurs, because if you give people decent education and some nice clothing to wear and maybe a roof over their heads, that's a beginning. But the real change occurs within ... what we believe ... *who we believe we are*"[49] (emphasis mine).

In 1969, the BPP set up liberation schools for young people and teenagers. San Francisco, Richmond, and Berkeley hosted these initial efforts. Most were informal affairs that resembled after-school or summer programs with teachers composed mainly of Party members and community volunteers.[50] As in the case of breakfast programs, the Bay Area Panthers relied on the support of local churches. The Ridgepost Methodist Church in Hunter's Point initially housed San Francisco's first liberation school, before it was relocated to the Fillmore area on Ellis Street.[51] The facility held classes throughout the year and served children between the ages of two and thirteen.[52] The combination of government pressure, limited funds, and local resistance made it difficult to sustain lasting programs.[53] On June 25, the BPP opened the first permanent liberation school above the national headquarters' office on Berkeley's Shattuck Avenue.[54] An average day started with a free breakfast or lunch. Instruction focused on current events, black history, and memorizing the Ten Point Program. Liberation schools soon expanded beyond the San Francisco Bay Area, and a number of cities developed their own programs to serve children between four and eleven years of age. These grassroots educational efforts had their greatest impact between 1969 and 1971. Initially, enrollment remained limited to Party members and functioned as an extension of communal child rearing, but as the school evolved, participation was opened up to the broader community.[55]

By placing African American history at the forefront of the curriculum, the liberation schools revealed the Panthers' ongoing ties to the Bay Area Black Studies movement. As colleges and universities reluctantly began setting up new programs in response to student pressure, the Black Panther Party established its own alternative schools to expose school-age children to revolutionary thought, BPP philosophy, and black history.[56] In contrast to cultural nationalists' teachings, Party education stressed class, multiculturalism, and the importance of interracial alliances. As Bobby Seale described the intended function of liberation schools: "We see the Liberation Schools as a supplement to existing institutions, which still teach racism to children, both white and black. The youth have to understand that the revolutionary struggle in this country that's now being waged is not a race struggle but a class struggle."[57] While the liberation schools shared a common ancestry with SNCC's freedom schools, at its core the BPP's focus was political education—critics might say "indoctrination"—as an end rather than a means. Like the Black Studies movement, the Panthers developed curricula to instill revolutionary consciousness, rather than directing young people toward a specific goal of voter registration, electoral politics, or social mobility.[58] A teacher in the San Francisco liberation school explained, "We are teaching the young brothers and sisters what 'Power to the People' means

Children of Party members attending class in the Intercommunal Youth Institute, Oakland, 1971. Photograph by Stephen Shames, courtesy of Stephen Shames / Polaris Images.

and we, the teachers, know that power belongs to the people and that youth makes revolution."[59]

The BPP made further inroads into Bay Area black communities by offering residents an alternative to the public school system. Like their use of police patrols several years before, the BPP's appeal stemmed from its ability to express black newcomers' long-standing aspirations, as well as their anger. Ericka Huggins explained why black people, and southern migrants in particular, invested education with such meaning: "Since the history of black people in the United States is such that we were not *allowed* to read and we were not *allowed* to write, then this was very important. And it was something that our parents—*all* of our parents, no matter, where, what class we came from—felt to be important. And we *knew* that the parents of the children that we were educating felt it to be important too. Even though many of them could not read or write, those parents, they wanted the best for their children."[60]

Founded in 1971, the Intercommunal Youth Institute represented the culmination of earlier Panther educational programs. Although it went through a series of location changes in its first years, the IYI became the first fully accredited Panther school.[61] Initially, the institute served only the children of Party members, but within several years its doors opened to the larger East Bay community. Throughout the history of the school, African Americans made up the majority of the student body; however, the IYI accepted children of all backgrounds, and in its latter years, Latinos formed a significant percentage of its enrollment.[62] By 1973, the BPP established a permanent home for the institute in East Oakland, where it remained until the school closed its doors in 1982. Under the direction of Ericka Huggins and Elaine Brown, the school grew rapidly and attracted a long waiting list. Its motto revealed its links to progressive, student-centered theories of education: "Learning *how* to think, not *what* to think."[63]

The institute was subsequently renamed the Oakland Community School, and by the late seventies, it had few obvious curricular or ideological ties to the Panther Party.[64] The OCS and its not-for-profit parent company, the Educational Opportunities Corporation, became an effective vehicle for broadening Party support and making inroads into larger progressive circles in Oakland and Berkeley. The Oakland Community Learning Center, a multiuse facility, housed the OCS as well as an adult night school for GED preparation.[65] Sixteen accredited instructors offered a full curriculum of math, science, social science, Spanish, environmental studies, physical education, and fine arts. OCS attracted a number of artists and contributors who volunteered their time, including jazz pianist and composer Sun Ra.[66] The school became overwhelmingly popular and could not meet the full demand for placements. At it height, its graduating class barely reached double-digit figures.[67] The OCS successfully provided poor children the scholastic excellence of private academies based on progressive models of nonauthoritarian, hands-on approaches to learning. Foundation grants and community support enabled the Black Panther Party to offer this excellent education tuition free. In designing the school, director Erika Huggins and the Panther leadership explicitly repudiated industrial-style education, which they blamed for reproducing racial and class disparity.[68]

Huggins's democratic vision of education shaped OCS's curriculum and administration. Among her most urgent concerns was countering the authoritarian model of education that black children, their parents, and the school's teachers had received. In order to do this, Huggins worked actively with the staff and discussed how to engage with students without harsh verbal or physical discipline. As a regular practice, the OCS director "patrolled the halls of the school" to carefully observe teachers' treatment of students and to make sure there was no "yelling, screaming, and terrorizing." Huggins also developed alternate means of discipline, including encouraging students to assume yoga poses to reestablish "the internal locus of control" and setting up a "justice committee" to have peers decide in a democratic manner how to respond to student infractions, like failure to complete homework.[69] She also worked hard to politicize the issue of public education itself for students, their parents, and the larger black community of the East Bay:

> Why should it be that a school in East Oakland, in the flatlands
> of East Oakland, should have a public school . . . [that is] poorly
> equipped and poorly cared for with little or no funding for extra
> programming? And a school in the same city, in the hills, run by the
> same school district would have all kinds of additional program-
> ming and funding? . . . Our feeling was that, "We'll bring in the best,
> no matter what it costs!" The parents have to take ownership of it by
> coming and helping, but we will not make them give the money they
> do not have. We will give the quality of a private school education to
> children who would ordinarily have to be in a public school.[70]

The successes of the Panther school stood as an implicit plaint against the floundering Oakland public school system under the direction of Marcus Foster in the early seventies. While the Oakland Community School had demonstrated that poor urban youth could receive high-quality educations, Oakland Unified was debating installing police on school grounds and the use of a mandatory pass system.[71] OCS even received a special commenda-tion from the California State Department of Education for its violence pre-vention program.[72]

Hoover Strikes Back

Despite the shift toward community action, the late sixties were years of unmitigated repression, thereby calling into question whether survival pro-grams constituted an even greater threat to the state than police patrols and displays of armed self-defense. By tapping into long-standing institutions of southern black communities—like the church and mutual-aid societies—BPP breakfast, health, and school programs fused the Party's Marxist vision of radical internationalism with organic forms of black self-help. Estab-lishing autonomous social services—and broadcasting their existence in a high-quality newspaper with national and international distribution—high-lighted the American government's negligence, while vastly broadening the Panthers' base of support.[73]

Local, state, and federal law enforcement watched these developments with alarm and responded with unprecedented force. In November 1968, FBI director J. Edgar Hoover declared that the Black Panther Party represented the single "greatest threat to the internal security of the country."[74] Between 1968 and 1969, the *Black Panther* reported that police arrested 739 people nationwide with the BPP subsequently paying nearly $5 million in bail.[75] In addition to Eldridge Cleaver's exile and Bobby Seale's trials in Chicago and New Haven, police also arrested David Hilliard for threatening President Richard Nixon during a Bay Area antiwar rally. In a fiery speech, the BPP's chief of staff lambasted Nixon as "the man that sends his vicious murdering dogs out into the black community and invade upon our Black Panther Party Breakfast programs. Destroy food that we have for hungry kids and expect us to accept shit like that idly. Fuck that motherfucking man. Richard Nixon."[76] The near hysterical tenor of Hilliard's remarks reflected the intense crisis the Party experienced at the close of the decade. By July 1969, the BPP had become the singular focus of COINTELPRO's division concerned with "Black Nationalist Hate Groups." Of the 295 actions authorized that year, 233 involved the Black Panther Party.[77]

While vanguardist Eldridge Cleaver criticized the Panthers' communitarian turn as reformist, J. Edgar Hoover wrote a memorandum warning of the unprecedented threat posed by free breakfast programs. As Huey Newton later recounted, the FBI director noted in his memo that this new form of outreach had "met with some success and resulted in considerable favorable publicity for the BPP." The program was dangerous precisely because it provided "the BPP with a ready-made audience composed of highly impressionable youths. . . . Consequently, the BCP [Breakfast for Children Program] represent[ed] *the best and most influential activity going for the BPP and, as such, [was] potentially the greatest threat to efforts by authorities.*" To roll back these efforts, Hoover urged law enforcement to act quickly to "*neutralize the BPP and destroy what it stands for*"[78] (Newton's emphasis in both quotations). In subsequent months, the FBI relentlessly targeted the survival programs and used its media division to promote a "disinformation campaign" in the press. Author G. C. Moore claimed that, contrary to the Party's populist appeal, the true function of the free breakfast programs was to "gain control of the ghetto community, poison the minds of ghetto children with anti-white propaganda and to cloak the illegal activities of the BPP with some segment of respectability."[79]

In addition to this war of words, Hoover and the FBI used a number of other disruptive tactics to sabotage food and school programs. Agents mailed anonymous letters to church administrators and local congregations to discourage their support.[80] When this failed, officials alerted Bay Area regulatory agencies of the dangers to public health posed by Panther food preparation. One letter warned of potential food contamination caused by "the recent information that several members at national headquarters have a social [venereal] disease."[81] Liberation schools suffered similar efforts at interference. The *Black Panther* reported that within a two-week period during the summer of 1969, the facilities housing the San Francisco and Richmond liberation schools abruptly evicted them, despite their initial enthusiasm.[82] Law enforcement also applied pressure to individuals, who could face not only arrest and incarceration but expulsion from public housing. Many women and children suffered as a result. In one instance, authorities succeeded at having a rank-and-file Panther evicted by informing the San Francisco Housing Authority that she used her "apartment for BPP Free Breakfast Programs."[83]

Split within the Party

By forcing the Panthers to expend immense amounts of energy simply maintaining programs, these tactics succeeded at eroding organizational resources and morale. The most damaging effect of federal counterintelligence, however, was more subtle and insidious. In response to violent repression and infiltration, the Panther leadership shifted into a reactive mode, responding to attacks defensively, rather than pushing forward to realize its own vision of social democracy. Even though the Party dropped self-defense from its name in 1968 in an attempt to distance itself from its earlier advocacy of police patrols and armed struggle, the leadership floundered and backtracked when presented with each new crisis. As in the case of Hilliard's angry rant against Nixon in 1969, the *Black Panther* responded to arrests, shootings, and sabotage with a strident and exaggerated rhetoric of urban guerrilla warfare that the Central Committee had neither the capacity, nor the intention, to fulfill.[84] Equivocating on the true nature of the Party's focus left the leadership vulnerable to misinterpretation by its own diverse membership and to manipulation from outside. Significantly, many of the FBI's most successful attempts at infiltration took place among the Party's armed "security" forces. A clear pattern emerged. In the name of militancy, agent provocateurs advocated illegal activities often involving firearms and offensive violence, which, in turn, justified further police repression of individuals and local chapters.[85] The cumulative effect of these joint FBI and police campaigns proved devastating. As historian Tracye Matthews has argued, "In hindsight, it is known that the actions of the FBI instigated as much if not more violence than they deterred, and diverted attention and energies away from the political and direct service activities of the BPP."[86]

In a desperate attempt to stop infiltration, the BPP closed its membership in January 1969 and began purging members under suspicion. Constant surveillance, infiltration, and disruption created an atmosphere of paranoia and distrust that aggravated personal, ideological, and regional divisions. Defensive measures intended to shield the organization only made matters worse by alienating whole segments of the membership who coalesced into rival factions. Ultimately, law enforcement's greatest blow to the Black Panther Party was its success in capitalizing on this growing internal conflict. Between 1969 and 1971, a partisan split cleaved the national organization, pitting a dissident group led by Eldridge Cleaver against the Oakland leadership. After fleeing into exile at the end of 1968 and establishing the International Section of the Black Panther Party, Eldridge Cleaver maintained a distant relationship with the Bay Area BPP largely through written correspondence. Recognizing this unique opportunity, the San Francisco office of the FBI worked together with J. Edgar Hoover to send a series of incendiary letters to Newton and Cleaver in hopes of pitting them against one another.[87]

Mounting tension between the Oakland leadership and some of its far-flung chapters aggravated this fracture in the Party's top leadership. The New York branches of the Party became increasingly dissatisfied with the Bay Area–dominated national headquarters. A conflict over how the Central Committee allocated monies exacerbated differences of geography and political sensibility. Sales of the *Black Panther* in New York City accounted for nearly a third of the Party's newspaper revenues. However, despite the city's large number of political prisoners, exorbitant legal fees, and high cost of living, the New York Panthers received only a fraction of their sales proceeds for operating costs.[88] Added to this conflict over resources was the more diffuse problem of political and cultural dissonance. From its inception, the New York chapter possessed a very different political flavor than their Bay Area predecessor. With their Panafricanist orientation and roots in the city's long-standing nationalist tradition that had nurtured diasporic movements from Marcus Garvey to Malcolm X, the New York Panthers found Newton and Seale's rants against cultural nationalism hard to accept. Many had chosen African-inspired names and sewed cowrie shells into their uniforms to signify their identification with black diasporic culture. Important continuities could also be seen between the membership of the New York chapter and its antecedent, RAM. As Huey Newton and Bobby Seale distanced themselves from their earlier support for revolutionary nationalism and armed self-defense, New York, New Jersey, and a handful of other East Coast chapters became disenchanted with the Oakland-based leadership.[89]

This potentially explosive situation came to a head when Huey Newton expelled Elmer Gerard Pratt from the Black Panther Party in February 1971.[90] Pratt, affectionately known as "Geronimo," was a southern migrant from Morgan City, Louisiana, who relocated to Los Angeles after serving a tour in Vietnam. Bunchy Carter approached the decorated military veteran about joining the southern California chapter while he was a student at UCLA in fall 1968.[91] Pratt used his martial expertise to help build the group's armed wing before officially joining the BPP the following year. In the aftermath of Carter's murder, Pratt assumed leadership of the southern California chapter and took on increased national responsibilities, including extending the BPP's reach throughout the South by helping to set up local chapters in Atlanta, Dallas, New Orleans, Memphis, and Winston-Salem. In August 1970, Pratt decided to go "underground" to develop the Black Liberation Army.[92] Like Orpheus, Pratt traveled back and forth between the two different realms of the Party, working tirelessly to expand "aboveground" branches, while also assembling a clandestine apparatus to shield members from police and foment armed rebellion. In the process, Pratt established close ties with some of the most militant sectors of the Panther Party across the nation. In addition to his links with Panthers in the historic southern "Black Belt," the New York chapter contained some of his closest allies.[93]

To fully understand the origins of the fratricidal split that emerged in the BPP, it is necessary to consider how Huey Newton's and Booby Seales's repeated arrests and incarceration helped to alienate the national leadership from the regional Panther chapters and their diverse rank and file. In the midst of the tide of repression and the increasing militarization of the Party that accompanied it, Newton was released from jail in August 1970. He found an organization that scarcely resembled the one he had left behind nearly three years before. Not only had the Oakland-based Party grown from a small group composed largely of childhood friends and neighbors into a national movement over 5,000 strong, Pratt and his allies had built an extensive underground organization with few formal ties to the public BPP. Even more disorienting was the increasingly antagonistic relationship between the Oakland leadership and the East Coast branches of the Party. In addition to their anger over the lack of Party democracy and the failure of the Party's Central Committee to incorporate homegrown organizers from outside the Bay Area, they also expressed an unwavering commitment to armed struggle and to its prophet, Eldridge Cleaver.[94]

Given the Oakland leadership's decision to renounce the military aspects of the Party and to focus all of their energies on community service programs, Newton attempted to demobilize the clandestine wing of the Party. He purged Pratt, publicly denounced him in the *Black Panther*, and forbade other members of the Party from associating with him. In March 1971, the leadership of the New York Party, many of them incarcerated as part of the Panther 21 case, wrote an "Open Letter to the Weathermen" in the *East Village Other*. They identified the armed faction of Students for a Democratic Society as the true vanguard for revolutionary change in the United States.[95] Newton immediately responded, first by expelling the seventeen members of the Panther 21 in early February and several weeks later by purging the whole International Section of the BPP, including three Central Committee members, D. C. Cox and Kathleen and Eldridge Cleaver.[96] Upon observing these developments, the FBI proudly claimed responsibility. An interdepartmental memo observed, "Analysis indicates the chaotic condition of the BPP and the split between BPP leaders Huey P. Newton and Eldridge Cleaver is possibly a direct result of our intensive counterintelligence efforts aimed at causing dissension between Newton and Cleaver and within the Party. We are closely scrutinizing developments in the BPP to fully exploit through counterintelligence in order to keep the BPP off balance."[97]

While law enforcement played a decisive role in fomenting dissension inside the organization, some structural aspects of the BPP left it susceptible to splits and infiltration. In many respects, "democratic centralism" was the Achilles heel of the Black Panther Party. The tendency toward top-down leadership structures reinforced preexisting cleavages in the Party, leaving it vulnerable to fractures in the edifice. Under the immense pressure of state and federal law enforcement, fault lines spread out in expanding concentric circles throughout the Party: at the most personal level, between men and women; at the institutional level, between the Central Committee and the rank and file; at the geographic level, between national headquarters and the local chapters. Regina Jennings, a young woman originally from Philadelphia, who flew to Oakland to join the Party in 1968, explained, "During the early years of the Panther Party, there was no democratic procedure for challenging an officer. This was one of the greatest flaws in my beloved organization. There was no external governing board to regulate how the individual offices operated."[98]

The Black Panther Party's failure to codify and disseminate a consistent ideological position through speeches, the newspaper, and inner Party directives proved equally distressing. As the BPP spread rapidly across the country, the Party's bombastic rhetoric created confusion and ambiguity. While the Cleaver faction could be faulted for its romantic investment in revolutionary violence, Newton and Seale's earlier pronouncements endorsing urban guerrilla warfare made this possible. Despite their shift to survival programs, articles calling for "organized self-defense groups" continued to appear in the *Black Panther* as late as February 1971.[99] Through their exaggerated bravado, the founders of the BPP set in motion political forces they ultimately could not control.[100] Tragically, when they witnessed the death or incarceration of young people like Bobby Hutton and tried to change direction by turning to community service, the Party—with the intervention of COINTELPRO—turned in on itself. Sadly the seeds of this were sown not only by state repression but also by the leadership's reliance on an armed wing earlier in its development. Moreover, the failure to establish democratic procedures within the organization proved equally damaging. Both of these tendencies left the BPP susceptible to counterintelligence measures and to factionalism.

. . .

IF LOWNDES COUNTY inspired the Oakland Black Panther Party's name and symbol initially, in this later phase of its history, the BPP drew on SNCC's organizing successes in Greenwood and McComb.[101] Ever reluctant to relinquish the Panthers' status as revolutionary vanguard, Huey Newton deemed this programmatic shift as "survival pending revolution."[102] A convergence of forces lay behind the BPP's turn to grassroots social welfare. State repression had crippled much of the Party nationwide, and by 1969 it became clear that direct confrontation with law enforcement was untenable. The political spectacle of men with guns and the mass arrests that followed had disastrous consequences for both the leadership and the rank and file, whose average age was a mere nineteen years old.[103] Moreover, the COINTELPRO-inspired split between Eldridge Cleaver and Huey Newton exposed the tensions and contradictions inherent in the original objectives of the Party. An abiding commitment to armed struggle ultimately proved incompatible with an ethos of community control and development.[104] After expelling the Cleavers, Newton explained why community service was essential to the Party's revitalization: "The original vision of the party was to develop a lifeline to the people, by serving their needs and defending them against their oppressors. . . . We knew that this strategy would raise the consciousness of the people and give us their support. . . . For a time the Black Panther Party lost its vision and defected from the community. . . . The only reason the Party is still in existence at this time is because of the Ten Point Program . . . our survival program. Our programs would be meaningless and insignificant if they were not community programs."[105]

In addition to ideological change, the shifting gender composition of the Party played a crucial role in its turn to "survival pending revolution." By 1969, women made up the majority of the rank and file, and their influence was clearly visible in the Party's survival and political education efforts. In keeping with the BPP's origins in the Bay Area's southern diaspora, the social services that the Panthers provided—food and clothing giveaways, free health clinics, community control of police, public education, and electoral representation—all addressed urgent needs of northern California's migrant population. However, in order to finance and expand these efforts, the BPP needed new allies. Cultivating ties with civil rights groups and black churches served the dual purpose of insulating the Party from attacks by law enforcement and building a supportive infrastructure for their community programs. By uniting with long-standing African American institutions, the Panthers' renewed focus on grassroots social welfare suceeded at increasing public support. Addressing the needs of children became the primary means through which the Panthers courted older and more conservative segments of the African American community. While the BPP achieved its aim of expanding its base of support between 1969 and 1972, it continued to suffer state repression that would ultimately damage many local chapters and force the national headquarters to refocus its attention on the Party's birthplace in Oakland, California.

7. A CHICKEN IN EVERY BAG

Much to the surprise of the press and national observers, Bobby Seale announced his decision to run for mayor of Oakland during a massive rally in the city's historic DeFremery Park on Saturday, May 13, 1972. The Panthers' new minister of information, Elaine Brown, also declared her candidacy for the Oakland city council. Not since the March on Sacramento had the Oakland Panther Party attracted so much attention. Brown later explained the media spectacle surrounding the Party's bid for elected office: "Entrance into the U.S. Establishment's game by its most vehement opposition was news."[1] Of particular interest was the political symbolism of Bobby Seale's new image. For the first time since his "early days as a black nationalist," the cofounder of the Panthers wore a conservative dark business suit and white dress shirt. In order to assume the respectable mantle of a municipal campaign, the political iconography of social movements and revolution had been shed. Gone was the leather jacket, black beret, and paramilitary title that made Seale and the Party (in)famous. When asked about his ability to project "the kind of image needed to win the Oakland mayor's race," Seale responded, "The dress doesn't make any difference. The people see me as one who wants to end their exploitation. That's real, beyond the surface image."[2]

While many in Oakland vigorously debated whether or not the Panther leadership had replaced the bullet with the ballot box by 1972, the Party's community survival programs laid the groundwork for their electoral campaigns years before.[3] Starting in early 1969, the BPP had focused nearly all of its efforts on mobilizing broader segments of the African American community. The BPP initiated this process by sponsoring their first breakfast program at St. Augustine's Episcopal; however, their carefully cultivated reconciliation with former adversaries reached its culmination in the Oakland municipal elections in the spring of 1973. In this latter phase of their history, the Panthers embraced the once-hated black middle-class establishment and remade themselves in its image. In August 1973, *Ebony* described in almost giddy tones how "[Bobby] Seale shocked the nation when, in an apparent switch from militance to middle-classism he donned bourgeois togs and ran for mayor of Oakland—winning a respectable 47,000 votes. . . . Seale's new image signaled an end to previous Panther paramilitarism and marked a unique stage in the organization's thrust for black liberation."[4] As is clear from the reaction by Johnson Publications, the Panther leadership jettisoned not only their uniforms and titles but also the biting class-conscious rhetoric of the "bootlickers gallery," choosing instead to join the larger national push for black electoral office. Buoyed by the presidential candidacy of Shirley Chisholm and the National Black Political Convention in Gary, Indiana, the BPP joined Amiri Baraka's Congress of African People and other radical groups who saw municipal government as a means to black political power. This decision earned the Panthers unprecedented support from national black leaders and former critics. Coretta Scott King, the Reverend Jesse Jackson, and California assemblyman and future mayor of San Francisco Willie Brown all endorsed Bobby Seale's bid for mayor of Oakland.[5]

The Panthers' increasing mainstream popularity extended beyond the African American community. By embracing the new philosophy of "intercommunalism," the BPP broke decisively with its origins in revolutionary nationalism to reach out to a series of new political constituencies, including the burgeoning movements for women's and gay liberation, Chicano rights, and international struggles for self-determination. While many of these tendencies emerged during the "Free Huey" movement, the early seventies witnessed their fullest expression.

Like the BPP's turn to community service, this new phase emerged in fits and starts. Although the leadership had clearly changed its organizing focus, Seale continued, on occasion, to argue that the BPP remained a revolutionary organization.[6] But the most serious challenge the organization faced was changing its own administrative structure. Launching a municipal campaign meant a large-scale internal reorganization eliminating nearly all of the regional chapters to divert resources and (wo)manpower to the national headquarters in the East Bay. Not everyone agreed. All over the country, black urban communities had shouldered police repression and personal sacrifice to establish their own Panther parties to address their local needs and problems. In the process, law enforcement jailed many young people, and individual Panther chapters provided much needed legal aid and support for political prisoners from their area. Establishing Oakland as "the base of operation" meant leaving these struggles behind to refocus attention on a single, and from the perspective of Panthers outside the Bay Area, unfamiliar regional theatre of struggle. It remained to be seen how the Party's historic base among migrant youth, college students, and the urban poor would respond to these momentous changes in Party ideology and structure.[7]

Intercommunalism and Community Control

Beginning in 1970, Newton coined the term "intercommunalism" to describe the current ideology of the Party. The new philosophy shifted political focus to "communities" rather than nation-states. Intercommunalism replaced the Party's earlier stance on internal colonization, which defined Afro-America as a subjugated colony within the mother country. Newton now argued that capitalist expansion and an increasingly integrated world system rendered the nation-state obsolete as a means of confronting power. Seizing control of national governments and redistributing wealth could no longer be the goal of revolution. The hierarchy between rich and poor nations meant that to do this in the United States would compromise the peoples of other countries. Instead Newton proposed that activists organize using a communitarian ideal in which resources would be mobilized to serve "communities" rather than nations. David Hilliard summarized Newton's position:

> In prison Huey developed an analysis of the present political moment. . . . Nationalist struggles, even revolutionary ones, [he said] are beside the point. Capital dominates the world; ignoring borders, international finance has transformed the world into communities rather than nations. Some of the these communities are under siege—like Vietnam—and others conduct siege, like the United States government. The people of the world are united in their desire to run their own communities: the Black people of Oakland and the Vietnamese. We need to band together as communities.[8]

Newton's formulation made it possible to link the Party's radical anticolonial and internationalist stance with its newfound commitment to domestic reform. Elaine Brown identified the death of George Jackson, the split with Eldridge Cleaver, and Newton's visit to Beijing as central factors in his reconceptualization of revolutionary method.[9] An encounter with Mozambique's Samora Machel reinforced the Panther leader's confidence in community-based programs for rebuilding the Party. Machal, a former military leader, now headed up FRELIMO, the nationalist organization that was attempting to drive out the Portuguese. He emphatically stressed the power of building social infrastructure, like schools and hospitals, to inspire widespread support. These mass organizing techniques would become the key to making the Party a revolutionary force of international significance.[10]

For much of the rank and file, the concept of "intercommunalism" remained elusive. "It was a phraseology that Huey Newton attempted to coin," Bobby Seale later explained. "It was lofty, pure abstract to most Party members. What the Party members learned on a firsthand basis was community control."[11] In the late sixties and early seventies, after three consecutive decades of black migration into northern urban centers, African Americans sought to transform local institutions and wrest control of governance. This ambition extended into a broad spectrum of civic life, including schools, housing, health, industry, social services, and transportation.[12] Although the Black Panther Party described its transformation as the product of internal contradictions, its turn to community control took place in the context of a national push for black political and civic representation in urban America. Given the relative weakness of African Americans' economic base, community empowerment necessitated an increasing reliance on local government. Groups throughout the country sought to achieve this ideal through a variety of methods: strengthening the power of individual neighborhoods and enabling them to assume a larger share in decision making; running local campaigns to increase black representation on the board of education, the police commission, city council, poverty programs, and in all levels of public service; fighting for parity in government hiring and contracting; and redirecting state resources toward black economic development.[13]

African Americans' drive for electoral power had strong affective dimensions that tapped into their collective history of displacement and exclusion. The hope was that new black majorities could transform cities in their own image and thereby redeem the long history of disfranchisement and expropriation.[14] On their album *Chocolate City*, the funk band Parliament epitomized this sentiment when they sang, "We may not have gotten our forty acres and a mule, but we did get you CC. You're our piece of the rock, and we love you CC."[15] Sadly, the racial structure of local economies made this promising vision a fiscal impossibility. African Americans sought political control at a time when cities faced an unprecedented budget crisis, precipitated largely by white flight. Between 1952 and 1959, spending by local governments increased at a rate nearly twice that of the gross national product, and their public debt rose at a rate forty times faster than that of the federal government. This trend would continue and deepen in the subsequent decade.[16]

Nevertheless, two important national developments empowered the Panthers to take on local municipal campaigns: the candidacy of Shirley Chisholm for president of the United States and the National Black Political Convention in Gary, Indiana.[17] The movement for black political representation created natural points of unity between the Black Panthers and other Black nationalist/Black Power groups and their more conservative counterparts from the civil rights movement and the Democratic Party. In the aftermath of King's murder, a united-front strategy emerged that came to fruition in the National Black Convention.[18] In 1969, nine black Congressmen met at the behest of Representative Charles Diggs of Detroit and formed the Democratic Select Committee (DSC) to fight Nixon's attacks on African Americans and other low-income people. Within two years, the original members of the DSC along with their newly elected colleagues, Representatives Ronald Dellums of Oakland, George Collins of Chicago, and Parren Mitchell of Baltimore, established the Congressional Black Caucus (CBC). Historian Manning Marable described its activities during these pivotal years:

> During 1971 and 1972, CBC attempted to represent a 'united voice for Black America' in the Congress, and to an extent, across the nation. CBC staff members supported local races of black candidates; lobbied for progressive reforms in job training, health care, welfare and social service programs; and attempted to fashion a national political strategy to increase black political power from local to federal needs. The Black nationalists at this point began a period of tactical cooperation with many CBC members, particularly Diggs, who was vice chairperson of the House Committee on African Relations, and Dellums, who was at the time the only avowedly socialist in Congress.[19]

Among many black political groups, both electoral and grassroots, a consensus began to emerge about the need for a new political formation that could mobilize the African American community and force the white leadership of the Democratic Party to be more responsive. On March 10, 1971, the National Black Political Convention met in Gary, Indiana—the city that had elected Richard Hatcher, the first black mayor in U.S. history. The theme, "Unity not Uniformity," called attention to the impressive spectrum of participants who ranged from civil rights luminaries like Coretta Scott King and SCLC leader Jesse Jackson to the militant cosponsor of the conference, Amiri Baraka. The quest for black political empowerment provided common ground for cultural and revolutionary nationalists, black liberals, and capitalists that would have been unimaginable several years before. Over

3,000 official delegates came together with an additional 9,000 participants to make the Gary meeting the largest black political convention ever held in North America. While deep cleavages developed over the course of the weekend about busing, labor, the Israeli-Palestinian conflict, and the proper relationship between black elected officials and the grass roots, the convention gave birth to the National Black Political Assembly, accompanied by a serious discussion of an independent black political party. Manning Marable has dubbed the Gary convention the "zenith not only of black nationalism, but of the entire black movement during the Second Reconstruction."[20]

Although the Panthers enthusiastically participated in this historic event, they later expressed ambivalence about their reception. A position paper written soon after the convention complained that Chairman Bobby Seale received insufficient time, after being upstaged by Isaac Hayes's musical performance. Given the BPP's seniority in the black revolt and the sacrifices of its membership, the Party felt that being included in an entertainment program was insulting. Moreover, the Panther leadership accused the chief organizers of faulty planning and of monopolizing the conference program. Despite these criticisms, the memo praised the Gary convention's historic attempt to create independent institutions and establish broad-based black unity. In order to disseminate the convention's message, the *Black Panther* agreed to reprint the full text of the National Black Political Agenda, thereby allowing readers to determine its value and relevance to their everyday lives.[21] Interestingly, the Panthers' assessment of the Gary convention ended with an affirmation of armed struggle: "In the last analysis, we believe that this change will come when the contradiction between Black people, all oppressed people and our oppressors is ultimately resolved, which we believe will be through violent conflict. It is with these ideas in mind that we offer this Agenda for the masses of Black people, for, as we have stated before, '. . . when (the people) are ready to pick up the gun, serious business will happen.'"[22] In the coming months, the BPP lobbied to be included in the National Black Political Assembly.[23] The Panthers actively enlisted Wisconsin state representative Lloyd Barbee, district representative Donald Hopkins, and Congressional representative Ronald Dellums to support their bid for one of the fifteen spots set aside for "Nationalist group membership."[24] Although Bobby Seale attended the Sacramento conference held a month after Gary, he did not become a permanent delegate to the assembly.[25] Nevertheless, these national developments fed the Party's ambition to secure a place in Oakland politics.

As the African American population in Oakland exploded in size, most avenues of political power remained closed, leaving the migrant community without substantive electoral representation. This historical feature of the East Bay combined with a faltering local economy, and the campus turmoil of the late 1960s helped foster the rich culture of Black radicalism that the Black Panther Party dominated. When the BPP turned its attention to local government, it confronted a long-standing history of political exclusion of both black and working-class residents. Despite African Americans' constituting over 40 percent of Oakland's population in the early seventies, only one councilman out of eight was black, and no people of color had been elected to a major office.[26] While the majority of voters registered as Democrats, the Republican Party dominated city politics. Stretching back to the Progressive Era, the conservative Knowland family operated the single citywide newspaper, the Oakland Tribune. The Tribune Building, known as the "Tower of Power," cast a broad Republican shadow across city hall. Joseph P. Knowland founded the family dynasty as "editor, publisher, and owner" of the paper. He fought and successfully defeated the liberal Republican machine politician Mike Kelley in the 1920s and helped elect Earl Warren as Alameda County's district attorney in 1925. Although J. P. Knowland never assumed political office, his Tower of Power anointed a succession of economically conservative, probusiness candidates in Oakland city government from the mid-1920s through the 1970s. The Tribune's political influence manifested itself most explicitly in local law enforcement. Knowland and his political network prevented the election of a Democrat or a liberal to the office of district attorney for over fifty years.[27]

Despite the huge demographic changes in postwar Oakland, J. P. Knowland's machine remained unshaken. In fact, it was powerful enough to propel his son into national politics. In 1946 William Knowland became one of California's U.S. senators, and after his reelection in 1952 he served as both Republican majority and minority leaders. This accomplishment led political scientist Edward C. Hayes to speculate that in the early 1950s William Knowland was "possibly the second most influential Republican in the country, after the President, Dwight D. Eisenhower."[28] The power of the Knowland machine foreclosed possibilities of local reform, resulting in a gaping power vacuum. This was nowhere more evident than in the successive defeats of the labor coalition between 1947 and 1952 and the failure to elect a black mayor until 1977 despite the rapidly changing population of the city.[29] In 1973, the incumbent mayor of Oakland, Republican John Reading, had served in office since 1966 when he was appointed to replace the then incumbent, shortly before the upcoming election.[30]

While black residents struggled to enter the political process with varying success at the county, state, and federal level, they faced nearly insurmountable barriers in the city governments of Berkeley, Oakland, and Richmond.[31] A decade before the changes ushered in by World War II, a small network of West Oakland politicians rooted in the unions and railway yards established their own patronage networks. A. Philip Randolph's lieutenant on the West Coast, C. L. Dellums, emerged as the most powerful figure among a tight-knit group of "oldtimers" that included Walter Gordon, Frances Albrier, Tarea Hall Pittman, William Byron Rumford, and D. G. Gibson. While he eschewed elected office—preferring instead to exert political influence as the head of the West Coast Brotherhood of Sleeping Car Porters and the Alameda County NAACP—Dellums and his associates dominated black politics until the mid-1960s. For this older generation, political clubs and fraternal organizations served as the mainstay for political power. In the 1920s, D. G. Gibson founded Oakland's first black political club, the Appomattox, and worked with its successors, like the East Bay Democratic Club and the Men of Tomorrow, to establish a political base in the Bay Area's tiny black middle class. Although a few successful newcomers entered this remote inner circle, it was not until the advent of the Panthers and the federal poverty programs that recent southern migrants exerted influence reflecting their large numbers. However, while southern newcomers made inroads into local consciousness through work with federal officials and the radical spectacle of the Panthers' police patrols, elected municipal office remained elusive.[32]

In the midsixties, members of the Afro-American Association and their wide circle of affiliates began laying the groundwork for a new generation of black electoral politicians. Influenced by the Black nationalist and Black Power ethos of their Bay Area study group, these U.C. Berkeley graduates promoted an independent African American electoral politics that repudiated the client and broker relations of the earlier generation of "Negro leadership." Running Otho Green for Byron Rumford's vacant seventeenth assembly district seat represented their first attempt to challenge Berkeley's older black elite.[33] To do this, they could not rely on established channels and instead searched for ways to interject "black populism" into the race. In a column in the *Oakland Post*, Donald Hopkins contrasted Otho Green with the hand-picked candidate, Berkeley school board president John J.

Miller. "Otho Green represents an effective people's candidate. . . . He attends their churches, walks along their streets, and knows scores by their first names due to a lifetime of association in the community. He represents that unique brand of Negro college graduate who has successfully bridged white and black culture, who speaks the language of business and the academy as deftly as he speaks the language of the ghetto."[34]

Historian Joseph Rodriguez described how Oakland's established "black elites often times formed committees which discussed problems of discrimination with white officials. Confrontation rarely, if ever, took place. Instead, prominent black elites used their personal influence and friendships with city officials to change public policy."[35] Green's embrace of the urban poor in Berkeley's flatlands contrasted with the traditional candidacy of his opponent. Members of the AAA assailed the accommodationist style of the older generation of black politicians for relying on personal ties with white officials to broker black community interests. Echoing through Donald Hopkins's condemnation of Miller was the biting critique of the assimilationist black middle class in E. Franklin Frazier's *Black Bourgeoisie*: "He is usually a Negro professional who has 'made it,' i.e., he is educated, articulate, lives in the hills and admits to strangers that he is Negro. He's your Dawson, your Diggs, your Hawkins, your Rumford."[36]

While Miller easily defeated Otho Green, the challenger's bid for office catalyzed a new commitment to electoral politics among his fellow AAA members. In January 1967, Green joined together with Ronald Dellums, Ernest Howard, Will Ussery, and Donald Hopkins to establish a black political caucus to promote their vision of electoral reform.[37] In contrast to the earlier group of politicians, who derived power from serving as middle-class intermediaries with the white power structure, this younger group came from outside the Bay Area and sought a broader base among college students, older white progressives, and black migrants. Ultimately, this cross-racial constituency launched Ronald Dellums's city council and Congressional campaigns. Student organizers and voters played an essential role in his election to the House of Representatives in 1970.[38]

Although tensions existed between these two different generations of politicians, both faced barriers to political power at the municipal level. As evidenced by the early careers of Rumford, Gibson, Dellums, and Brown, most black electoral gains took place at the state or national level, as city governments remained largely impervious to changing racial demographics.[39] By the early seventies, however, clear signs emerged that the East Bay's Republican citadel was no longer invincible. The Black Panther Party's ability to mobilize young migrants on a mass scale, combined with the election of Berkeley's progressive black mayor, Warren Widener, in 1971, revealed that Oakland city politics could no longer ignore the growing black population, which was quickly approaching a majority.[40]

Oakland Base of Operations

To combat both the particular barriers to black electoral participation in Oakland and the long history of disfranchisement, the BPP used a multifaceted political strategy. The Panther leadership developed new forms of outreach, while simultaneously transforming their community programs into venues for voter registration and electoral outreach. In fact, Huey Newton specifically chose Bobby Seale as the BPP's mayoral candidate because he was so closely associated in people's minds with the Party's survival programs.[41] Through redistribution of goods and services, the Panthers hoped to mobilize Oakland's low-income black majority, who consisted largely of southern migrants and their children. In the past, these newcomers had little reason to vote; the Republican domination of the heavily black and Democratic city made electoral politics seem hopeless. Now, the Panthers' offers of free food, education, and medical care provided a concrete alternative. Fighting black political entropy created by years of southern disfranchisement and northern "personal politics" that elevated a small elite while marginalizing southern newcomers required aggressive measures. The Panther leadership understood that without broadening the electorate, victory was impossible. Even before Seale's and Brown's announcement of their candidacies, the Black Panther Party had already begun registering black residents to vote in the Bay Area.[42]

Starting in spring 1972, the Party sponsored large rallies with food giveaways called "survival conferences." In order to participate in these mass gatherings, people had to show their voter registration cards. If they did not have one, volunteers helped them register. This ingenious form of organizing served multiple purposes. In addition to swelling the rolls with thousands of new black voters, the survival conferences made the link between the Party's survival programs and their new electoral agenda explicit.[43] Sponsoring rallies that combined voter registration and consciousness-raising with massive giveaways of essentials—food, shoes, clothing, and health-care services—became the core of their political strategy. The press reacted immediately to these innovative tactics, proclaiming the birth of the "New

Women participating in the People's Free Food Program, Palo Alto, California, 1972. In the early seventies, the Black Panther Party gave out thousands of bags of groceries during their "survival conferences" in the San Francisco Bay Area, evoking President Hoover's Depression-era promise, the BPP included "a chicken in every bag." Photograph by Stephen Shames, courtesy of Stephen Shames / Polaris Images.

Panthers." Even the Party's eternal critic, Roy Wilkins, extended "a cautious welcome . . . [to] these new recruits to the banner of voter action."[44]

Like the Afro-American Association a decade before, the Panthers targeted black population centers throughout the Bay Area for outreach. On the weekend of March 29, 1972, the Panthers sponsored their first survival conference, which attracted over 16,000 people. During this three-day extravaganza featuring Shirley Chisholm, the BPP distributed 10,000 bags of groceries stamped with the Panther logo. Each package contained a whole chicken and two dozen grade AA eggs. In addition, volunteer medical personnel screened 3,600 people for sickle cell anemia, while Party members registered 2,071 new voters. The event extended beyond West Oakland. A diverse range of political figures spoke in a variety of venues spanning the breadth of the East Bay's black population settlements from the Oakland Auditorium near Lake Merritt to Greenman Field in East Oakland and San Pablo Park in West Berkeley. Bobby Seale, Elaine Brown, and the head of the national Welfare Rights Organization, Johnnie Tillman, addressed enthusiastic crowds. The headline event featured the United States' first black female Congresswoman and presidential candidate, Shirley Chisholm.[45] Her speech stressed the importance of voter registration and emphasized the radical nature of black electoral participation: "On this momentous occasion . . . [we] are breaking down barriers to black participation in the political system. . . . By joining the system, we are hitting white America below the belt, hurting them where they are most vulnerable. Blacks are learning to be sophisticated about power."[46]

Two months after Chisholm's visit to the Bay Area, Bobby Seale and Elaine Brown declared their candidacies in a large rally in historic DeFremery Park. Elaine Brown later described the significance of this location: "We started appropriately in the middle of West Oakland. The party had been born there, Bobby Hutton had been slain there, and Huey had been raised there." In addition to the neighborhood's symbolism of shared memory and struggle, Brown emphasized its proximity to one of the largest containerized ports in the United States. Through taking control of Oakland city government, the Panthers planned to harness the vast trade and wealth of the Port of Oakland to remedy the historical disappointments of Bay Area migrants. Brown explained, "They came from sharecroppers shanties in the South in response to Kaiser's promised of good wages on the wharfs and docks of Oakland. . . . The blacks in Oakland found that the end of the war brought a return to joblessness . . . to the realities of racism . . . [and] abject poverty in most cases. Our campaign was designed to inspire our people to take control of their own destinies, without reliance on the Henry Kaisers . . . to engender the idea of revolutionary change."[47]

The Panthers effectively integrated the particular history of the Bay Area's southern black diaspora with a vision of radical internationalism. On June 24, 1972, the BPP sponsored the "Anti-war, African-Liberation-Voter Registration Survival Conference." As the name revealed, the Panthers emphasized their ongoing ties with anticolonial movements around the world. Featured speakers included Congressman Ronald Dellums and a representative from the Provisional Revolutionary Government of South Vietnam.[48] In spite of the expulsion of the International Section of the BPP headed up by the Cleavers, the Party continued to maintain a thick network of transnational solidarity and support. The Panthers' radical internationalism, combined with their street-level outreach to Oakland's poor, created a compelling vision for a grassroots political campaign. With their slogan, "a chicken in every bag," evoking the Depression-era promise of "a chicken in every pot," the Panthers' masterfully blended old-style machine politics and sixties radicalism.[49] In less than a year, the Party registered over 35,000 new voters. Black migrants, Latinos and Asians, college students, and the more amorphous category of the "youth vote" coalesced into the Panthers' emerging political base.[50]

While the Black Panther Party had run political campaigns in the past, their bids for a city council seat and the mayoralty of Oakland represented a departure from previous efforts that were largely a medium for political education and fundraising.[51] The Party's ongoing struggle for its own survival was essential to its strategic calculus, but in 1972 the electoral turn was not a means to an end but an end in itself. The BPP hoped to become a major player in Oakland municipal politics by winning two major offices in the city. The Party's success in running candidates for Bay Area antipoverty agencies represented the first test of its political muscle. With the election of Ericka Huggins, Herman Smith, Audrea Jones, and William Roberts, the BPP won four seats on the Berkeley Community Development Council in May 1972. Two months later, the Central Committee ran a ten-candidate slate for the West Oakland Planning Committee (WOPC), the policymaking board for Oakland's Model Cities Program. Announcements in the *Black Panther* promised voters free bags of food, sickle cell anemia testing, and "brand new women's shoes" at polling places. A BPP press release declared, "The voting unity: is Power of the People: the only means to begin implementing community control." Building on years of black struggle for local representation in antipoverty agencies, the BPP promised that they would "force" Model Cities to use the $4.9 million budget "to begin serving us, the poor of Oakland." By placing John Seale, Ruth Jones, Mariah Hilliard, Steve McCutchen, Millicent Nelson, and Samuel Castle on the WOPC, the Black Panther Party made an impressive showing by winning six out of the eighteen available seats.[52]

Even more important than representation in the Bay Area poverty agencies was the Party's ability to reach out to the public through its own media. In July 1972, the *Black Panther* started publishing a multipart series entitled "Oakland—The Base of Operation." The title had a double meaning that referred both to the Party's decision to focus all of its resources on the city of its birth and to Oakland's status as a major disembarkation port for the Vietnam War. The *Black Panther* explained, "Sitting on the northern coast of America's most militarized, industrialized, most technologically developed state, California, Oakland operates as a base for much of America's dirty work, with relatively little attention."[53]

With the destructive effect of urban renewal on West Oakland as its starting point, the newspaper's weekly reports provided a running critique of the city government's institutional racism and its failure to use tax dollars to serve black residents and other low-income groups. From the summer of 1972 through the April 17 primary, the *Black Panther* described in detail how the Knowland regime had systematically destroyed the world the older migrants had known. The building of the Grove Shafter Freeway, Acorn housing, and the Oak Center project decimated West Oakland by destroying the thriving black business district of Seventh Street and reducing its population by over 25 percent. Similarly, the city's schools squandered black residents' hard-earned wages by failing to educate their children and routinely expelling them for minor offenses. With its colorful style that portrayed the problems of race and political economy in accessible terms, the newspaper mobilized potential voters by giving voice to the migrant community's repository of anger and disappointment from the past thirty years.[54]

In addition to using their newspaper to attack the status quo, the Party ran a remarkable street-level campaign. A virtual army of college students, Party members, and community volunteers blanketed the city with campaign leaflets, door hangers, and posters. The resettlement of the Panthers' most talented organizers from all over the country made this massive grassroots effort possible. In order to transform Oakland into the Party's national "base of operation," the BPP closed many of its local chapters and transferred this infrastructure to the East Bay. The leadership initiated this process during its turn to survival programs in 1969; however, the internal migration of Party members to the Bay Area reached its height during the electoral campaign. Three of the Party's most gifted activists, Audrea Jones (Boston), Joan Kelley (Los Angeles), and Herman Smith (Philadelphia) were part of this group, and their talent and experience shaped the campaign strategy in crucial ways.[55] Several other Party members, who later ran for office in their home cities, traveled back and forth to the Bay Area to work on the Oakland campaign, including Larry Little (Winston-Salem) and future congressman Bobby Rush (Illinois).[56]

Like much of the grassroots leadership from outside the Bay Area, Herman Smith first came to the Bay Area to participate in the national headquarters' Ideological Institute. Shortly after Newton's release from jail in August 1970, the BPP initiated this more structured form of political education to bring local branches into line with the Central Committee. Prior to relocating to the East Bay, Smith served as an officer for the Philadelphia chapter and helped to administer its free breakfast for children program. Smith later explained how he and fellow activists came to work in Oakland: "At that point, myself and several other branch captains across the country were sort of all summoned out to California . . . to begin this movement. They told me to pack up enough things for about two weeks. It would be two weeks of training, and then you would return," Smith remembered. "I think I went out there and stayed almost five years. Came back one time to officially close the chapter back here [in Philadelphia]."[57]

Intensive study marked the true beginning of the Panthers' electoral campaign. "It was clear to me that we were really going to lay out something very serious, and we would really approach Oakland, because the first thing that we did in the political education classes was to study the city," remembered Smith. "Many of us were new to Oakland. . . . We had to learn about what Oakland was, how its government operated, who was the key leadership. . . . We studied the budget of Oakland . . . the census tracts and . . . the population breakdowns."[58] Through research, discussion, and debate, young Party members identified the city's long-standing barriers to black political power and their points of vulnerability. The city manager form of government represented one of the most daunting obstacles. To reduce the power of political machines following a corruption scandal, Oakland adopted a new city charter in 1930 to insulate large segments of decision making from elected officials, thereby vastly reducing the mayor's actual powers of governance. The charter also limited districts to nominating rather than electing city council members. At-large elections were prohibitively expensive to run and diluted the vote of minority constituencies. Activist Paul Cobb summed it up well: "You have to be rich, white, and Republican in the city council."[59] Ultimately, these institutional barriers ensured a self-reproducing municipal government that could largely ignore the shifting political and social vicissitudes of the city. In response, the Black Panther Party crafted a strategy that spoke not only to the painful grievances of Oakland's migrant community but also to the "veil of secrecy" and privilege that enveloped much of Oakland's official political culture.[60]

The Panthers' antidote to apathy and exclusion was to once again take to the streets. Although Herman Smith, like most of the campaign staff, was only a few years past high school, the Panther leadership appointed him as the campaign manager. Not long after arriving in the Bay Area, he immediately distinguished himself by setting up an office in East Oakland and recruiting local people to work with the Party. Drawing on the Panthers' 10/10/10 organizing model first pioneered by SNCC, Smith modified this formula for Oakland's diffuse "suburban" neighborhoods. The built environment of the East Bay flatlands was a stark contrast to the dense "row house community" of Philadelphia. Many black people owned homes or rented "private houses," and the problems of poverty and unemployment were not as immediately apparent as in the urban centers of East Coast cities.[61] In order to mobilize the spread-out neighborhoods that encompassed radically different social and geographic terrain, the BPP broke Oakland into eight sections and set up an office in each one. In an attempt to recreate a ward-based system, Panther staff partitioned each section into forty-five subsections composed of smaller neighborhood units. A Party directive explained, "We must first organize the block, then the neighborhood, gradually expanding to the city." Historian Robert Self noted the effectiveness of the Panthers' grassroots campaign, stating, "It was a creative response to the city's lack of a true political apparatus in the neighborhoods, and by all accounts it worked extremely well."[62]

With the same attention to public culture that inspired the Afro-American Association's street speaking and the BPP's earliest police patrols, Brown and Seale took their campaign to the people. Initially, Panthers drove through neighborhoods in a motorcade with ten or twelve cars. They would park, get out, and knock on every door, always leaving behind rows of "doorhangers" and other campaign material. Bobby Seale made short, impromptu speeches from a bullhorn. He and his entourage would then get back into their cars, ride four or five blocks, and do the same thing again. As the campaign progressed, they increasingly made their presences felt not only in the heavily black neighborhoods of East, West, and North Oakland but in the downtown area itself. The captive audience of city bus riders also became one of their favorite targets. "We would get on all the major lines . . . and get on those buses," remembered Herman Smith. "And we would stage it out so that we had a film crew, or a camera guy at one corner. And then the next guy would get on with some flyers. And then I would get on and say, 'The next Mayor of the City, Bobby Seale, will say hello to you sooner or later.' . . . And then the next person you see was Bobby saying, 'Good morning, everyone. My name is Bobby Seale, and I'm running for Mayor of Oakland. And here's why.'"[63]

In addition to using public space and transportation, the BPP also reached into people's homes. Frequently, community supporters hosted "sit-downs." One person would invite ten people they knew, and Bobby Seale or Elaine Brown would come, have coffee, and sit down to talk with them about the issues and distribute campaign literature. They, in turn, encouraged all attendees to invite ten other people and sponsor gatherings in their homes. In this way, the BPP built an extensive network of supporters with little money or use of commercial media. Herman Smith summed it up well: "The elected

Bobby Seale's campaign car during the BPP mayoral campaign in Oakland, 1973. Photograph by Stephen Shames, courtesy of Stephen Shames / Polaris Images.

officials were stunned. The media was stunned, because . . . we created our own media backdrop by literature distribution. So if the TV was going into 1,000 households, then we'll go into 1,000 households with this flyer."[64]

Class Conflict

Much of Bobby Seale's appeal to Oakland's emerging black majority stemmed from his public persona. As a southern migrant, who proudly embraced vernacular speech and dress, he was deeply recognizable to his constituents. His willingness to use familiar idiom not only on the campaign trail but in larger venues valorized the cultural distinctiveness of the East Bay's southern newcomers. Thus he turned what had been cause for ridicule into a source of pride. In fact, Seale's "down home" tendencies, combined with his background as a stand-up comic, even created tensions with his running mate, Elaine Brown, who was frequently embarrassed by his "antics." She later described her persistent irritation over his "refusal to use standard English, even though his speeches were always strong and spirited [and] delivered with passion. . . . His verbal clowning had always elicited foot-stomping responses from black people. . . . [He] would announce each day that we had 'shooken' the hands of so many potential voters and 'tooken' so many press photographs," remembered Elaine. "For one whole year, however, I would

Bobby Seale campaigns on a city bus, Oakland, 1973. Photograph by Stephen Shames, courtesy of Stephen Shames / Polaris Images.

have to stand by Bobby's side listening to him say over and over that when he became mayor, the big 'cooperations' were in for 'boo-coo' trouble."[65]

While Seale received widespread support from Oakland's southern black working class and poor, the East Bay's black middle class was another matter altogether. With the exception of Congressman Ronald Dellums, who had been a staunch ally of the Party since his earliest days in Berkeley politics, most of the Bay Area's black political establishment supported Seale's Democratic opponent, Otho Green. There were many reasons for this, ranging from personal histories and ideological differences to the exigencies of Democratic Party coalitions. But all these issues paled in comparison to the Panthers' biggest obstacle: their ongoing conflict with black businesses over funding their survival programs. From the beginning, demanding support was risky. The Party's antagonistic class rhetoric and its singular focus on the urban poor provided little benefit to the small group of affluent blacks who had abandoned the impoverished flatlands for the East Bay hills.[66] And although the Panthers always had strong allies, a segment of black middle-class opinion remained decidedly unsympathetic to the Party. The East Bay's black newspapers, the *Oakland Post* and *California Voice*, carried little or no mention of the Party's community programs between 1969 and 1973, and black publisher Tom Berkeley emerged as one of the Party's harshest critics.[67]

Private donations and sales revenues from newspapers and books proved insufficient to support the BPP's growing infrastructure of schools, food programs, and health clinics. By October 1971, the Panthers sponsored a total of fourteen separate programs in the Bay Area that included not only the popular food and clothing giveaways but also legal aid and busing to California's state prisons. Indeed, some speculated that the escalating costs of running the BPP's ad hoc welfare system motivated the Panthers' mainstream turn to Bay Area poverty programs and municipal office.[68] When other funding sources proved scarce, the leadership of the BPP approached black businesses for help. The *Black Panther* declared, "The Breakfast for School Children Program, and all other Survival Programs, must be supported and donated to by Black Businesses, every week, for greater unity in the Black community."[69] Initially, local merchants agreed to make intermittent donations on their own terms. They refused, however, to do this on a regular basis.

In the summer of 1969, the BPP organized a boycott against the Safeway store in West Oakland, because the supermarket chain refused to donate $100 worth of food weekly. "This avaricious (greedy exploiting) businessman . . . must come forth and donate to the Breakfast for School Children Program. We the people shop there, making the businessman fat and rich," declared the *Black Panther*. "The Breakfast [program] will survive because people's power will make the avaricious businessman donate or we will run the exploiters out of business." While many supported the Panther boycott, ultimately the BPP leadership found it too difficult to leverage influence with white-owned supermarket chains, and instead, they turned to local black businesses within familiar neighborhoods.[70]

Two years later, the Panthers became involved in a protracted struggle with Bill Boyette, the president of the Cal-State Package Store and Tavern Owners Association.[71] In early July 1971, the BPP worked with the black business leader to boycott liquor distributors for failing to hire African Americans. Within a few weeks, their alliance soured when Boyette reneged on his agreement to contribute regularly to the BPP's survival programs. As the conflict deepened, Boyette went on the offensive—questioning the value of free busing to prisons and other Panther services to Oakland's poor. In leaflets distributed to customers, Boyette complained that if "a man had come into his store and robbed it, he did not see why he should support a program which would send that man's family to visit him." In response, the BPP organized a boycott of its own. On July 31, Party members set up picket lines on the sidewalks outside of "Bill's Liquor" stores; protestors carried signs declaring "Support Those Who Serve the People." Many ordinary citizens expressed strong support for the Party's actions.[72]

Boyette retaliated by charging the BPP with harassment and extortion, and soon the explosive conflict triggered a new round of negative publicity.[73] In the East Bay, local black newspapers immediately jumped to the businessman's defense. In an interview published in the *Oakland Post*, Berkeley civil rights activist Frances Albrier lamented, "Some of the Panther programs are excellent and good but this is wrong, quite wrong."[74] Similarly, an ever-vigilant Roy Wilkins warned, "The five-year-old party now uses the powerful, but two-edged weapon, the economic boycott. The money clubbed out of small businesses each month will be but a drop in the bucket."[75] Black entrepreneurs banded together in the Ad Hoc Committee for Promotion of Black Business to oppose the Panthers' boycott, and local businessman Jim Hadnot complained, "I feel that the Panther breakfast program and the other survival programs are worthy of our support. But it is unfair to demand that we continue to pay in cash money for an indefinite time until all Black problems are solved."[76] Just as Boyette teetered on the brink of financial ruin and the BPP became mired in the latest salvo of the black class war, Congressman Ronald Dellums negotiated a truce. His administrative assistant, Donald Hopkins, who was a founding member of the Afro-American Association, played a crucial role in the talks. On January 15, 1972, the two sides agreed to establish the "United Black Fund of the Bay Area" as a community trust in which donations would be solicited regularly from black businesses and used to support the Panther survival programs and other grassroots initiatives. Father Earl Neil of St. Augustine's Church agreed to administer the fund, and it appeared as if the conflict had been resolved. In the coming election year, however, residual tensions flared up between the BPP and Oakland's black establishment. In a striking gesture, the publisher of the *Oakland Post*, Tom Berkeley, announced his support for the incumbent Republican mayor over Bobby Seale in the general election.[77]

To repair the damage to a much-needed political constituency, the BPP cultivated a kinder, gentler Black radicalism. Much as the survival programs necessitated a revision of the Party's view of the black church, so it was with the municipal campaign, black business, and the "bourgeoisie." In an attempt to reconcile with the significant portion of Oakland's African American elite that the Party had alienated, the BPP consciously changed not only its image, but its rhetoric. Downplaying the confrontational aspects of Party ideology, the BPP retracted its long-standing criticisms of the black "bourgie." In 1973, Bobby Seale declared, "I have criticized the black middle class in the past but not in a negative sense. It was the income of the black middle class grass-roots people criticized—the clothing, the residences. But now we realize that its not your income; its your relationship to the slave master. Are you with the slave master or are you against him? It's not your residence, it's your politics."[78] Similarly, Elaine Brown stressed that the turn to electoral politics itself legitimated the Party in the eyes of the black middle class and expanded its base. "Working black people were joining our constituent lumpen, as the so-called black middle class became more than a smattering of Survival Program supporters. Our electoral campaign was one all of them could openly support. It was that support we sought."[79]

Rainbow Coalition

In addition to reaching out to the black middle class, the BPP election campaign cultivated a broad range of alliances with feminist organizations, gays and lesbians, and Latinos. Charles Garry summed up the Party's transformation when he told the press, "By participating in the system, the Panthers will be much more of a threat than they ever were when they were carrying guns. They will become more acceptable to all groups."[80] The BPP had a long-standing relationship with both feminist and gay and lesbian activists in the Bay Area. In August 1970, immediately following his release from prison, Huey Newton issued a statement addressed to "The Women's Liberation and Gay Liberation Movements." He embraced both constituents as "oppressed groups" and declared that the Panthers and their supporters "should try to unite with them in a revolutionary fashion."[81] Furthermore, during the Revolutionary People's Constitutional Convention in Philadelphia, "women[,] . . . lesbians [and] male homosexuals" were identified as core "social groups" needed to organize for a new society. During the municipal election in 1973, the Party sought to translate this political affinity into a concrete electoral strategy. To mobilize feminist and gay voters, the candidates advocated new legislation to ban police brutality and discrimination based on gender and sexual orientation in jobs and housing, adoption and child custody, taxation, and inheritance laws. Similarly, the BPP reached out to Mexican Americans and other Latinos by advocating the use of bilingual ballots for local elections. Cesar Chavez of the United Farm Workers endorsed Brown and Seale and co-sponsored rallies and fundraisers.[82]

While the Panthers forged ties with a variety of emerging constituencies, their most consistent sources of support came from student groups.

The newly established networks of black student unions provided the Black Panther Party with a ready-made campaign infrastructure. Urban campuses supplied large numbers of skilled volunteers along with regular speaking venues and other facilities. Another important factor was the relative youth of the Panther candidates. Bobby Seale, thirty-six, and Elaine Brown, twenty-nine, successfully targeted young voters and received collegiate support throughout the East Bay, including a substantial amount from progressive whites.[83] Whether by design or coincidence, Brown attended Mills College while running for city councilwoman.[84] Several other Party members followed suit, and in the early seventies, over two dozen Panthers enrolled in Bay Area colleges and universities under the Educational Opportunity Program. They used their status as students to set up campus groups to assist in the BPP's election campaign. In May 1972, the same month the Party declared its candidacy, organizing cadres on campuses throughout the Bay Area came together to form the Black Student Alliance (BSA). Although youth from U.C. Berkeley, California State Hayward, and Mills College participated, the local community colleges of Laney, Merritt, and Grove Street provided the core membership.[85] In December, individual BSAs at junior colleges issued endorsements for the Seale and Brown candidacies. According to the Berkeley community newspaper, *Grassroots*, some 500 captains and a large portion of the 3,000 workers needed to cover Oakland's voter precincts came from these schools.[86] Their involvement was not limited to traditional voter registration and canvassing. Black student unions sponsored many different functions, including dance parties with colorful titles like "Got Ants in My Pants and I Need to 'Vote' Dance" or "'Itch and Scratch' at the Black House." Without this enthusiastic pool of young campaign workers, the Panther's strategy of comprehensive community outreach would have been impossible.[87]

Election of 1973: Victory in Defeat

Through the tireless work of students, community members, and the rank and file, the BPP built a resilient political machine that had a charming and anachronistic appeal that evoked the thriving political culture of nineteenth-century party politics. Organizers sponsored dances and barbecues, rallies and marches, shoe giveaways and free meals, while the candidates stumped college campuses, churches, streets, public parks, city buses, and labor unions, reaching out to anyone who would have them. Their young army of campaign workers distributed mountains of leaflets and flyers with

Laney Black Student Union   presents:

GOT ANTS IN MY PANTS
AND I NEED TO "VOTE" DANCE

FRIDAY, MARCH 30th
4402 E. 14th ST.
10pm - UNTIL
DONATION - 50¢
REFRESHMENTS

Get out and vote April 17th for
Bobby Seale and Elaine Brown

"Ants in My Pants Dance," electoral campaign flyer, Oakland, 1973. Community colleges throughout the Bay Area played a crucial role in the Panthers' voter outreach and registration drives. Black student unions, such as the one at Laney Institute, often threw dances and parties to raise funds, as well as providing scores of volunteers to the Panther organization. Courtesy of the Dr. Huey P. Newton Foundation and of Stanford University's Department of Special Collections.

such catching sayings as "Want a Job, Vote for Bob!" or "Keep *Un*-Employment Down, Vote for Elaine Brown!" Sponsoring events like the "People's Barbecue" served the dual purpose of raising money and furthering voter registration.[88]

Brown and Seale hoped to attract a broader constituency by championing antisecrecy policies and redistributive economic reforms. Their "fourteen point" campaign plank consisted of two different parts. In keeping with the symmetry of the Ten and Twenty Point Programs, the first part laid out seven far-reaching strategies for generating revenue while the second half proposed new programs that would improve city services. Vastly increasing the city payroll and levying a 1 percent tax on owners of stocks and bonds would bolster city revenues by $5–10 million.[89] Transfers of income property or corporate property would be subjected to a capital-gains tax of 5 to 10 percent.[90] In addition, more aggressive investment strategies would replace monies lost from Nixon's cuts to cities. Plank four in the Seale-Brown plan harkened back to their earlier struggle to end police brutality and cease law enforcement's occupation of African American communities. Oakland's police and firemen would face a mandatory residency requirement. Part of the rationale was economic. The municipal salaries for these two groups totaled over $8 million, which benefited the suburban communities where they resided almost exclusively.[91]

Seale's proposal to transform city government's relationship to the Port of Oakland represented the greatest threat to the established order. The port complex spanned nineteen miles of Oakland's bay front and brought income of over $80 million per year, while contributing less than a tenth to city revenues. Seale proposed that the port should contribute four times that amount to the city budget and be required to hire more minority workers.[92] Other campaign promises included ending property-tax exemptions for "public utilities" like the Southern Pacific Railroad, raising lease payments on the Oakland Coliseum to offset the multimillion dollar operating budget, and increasing the hotel-motel tax by one half. These funds would be used to offer low-income families loans and grants to rehabilitate private homes and rental property, support mobile health clinics, expand child-care services, provide seniors with round-the-clock transportation, prevent crime through improved street lighting, and increase funding to schools. In essence, capturing city government would allow the Party to vastly extend its network of survival programs.[93]

Mayor John Reading's campaign slogan, "Don't Let Oakland Become Another Berkeley," summed up his exploitive relation to Bobby Seale's campaign. As the election approached, the candidate that Republicans had initially welcomed to divide the Democratic vote was increasingly seen as their prime opponent.[94] Neither Ortho Green, a former member of the Afro-American Association and owner of a management consulting firm, or John Sutter, current city councilman, was making a strong showing in the polls. By April 5, Bobby Seale was the Democratic frontrunner. Like future black mayor Tom Bradley's opponent, Sam Yorty, in Los Angeles, the Republican incumbent framed the election as a takeover by radicals. His campaign literature on the eve of the election warned, "The Radicals Will Vote, Will You?"[95]

The election returns on April 17 revealed mixed results for the BPP. Elaine Brown had not been able to take Joshua Rose's city council seat and had only received 38,845 votes, roughly one-third of the total. Bobby Seale received 21,314 votes compared to John Reading's 55,342 in his bid for mayor. The large turnout of Democratic voters prevented Reading from capturing a plurality, and he and Seale were forced into a run-off election on May 15.[96] Given the limited financial resources of the BPP, and the long-standing exclusion of African Americans from local politics, the Panthers' showing was remarkable. In a celebratory editorial, the *Sun Reporter* proclaimed, "Bobby's accomplishment is probably greater than their knowing. He and the Panthers have achieved a high level mark in which is destined to be an exciting history of social mobility of Blacks in not only Oakland but also California and throughout the nation."[97]

In the runoff, Reading received 77,476 votes compared to Seale's 43,719.[98] While the Panthers did not win, the most striking outcome of the elections was the unprecedented rate of voter participation. The BPP's innovative campaign vitalized local politics and mobilized whole new sectors of the electorate. Over 70 percent of registered voters had turned out for the runoff, thereby demonstrating that African American and working-class electoral apathy was not inevitable.[99] The concrete ideological alternative provided by the Black Panther Party combined with its aggressive community outreach showed that the "flatlands" could be a major source of political power. Bobby Seale conceded defeat by claiming a "symbolic" victory and declared he would run again in 1977. The Black Panther Party's success in winning nearly 40 percent of the vote in the municipal elections indicated that a new era had come in Oakland politics. The *Oakland Tribune*'s stranglehold had finally been broken, and when moderate African American candidate Lionel Wilson launched a successful bid for mayor four years later, he turned to Elaine Brown and other Party members to get out the vote. In this late phase of the Party's history, from 1974 to 1977, the BPP became a powerful broker in Democratic Party politics. Brown launched a second city council campaign in 1975 and forged close ties with California's liberal elite. While Panther candidates never attained elected office higher than antipoverty councils and the Oakland school board, by the late seventies Elaine Brown had become a political insider.[100]

Coda: The Road to Power and Its Price

The Black Panther Party's remarkable showing in the Oakland elections was undeniable; however, the BPP's shift toward the center had come at a price. In a process that started with the programmatic turn to "survival pending revolution," the BPP leadership increasingly viewed its community programs as a means to achieve political power. While Seale's mayoral campaign enabled the Party to gain greater legitimacy, in the long run, narrowing its focus to electoral politics undermined the Party's ties with its black student and working-class base. This was nowhere more evident than in the two major confrontations that took place on the Merritt campus in the years leading up to the Panther election campaigns.[101]

Despite the BPP's reliance on the community college—or perhaps because of it—conflict emerged with faculty and students who defied the Panther leadership. As was clear with the Party's confrontation with black businesses, the BPP's aggressive pursuit of its own interests sometimes strained relationships with its allies. While the Panthers emerged directly from Merritt's thriving black political culture and the struggle to establish Black Studies, as the organization grew and matured, the leadership separated itself from its roots and viewed the campus as a resource to be mined for political goals. After 1966 when Huey and Bobby left the campus for the "street," Merritt students continued to fight for a Black Studies department and increased representation at the highest levels of the college administration. When campus protest and a takeover of the faculty senate by the Black Student Union (BSU) forced Merritt president Edward H. Rutherford to step down in 1968, campus activists celebrated their victory. Bowing to pressure, the Peralta Community College District appointed California's first black college president, Norvel Smith.[102]

For a brief moment, the urban campus affectionately known as "Grove Street" became a resplendent example of community control. Through student organizing and protest, migrant youth had succeeded in remaking the college in their image with a full-fledged Black Studies department and substantial numbers of African American faculty and administrators.[103] However, within a few short years, the district started the process of relocating Merritt from the flats of northwest Oakland to a distant, and not easily accessible, hill campus. President Norvel Smith's coordination of the move made the prospect particularly bitter; after all, the constant protest of students and residents from the surrounding community made his appointment possible. This painful truth was not lost on student activists, and the destruction of their beloved "Grove Street" became a symbol of black powerlessness in the face of elite betrayal. Merritt's Black Student Union, headed up by rank-and-file Panthers and their sympathizers, responded immediately by organizing to prevent the closing of the campus. Within months, the struggle to preserve Merritt propelled this group into a vortex that pitted them against local authorities, on the one hand, and the BPP hierarchy, on the other. Their experience revealed much about the Party in this latter phase of its history, and how top down and authoritarian leadership remained its greatest flaw.[104]

In late December 1969, Andre Russell moved to the Bay Area to join the

Black Panther Party. The college senior had recently dropped out of Hiram Scott in Nebraska and decided to make the sojourn to Oakland after reading press accounts of Fred Hampton's brutal murder in Chicago. When Russell arrived in Oakland, a rectification campaign prevented the Party from accepting new recruits, and so he initially joined the National Committee to Combat Fascism.[105] Several months later, the Central Committee assigned Russell and the former branch captain of the Boston chapter, Douglas Miranda, to organize the students on the Merritt campus. Along with Jim Evans and Joe Stephens, these young activists enrolled full time and participated in Merritt's Black Student Union, while continuing to work for the Party selling newspapers and carrying out other rank-and-file duties. By all accounts, they excelled at bridging the Party's agenda to student concerns. Jim Evans became president of the Merritt BSU in 1970, and under his leadership the organization established a free breakfast program at Forty-second and Grove. They also founded a campus newspaper called the *Lumpen*, which publicized the campaign to save Merritt. The November 17 issue denounced the planned move as an attempt "to separate an increasingly powerful student movement at Merritt and the community that nurtures it. They either had to move Merritt or build a moat around it." Linking Merritt's destruction to the larger struggles of Bay Area black communities, the article stressed, "The principle of community control of education is every bit as important as community control of police. It's about people controlling the institutions that affect their lives."[106]

As the battle escalated, the BSU staged regular protests that brought together a broad coalition that included the Asian alliance, the Revolutionary Studies Group, and the Chicano Student Union. Together they organized a campus referendum on the move and documented overwhelming opposition among the student body and faculty.[107] Berkeley city councilmen Anthony Camejo and D'Army Bailey met with the BSU and expressed support. Although Merritt's administration engaged in negotiations with the activists, in the midst of these talks, they hired a company to begin dismantling campus facilities, thereby turning the move to the hills into a fait accompli. In response, the BSU and other campus groups staged a large demonstration that shut down not only the Merritt campus but the rest of the Peralta system. With over 100 students participating, the BSU's large-scale civil disobedience proved effective, because it capitalized on the yearlong battle to keep the school in the flatlands. A thick perimeter of picket lines ringed the small campus, creating a buffer for the students who occupied the library and administrative buildings. Andre Russell remembered,

At that point we called a student strike . . . and this was the last one at Merritt. There had been these before. But with this student strike, it was a little different because for one, when we took over the school, we took over the library. And the library was the computer center for the whole Peralta school district. So by taking over one school, we shut down the functioning of the whole. . . . Then as the issue became more popularized and the news got out of it, then everybody started saying, "Well they've got a school already built. The students are striking to *not* go there. And there's this big problem with Peralta . . . because they had built a school that nobody wanted to go to."[108]

At night a skeleton crew remained barricaded inside the library. On March 17, 1971, the police forcibly cleared the school in the early morning hours. Although most of the BSU's leadership eluded law enforcement, in the subsequent weeks and months, authorities arrested Jim Evans and Doug Miranda and charged them with assault.[109]

Paradoxically, the BSU's defense of the "Grovestreet" campus set them on a collision course not only with police but also with Huey Newton and the Panther leadership. In spring 1971, the founder of the BPP had been recently freed from jail and was anxious to assert his status as peacemaker and powerbroker in Oakland politics. During the police siege of Merritt, Huey Newton insisted that the Merritt BSU immediately stand down and threatened the young Panthers with retaliation if they disobeyed his orders. The BSU leaders listened in disbelief. After all, when authorities released Newton, "Grove Street" had been one of his first destinations.[110] The Party's roots were there, and for many years the campus provided the political and intellectual moorings of the "Free Huey" campaign and the East Bay's larger Black Power movement. Nevertheless, as Russell, Miranda, and a half dozen other rank-and-file Panthers manned the picket lines and fought to keep Merritt in the community, Newton sided with Norvel Smith and the Peralta school district. When the BSU activists ignored his orders, the Party immediately purged them. Threats of retaliation forced Russell and Stephens underground, while others resigned from the BPP deeply disillusioned. Oakland police prosecuted Douglas Miranda on assault charges for removing Merritt's president from his office. Miranda's expulsion meant that he—like other Panther dissidents—faced his legal troubles in isolation. This internal conflict became another example of how the Party's "democratic centralism" functioned at the expense of its rank and file and network of young supporters. When its top-down structure was combined with a new focus on electoral politics in the city of Oakland, the leadership endorsed people and institutions they had previously opposed at the expense of their student and black working-class base.[111]

The following year, the Panthers' attack on Fritz Pointer further illustrated how "old Merritt" fell victim to the Party's strong-arm tactics and authoritarian tendencies. Almost a year after the forcible removal of the main campus, the school on the edge of northwest Oakland had been reduced to a shadow of its former self. The Peralta District successfully relocated the main campus to the hills but bowed to community pressure by maintaining Grove Street in North Oakland. While its doors remained open, the school was severely defunded and steadily hemorrhaging both faculty and students. The facilities now consisted largely of metal portables that students had decorated with colorful murals and stark monochromatic stencils reminiscent of Panther artist Emory Douglas. Despite its limited resources, the old Merritt retained some of its previous vitality and continued to be a launching pad for radical activism, including the Panthers' fast approaching mayoral campaign. Although its days were clearly numbered, Grove Street retained hints of its former glory. In this atmosphere, Fritz Pointer taught a class on the "literature of dissent" during the spring semester of 1972. Bobby Seale and his brother John, Steve McCutchen, and some other Panthers enrolled. Conflict emerged when a student in the class made a critical remark about the BPP, and the instructor defended his right to voice an opinion.[112]

Fritz Pointer had a long history with the Party's leadership. Huey Newton's family occasionally attended his father's church, and the two had come of age together in West Oakland. As teenagers, they met once again in the halls of the CYA, and Pointer later joined the Oakland Panthers' rival faction, the Black Panther Party of Northern California. By 1972, Pointer identified as a "Panafricanist," and, like Stokely Carmichael before him, he chafed at the Panthers' ties with white radicals. In class, he repeatedly questioned the BPP's "nationalist credentials" and argued that the organization was not revolutionary at all, alternately referring to its members as "violent integrationists" or "integrationists in flight jackets."[113]

The Panthers in the class became incensed and decided to teach him a lesson. Before the next period, they brought additional members, including strongmen Flores Forbes and Elbert Howard, and waited behind the door for the instructor. The cadre ambushed Pointer, pummeling and kicking him in the center of the classroom, ultimately leaving him unconscious and badly bruised. The event so traumatized the young professor that he left Oakland permanently and relocated to a suburb an hour from the city.

Afterward, the *Oakland Tribune* and other local newspapers reported the incident, which threatened to mushroom into a local scandal that could capsize the Party's upcoming mayoral campaign. However, in the days after, Pointer publicly denied the incident and sponsored a joint press conference with Huey Newton to demonstrate his solidarity with the Party. Whether or not this was done out of fear or a desire for a united black front remains unclear. Nevertheless, the beating sent a clear message to other Black radicals and members of the community: public criticism of the Party would not be tolerated. Despite their turn to electoral politics and search for greater mainstream support, strong-arm tactics remained a mainstay of the Party's political culture and were used to silence dissent within and outside their ranks.[114]

Given the transient nature of students, the historical memory of colleges and universities was notoriously short, sometimes little more than a single school year. At institutions like Merritt with associate degree programs, a complete turnover of the student body took place regularly. And so, despite these intense conflicts with Merritt's BSU, the Party continued to work with fresh generations of campus activists. After the expulsion of the campus leadership, few traces remained, and a new group of Party members and students replaced the dissidents. As was evident from the high levels of support for Seale and Brown's candidacies in 1973, much of this history was lost or forgotten. Nevertheless, the confrontation with the BSU and Fritz Pointer symbolized how the Black Panther Party had changed and evolved since its founding in 1966. By the early seventies, the Panthers had come full circle from their roots in the Bay Area black student movement and now focused their attention almost exclusively on gaining power in local government. As the BPP transformed itself from a youth group into a municipal player, students represented raw material for its larger ambitions. The betrayal of Merritt served as an unfortunate reminder that absorption into the political status quo could undermine the integrity of social movements in ways as subtle and damaging as direct state repression. While the Panthers' origins lay firmly in the early push for Black Studies at Merritt, by this last phase of its history, the Party stood outside the ongoing student movement in favor of using campus organizations to achieve Party aims. The Panther leadership viewed the college and other Bay Area black student unions as political resources to be mined for their day-to-day organizational needs, survival programs, and as a ready-made political infrastructure for their electoral forays from 1971 to 1975.[115]

While the increasing authoritarianism of the Party and its movement toward the mainstream would seem to be opposites, in the Party's final years these contradictory impulses grew stronger, taking on an almost schizophrenic quality. Under the leadership of Elaine Brown, the Party gained greater legitimacy in mainstream political circles. When she staged a second bid for city council in 1975, her campaign brought together a powerful coalition that laid the groundwork for the election of Lionel Wilson. Brown worked closely with Congressman Ronald Dellums and his aide Barbara Lee and drew on the strong political networks of the West Oakland Planning Committee. Bobby Seale's former opponent Otho Green cochaired her campaign, while Dellums's aide Brenda Meador served as campaign manager. Historian Robert Self praised Brown's exceptional ability to assemble a broad interracial coalition that attracted large numbers of women: "More than any other individual, she constructed a bridge between the Panthers and the liberal community, black and white." Her growing cachet within northern California's political elite was evident in her selection as a delegate to the 1976 Democratic National Convention.[116]

Despite politicians' embrace of Brown and the newly reformed face of the Black Panther Party, as was evident in the Party's conflict with the Merritt BSU, the mainstreaming of the BPP contained a paradox. In precisely the period that Brown helped the BPP make deeper inroads into the Bay Area's liberal political establishment, she *also* presided over a centralization of power inside the Party that made its internal workings profoundly undemocratic. While Brown courted liberals outside, within the BPP she and Huey Newton implemented a brutal top-down hierarchical organization that led to many abuses of the rank and file. She later explained her rationale, stating, "The party was, I believed, the true vanguard of a new revolution in America. The reactionary forces against change were so strong, we had to use a closed fist to break through. The individual rights that were forfeited were inconsequential to the task before us." Newton and Brown's heavy-handed leadership style was combined with a growing involvement in illegal activities that exposed black residents and business owners to strong-arm tactics and arbitrary violence. While an authoritarian strain had always existed in the Party, this tendency became much worse after the municipal campaign and led directly to the Party's dissolution in 1980.[117]

Originally born and raised in Philadelphia, Elaine Brown entered the Black Panther Party through the Los Angeles chapter in 1967. Prior to joining the Party formally, she worked with the Black Student Union at UCLA and helped organize the Southern California College Black Student Alliance. Brown served first as deputy minister of the Los Angeles chapter in 1969 following the murder of Bunchy Carter and rose quickly through the Party's ranks to become minister of information after Cleaver's expulsion from the Party in 1971. A talented singer, Brown recorded two albums while working with the Party, *Seize the Time* (1969) and *Until We're Free* (1973).[118] The outstanding development of the Party newspaper and the Intercommunal Youth Institute under her hand showcased her exceptional abilities as an administrator and editor. While clearly talented, Brown had a complex and antagonistic relationship with many members of the Party. Although she and Bobby Seale ran for office together, they remained distant and mistrustful of one another, and Brown often questioned Seale's competence. In many respects, Elaine Brown never entirely reconciled herself to Oakland's southern migrant political culture. She chafed at Bobby's use of the vernacular and often saw the black communities of the East Bay as a backwater.[119]

As Elaine Brown consolidated her personal power in the larger world of California Democratic Party politics, inside the BPP she aligned herself with Huey Newton's inner circle. In the early seventies, several organizational changes left the BPP vulnerable to abuses. The first was Newton's cultivation of a brutal group of bodyguards, euphemistically known inside the Party as the "goon squad." This group of men acted as enforcers for the leadership, and their use of violence and strong-arm tactics increasingly focused on squelching dissent within the BPP. Historian Robyn Spencer described how Newton set himself apart from the rest of the Party and even acted at their expense: "Newton and his clique lived radically different lives than most Party members, untouched by Party rules or regulations. Whereas rank and file Panthers sacrificed individual rights to the collective structure, sought to implement criticism and self-criticism, and faced financial hardship, Newton and his clique practiced self-indulgence and excess, and met criticism with the threat of retribution."[120]

In a related development, Newton and the Central Committee established a "Board of Corrections" to discipline members who violated Party rules or misrepresented BPP ideology.[121] Physical punishment of members was common and employed the notorious use of bullwhips; the racial symbolism of this brutal practice spoke to the continuing and undigested role of southern violence in Party culture.[122] Bobby Seale suspended the board's operations during the election, but with his departure from the Party in 1974, Brown and Newton reinstituted corporal punishment with renewed vigor. Equally ominous, the constant search for regular funding led them into the twilight world of Oakland's after-hours clubs and vice industry. In her controversial 1992 autobiography *A Taste of Power*, Brown confessed, "Bobby Seale and I remained, however, examples of a new, more moderate Panther. It was generally believed that we had no knowledge of or relationship to the kicked-in doors of the shot-up facilities of reluctant after-hours-club contributors. Indeed our electoral campaign had created illusion that Bobby and I were separate from rough activity, it was as though there were two arms of the party; the militant dark side and the more moderate, reformist side. I felt we had achieved a state of perfection. Bobby was confused."[123]

In contrast to Seale, who was kept isolated from these developments and largely excluded from the lurid intrigues of Newton's penthouse apartment, Brown participated in all dimensions of Panther activity and relished their varied assertions of power. Huey Newton's writings from this period reflect his inner turmoil and growing immersion in drugs and vice. He insisted, for example, that the rank-and-file members study *The Godfather* in political education classes, while he published an extended essay on Mario Van Peebles's proto-blaxploitation epic, *Sweet Sweetback's Baadasssss Song*. The film's hero, Sweetback, a young man born and raised in a brothel, is forced to revert to the basest means of survival—pimping and performing sex for money. Newton interpreted the film as a profound allegory of black community struggles in a time of increasing economic obsolescence. While the Party leadership had always embraced lumpen iconography, in this later period of decline and corruption, Newton and his supporters used it as a self-justifying rationale.[124]

The Party's most principled and dedicated activists found these developments alarming. The volatile behavior of Newton's faction, combined with their deepening ties to Oakland's underworld, prompted Raymond "Masai" Hewitt to leave the organization. Originally from Los Angeles, Hewitt was adored by many as the organization's heart and soul. Despite his status as Central Committee member and minister of information, he spent almost all of his time working and socializing with the rank and file. In contrast to some of Newton's oldest associates, Hewitt never used his status in the Party for personal gain and chose instead the spare accommodations and collective living of the "panther pads." In January 1973, Hewitt assailed the growing corruption inside the Party, and the devolution of the BPP's democratic centralism into one man rule. Newton responded by stripping him of his position on the Party's Central Committee and demoting him to rank-and-file status. Within weeks, Hewitt left the Party.[125] In July 1974, Bobby

Seale followed, after Newton expelled him during a drug-induced rage. He left amid rumors that Huey Newton was attempting to take over the narcotics trade in Oakland.[126] Mass purges accompanied these departures, and between April and January 1974, the Party purged twenty-eight members from its ranks. Huey Newton subsequently appointed Elaine Brown—his closest ally and former lover—to replace Bobby Seale as chairman of the Party.[127]

Ultimately, the leadership's misdeeds ultimately depleted the Party's most valuable resource—its rank and file. From its height of 5,000 members during the "Free Huey" movement, in the aftermath of the Oakland election the BPP's total membership dwindled to fewer than 200 people and was rapidly declining from there.[128] Roni Hagopian described the forbearance of this group who endured the mounting abuses of the internal hierarchy because they believed in the idea of the Black Panther Party: "We just accepted the Party's leadership, some of us dogmatically. I know for myself, I didn't question. I was very young and full of dreams." Panther Terry Cotton went a step further, arguing that in the final years of the Party the rank and file persisted despite the Party hierarchy. "[We] were the foundation of that Party. They couldn't exist without us. We were the ones who kept the party up. The disruption, the corruption, that came from the leadership."[129]

While Elaine Brown and Huey Newton hastened the Party's decline, many of the problems that erupted under their watch could be traced back to the earlier period of state repression. The cult of personality that the Cleavers and Bobby Seale constructed in order to mobilize the "Free Huey" campaign became a dangerous liability upon his release from jail in August 1970. Cut off from the developments that transformed the Party from a small local group into an expansive national organization, Huey Newton became unmoored. Friends who had known him for many years felt that his years in prison had profoundly changed him.[130] Although the diminutive boy with a beautiful face had always pretended to be "street"—partially to counter the unwanted attention inspired by his honey-colored skin, perpetual baby face, and tenor voice—the disjuncture between the projection and the reality was not only obvious but a source of quiet amusement for those who loved him. Childhood friend and former Panther Shirley Hewitt remembered how Newton convinced her to join the Party by walking her back and forth to Merritt, talking for hours about his hopes and dreams for black people. His sensitivity and commitment impressed her as much as his ideas.[131] Like many, playwright Donald Freed observed Newton's vulnerability and earnestness. "He had a nervous system that the world impinged on with very

Bobby Seale speaks at the Black Community Survival Conference, Oakland, March 30, 1972.
Photograph by Stephen Shames, courtesy of Stephen Shames / Polaris Images.

great intensity. Some people are cursed with that and blessed with that. You
know, artists and others have that kind of extra sensitivity."[132]

But the person that emerged in 1970 from months and even years in solitary confinement was markedly different and foreign to many of his old
friends and comrades. He was distant and mistrustful, and in a perverse
twist of fate, many likened his changed persona to his nemesis Eldridge
Cleaver. As Huey Newton spiraled out of control, his mythic status inside
the BPP meant that no one, including his BPP cofounder Bobby Seale, had
the institutional authority to check his behavior. The top-down, democratic
centralist structure meant that the Party was indistinguishable from the
man. Huey Newton fled into exile in 1974 after being charged with the assault and murder of a local prostitute. Upon returning to the United States,
he was immediately tried, and the negative publicity combined with his attempt to wrest control of the BPP leadership led to the Black Panther Party's
dissolution in 1980. Elaine Brown resigned in disgust. Through the hard
work of Ericka Huggins, Jonina Abron, and other female party members,
the Oakland Community School remained open until 1982, making it the
longest-running survival program in the Black Panther Party's history.[133]

Disentangling the Black Panther Party's true motivations was always difficult. Three levels of information existed within the organization: "mass line," "party line," and "the truth." In practice, this system translated into different messages for different audiences. At the most superficial, "mass line," the BPP prepared set talking points for the press and public. At the next level were the internal workings of the Party with the official word of the Central Committee issued to the rank and file of the organization. Finally, individuals made their own assessments of what was really happening. In the case of the election, the "mass line" announced that Bobby Seale and Elaine Brown were staging an unprecedented campaign and would assume their new positions as mayor of Oakland and city councilwoman in spring 1973. "We are not just sideline players for the first time, not just voters," declared Bobby Seale. "But we could actually be the candidates, and win one."[134] In hindsight, both the "party line" and "the truth" were less clear. According to Bobby Seale and his campaign manager, the real focus of the mayoral bid was "voter education." In 1978, Seale's second autobiography, *A Lonely Rage*, revealed, "Actually becoming Mayor was not the major point—most of the time we told each other that the point was an educational campaign, getting the issues stated and known. We hoped that this would put pressure on who- ever ended up mayor to do things right, to do what the people needed and wanted and felt."[135]

In the final phase of its history, the Panthers faced a new set of obstacles. By 1973, the threat of obsolescence was even more daunting than the state re- pression that dominated the BPP's first years. Through resilience and adapta- tion, the BPP outlasted many of the social movements that helped produce it. Yet, as an expression of youth activism, its lifespan was also limited. As Party members grew older, it was inevitable that the organization would change and evolve. Whether occasioned by the death of J. Edgar Hoover or the Par- ty's electoral turn, the Panthers witnessed a decline in police violence after 1972. With the Watergate scandal, the Pennsylvania break-in that prompted the Church Committee, and the failure of "Vietnamization," the country's mood had shifted. In contrast to 1968, five long years later the Black Panther Party was no longer seen as a national threat.[136] For an organization that had relied so much on the dialectic between repression and resistance, in its later years the BPP fought to remain relevant to the Bay Area black community from which it sprang. Black electoral politics and voter registration pro- vided this medium. Elaine Brown situated the Panthers' electoral campaign in African Americans' centuries-long battle for voting rights that spanned the wages of southern segregation and the gerrymandering of northern cit- ies: "Blacks, in the South particularly, were murdered attempting to vote.

They were legally kept from voting by grandfather clauses and literacy tests. Blacks who actually made it to the ballot box found their voices decimated by the might of white political machines. Thus, blacks had come to the realization that black votes, like black lives, were always extinguished by majority rule of the whites. Voting for the Black Panthers was another matter."[137]

While many think of the Oakland Panthers' activities in the 1970s as a repudiation of their earlier revolutionary stance toward the police and other sources of African American oppression, their electoral campaign revealed an intriguing continuity. At their very core, the Panthers were mass mobilizers who chose various forms of community organizing and political spectacle to engage public attention. Whether it was large-scale screenings for sickle cell anemia or patrolling the police, the object was the same: to demonstrate the Black Panther Party's relevance to the everyday lives of African Americans. Their allure stemmed from their ability to dramatize aspects of African Americans' lived experience that legal remedies had not or could not address. The issues that the BPP attempted to confront—police brutality and the carceral state, wealth distribution and reparation, inferior infrastructure and global inequality, and the winner-take-all, two party system's erasure of black political interests—remain among the most intractable racial issues in the post–civil rights era.

Ultimately, the Black Panther Party reached its high-water mark in Oakland politics during its electoral campaign. The leadership registered over 35,000 new voters who had not previously participated in the political process.[138] A month before Oakland's mayoral election in April 1973, the *San Francisco Examiner* noted a distinct change in the Panthers' base. "To many the most surprising thing of all was the presence at these meetings of a large number of middle-aged and elderly blacks, the hard-working family types, usually approachable to politicians via some Sunday morning speech from a Baptist or Methodist pulpit. It appeared the Panthers had pulled a coup."[139] The Party's broad support represented the culmination of years of community service programs and of rebuilding ties to the local African American population. In the years to come, this substantial increase in black electoral participation combined with the organizing precedent for mobilizing young, poor, and working-class residents helped enable the election of Oakland's first black mayor, Lionel Wilson, in 1977. Although the Bobby Seale and Elaine Brown campaigns did not result in victory, both won over 35 percent of the total vote and mobilized much broader sections of the local black community. The types of organizational strategies employed by the Party paralleled successful black mayoral campaigns in other cities. In the same year that Seale ran, Los Angeles elected former policeman Tom Bradley. And the most immediate precedent occurred in Newark several years before, when Amiri Baraka's cultural nationalist NewArk movement helped propel Mayor Kenneth Gibson to victory.[140] The Seale and Brown campaigns placed the Black Panther Party squarely within the larger push toward political incorporation of African Americans in urban centers. Bobby Seale summarized their accomplishment: "Our objective was to create a grass-root based political organization which would attract the less fortunate and teach them to use the electoral process as one avenue of gaining community control of the institutions that affect their lives, especially on the local level. Most people don't realize it but Huey and I had a certain respect for Dr. King."[141]

The transformation of the Black Panther Party from a grassroots youth movement into a more traditional urban political party in the seventies, while remarkable, entailed loss as well as gain. By narrowing their political horizon to a municipal campaign in Oakland, the leadership disappointed many among its hard-working rank and file. Already decimated by the splits that alienated two of the Party's most vital chapters in New York and Los Angeles, by 1972 the BPP's membership was sharply declining. While this dynamic was strongest outside Oakland, even segments of the Bay Area rank and file remained sympathetic to the dissidents.[142] The increasing tension within the Party was not an isolated phenomenon; it spilled out into the larger solidarity networks the Panthers had established since the "Free Huey" campaign. Once again, black students on urban campuses played a crucial role. But by the early seventies, the leadership had grown older and increasingly viewed black student unions simply as tools for increasing its power in local politics. Through subordinating the aspirations of students and faculty to the larger goals of the Panther leadership, the BPP broke with its organic roots in the black student movement at Merritt College. After exhausting its most important resource—the rank and file drawn from both the campus and the street—the Party would never again accomplish projects on the scale it had between 1968 and 1973.

CONCLUSION

While many observers of the 1960s have defined Black Power as a radical break from the past, the story of Bay Area Black radicalism points in a different direction.[1] Youth activists from the Afro-American Association to the Black Panther Party did not emerge in a vacuum. Composed largely of recent arrivals from the South, they drew on southern migrant communities' long-standing investments in the black church, educational access, and the tradition of creating parallel institutions.[2] The impulses and commitments of this younger group of migrants who formed the Bay Area's Black Power generation reflected enduring values of self-help, black pride, and armed self-defense. Strikingly, many of their families hailed from central Louisiana where Garveyite and indigenous armed defense movements were strong.[3] However, rather than simply transplanting or reproducing their southern past, Bay Area youth created organizations that were truly diasporic. They reflected not only the culture migrants carried with them but also responded to the particulars of California cities at midcentury. What emerged was a complex blending of two seemingly irreconcilable worlds—the heavily rural, deeply religious, and tight-knit fabric of southern black communities transplanted to the Cold War expanse of defense industries and "multiversities," urban deindustrialization, and an increasingly punitive carceral state. The Black Panther Party exemplified the contradictions that resulted from this historic, and improbable, collision.

In many respects, the Black Panther Party is an enigma that confounds the discrete categories of ideology and region that historians have superimposed on an unruly past. Often embraced as the quintessential northern urban Black Power movement, the Oakland Panthers consisted largely of southern rural migrants. Although the BPP declared itself the vanguard of the lumpen proletariat, community college students founded the organization after participating in a U.C. Berkeley study group. While the Panthers were avowedly secular and even anti-Christian in their early rhetoric, black churches furnished the infrastructure for their survival programs in Oakland and other cities after 1968. Finally, the Black Panther Party advocated armed revolution, but a primary school for children was its longest-running institution and, arguably, its most important legacy. Rather than attempting to reconcile these apparent contradictions, *Living for the City* explores the remarkable breadth of the Party's activism and the many conflicting elements that produced it. Perhaps more than anything else, the BPP was a testament to the ingenuity of black newcomers to postwar California. In less than a generation, southern migrants who relocated to the Bay Area to work in federal defense industries gave birth to one of the nation's most compelling anti-imperialist movements for social and economic justice. Strikingly, the BPP articulated a critique of American government that drew its power and poetry from the cadences of the southern vernacular.

The melancholy of Stevie Wonder's "Living for the City" comes not only from the displacement of migration but the recognition that the longed for escape from Jim Crow had not materialized. Southern migrants to the Bay Area found themselves in a world quite different from those they left behind with possibilities unimaginable in the segregated South. Nevertheless, the newcomers who settled in the East Bay faced stark divisions of race and class that thwarted their dreams for social mobility and property ownership in California's "industrial garden."[4] Employment and housing discrimination limited economic opportunities for migrant families, who found themselves isolated and impoverished within the expanding metropolitan economy. For younger migrants and the first generation born in California, schools and juvenile authorities represented separate poles of opportunity and danger as they came under the increasing scrutiny of state agencies. Conflict with the police represented only one aspect of a larger confrontation with a disciplinary state apparatus that viewed black migrants as the catalyst for white flight and social decay. As former Panther Kilu Niyasha explained, "California didn't want us," and it found myriad ways to contain and criminalize black newcomers.[5] Of all the barriers facing migrant communities, the carceral state proved to be the most destructive and enduring, and it exacted a far-reaching toll not only on the political organizations that emerged in the 1960s but on the black population as a whole.

From its inception to its demise, the tentacles of the carceral state shaped every aspect of the Black Panther Party's history. Many of the young men who joined the Party from both the campus and the street had spent time in the halls of the California Youth Authority. Even more important, adult activists' repeated incarcerations profoundly influenced both their personal

Huey P. Newton in the
Alameda County Courthouse
jail in Oakland, September 26,
1968. Photograph by Ruth-
Marion Baruch. © Pirkle Jones
Foundation, estate of Ruth-
Marion Baruch.

development and that of the Party. While the negative impact of imprisonment on the Party was obvious in its drain of financial resources and the
constant crisis of leadership, incarceration also had dramatic effects on the
people themselves. Huey Newton's steady deterioration after 1971 cannot be
separated from the relentless state violence that he and the Party had been
subjected to for over a decade. His description of solitary confinement as the
"soul breaker" spoke to the psychic ordeal of prison that left marks deeper
than physical scars.[6]

In order to fully excavate this history, we can draw insights from other
time periods and subject fields. In her groundbreaking essay, "Soul Murder
and Slavery," historian Nell Irvin Painter has argued for the development
of interdisciplinary methods to compile a "fully loaded cost accounting" of
the far-reaching effects of slavery's regime of violence. Similar wide-ranging inquiry is needed into the cumulative impact of the criminalization of
African Americans, not only in the Jim Crow South, but also throughout
the southern diaspora of the postwar North and West.[7] The Black Panther
Party provides a window onto this process, because in each period of its

evolution the BPP both challenged and reflected the brutality of the carceral state.[8] California imprisoned three of the Black Panther Party's major leaders as juveniles—Eldridge Cleaver, Huey Newton, and George Jackson—and their experience in the state's youth authorities, and later in the adult penal system, left a profound impression on their political thought. While much recent scholarship has focused on the failures of growth liberalism to provide jobs and redistribute New Deal opportunity, no discussion of black radicalization can ignore the disciplinary regimes of local, state, and federal government. This history encompasses both the political economy of police and penal institutions *and* their reach into the interior lives of black and working-class people and communities.[9]

The devastating consequences of incarceration and state repression is the most painful lesson to be learned from the history of the Black Panther Party, but there are many others. Contained within the very idea of the BPP was the city of migrants that witnessed its birth and demise. The Black Panther Party was inseparable from the particulars of the East Bay from the onset of World War II to the election of the first black mayor in 1977. In this short time span, the black population rose from 8,462 to over 157,484 in less than four decades.[10] The optimism that drew hundreds of thousands of black southerners to California in search not only of jobs but high-quality public education was a driving force in the Party's development. With its roots in the university-based Afro-American Association and the Merritt College student movement, the Oakland Panther Party and other local Black Power/Black Studies groups spoke to the hunger for a "relevant" education that could explain southern migrants' past and present. Merritt student Brenda Byes, whose mother migrated from Darnell, Louisiana, explained how attending community college changed her life: "I've always been distant and so the education was . . . very relevant, it was very close to me, it was very dear. And it's been something that I've been longing for. I've been whitewashed and now I get to be involved with my blackness, my African-ness and that happened at Merritt College when I was there. I was brought up being told I was African and that I have a lot to be proud of in my heritage . . . by my mother. She brought me up that way, but it was never reinforced *anywhere*, until I got to Merritt."[11]

Although Brenda never formally joined the BPP or other groups in the Bay Area, many of her friends did and her recollection of education's transformative power was common.[12] Behind these very personal memories lay a larger truth. Under the 1960 Master Plan, the State of California promised to provide every resident with a high school diploma access to higher education. This attempt at social engineering had far-reaching effects, many of which the state could neither predict nor control. As historian Jeremi Suri has demonstrated, Cold War liberalism simultaneously expanded access to higher education and scrambled to contain the social upheaval that democratization engendered. Black migrants from the south recognized this opportunity and began using urban campuses for political organizing. African American youth like Huey Newton and Bobby Seale—who faced hostile primary and secondary schools and rebelled against the disciplinary culture of the East Bay's segregated education system—thrived in local community and state colleges. They developed a variety of tactics to lobby for Black Studies programs to inject their own political and cultural agenda into the curriculum. In a surprising twist of fate, black urban populations exercised greater influence on local colleges and universities than on municipal school districts in the East Bay.

From the Panthers' first advocacy of police patrols through their electoral campaign of 1973, urban campuses provided Black radicals with a base of operation. In earlier writings on the BPP, scholars and journalists' singular focus on men with guns obscured the most enduring strain of BPP activism: political education. The organization started with a study group and ended with a primary school for children that outlived the BPP by over a year.[13] In addition to their engagement with the carceral state, the BPP and its fellow Black Power groups were integral to African Americans' national struggle for community control in education. Like the Afro-American Association's use of street speaking before them, the Panthers defined education in new and unconventional ways that reached beyond formal schooling. Rather than simply criticizing government failure, in its later years, the Party developed independent media and educational institutions. Publishing an internationally distributed newspaper, creating innovative political and vernacular art, sponsoring community programs, and even staging election campaigns all served to inform the public of radical alternatives to the two-party system. Arguably, this spirit of invention remains the Black Panther Party's most important legacy. The BPP's efforts demonstrated the ability of black youths— many of them recent migrants from the South—to serve the needs of their communities. From its inception, Panther founder Huey Newton argued that the Panthers would educate by example. By dramatizing the relatively small and underfunded Party's ability to help the urban poor through massive survival conferences, health clinics, and a variety of welfare services, the BPP simultaneously raised consciousness through action *and* exposed government neglect. Finally, and perhaps most compellingly, the BPP linked these efforts to global struggles for nationalism and self-determination. By invoking Samora Machel in Mozambique, Fidel Castro in Cuba, and Ho Chi Minh in Vietnam, they tied their own vision of "intercommunalism" to anti-colonial liberation movements across the globe.

While *Living for the City* focuses on the genesis of postwar Black radicalism in the East Bay, this book also calls for a broader range of inquiry in future studies of the Panthers and other Black Power groups. As scholar and former Party member Kit Kim Holder has argued, the BPP "developed in order to address specific needs of a particular community."[14] As a result, the Party's early recruitment efforts flowed through Huey Newton and Bobby Seale's personal networks in the Afro-American Association and Merritt College, the surrounding high schools, neighbors and family, and the facilities of the California Youth Authority. In this sense the Party was initially composed of a small group of young people who knew each other well. By contrast, for black communities beyond the Oakland Panthers' immediate orbit, much of their exposure to the BPP was filtered through print, electronic media, and word of mouth.[15] After the press blitz following the March on Sacramento and the "Free Huey" campaign, individual branches sprang up around the country. While the Central Committee tried to control this process, they had neither the resources nor manpower to truly centralize the organization. By 1970, the result was a great deal of diversity among the fifty-plus national affiliates, which often had tenuous links with the national headquarters in the East Bay.[16]

As the Black Panther Party grew rapidly with little coordination from the top, each chapter reflected the particular conditions of regional black communities, leading historian James Campbell to describe the national BPP as "a congeries of local movements."[17] The Portland, Oregon, Panthers, for example, consisted almost exclusively of students from the state university, while Charlotte O'Neal of Kansas City remembered her local chapter as "downright lumpen."[18] Scholars and former activists have just begun excavating and preserving this rich history of local struggle.[19] *Living for the City* seeks to contribute to this work of historical recovery and to expand the parameters of inquiry. Too often, writing about the Black Panther Party has relied on facile assumptions about the group as gang, an extension of "street culture," or the theatrics of an urban underclass.[20] This narrow focus led many to ignore the broader culture of struggle that the Panthers emerged out of in the Bay Area, and more specifically, their base in a black student movement at California's public colleges and universities. In addition to focusing on northern civil rights organizations, labor/fair-employment campaigns, and antipoverty programs as the prehistory to the BPP and other radical groups of the late sixties, much greater research is needed into how battles over public education in primary, secondary, and especially higher education laid the foundations for the Black Power movement.

Ultimately, the Black Panther Party's national history represented a complex dialectic between particular local conditions and the mass media. The sensational portrayal of the Panthers left its own ambiguous imprint on the organization's growth, while simultaneously making it possible. Media spectacle often obscured the Party's abiding commitment to community service and political education. In the 1980s, Kathleen Cleaver described the Janus-faced effect of Panther fame: "More systematically than any other black group, the Black Panther Party exploited television's power to publicize its aims and programs—and used television to counter attempts by authorities to discredit and dismantle the organization. But the Panthers paid a heavy price: as membership boomed, many recruits fatally confused their flamboyant tactics with the substance of their goals. Unfortunately, the fundamental concerns of the Black Panther movement would never be transmitted by television."[21] Seductive images of masculine power sometimes prompted young people to pick up guns with tragic consequences. In conservative cities, like Los Angeles and Chicago, with long and brutal histories of police violence, the mere posture of armed resistance proved deadly.[22]

The problems experienced by the Black Panther Party were certainly not unique. Social movements and grassroots efforts that mobilize large numbers of people often flounder when they expand beyond their point of origin into broader geographic or social terrain. As organizations evolve over time, they often reach out to populations quite different from the place where they originated. Without question, this was the case with the BPP. From their beginnings at Merritt College and the North Oakland poverty center to their demise in the early eighties, the Panthers were integral to the political culture of the East Bay's migrant community. Indeed, the democratic failure to open up the Party hierarchy to its rank and file and the "bridge leadership" that developed across the country proved the BPP's tragic flaw. Despite their self-conception as revolutionary vanguard, the Panthers' true power derived not from their ability to lead the East Bay's southern diaspora but to reflect its deepest and most abiding faith in education, self-reliance, and collective struggle.

NOTES

ABBREVIATIONS

In addition to the abbreviations used in the text, the following source abbreviations are used in the notes.

BPN   *Black Panther Newspaper*
HPN   Dr. Huey P. Newton Foundation Papers, Department of Special Collections, Stanford University, Palo Alto, Calif.

INTRODUCTION

1. Johnson, *Second Gold Rush*; Lemke-Santangelo, *Abiding Courage*; Hayes, *Power Structure and Urban Policy*; Lotchin, *Fortress California*; Self, *American Babylon*; Moore, *To Place Our Deeds*; Newton, *Revolutionary Suicide*; Seale, *Lonely Rage*; Hall, "Long Civil Rights Movement."

2. Hobsbawm, *Primitive Rebels*; Gabaccia, *Militants and Migrants*.

3. The traditional view of the modern black freedom struggle narrates a peaceful nonviolent southern movement that achieved the legislative victories of the Civil and Voting Rights Acts, only to be disrupted by the unexpected outbreak of violence in Watts. In this account, the Los Angeles rebellions inaugurated a new era of struggle focusing on Black Power and armed struggle in the urban North. This narrative of progression, however, creates a false dichotomy. In the mid-twentieth century, large numbers of southern migrants transformed the face of urban California. As in the case of the Black Panther Party, they carried southern life ways and political culture with them, and this profoundly influenced the new forms of politics that emerged on the West Coast. Although *Living for the City* is the first book to examine the significance of the southern migration to the West Coast Black Power movement, my study draws on a recent body of literature that has challenged the singular focus on liberal, nonviolent civil disobedience in the southern black freedom struggle. For new scholarship documenting the history of the northern civil rights movement, see Sugrue, *Sweet Land of Liberty*; Gregory, *Southern Diaspora*; Countryman, *Up South*; Hall, "Long Civil Rights Movement"; Biondi, *To Stand and Fight*; Woodard and Theoharis, *Freedom North*; and Self, *American Babylon*. For recent scholarship documenting traditions of armed self-defense, Black nationalism, and Black radicalism indigenous to southern black communities, see Crosby "Calculus of Change"; Jeffries, *Bloody Lowndes*; Gilmore, *Defying Dixie*; Rolinson, *Grassroots Garveyism*; Wendt, *Spirit and the Shotgun*; Dirk, "Between Threat and Reality"; Strain, *Pure Fire*; Hill, *Deacons for Defense*; Hahn, *Nation Under Our Feet*; Umoja, "1964"; Umoja, "'We Will Shoot Back'"; Tyson, *Radio Free Dixie*; Umoja, "Ballot and the Bullet"; and Umoja, "Eye for an Eye."

4. Williams, "Exploring Babylon." For works that have incorporated multiple vectors of black identity in postwar African American history and urban studies, see Green, *Battling the Plantation Mentality*; Orleck, *Storming Caesar's Palace*; Williams, *Politics of Public Housing*.

5. For contrasting accounts of East Bay Black radicalism focusing on urban space and institutional arrangements, see Self, *American Babylon* and Rhomberg, *No There There*.

6. More research is needed into how generational tensions engendered by southern migration contributed to postwar Black radicalism in cities throughout the North and West. For a more general discussion of youth culture, see Austin and Willard, *Generations of Youth*; May, *Golden State, Golden Youth*.

7. For a framework for understanding internal divisions within northern black communities based on migration status, see Marilynn Johnson's discussion of a newcomer/old-timer schism in the wartime East Bay in *Second Gold Rush*, 4–5, 49, 231–32.

8. Kelley, *Freedom Dreams*.

9. The exception to this generalization is the Afro-American Association, which in its earliest years was composed largely of black students from outside the Bay Area. However, after the AAA started holding street rallies and doing outreach to local black population centers in the East Bay, the association developed a large following of southern-born black youth. See chapters 3 and 4.

10. Newton, *Revolutionary Suicide*, 14.

11. While a series of new studies have recently been published documenting the local and regional diversity of the national BPP chapters, much more research is needed into the international dimensions of Party activism, including the Panthers' transnational solidarity networks and shared influences from contemporaneous Third World nationalist, Maoist, and anticolonial movements. For current scholarship, see Frazier, "Revolution is Not a Dinner Party"; Ho and Mullen, *Afro Asia*; "New Black Power Studies: National, International, and Transnational Perspectives"; Johnson, *Revolutionaries to Race Leaders*; Joseph, *Waiting 'til the Midnight Hour*; Maeda, "Black Panthers, Red Guards, and Chinamen"; Ogbar, *Black Power*; Singh, *Black Is a Country*; Elbaum, *Revolution in the Air*; Meriwether, *Proudly We Can Be Africans*; Kelley, *Freedom Dreams*; Prashad, *Everybody Was Kung-Fu Fighting*; Cleaver, *Liberation, Imagination and the Black Panther Party*; Wilkins, "In the Belly of the Beast"; Kelley and Esch, "Black Like Mao"; Smith, *International History of the Black Panther Party*; Williams, "American Exported Black Nationalism"; Etzioni-Halevy, "Protest Politics in the Israeli Democracy"; Cohen and Shemesh, "Origin and Development of the Israeli Black Panther Movement."

12. By 1970, California had the single largest number of southern-born African Americans in the nation. This was also true for the white population. Gregory, "Southern Diaspora and the Urban Dispossessed"; Murch, "When the Panther Travels"; Gilmore, *Defying Dixie*; Rolinson, *Grassroots Garveyism*; and Woodruff, *American Congo*. For a more extensive discussion of the connections between the SNCC-sponsored Lowndes County Freedom Organization and Oakland's Black Panther Party for Self Defense, see chapter 5.

13. For an overview of current literature on the Black Panther Party, see Williams, "Black Panther Party" and Garrow, "Picking Up the Books." For more traditional organizational histories focusing exclusively on the BPP, see Alkebulan, *Survival Pending Revolution*; Austin, *Up Against the Wall*; Spencer, "Repression Breeds Resistance"; Pearson, *Shadow of the Panther*; Holder, "History of the Black Panther Party"; and Hopkins, "Deradicalization of the Black Panther Party." For thematic histories and local studies of the BPP, see Williams and Lazerow, *Liberated Territories* and *In Search of the Black Panther Party*; Jeffries, *Comrades*; Rhodes, *Framing*

the Black Panthers; Williams, *Black Politics/White Power*; and Jones and Jeffries, *Black Panther Party Revisited*.

14. For a national history of the Black Power movement focusing on New York, see Joseph, *Waiting 'til the Midnight Hour*.

15. Farred, *What's My Name*; Moses, "Segregation Nostalgia and Black Authenticity"; Joseph, *Waiting 'til the Midnight Hour*.

16. Hilliard and Lewis, *This Side of Glory*, 26–27.

17. The Master Plan for Higher Education had remarkably different effects on the various tiers of California's tripartite system. In response to financial pressures created by rapid population growth and the postwar baby boom, planners used a combination of local bond issues and state funding to expand the number of junior colleges. In order to transform these local schools into full service "community colleges," the Master Plan provided for increased funding, faculty hiring, and a new pool of resources that black student activists hoped to divert into Black Studies programs. However, for California's state university system, the Master Plan strained its already limited resources. Several historians of the San Francisco State strike have argued, in fact, that it dramatically decreased black student enrollments on California state campuses. Ferreira, "All Power to the People"; Douglass, *California Idea*; Brenner, "Public Higher Education"; Brossman and Roberts, *California Community Colleges*; Barlow and Shapiro, *End to Silence*; Allen, *Black Awakening*; Wollenberg and Allen interviews.

18. Smith and Horton, "Completion Levels," 530.

19. For a contrary view, see Rojas, *From Black Power to Black Studies*.

20. Ronald Dellums attended Oakland City College nearly a decade before the other participants in the Afro-American Association. However, although he did not formally join the AAA, he retained strong ties to its founders and to the Merritt campus. Bazille, Hopkins, and Harris interviews; Dellums and Halterman, *Lying Down with the Lions*, 24–25.

21. Although this study focuses on the Bay Area's early Black Studies and black student movements, in the national arena historically black colleges and universities played a crucial role in this process. Students at Central State in Ohio formed the Revolutionary Action Movement (RAM) in 1962, and the group quickly expanded to cities throughout the country, serving as the national framework for Black radicalism until the ascendance of the Panthers in 1967. As is evident from RAM, the link between black student activism and Black Power was not unique to California, but the state's expansive and well-funded system of higher education provided abundant resources. Peck, "Educate to Liberate"; Muhammad Ahmad interview; Ahmad, *We Will Return in the Whirlwind*.

22. One of the most striking aspects of early study groups was the diversity of opinion and ideology. Personalities and political tendencies that later erupted in conflict shared common ground in this early movement of consciousness. Future cultural and revolutionary nationalists, Black radicals, and reformers shared a common ancestry in campus activism. In some cases, individuals passed fluidly through several different tendencies in their political lifetimes. Bazille, Williams, al-Mansour, Hopkins, and Allen interviews; Newton, *Revolutionary Suicide*; Seale, *Seize the Time*.

23. Williams interview.

24. For a contrary view, see Self, *American Babylon*; Rhomberg, *No There There*.

25. The most notable example besides Oakland's Black Panther Party is the US organization established in Los Angeles in 1965. Its founder, Maulana Karenga, was an early participant in the Afro-American Association. Brown, *Fighting for Us*, 26–28, 83. While several recent works

explore the links between Black Power and Black Studies, they do not examine in any depth the contributions of the U.C. Berkeley–based Afro-American Association, Merritt College, or other East Bay community colleges. Instead, the San Francisco State strike is identified as the beginning of the modern Black Studies movement. See, for example, Rojas, *From Black Power to Black Studies*, and Joseph, "Black Studies, Student Activism, and the Black Power Movement," 251–77.

26. Dellums and California Fair Employment Practices Commission, *Report on Oakland Schools*, 1–32.

27. Huey Newton interview in Hampton and Fayer, *Voices of Freedom*, 351.

28. A wealth of primary and secondary source material reveals that traditions of armed self-defense were strong in many southern rural communities. Similarly, life histories of migrant activists in California demonstrate how they carried these ideas with them as they settled in West Coast cities. For armed self-defense, the southern diaspora, and direct influence on the Panthers, see Seale interview by Williams, and Pratt, *Last Man Standing*. For the broader secondary literature on armed self-defense in the South, see the sources cited in n. 3 above. For primary sources on armed self-defense in the South, see Carson, *Eyes on the Prize: Civil Rights Reader*; Sellers, *River of No Return*; Sugarman, *Stranger at the Gates*; Farmer, *Lay Bare the Heart*; Salter, *Jackson, Mississippi*; Rural Organizing and Cultural Center, *Minds Stayed on Freedom*; Raines, *My Soul Is Rested*; and Forman, *Making of Black Revolutionaries*.

29. For an overview of popular literature on the Panthers, see Williams, "Black Panther Party"; Jeffries, *Huey Newton*; Kaskins, *Power to the People*; Pearson, *Shadow of the Panther*; Newton, *Bitter Grain*; Van Peebles, Taylor, and Lewis, *Panther*.

30. For contrasting interpretations, periodizations, and analyses of postwar Black radicalism and Black Power, see Fergus, *Liberalism, Black Power*; Rojas, *From Black Power*; Rooks, *White Money*; Rhomberg, *No There There*; and Self, *American Babylon*.

31. Jeffries, *Lowndes County*; Gilmore, *Defying Dixie*; Rolinson, *Grassroots Garveyism*; Green, *Battling the Urban Plantation*; Orleck, *Storming Caesar's Palace*; Crosby, *Little Taste of Freedom*; Gregory, *Southern Diaspora*; De Jong, *Different Day*; Hahn, *Nation Under Our Feet*.

32. Lemann, *Promised Land*; Moynihan, *Negro Family*.

CHAPTER 1

1. Haywood, *Negro Liberation*, 11.

2. Broussard, "In Search of the Promised Land," 192.

3. Marable, *New Black Vote*, 3.

4. Lemann, *Promised Land*, 6. For more scholarship on postwar black migration, see Johnson and Campbell, *Black Migration in America*; Kirby, *Rural Worlds Lost*; Trotter, *Great Migration in Historical Perspective*; Jones, *Dispossessed*; Johnson, *Second Gold Rush*; Broussard, *Black San Francisco*; Moore, *To Place Our Deeds*; Lemke-Santangelo, *Abiding Courage*; Tolney, *Bottom Rung*; Gregory, *Southern Diaspora*; Rodriguez, *Repositioning North American Migration History*; Flamming, *Bound for Freedom*; Orleck, *Storming Caesar's Palace*; and Green, *Battling the Plantation Mentality*.

5. Johnson, *Negro War Worker*, 1.

6. Broussard, "In Search of the Promised Land," 190; Lane, *Ships for Victory*; Lotchin, *Fortress California*.

7. Bureau of the Census, *Population by Age, Race, and Sex in Oakland, Calif., by Census Tracts: 1940*; Bureau of the Census, *1950 Population Census*.

8. Department of Labor, "Data from Census Bureau Estimates for Oakland, California," 4.

9. Gregory, "Southern Diaspora," 75.

10. Lotchin, *Fortress California*.

11. Johnson, *Second Gold Rush*, 31–33.

12. Self, *American Babylon*, 170.

13. Wright, *Old South, New South*, 245.

14. Ibid., 245–49.

15. Ibid., 228, 230.

16. Kirby, *Black Americans in the Roosevelt Era*, 141; Sullivan, *Days of Hope*.

17. De Jong, *Different Day*.

18. Wright, *Old South, New South*, 232.

19. Ibid., 237.

20. Ibid., 241.

21. De Jong, *Different Day*, 118–22.

22. Wright, *Old South, New South*, 245.

23. Ibid., 242–47.

24. Broussard, "In Search of the Promised Land," 192; Johnson, *Negro War Worker*; Lemke-Santangelo, *Abiding Courage*.

25. Johnson, *Negro War Worker*, 5; Wollenberg, *Marinship at War*.

26. Johnson, *Negro War Worker*, 6.

27. Lemke-Santangelo, *Abiding Courage*, 23–24.

28. Ibid., 24; Fairclough, *Race and Democracy*.

29. Moore, *To Place Our Deeds*, 51. There is some disagreement about the rural/urban composition of Bay Area migrants during World War II and after. Following Carole Marks and Clyde Kiser, Shirley Ann Moore argued that the majority of war migrants entered Richmond shipyards as part of "ever widening circles of secondary migration moving from the rural South, to southern urban areas, to northern and midwestern cities." If this is true, while war migrants' origins lay in the rural South, the majority worked in southern cities before relocating West. Comparable migration studies of Oakland, San Francisco, and other Bay Area communities have not yet been done. For the texture of larger historiographical issues, see Gregory, "Southern Diaspora," 69–70; Kiser, *Sea Island to City*; and Rhomberg, *No There There*, 97–98.

30. Johnson, *Negro War Worker*, 7.

31. Ibid., 18.

32. California Department of Transportation, *West Oakland—A Place to Start From*, 57.

33. Ibid., 65.

34. Ibid., 98.

35. Johnson, *Second Gold Rush*, 14; California Department of Transportation, *West Oakland—A Place to Start From*, 44–45.

36. Brown, "Class Aspects," 83.

37. Hausler, "Blacks in Oakland," 68.

38. Johnson, *The Second Gold Rush*, 16.

39. Brown, "Class Aspects," 82–83.

40. Hausler, "Blacks in Oakland," 68.

41. Self, *American Babylon*, 79–81.

42. Brown, "Class Aspects," 101–2.

43. Hausler, "Blacks in Oakland" 123; Crouchett, Bunch, and Winnacker, *Visions Toward Tomorrow*, 15.

44. Brown, "Class Aspects," 83.

45. De Graaf and Taylor, *Seeking El Dorado*, 24.

46. Hunter, *Housing Discrimination in Oakland, California*, 14.

47. Brown, "Class Aspects," 86.

48. Bachemin interview.

49. Brown, "Class Aspects," 105–6.

50. Self, *American Babylon*, 50.

51. Ibid., 51.

52. Johnson, *Second Gold Rush*, 93.

53. Ibid., 90–95; Bureau of the Census, *1950 Population Census*; Self, *American Babylon*, 131.

54. Rose interview by McGrew.

55. Hill interview by Wilmot, 13.

56. Self, *American Babylon* 68–69.

57. Hausler, "Blacks in Oakland," 117.

58. Hunter, "Housing Discrimination in Oakland, California," 12.

59. Hausler, "Blacks in Oakland," 122.

60. Brown, "Class Aspects"; Watkins interview.

61. Boone interview, 9.

62. Berkeley, "On the Sidewalk," *Oakland Post*, March 12, 1975; Moore, *To Place Our Deeds*, 131.

63. Moore, *To Place Our Deeds*, 137; Starks interview, cited in ibid.

64. Watkins interview, 30.

65. Hildebrand, "West Side Story."

66. Watkins interview, 17.

67. Ibid., 16.

68. Hildebrand, "West Side Story," 3.

69. Ibid.

70. Angelou, *I Know Why the Caged Bird Sings*, 207.

71. Gregory, *Southern Diaspora*, 197–236; Hausler, "Blacks in Oakland"; Best, "South and the City," 314.

72. Pointer interview, 1–2.

73. Ibid., 13.

74. Ibid., 13–14.

75. Moore, *To Place Our Deeds*, 142–43.

76. Gregory, *Southern Diaspora*, 197.

77. Rose interview by McGrew, 5.

78. Watkins interview; Johnson, *Second Gold Rush*, 96.

79. Hildebrand, "West Side Story," 3.

80. Rose interview by McGrew, 7.

81. Himes, *If He Hollers Let Him Go*, 4.

82. Committee of Fair Employment Practices, *Final Report*, 77.

83. Wollenberg, *Marinship at War*, 70.

84. Quoted by Broussard, *Black San Francisco*, 40.

85. Nash, *American West Transformed*, 17; Lotchin, *Fortress California*.

86. Dellums, "International President," 97.

87. Johnson, *Second Gold Rush*, 30.

88. Coletta and Bauer, *United States Navy and Marine Corps Bases*, 686–704.

89. Johnson, *Second Gold Rush*, 32.

90. Here Dellums is referring to the precursor to the Federal Employment Practices Committee. Dellums, "International President," 97.

91. Ibid.

92. Reed, *Seedtime for the Modern Civil Rights Movement*, 269.

93. Dellums, "International President," 98.

94. Johnson, *Negro War Worker*, 19.

95. Dellums, "International President," 98.

96. Johnson, *Second Gold Rush*, 22.

97. Dellums, "International President," 103.

98. Ibid., 104.

99. Harris, "Federal Intervention in Union Discrimination," 339–43.

100. Wollenberg, *Marinship at War*, 71.

101. Ibid.; Harris, *Harder We Run*, 95.

102. Johnson, *Second Gold Rush*, 51.

103. Dellums, "International President," 99.

104. Murch, "Problem of the Occupational Color Line."

105. Scholars have debated the precise causes and timing of the city's deindustrialization. Some point to the immediate impact of the closing down of wartime shipyards, while others stress larger trends such as white flight, corporate relocation, and tax incentives for suburbanization. Walker, "Industry Builds the City"; Hayes, *Power Structure and Urban Policy*; Self, *American Babylon*.

106. Hayes, *Power Structure and Urban Policy*, 49; Self, *American Babylon*, 170.

107. Hayes, *Power Structure and Urban Policy*, 49.

108. Ibid., 48.

109. Ibid., 44.

110. Ibid., 46; Bureau of Labor Statistics, *Monthly Labor Review*, March 1965, 249–55.

111. City of Oakland Police Department, "History 1941–1955," Part 6, 23.

112. Johnson, *Second Gold Rush*, 167–68.

113. Thompson interview, 29; Himes, *If He Hollers Let Him Go*.

114. City of Oakland Police Department, "History 1941–1955," Part 6, 36–40.

115. For a more extended discussion of the police interactions with the African American community, see chapters 2 and 5 in May, "Struggle for Authority."

116. Johnson, *Second Gold Rush*, 167.

117. Street, "Nightstick Justice in Oakland," 15–16.

118. City of Oakland Police Department, "History 1941–1955," Part 6, 14–15; Murch, "Problem of the Occupational Color Line"; Thompson interview.

119. Thompson interview, 34.

120. Salamunovich, "Party and the People," 18.

121. Moore, *To Place Our Deeds*, 121.

122. Hunter, "Housing Discrimination in Oakland," 10; Hinckle, "Metropoly," 32–37.

123. Hunter, "Housing Discrimination in Oakland," 12.

124. May, "Struggle for Authority"; Self, *American Babylon*.

CHAPTER 2

1. The Community of Oakland, "Proposal to the Ford Foundation for a Program of Community Development with Special Reference to Assimilation of the Newcomer Population," December 1961, 1–43, Ford Foundation Archives, PA 0620-0105, reel 2957. Although the grant proposal listed a corporate author, it was widely recognized that Evelio Grillo was the principal author.

2. In addition to migration studies previously listed, see for example Countryman, *Up South*.

3. Self, *American Babylon*.

4. "Back from Skid Row."

5. Orleck, "I Decided To Marry the First Man Who Asked," 357; Katz, "Urban 'Underclass' as a Metaphor of Social Transformation."

6. "Back from Skid Row."

7. Williams interview, 4.

8. Ibid., 72.

9. Ibid., 19.

10. Johnson and Campbell, *Black Migration in America*, 141–42.

11. Boone interview, 1.

12. Ibid., 16.

13. Ibid.

14. Seale, *Seize the Time*, 4–7; Seale, *Lonely Rage*, 3–50; Boone interview, 1; Seale interview by Williams.

15. Williams interview, 16; Bertha Byes and Brenda Byes interviews.

16. Newton, *Revolutionary Suicide*, 11–13.

17. Ibid., 37.

18. Ibid., 58.

19. Pointer interview, 10.

20. Here I am borrowing a phrase from Lotchin's *Bad City in the Good War*.

21. Sanchez, *Becoming Mexican American*, 266–67.

22. Ibid., 266; Johnson interview.

23. Newton, *Revolutionary Suicide*, 26.

24. Schneider, *Vampires, Dragons and Egyptian Kings*, 246–55; Wilson and Johnson interviews.

25. Johnson interview; Self, *American Babylon*, 144, 146–49.

26. Johnson interview, 23.

27. In researching Oakland's black youth culture in the 1950s, I was struck by the stark differences in the racial dynamics between East Bay youth gangs and their counterparts in Los Angeles and New York. For an account of white flight in Oakland during the 1940s and 1950s, see Self, *American Babylon*. For subjective accounts, see Vanucci, Gianini, and Johnson interviews; Schneider, *Vampires, Dragons and Egyptian Kings*; Sloan, "Bastards of the Party," HBO film, 2006. Self, *American Babylon*.

28. Johnson interview, 21.

29. After 1968, DeFremery was rechristened "Bobby Hutton Memorial Park" in tribute to the Black Panther Party's first member, who was shot by police. See, for example, Baruch and Jones, *Black Panthers 1968*, 138–41.

30. Johnson interview, 27.

31. Pointer interview, 5.

32. Newton, *Revolutionary Suicide*, 28.

33. Garrett interview, 6, 8.

34. Ibid.

35. Brilliant, *Color Lines*, 5.

36. Ibid., 43.

37. Ibid., 39.

38. In 1940, California's black population total was 124,306 out of a total state population of 6,907,387. See Taylor, *In Search of the Racial Frontier*, 253.

39. Johnson, *Second Gold Rush*, 170.

40. Theoharis, "Alabama on Avalon," 36; Spencer, "Caught in Crossfire," 354–62.

41. Wollenberg, *All Deliberate Speed*, 136–37.

42. Kirp, *Just Schools*, 219.

43. Hayes, *Power Structure and Urban Policy*, 10–14. See chapter 7 for a detailed discussion of Republican-dominated electoral politics in Oakland.

44. Kirp, *Just Schools*, 219.

45. Spencer, "Caught in the Crossfire," 355; Self, *American Babylon*.

46. Bureau of the Census, *Population by Age, Race, and Sex in Oakland, Calif., by Census Tracts: 1940*; Bureau of the Census, *Population by Age, Race, and Sex in Oakland, Calif., by Census Tracts: 1950*; Spencer, "Caught in the Crossfire."

47. Kirp, *Just Schools*, 220.

48. Dellums and California Fair Employment Practices Commission, *Report on Oakland Schools*.

49. Spencer, "Caught in the Crossfire," 362.

50. Ibid., 363.

51. Boone interview, 17. For more contemporary history of McClymonds, see Ginwright, *Black in School*.

52. Born in Wharton, Texas, Edwin Kelly learned to play piano in his father's church, and after migrating to Oakland at age eight, he became interested in jazz. An alumnus of McClymonds, Kelly graduated in 1953, going on to found his own quintet and run the jazz program at the DeFremery Park Recreation Center. Boone interview, 15, 21; "Edwin Kelly—RIP"; "Pipes."

53. Johnson, *Negro War Worker*, 7.

54. Ritterhouse, *Growing Up Jim Crow*, 183.

55. Anderson, *Education of Blacks in the South*, 188.

56. Quoted from Spencer, "Caught in Crossfire," 361.

57. Ibid., 361–63.

58. Turner and McKee, "High School Planned"; Spencer, "Caught in the Crossfire," 361.

59. Dellums and California Fair Employment Practices Commission, *Report on Oakland Schools*.

60. "Clint White Blasts Phasing Out of McClymonds High," *California Voice*, January 22,

1965; "Oakland Board of Education Against Mack Phase-Out," *California Voice*, January 29, 1965; May, "Struggle for Authority."

61. Newton, *Revolutionary Suicide*, 9.

62. Dellums and California Fair Employment Practices Commission, *Report on Oakland Schools*, 10–11.

63. Ibid., 16.

64. Ibid., 11–12.

65. Ibid. The determination of a "Negro school" is a school with 75 percent or more African American pupils.

66. Ibid., 12–13.

67. Ibid., 14.

68. Ibid.

69. Ibid., 20.

70. Ibid., 18.

71. Ibid., 19.

72. NAACP West Coast Region Files, Box 16, September 12, 1962, Bancroft Library.

73. James Brent, "Her Day in Court—Teacher vs. System," *San Francisco Chronicle*, February 14, 1966; Roy Wilkins, "A Teacher Fights for Her Negro Pupils," *Detroit News*, February 27, 1966.

74. Dellums and California Fair Employment Practices Commission, *Report on Oakland Schools*, 20.

75. Community of Oakland, "Proposal to the Ford Foundation," 13; May, "Struggle for Authority."

76. Walker, *Popular Justice*, 175.

77. Gilbert, *Cycle of Outrage*, 72.

78. May, "Struggle for Authority," 115.

79. Ibid., 117.

80. Ibid.; Grillo, *Black Cuban, Black American*, 131.

81. May, "Struggle for Authority," 117.

82. Ibid., 124.

83. Ibid.,123.

84. Ibid., 84.

85. Ibid., 128.

86. Ibid., 131–35; For an overview of the history of and twentieth-century discourse on juvenile crime, see Austin and Willard, *Generations of Youth*.

87. May, "Struggle for Authority," 127.

88. Community of Oakland, "Proposal to the Ford Foundation," 22.

89. Pitts and McKinney, *Special Place for Special People*, 4.

90. Ibid.

91. Ibid., 3–26, 73–96.

92. Ibid., 72.

93. Ibid., 6.

94. Ibid.; Community of Oakland, "Proposal to the Ford Foundation."

95. Dellums and Halterman, *Lying Down with the Lions*, 26–30.

96. Tate, "New Black Urban Elites." For a broader discussion of the black class politics of the postwar welfare state, see Reed, *Stirrings in the Jug*.

97. May, "Struggle for Authority," 130; City of Oakland Police Department, "History 1941–1955," Part 6, 36–40.

98. May, "Struggle for Authority," 130–35.

99. Ibid., 130; Rhomberg, *No There There*; Douglas interview; Thompson, City's War on People Problems."

100. Community of Oakland, "Proposal to the Ford Foundation," 8; Thompson, "City's War on People Problems," 210–16.

101. Johnson interview, 30.

102. There is a great deal of variation both between institutions in CYA and among the experiences of young people themselves. For a counterpoint to Johnson's experience, see Pointer interview, 8.

103. Mihailoff, "Protecting Our Children," 235.

104. Ibid.

105. Ibid., 237; Johnson interview, 29.

106. Johnson interview, 28.

107. Douglas interview, 1–3; Doss, "'Revolutionary Art,'" 179.

108. Douglas interview, 1–8.

109. Cleaver, *Soul on Ice*, 38; Horne, "Black Fire," 381–82.

110. Cleaver, "The Following Is an Address by Eldridge Cleaver," 8; Cleaver and Cleaver, *Target Zero*, 9–38.

111. Cleaver, "The Following Is an Address by Eldridge Cleaver," 8.

112. Ibid., 27–31. For a more general source on race relations, law enforcement, and the incarceration of black youth in postwar Los Angeles, see Jeffries and Foley, "To Live and Die in L.A.," 272–77.

113. Johnson interview, 27–31.

114. This term was especially common in southern California. In Oakland, interview subjects referred to the CYA as "juvy." Garrett interview, 15.

115. Cleaver, "The Following Is an Address by Eldridge Cleaver," 8.

CHAPTER 3

1. "Profs. Gather 161 Signatures Protesting Black Muslim Ban," *Daily Californian*, May 16, 1961.

2. The YMCA's auditorium had a special place in the history of campus free speech since the left student movement of the 1930s when Stiles hosted speakers banned from the U.C. Berkeley campus. Rorabaugh, *Berkeley at War*, 14–15; Somerville interview.

3. Somerville interview.

4. Al-Mansour interview; Hopkins interview by Rubens.

5. Freeman, *At Berkeley in the '60s*; Kerr, *Gold and the Blue*; Rorabaugh, *Berkeley at War*.

6. Lawson, *Running for Freedom*, 89; Luker, *Historical Dictionary of the Civil Rights Movement*, 27–28; Branch, *Parting the Waters*, 793–802; Meriwether, *Proudly We Can Be Africans*, 150–80.

7. Allen interview. Ernest Allen's seemingly limitless recall and knowledge of the period has informed nearly every aspect of this research.

8. Ibid.; Seale, *Seize the Time*, 19–29; Brown, "Politics of Culture," 226.

9. Freeman, *At Berkeley in the '60s*, 40; Rorabaugh, *Berkeley at War*, 16.

10. Kerr, *Gold and the Blue*, 6; Gilman, *Mandarins of the Future*, 107–12.

11. Kerr, *Uses of the University*.

12. Ibid.

13. Rorabaugh, *Berkeley at War*, 12.

14. Douglass, "Brokering the 1960 Master Plan"; Kerr, *Gold and the Blue*, 6.

15. Rawls and Bean, *California*, 426; May, *Golden State, Golden Youth*, 21.

16. Brenner, "Public Higher Education," 210–11.

17. Rorabaugh, *Berkeley at War*, 12.

18. Ibid., 10.

19. Rawls and Bean, *California*, 428–34; Freeman, *At Berkeley in the '60s*; Rorabaugh, *Berkeley at War*; Suri, *Power and Protest*.

20. Morris, *Head of the Class*, xvii–xviii.

21. Lewis interview, 8.

22. Freeman, *At Berkeley in the '60s*, 34.

23. Lewis interview, 8.

24. Donald Warden, "Letters to the Ice Box," *Daily Californian*, March 1, 1961.

25. Ibid.; *Daily Californian*, March 22, 1961.

26. Hughes, *Fight for Freedom*, 122.

27. Daniel Watts, publisher of the *Liberator*, identified the African American reaction to Lumumba's murder as an important "turning point. . . . The spontaneous demonstration in the Security Council marked the beginning of the departure of Negro militants from passive, peaceful, largely legalistic protests." Plummer, *Rising Wind*, 300–305.

28. Meriwether, *Proudly We Can Be Africans*, 233.

29. Al-Mansour interview, 16. The Congolese leader had forged a special relationship with African Americans by making Harlem one of his first stops on an official visit to President Eisenhower. As reporters looked on, Lumumba danced with women outside the Theresa Hotel while drummers played. The warmth of his gesture was not easily forgotten. As Warden later explained his own deep investment in the Congo crisis, "We identified with Lumumba because of his identification with us."

30. Plummer, *Rising Wind*, 304; Lincoln, *Black Muslims in America*, 244.

31. Lincoln, *Black Muslims in America*, 243–44.

32. Blake interview, 2–3.

33. Ibid.

34. Dashiell interview, 21; Robinson interview.

35. Warden, "Letters to the Ice Box," *Daily Californian*, April 17, 1961.

36. Quote not directly from Warden but quoted from the text of the *Daily Californian*, April 17, 1961.

37. Blake interview, 4.

38. Ibid.; *Daily Californian*, April 17, 1961.

39. Al-Mansour, *Black Americans at the Crossroads*, 27.

40. Ibid., 29.

41. Al-Mansour interview, 11.

42. Ibid.

43. Frazier, *Black Bourgeoisie*, 237.

44. Al-Mansour, *Black Americans at the Crossroads*, 34.

45. Dashiell interview, 29. This dualism manifested itself long after his student days and

later caught the attention of Huey Newton, who charged in his autobiography that Warden carried this model into Oakland politics. Newton explained, "Wanting whites to believe that blacks were behind him, Warden talked up Black Power and Black history using the people to gain their support. Downtown, he looked for whites to support him out of their fear of organized blacks. Warden gathered the people around him to lead them like sheep." Newton, *Revolutionary Suicide*, 65.

46. Dawson interview, 1.

47. Dawson, Allen, and Blake interviews.

48. There were exceptions to this rule. While black and white students tended to socialize in separate groups, there were some parties with mixed attendance. The Greek system dominated social life on campus, and in most cases black people were unwelcome. However, Jewish fraternities and sororities were an exception to this rule, and Maurice Dawson reported that black students often attended their functions. Dawson interview, 5.

49. Al-Mansour interview, 9; Smethurst, *Black Arts Movement*, 259.

50. Hopkins interview by Rubens, 24.

51. Dawson interview, 5.

52. Labrie, Dawson, Lewis, al-Mansour, and Dashiell interviews.

53. Dawson interview, 24.

54. Hopkins interview by Rubens, 12; Robinson, Dawson, and Dashiell interviews.

55. Dashiell, Blake, and Robinson interviews; al-Mansour, *Black Americans at the Crossroads*.

56. Veatch, "African Students in the United States," 168; Dudziak, *Cold War Civil Rights*, 153.

57. Veatch, "African Students in the United States," 168; McKown, "Kenya University Students and Politics," 215–21; Dudziak, *Cold War Civil Rights*; Lipset, foreword to *University Students and African Politics*; Hanna, "Students, Universities, and Political Outcomes," 1–22.

58. The majority came from Nigeria, Ethiopia, and Kenya, and over half received federal development subsidies; McKown and Hanna, *University and African Politics*.

59. Dashiell interview.

60. Maurice Dawson mentioned Crossroads Africa as one of the organizations that helped to raise his consciousness of decolonization in Africa. According to him, they held meetings on campus. Dawson interview, 3.

61. Sales, *From Civil Rights to Black Liberation*, 36.

62. Blake interview, 8.

63. Lincoln, *Black Muslims in America*, xvii.

64. Ibid.; Haley and Malcolm X, *Autobiography of Malcolm X*, 283–85.

65. Baldwin, *Fire Next Time*.

66. Interestingly, a number of non-Muslim journalists contributed regularly and worked for the editorial staff. Veteran newspaperman Dan Burley and former CIO organizer and playwright Richard Dunham, who went on to write Muhammad Ali's biography, *The Greatest*, served as editors-in-chief after Malcolm X. In the late sixties former *Ebony* editor-writer John Woodford served as editor-in-chief between 1969 and 1972 before leaving for the *Chicago Sun-Times* and later the *New York Times*. Gardell has argued that the charge that the NOI succeeded at achieving such high circulation figures through mandatory sales minimums is overstated. Its content on both domestic and international reporting reveals that it was simply one of the best black weekly newspapers of the period. Gardell, *In the Name of Elijah Muhammad*, 64; Dawson interview, 11.

67. Dawson interview, 6.

68. Frazier's claim is more conservative than Warden's recollection. In the introduction to *Black Bourgeoisie* he states, "In their disillusionment many of them [northern migrants] joined the Garvey Movement, the only serious Negro nationalist movement to arise in the United States." Frazier, *Black Bourgeoisie*, 21.

69. Al-Mansour interview.

70. Robinson interview, 6.

71. Tyson, *Radio Free Dixie*.

72. Blake interview, 5.

73. Richard Fallenbaum, "Muslims," "Letters to the Ice Box," *Daily Californian*, May 11, 1961.

74. Blake interview, 5.

75. Ibid., 14.

76. Ibid.

77. Robinson interview, 2–4.

78. Lacy, "African Responses to Malcolm X," 25.

79. Blake interview, 9–10; Warden, "Black Negro," 8.

80. Blake interview, 9–10.

81. Ibid.; Cleaver, *Soul on Ice*.

82. Dawson interview; Lincoln, *Black Muslims in America*, 6.

83. Baldwin, *Fire Next Time*, 84.

84. Du Bois, *Souls of Black Folk*, 5.

85. Al-Mansour interview, 4.

86. Ibid., 6. This view is clearly self-serving but may nevertheless be accurate. According to James Smethurst, "The West Coast saw perhaps the most influential of all regional expressions of the Black Arts and Black Power Movement. A complicated and even contradictory network of cultural activists and institutions served as an incubator of African American cultural nationalism and revolutionary nationalism and as a progenitor of the multicultural movement." Smethurst, unpublished manuscript, 258.

87. Thompson interview, 36.

88. Al-Mansour interview, 21.

89. Dawson interview, 13; al-Mansour interview, 20.

90. Dawson interview, 25–26; al-Mansour interview, 7.

91. Scott, *Contempt and Pity*, 60–61.

92. Herskovits, *Myth of the Negro Past*, xx.

93. Lemelle and Kelley, *Imagining Home*, 8.

94. Scott, *Contempt and Pity*, 104–14.

95. Ibid. Herskovits acknowledged the tie between his work and decolonization in his 1958 preface to the reprinting of his book. "For generations, America was indeed the dark continent in so far as concerns any sound knowledge of Africa. But with increased interest in Africa, greater opportunity to meet and to know Africans, especially those who came to our institutions of higher learning, and, above all with the realization that the nationalist movements of Africa were directed by men of maturity and competence, it was inevitable that attitudes would change. For the Negroes in the United States, Ghana has become a symbol." Herskovits, *Myth of the Negro Past*, xxviii.

96. Lemelle and Kelley, *Imagining Home*, 8.

97. Al-Mansour interview, 18.

98. Warden, "Black Negro," 20.

99. Al-Mansour interview, 18–19; Martin, "Shades of Brown," 230–53.

100. Scott, *Contempt and Pity*, 78–79, 109–10.

101. Ibid.; Warden, "Black Negro," 2; al-Mansour interview, 8–9; Allen interview, 11–14.

102. Dawson interview, 15.

103. Hopkins interview by Rubens, 24.

104. Al-Mansour interview, 7; Dawson interview, 18.

105. Al-Mansour, Dawson, and Allen interviews; Hopkins interview by Rubens.

106. Smethurst, *Black Arts Movement*, 260–62.

107. Sales, *From Civil Rights to Black Liberation*, 60; al-Mansour and Dawson interviews.

108. Dawson interview, 5.

109. Ibid., 1–5.

110. Ibid., 32; al-Mansour interview, 22.

111. Dawson interview, 5–20; al-Mansour interview, 20–22.

112. Allen interview, 10.

113. Ibid.

114. Al-Mansour, *Black Americans at the Crossroads*, 108.

115. Ibid.; al-Mansour interview, 32. In his interview, al-Mansour called this album *Go Brother Go*, but according to my research its real title was *Speak, Brother, Speak.*

116. Al-Mansour, *Black Americans at the Crossroads*, 78–79.

117. Dawson interview, 31.

118. Ibid.

119. Ibid., 32. According to Jamila al-Mansour, Ray Dobard of Music City in Berkeley produced the album for a private label called the African American Association in August 1965, shortly after the Watts Rebellion; email correspondence with Jamila al-Mansour, August 19, 2009.

120. Al-Mansour interview, 23.

121. Dawson interview, 6–14; al-Mansour interview, 36.

122. Irvin, *Unsung Heart of Black America*, 1.

123. Al-Mansour interview, 23.

124. Irvin, *Unsung Heart of Black America*, 5–12.

125. Al-Mansour, *Black Americans at the Crossroads*, 92.

126. Ibid. Warden also claimed that Marvin Gaye agreed to become an honorary member of the AAA along with Olatunji and Miriam Makeeba, who attended an association meeting after performing in the Bay Area.

127. Al-Mansour interview, 24.

128. Al-Mansour, *Black Americans at the Crossroads*, 122.

129. Al-Mansour interview, 26.

130. Al-Mansour, *Black Americans at the Crossroads*, 92–93.

131. Al-Mansour interview, 24.

132. Ibid., 8.

133. Discussions with Ernest Allen provided this framework.

CHAPTER 4

1. Woodard, *Nation within a Nation*; Douglass, *California Idea and American Higher Education*; Dupree and McAllister, "A Campus Where Black Power Won"; al-Mansour, *Black Americans at the Crossroads*; Allen interview; Cruse, *Rebellion or Revolution*, 68; Clarke, "The New Afro-American Nationalism."

2. Douglass, *California Idea and American Higher Education*; Brossman and Roberts, *California Community Colleges*.

3. Douglass, *California Idea and American Higher Education*, 314–25.

4. Ibid.

5. O'Neill, *Coming Apart*, 233.

6. Douglass, *California Idea and American Higher Education*, 1.

7. Smith and Horton, "Completion Levels."

8. Brown, "US Organization"; Murch, "The Campus and the Street."

9. Huntington, *Crisis of Democracy*, 59–64; Murch, "The Campus and the Street"; "Special Report on Minority Group Relations Presented to the Trustees."

10. Rauber, "The Case of the Languishing Landmark."

11. Ibid., 13.

12. Ibid.

13. Ibid.; Kraft, "Oakland City College New Campus Planning and Development," 10–14.

14. Wallenstein interview.

15. Wollenberg interview.

16. Ibid.

17. Ibid.; Mills interview.

18. Polt, "School Daze."

19. Newton interview, 2–3; Bazille interview.

20. Polt, "School Daze."

21. Newton interview, 3.

22. Ibid., 2; Dellums and Halterman, *Lying Down with the Lions*, 25.

23. Newton and Love interviews.

24. Love interview; Research Staff of the School of Criminology, *Oakland City College Workshop on Cultural Diversity*, 69.

25. "Special Report on Minority Group Relations Presented to the Trustees," 2.

26. Research Staff of the School of Criminology, *Oakland City College Workshop on Cultural Diversity*, 1–2.

27. Ibid.

28. Hobsbawm, *Primitive Rebels*, 108.

29. Newton interview, 5.

30. Ibid., 2–3.

31. Newton, *Revolutionary Suicide*, 54.

32. Research Staff of the School of Criminology, *Oakland City College Workshop on Cultural Diversity*, 3.

33. Ibid.; Huntington, *Crisis of Democracy*; Newton, *Revolutionary Suicide*.

34. "Special Report on Minority Group Relations Presented to the Trustees," 2.

35. Ibid.; "This Course Is for Black Students Only," 58.

36. Allen interview, 12.

37. Ibid.

38. Seale, *Seize the Time*, 10.

39. Ibid., 3–6.

40. Ibid., 3–12.

41. Research Staff of the School of Criminology, *Oakland City College Workshop on Cultural Diversity*, 35–38.

42. Ibid.

43. Al-Mansour interview, 23.

44. Al-Mansour, *Black Americans at the Crossroads*, 93; al-Mansour interview.

45. Al-Mansour interview, 5.

46. Ibid.

47. National statistics on foreign enrollment did not bear out Warden's perception of nation building. Over half of the African students attending U.S. universities majored in social science or humanities programs, and less than 10 percent chose degrees in medicine and agriculture. This first generation of independence scholars relied heavily on a liberal arts education as preparation for service-oriented careers. Jacqz, *African Students at U.S. Universities*, i; Veatch, "African Students in the United States," 18.

48. Gaines, *Uplifting the Race*, 2.

49. Al-Mansour, *Black Americans at the Crossroads*, 109.

50. Williams interview, 3–4.

51. Ibid. Student organizers Lavey Laub and Fred Jerome subsequently became influential activists in the Progressive Labor Party.

52. Ibid., 4, 33–34; De La Cova, *Moncada Attack*; Umezaki, "Breaking Through the Cane Curtain."

53. Williams interview, 30–68.

54. Allen interview, 10.

55. Newton interview, 2.

56. Bazille and Newton interviews; Polt, "School Daze."

57. Newton interview; Allen interview, 9.

58. Newton, *Revolutionary Suicide*, 67–77; Dupree and McAllister, "A Campus Where Black Power Won"; Marvin X, *Somethin' Proper*; Allen interview; Seale, *Seize the Time*.

59. Bazille and Thorton interviews.

60. Bazille interview; Newton interview, 3–8; Makinya interview, 1–2; Thortnton interview; Walton, *Black Curriculum*. *The Black Curriculum* includes reproductions of original documents concerning the fight to establish Black Studies at Merritt.

61. Thornton interview.

62. Walton, *Black Curriculum*.

63. Ibid.

64. Ibid., 51–96.

65. Ibid., 52.

66. Ibid.

67. "Letter to Dr. Carl Larsen Chief Bureau of Teacher Education & Certification from Edward O. Pete Lee President of Bay Area Black Educators," May 3, 1968, ibid., 74–76.

68. "Resolution II Bay Area Black Educators, Merritt College," May 29, 1968, ibid., 79.

69. Excerpt from "Recruiting Minority Teachers" handbook, table VIB, "Racial Distribution by Campus," ibid., 62.

70. "Memo to Board of Trustees Ravenswood City School District from Mr. John A. Minor, Superintendent," February 13, 1968, ibid., 56–59.

71. "Letter to the Faculty from Norbert S. Bischof, Faculty Senate President," May 7, 1968, ibid., 342–43.

72. "Letter from Carl Larsen to Sidney Walton," October 4, 1968, ibid., 95–96.

73. "Proposed Resolution from the State Board of Education," September 27, 1968, ibid., 86.

74. "Proposed Resolution (2) from the State Board of Education," September 27, 1968, ibid., 90–91.

75. Letter from Edward H. Redford Dr. John W. Dunn, Recommended Dismissal of Walton," June 28, 1968, ibid., 345–56 (quotation on 353).

76. Ibid.

77. Newton, *Revolutionary Suicide*, 72; al-Mansour interview.

78. Dupree and McAllister, "A Campus Where Black Power Won."

CHAPTER 5

1. For a sustained discussion of the constraints of Great Society programs on remedying problems of unemployment and poverty, see Self, *American Babylon*.

2. Bradford, *Oakland Is Not for Burning*.

3. Carson, *In Struggle*, 215–28.

4. Hilliard and Lewis, *This Side of Glory*, 117.

5. Seale, *Seize the Time*; Newton, *Revolutionary Suicide*.

6. Newton, *Revolutionary Suicide*, 14.

7. Hill, *Deacons for Defense*, 4–5; Wendt, *Spirit and the Shotgun*.

8. Carmichael and Thelwell, *Ready for Revolution*, 474.

9. Austin, *Up Against the Wall*, 15.

10. Davis, *Autobiography*, 160–67; Anthony, *Picking Up the Gun*; Allen interview.

11. Horne, *Fire This Time*; Horne, "Black Fire," 377–404.

12. Murch, "When the Panther Travels"; Gilmore, *Golden Gulag*; Mihailoff, "Protecting Our Children."

13. Mitford, *Fine Old Conflict*, 107. Jessica Mitford argues that whites formed a parallel migration to blacks and found work in the building trades and Bay Area police departments; Major, *Panther Is a Black Cat*, 1, 22–56; Newton, *Revolutionary Suicide*, 112; Hayes, *Power Structure and Urban Policy*, 39;

14. Karmin, "Federal Study Finds Unrest Among Negroes Rising"; Bradford, *Oakland Is Not for Burning*.

15. Karmin, "Jobs vs. Training."

16. Wollenberg, "California and the Vietnam War," 15; Gilbert, "Next Stop—Silicon Valley," 24–33.

17. Gilbert, "Next Stop—Silicon Valley."

18. Lustig, "War at Home," 59–82.

19. Rodriguez, "Rapid Transit and Community Power," 216.

20. "Racial Tinderbox," *Wall Street Journal*, January 5, 1966.

21. Karmin, "Jobs vs. Training."

22. Hinckle, "Metropoly," 26, 28.

23. Bradford, *Oakland Is Not for Burning*.

24. The history of Watts and black Los Angeles is the source of some contention. For competing viewpoints on its levels of political organization prior to the rebellions, see Horne, *Fire Next Time* and Willard, "Urbanization as Culture."

25. Carmichael and Thelwell, *Ready for Revolution*, 457.

26. Stokely Carmichael, "What We Want," *New York Review of Books*, October 17, 1966.

27. Carson, *In Struggle*, 166.

28. Prior to Stokely Carmichael's invitation to speak on "Black Power Day," the Bay Area Committee to Support Lowndes County circulated flyers throughout the East Bay with the Panther logo. Also, members of the Harlem Black Panther Party, a more direct outgrowth of SNCC in northern cities, corresponded briefly with Newton and Seale prior to their founding of the BPPSD. Murch, "When the Panther Travels." For a detailed account of Carmichael's visit, see also Murch, "Urban Promise of Black Power."

29. The sectarian conflict among California's different Panther parties made the question of derivation a highly charged one. For varying accounts, see Newton, *Revolutionary Suicide*, 113; Seale, *Seize the Time*; and Austin, *Up Against the Wall*, 12–15.

30. Carmichael and Thelwell, *Ready for Revolution*, 475.

31. For nearly six months, committee members met regularly with owner William Knowland, who refused to disclose the total number of black employees. The committee charged that fewer than thirty of 1250 employees were African American. See Self, *American Babylon*, 183–84.

32. Ibid.; Bradford, *Oakland Is Not for Burning*, 19, 154.

33. *Spider Magazine*, May 24, 1965.

34. Ibid.

35. Bradford, *Oakland Is Not for Burning*, 48.

36. Ibid., 19, 67, 154; *Spider Magazine*, May 24, 1965; *Slate Newsletter*, April 5, 1965; SNCC of California, "Oakland Is a Powder Keg" and "Negroes Should Stop Fighting."

37. *Slate Newsletter*, April 5, 1965; Pearson, *Shadow of the Panther*, 105; Carmichael and Thelwell, *Ready for Revolution*, 475–76.

38. Carmichael and Thelwell, *Ready for Revolution*, 475.

39. Ibid., 475–76.

40. Wilson, "Free Huey," 39. Newton, *Revolutionary Suicide*; Austin, *Up Against the Wall*, 31.

41. Newton, *Revolutionary Suicide*, 56–59.

42. Marine, *Black Panthers*, 33. Ronald Stone changed his name to Yusef Rahman. See *Blackfire*, 386–88.

43. Wilson, "Free Huey," 40; Seale, *Seize the Time*, 38.

44. Seale, *Seize the Time*, 26.

45. Ibid., 23.

46. Newton cited a series of texts as major influences, including Robert F. Williams's *Negroes with Guns*, Frantz Fanon's *Wretched of the Earth*, Che Guevara's *Guerilla Warfare*, contemporary writings on the Deacons for Defense and Justice in Louisiana, and most important, Malcolm X's program for the Organization of Afro-American Unity, which he interpreted as an unambiguous call for black people to take up arms. Newton, *Revolutionary Suicide*, 111–13.

47. Seale, *Seize the Time*, 30–31.

48. Newton, *Revolutionary Suicide*, 108–9.

49. Seale, *Seize the Time*, 27.

50. Newton, *Revolutionary Suicide*, 109.

51. Ibid., 64–65.

52. Seale, *Seize the Time*, 33.

53. Newton, *Revolutionary Suicide*, 115.

54. Ibid., 70, 116–19.

55. "What the Muslims Want," *Muhammad Speaks*, October 22, 1968, Merritt College, "1969 Folder," Merritt College Archives, Merritt College, Oakland, Calif.

56. Alkebulan, "Role of Ideology," 25; "What the Muslims Want"; Newton, *Revolutionary Suicide*, 116–19.

57. "What the Muslims Want"; Spencer, "Repression Breeds Resistance," 32–34; Newton, *Revolutionary Suicide*, 117.

58. Seale, *Seize the Time*, 62.

59. Newton, *Revolutionary Suicide*, 105–13.

60. Seale, *Seize the Time*, 62–63.

61. Newton, *Revolutionary Suicide*, 116.

62. Spencer, "Repression Breeds Resistance," 33.

63. Alkebulan, "Role of Ideology," 7.

64. Ibid.

65. Horne, *Fire This Time*, 129; Malcolm X, "Ballot or the Bullet," 23–44.

66. Horne, *Fire This Time*; Malcolm X, "Ballet or the Bullet"; Lincoln, *Black Muslims in America*.

67. Newton, *Revolutionary Suicide*, 113.

68. Dawson interview, 16.

69. Bazille interview, 2; Pearson, *Shadow of the Panther*, 108.

70. Spencer, "Repression Breeds Resistance," 42; Hilliard and Lewis, *This Side of Glory*, 114.

71. "Berkeley Conference on Black Power," flyer, October 27, 1966, Eddie Yuen Collection, Institute for Social Change, University of California, Berkeley; Bazille interview; *Daily Californian*, November 4, 1966.

72. Newton, *Revolutionary Suicide*, 120.

73. Ibid.

74. Hilliard and Lewis, *This Side of Glory*, 115–16.

75. Ibid.

76. Spencer, "Repression Breeds Resistance," 41.

77. *Little Red Book* refers to a popular collection of short sayings and political aphorisms from Chairman Mao Tse-tung. The proper title for the English translation was *Quotations from Chairman Mao Tse-tung*. Kelley and Esch, "Black Like Mao," 7.

78. Newton, *Revolutionary Suicide*, 121.

79. Ibid., 120–21.

80. Marine, *Black Panthers*, 37.

81. Seale, *Seize the Time*, 30.

82. Booker, "Lumpenization," 337–62.

83. Douglas interview, 6.

84. Spencer, "Repression Breeds Resistance," 40; "Police Vow Court Battle on Review," *Oakland Tribune*, ca. 1966, Clippings File, Oakland History Room, Main Public Library, Oakland, Calif.

85. Newton, *Revolutionary Suicide*, 68.

86. Hilliard and Lewis, *This Side of Glory*, 319.

87. Ibid., 116.

88. *Eyes on the Prize* transcript.

89. Newton, *Revolutionary Suicide*, 166.

90. Ibid., 167.

91. Spencer, "Repression Breeds Resistance," 44.

92. Payne, *I've Got the Light of Freedom*.

93. Austin, *Up Against the Wall*, 40.

94. Spencer, "Repression Breeds Resistance," 43; Austin, *Up Against the Wall*, 40; Seale, *Seize the Time*, 38–39; Hilliard, *Huey*, 29–30.

95. Seale, *Seize the Time*, 77.

96. Spencer, "Repression Breeds Resistance," 45.

97. Spencer, "Repression Breeds Resistance"; Alkebulan "Role of Ideology."

98. Salamunovich, "People and the Party," 4; *BPN*, February 7, 1970.

99. Newton interview, 1–2; Seale, *Seize the Time*, 101–3.

100. Huey Newton interview in Hampton and Fayer, *Voices of Freedom*, 361. For another example of the central role of black veterans in armed struggles in the South, see Tyson, *Blood Done Sign My Name*.

101. Seale, *Seize the Time*, 7–11.

102. Aoki interview; Hilliard, *Huey*, 41.

103. Austin, *Up Against the Wall*, 40.

104. Hilliard, *Huey*, 20; Aoki and Billy X interviews; Austin, *Up Against the Wall*, 40–41; Howard, *Panther on the Prowl*, 28–29.

105. Russell interview, 2; Tyson, *Radio Free Dixie*, 26–27; Austin, *Up Against the Wall*, 49; Billy X and Johnson interviews.

106. Quoted from interview in Spencer, "Repression Breeds Resistance," 44.

107. Hilliard and Lewis, *This Side of Glory*, 228.

108. Spencer, "Repression Breeds Resistance," 59; Newton, *Revolutionary Suicide*, 129–31; Douglas interview, 4.

109. Seale, *Seize the Time*, 113–32.

110. Hilliard and Lewis, *This Side of Glory*, 119.

111. Carmichael and Thelwell, *Ready for Revolution*, 475–76.

112. Seale, *Seize the Time*, 113–32; Allen interview, 15–19; Alkebulan, "Role of Ideology," 97.

113. Historian Scot Brown has stressed the role of partisanship in the Black Panthers' conflict with cultural nationalist organizations. See Brown, "US Organization." Allen and Pointer interviews.

114. Salamunovich, "Party and the People," 4; Brown, "US Organization." The BPPSD's support for interracial organizing also set the Panthers outside much of the nationalist spectrum and proved to be a source of friction not only with Warden but also with SNCC, ultimately making a merger in 1968 impossible. Clayborne Carson, "Interview with Cleavers," Martin Luther King Papers Project, Martin Luther King Research and Education Institute, Stanford University, Palo Alto, Calif.

115. One reason for Stanford's opposition was clearly his link to the BPPNC, which had close ties to RAM. However, the decentralized structure of the organization meant that local cells functioned independently, acting largely as separate organizations. Murch, "When the Panther Travels"; Ahmad, *We Will Return in the Whirlwind*; Muhammad Ahmad interview, 26–30.

116. Muhammad Ahmad interview, 26–30.

117. *New York Times*, June 22, 1967; Muhammad Ahmad interview; Ahmad, *We Will Return in the Whirlwind*.

118. Douglas interview, 5.

119. Scheer, Introduction to *Post-Prison Writings*, ix.

120. Newton, *Revolutionary Suicide*, 128–36.

121. Cleaver, *Post-Prison Writings*, 28.

122. DeLeon, "Eldridge Cleaver," 67; Cleaver, *Soul on Ice*, 17–29; Newton, *Revolutionary Suicide*, 328–33; Cleaver and Cleaver, *Target Zero*.

123. Hilliard, *Huey*, 52; Austin, *Up Against the Wall*, 77.

124. Hilliard, *Huey*, 55; Seale, *Seize the Time*, 138–39.

125. Newton, *Revolutionary Suicide*, 137.

126. Seale, *Seize the Time*, 136; Austin, *Up Against the Wall*, 77.

127. Marine, *Black Panthers*, 70–71; Seale, *Seize the Time*, 141.

128. Austin, *Up Against the Wall*, 79.

129. Ibid., 78.

130. Newton, *Revolutionary Suicide*, 143; Rhodes, *Framing the Black Panthers*, 98; BPN, April 25, 1967. Hereafter, the newspaper will be referred to in the text as the *Black Panther*.

131. Hilliard, *Huey*, 62, 65.

132. Hilliard, *Huey*, 62–74; Newton, *Revolutionary Suicide*, 148; Spencer, "Repression Breeds Resistance," 64; Peebles, Taylor, and Lewis, *Panther*, 35–41.

133. Hilliard, *Huey*, 65.

134. Newton, *To Die for the People*.

135. Jones and Hancock, "Preliminary Investigation," 7; Rhodes, *Framing the Black Panthers*, 77.

136. Newton, *Revolutionary Suicide*, 150.

137. Holder, "History of the Black Panther Party," 36; Spencer, "Repression Breeds Resistance," 73.

138. Hilliard and Lewis, *This Side of Glory*, 70.

139. Quoted by Rhodes, *Framing the Black Panthers*, 88–89.

140. Jones and Hancock, "Preliminary Investigation"; Spencer, "Repression Breeds Resistance."

141. Jones and Hancock, "Preliminary Investigation," 7.

142. While many local newspapers reflected the viewpoints of city leaders, in Oakland this was true to the extreme. For nearly half a century, *Tribune* publisher J. R. Knowland and his son and successor, Senator William Knowland, served as the keystone to Oakland's Republican government. Historically, the *Tribune* actively supported its own state and municipal candidates, with some of its most pointed influence brought to bear on the courts and law enforcement. From the late twenties onward, the Knowland machine succeeded in preventing the election of a liberal or Democrat to the office of district attorney, and by the late sixties, the *Tribune* had earned a national reputation as a right-wing mouthpiece. For a more detailed discussion of the Knowland machine, see chapter 7. Hayes, *Power Structure and Urban Policy*, 15. For the history of the *Oakland Tribune* and its central roll in California Republican politics, see also Montgomery and Johnson, *One Step from the White House*, 280.

143. Spencer, "Repression Breeds Resistance," 73; Jones, "Political Repression of the Black Panther Party," 415–34.

144. Newton, *Revolutionary Suicide*, 173–75; Marine, *Black Panthers*, 75–90; Spencer, "Repression Breeds Resistance."

145. See image in photo insert in Newton, *Revolutionary Suicide*, 146–47.

146. Newton, *Revolutionary Suicide*, 179; Spencer, "Repression Breeds Resistance," 74.

147. Wilson, "Free Huey."

148. Marine, *Black Panthers*, 78.

149. Pointer interview.

150. Rhodes, *Framing the Black Panthers*, 85.

151. Allen, Bazille, and Watkins interviews; Rhodes, *Framing the Black Panthers*, 85–86.

152. Rhodes, *Framing the Black Panthers*, 86.

153. Ibid.

154. In 1968, the Party shortened its name from Black Panther Party for Self Defense to simply Black Panther Party. "Transcript from 40th Anniversary," Black Panther Party reunion, October 2006.

155. Ibid.

156. This figure is taken from Bobby Seale's introduction to the 1991 edition of his autobiography. David Hilliard's memoir chooses the more conservative estimate of 10 to 15. For the competing figures, see Seale, *Seize the Time*, ii; Wilson, "Invisible Cages," 216–17n15; Hilliard and Lewis, *This Side of Glory*, 139; Spencer, "Repression Breeds Resistance," 76. Spencer does not cite Seale's autobiography, instead using a 1997 interview she conducted with Seale.

157. Earlier in July, Neal organized the Black Student Conference at Fisk University, where she met Eldridge Cleaver, who had traveled to Nashville to write an article on Stokely Carmichael for *Ramparts*. Cleaver interview by Carson, 8; Carson, *In Struggle*, 279.

158. Cleaver interview by Carson, 7, 9; Spencer, "Engendering the Black Freedom Struggle," 97.

159. Cleaver interview by Carson, 10; A regular campaign of police harassment had effectively depleted the BPP's financial resources and created a cycle with the leadership and rank and file passing in and out of jail. See Jones, "Political Repression of the Black Panther Party," 415–34.

160. Cleaver interview by Carson, 10.

161. Brown, "Kathleen Neal Cleaver," 252.

162. Cleaver interview by Carson, 19.

163. The Black Panthers' Central Committee was formed in December 1967 with an initial membership of five people. Brown, "Servants of the People," 23.

164. A substantial body of literature has emerged documenting the "Free Huey" movement, spanning journalistic accounts from the period through more recent scholarly monographs and dissertations. See, for example, Keating, *Free Huey*; Marine, *Black Panthers*; Wolfe, *Radical Chic & Mau-Mauing*; Lester, "SNCC and the Black Panthers," 144–49; Carson, *In Struggle*; Wilson, "'Free Huey.'"

165. Marine, *Black Panthers*, 106.

166. Brown, "Servants of the People," 21.

167. Eldridge Cleaver, "Cleaver Speaks," pamphlet, vertical files, Civil Liberties–Negroes–Black Nationalism–Black Panthers–Eldridge Cleaver, Joseph A. Labadie Collection, Harland Hatcher Graduate Library, University of Michigan, Ann Arbor, 11.

168. Ibid.

169. The *BPN* was published regularly until 1978, when its circulation began to falter. See

Davenport, "Reading the 'Voice of the Vanguard.'" There is significant evidence that Kathleen Cleaver was the catalyst in revitalizing the *Black Panther* and increasing its production to a regular weekly. Eldridge Cleaver was the first editor of the paper, and until Kathleen Neal's arrival in the Bay Area, its publication was irregular. See Cleaver interview by Carson, 26–27; Abron, "Serving the People," 181–82; Abron, "Raising the Consciousness of the People," 343–60; Brown, "Servants of the People," 23–24.

170. Emory Douglas, "Art for People's Sake," *BPN*, October 21, 1972, 4–5; Abron, "Raising the Consciousness of the People," 350, 357.

171. Jones, "Political Repression of the Black Panther Party," 426; Abron, "Raising the Consciousness," 352.

172. Davenport, "Reading the 'Voice of the Vanguard,'" 196.

173. Abron, "Raising the Consciousness of the People," 350.

174. Davenport, "Reading the 'Voice of the Vanguard,'" 196; Alkebulan interview; Brown, *Taste of Power*, 275.

175. Abron, "Raising the Consciousness of the People," 350.

176. Cleaver interview by Carson, 3; *BPN*, October 26, 1976, G; U.C. Berkeley Library Social Activism Sound Recording Project, transcript, 7.

177. In response to conflict within SNCC, Carmichael's title was alternately changed to "Prime Minister of Foreign Affairs," or simply "Prime Minister," of the Black Panther Party. Foreman, *Making of Black Revolutionaries*, 529; Lester, *Revolutionary Notes*, 146; Cleaver interview by Carson, 15.

178. A working coalition between the PFP and the Panthers emerged in December 1967. KPFA Radio Recording, February 15, 1968, Pacifica Radio Archives; Seale, *Seize the Time*, 207–11; Rorabaugh, *Berkeley at War*, 81; Peters, "Peace and Freedom Party."

179. Wilson, "Free Huey," 81.

180. Cleaver, "Fire Now."

181. Stokely Carmichael, "Free Huey Rally," U.C. Berkeley Library Social Activism Sound Recording Project, transcript, 3.

182. Carmichael, "Free Huey Rally," transcript, 7.

183. Brown, "Free Huey Rally," transcript, 1.

184. According to Kathleen Cleaver, the relationship with SNCC was always tenuous, because it focused almost exclusively on Stokely Carmichael at a time when his power and influence were declining in SNCC. From the beginning, tensions existed with James Foreman. See Cleaver interview by Carson, 13–15.

185. The coalition between SNCC and the Panthers has been the subject of much historical debate. Scholarship tends to follow in the same vein as the history itself, representing the conflict either from the point of view of SNCC or the Black Panther Party. For competing views of the BPP-SNCC alliance, see SNCC-centered scholarship and memoirs by Carson, *In Struggle*, 272–86; Carmichael and Thelwell, *Ready for Revolution*, 659–71. *New York Times* journalist Gerald Fraser used sources from "federal authorities" to allege that members of the Black Panther Party threatened James Forman with a gun. Although Foreman denied this incident in his autobiography, *Making of Black Revolutionaries*, Kwame Ture (Stokely Carmichael) later criticized the Panthers for this action. See Carmichael and Thelwell, *Ready for Revolution*, 671; *New York Times*, October 7, 1968; Foreman, *Making of Black Revolutionaries*, 522–43. Sources providing the BPP perspective include Seale, *Seize the Time*, 217–22; Marine, *Black*

Panthers, 106–23; Cleaver, "My Father and Stokely Carmichael," 43–56; Cleaver interview by Carson.

186. As subsequent events proved, when SNCC voted on ratifying the Ten Point Platform in June 1968, significant resistance emerged from the organization's staff. Carson, *In Struggle*, 280–84.

187. By July 1969, Stokely Carmichael himself became disillusioned with the BPP's authoritarian leadership structure and its use of strong-arm tactics to intimidate rivals and dissenters. He subsequently resigned from the organization. Cleaver interview by Carson, 13.

188. Ibid., 3; Carson, *In Struggle*, 283.

189. Huggins interview, 9; Carmichael and Thelwell, *Ready for Revolution*, 663.

190. Cleaver interview by Carson, 5; Holder, "History of the Black Panther Party," 256.

191. The intended goal of the campaign was to raise awareness of political prisoners, incarceration, and the particulars of Newton's case. Brown, "Servants of the People," 26–27; Matthews, "No One Ever Asks," 179; Seale, *Seize the Time*, 208–9.

192. Ultimately, the Panthers' working relationship with PFP also erupted in conflict. See Wilson, "Invisible Cages," 191–222; Barber, "Leading the Vanguard," 223–51; Heath, *Off the Pigs*, 83; Hall, *Peace and Freedom*, 154; *BPN*, November 16, 1968, 11.

193. A staff reporter for *Ramparts* described Cleaver as "the man who did [the] most to unbend the minds of white radicals, first in California, then across America." Carson, *In Struggle*, 283–86; Hilliard and Lewis, *This Side of Glory*, 141. Cleaver's use of wit, humor, and outrageousness rivaled Abbie Hoffman's. On one occasion, Cleaver threatened to beat California's Republican governor to death with a marshmallow; on another he convinced an auditorium of nuns to shout "Fuck Ronald Reagan! Fuck Ronald Reagan!" over and over in a rhythmic chant. He concluded by telling the group of Catholic sisters, "Now you're liberated in speech. You've freed yourself from your fathers." Hilliard and Lewis, *This Side of Glory*, 128.

194. Cleaver, "Education and Revolution," 46; Cleaver, "On Lumpen Ideology," 8; Rout, *Eldridge Cleaver*. Cleaver's later writings break with his 1968 essay "On the Ideology of the Black Panther Party" and call for a broader definition of the category of lumpen, repudiating the narrow definition by Marx. The essay argues that leftist thought should move from production to consumption/distribution as determinant of the American class structure. The implication is that, because college students have not yet entered into the labor market, they, like the traditional lumpen, are excluded from the ruling class.

195. One of my greatest surprises as a young researcher was conducting oral histories with members of the Oakland Party and asking them to explain how they understood the BPP as part of the larger Black Power movement, only to have them deny adamantly that this was the case. Erica Huggins stressed that this assumption is one of the greatest historical misconceptions about the Black Panther Party. "Most young people don't know that the Party wasn't a Black nationalist organization. It just wasn't. It didn't even continually call itself a Black Power organization. . . . That might have been where we were conceived . . . at that juncture in history. . . . Remember, our slogan was 'All Power To the People!'" Huggins interview, 6.

196. Murch, "When the Panther Travels"; Marable, *Race, Reform and Rebellion*; Joseph, *Waiting 'til the Midnight Hour*; Woodard, *Nation within a Nation*.

197. Rorabaugh, *Berkeley at War*; al-Mansour, *Black Americans at the Crossroads*; Brilliant, *Colorlines*; Heath, *Off the Pigs*, 83.

198. Cleaver, "Education and Revolution," 49–50.

199. Marine, *Black Panthers*, 127; Parenti, *Lockdown America*, 3–26. Cleaver interview by Carson, 18, 19.

200. Counterintelligence Program, Black Nationalist—Hate Groups, Racial Intelligence, J. Edgar Hoover Memo, March 4, 1968; U.C. Berkeley Library Social Activism Sound Recording Project, transcript, 8–9.

201. Matthews, "No One Ever Asks," 181nn87–88, 434–37.

202. Grady-Willis, "Black Panther Party," 368–71.

203. Counterintelligence Program, Black Nationalist—Hate Groups, Racial Intelligence, J. Edgar Hoover Memo, August 25, 1967.

204. Cleaver interview by Carson, 23. The trial was later postponed until July 15, 1968; *BPN*, October 16, 1976, G.

205. Marine, *Black Panthers*, 132.

206. Abron, "Raising the Consciousness of the People," 350–52; Jones, "Political Repression of the Black Panther Party," 426–27; Grady-Willis, "Black Panther Party," 368–69; *BPN*, March 20, 1976.

207. Brown, "Servants of the People," 30; *BPN*, March 16, 1968, 1, 11.

208. Austin, *Up Against the Wall*, 119; Newton, *Bitter Grain*, 70; U.C. Berkeley Library Social Activism Sound Recording Project, transcript, 8.

209. Austin, *Up Against the Wall*, 125; U.C. Berkeley Library Social Activism Sound Recording Project, transcript, 8. In less than a year, his brother Alprentice Bunchy Carter was killed in a shootout on the UCLA campus by members of the US organization. While decisive documentation has yet to be found, many assert that the US-Panther split resulted from COINTELPRO involvement. For further discussion, see Austin, *Up Against the Wall*, 225–40. This figure is a conservative estimate. The number that is usually cited for total Panther deaths is twenty-eight. Garry, "Survey of the Persecution of the Black Panther Party," 257–62. For an opposing view, see Epstein, "Black Panthers and the Police."

210. Marine, *Black Panthers*, 132.

211. *BPN*, March 16, 1968, 1.

212. Pacifica Radio Archives, "Black Panther Press Conference," BB5475, April 7, 1968; Neil, "Black Panther Party and Father Neil," printed transcript, 2.

213. *San Mateo Times*, April 5, 1968; *Oakland Tribune*, April 5 and 6, 1968.

214. *Oakland Tribune*, April 5 and 6, 1968.

215. Although Cleaver claimed at the time that the police attacked his small band of followers on April 6, 1968, he later admitted to planning an offensive assault on the OPD. See Cleaver and Newton interviews in Hampton and Fayer, *Voices of Freedom*, 514–18; Austin, *Up Against the Wall*, 165–66; Hilliard and Lewis, *This Side of Glory*, 182–95.

216. In his summary report for the National Advisory Commission on Civil Disorders, criminologist Jerome H. Skolnick even praised the Panthers for "keeping Oakland cool after the assassination of Dr. King." Skolnick, *Politics of Protest*, 153; Jeffries, *Huey Newton*, 30.

217. Cleaver interview in Hampton and Fayer, *Voices of Freedom*, 515.

218. Marine, *Black Panthers*, 136–; Hilliard and Lewis, *This Side of Glory*, 181–92.

219. Allen, "Dialectics of Black Power," 18.

220. Seale, *Seize the Time*, 269.

221. Spencer, "Repression Breeds Resistance," 43; Austin, *Up Against the Wall*, 165–68; Seale, *Seize the Time*, 38–39; Hilliard, *Huey*, 29–30; Marine, *Black Panthers*, 137. For competing

accounts of the shootout closer to the period, see Epstein, "Black Panthers and the Police"; Marine, *Black Panthers*, 136–73; Pacifica Radio Archives, "Black Panther Press Conference," BB5475, April 7, 1968.

222. Austin, *Up Against the Wall*, 165–68; *Oakland Post*, August 2–8, 2006.

223. Austin, *Up Against the Wall*, 165–68; *Oakland Post*, August 2–8, 2006. For the shift in the name of DeFremery Park, see Baruch and Jones, *Black Panthers 1968*, 138–41.

224. Austin, *Up Against the Wall*; Gitlin, *Sixties*; Pearson, *Shadow of the Panther*; Wolfe, *Radical Chic & Mau-Mauing*; Self, *American Babylon*; U.C. Berkeley Library Social Activism Sound Recording Project, transcript, 13; Matthews, "No One Ever Asks."

225. There is compelling evidence that anti–juvenile delinquency campaigns and youth incarceration were even more pronounced in Los Angeles and Chicago than in Oakland. Much more local research needs to be done on these two cities to fully understand the impact of law enforcement and the carceral state on the Party's development. Olsen, *Last Man Standing*; Posey and Nyasha interviews; Austin, *Up Against the Wall*; Wilkins, *Search and Destroy*; Rice, "Black Radicalism."

226. Nearly all of Oakland's male Panther leadership had encounters with the criminal justice system throughout their teens and young adulthood. Huey Newton was jailed several times before founding the Party, and he spent a considerable portion of his sentence in isolation. Similarly, Bobby Seale was incarcerated after an altercation with his commanding officer; he later received a dishonorable discharge from the air force. George Jackson's story reflected the tragedy of arbitrary sentencing laws; after being convicted on a petty-theft charge in 1960, he received a sentence of one year to life, which he served out at Soledad Prison and later San Quentin, where he was shot by guards in 1971. Eldridge Cleaver had the most extensive prison record, and spent nearly all of his adolescence behind bars. Newton, *Revolutionary Suicide*, 99–104; Seale, *Seize the Time*, 9–10; Cleaver, *Soul on Ice*; Jackson, *Soledad Brother*, ix–xi; Olsen, *Last Man Standing*; Posey and Nyasha interviews; Austin, *Up Against the Wall*; Wilkins, *Search and Destroy*; Rice, "Black Radicalism."

227. Douglas and Pointer interviews; Cleaver, "The Following Is an Address by Eldridge Cleaver," 6–10. The theme of juvenile incarceration appeared repeatedly in the interviews I conducted with Black Panther Party members and other Black Power groups in Oakland (see chapter 2). This is, of course, a highly select group that may not be representative of the larger pool of migrants. More qualitative and quantitative research is needed to understand how antidelinquency efforts, youth authorities, and other forms of juvenile detention and incarceration affected southern migrants in northern cities. Another important and largely unexplored area of inquiry is a gendered analysis that considers the different outcomes and effects for male and female migrants.

228. Although most of the recent work on the American carceral state has been done in sociology and focuses on the period from the 1980s forward, there are several new historical monographs and manuscripts in progress. See McLennan, *Crisis of Imprisonment*; Gottschaulk, *From the Gallows to the Prisons*; Simon, *Governing through Crime*; Thompson, "Attica"; Thompson, "Rethinking 1968"; Gilmore, *Golden Gulag*; Wacquant, *Deadly Symbiosis*; Parenti, *Lockdown America*.

229. Newton, *Revolutionary Suicide*, 129, 133. For a compelling debate about historical memory, masculinity, and the Black Panther Party, see the exchange between Alice Walker and Elaine Brown in the *New York Times*, May 5, 1993.

230. Hilliard and Lewis, *This Side of Glory*, 141.

231. David Hilliard's recollection of the intellectual differences between Eldridge Cleaver and Huey Newton made this point with remarkable insight: "But Eldridge seems forged by his own experience in prison, where you want to control people because you don't know who you can trust. For all of Huey's madness, one thing is always true about him: he loves knowledge, loves knowledge for its own sake. That's why he can go on for so long. He loses himself in exploring things, trying to understand them. Not Eldridge. Not that he isn't smart. But for him knowledge always means control. For Huey knowledge is a tool of power. For Eldridge knowledge is a tool of manipulation." Hilliard and Lewis, *This Side of Glory*, 129–30.

232. Cleaver, *Soul on Ice*, 12; Avrich, "Legacy of Bakunin," 129–42; Cummins, *Rise and Fall of California's Radical Prison Movement*; Yee, *Melancholy History of Soledad Prison*; Jackson, *Soledad Brother*; Armstrong, *Dragon Has Come*; Mann, *Comrade George*; Carr, *Bad*.

233. With the constant incarceration of the male leadership, Eldridge Cleaver increasingly became the public face of the Party. This visibility brought his ideas about gender, revolution, and the nature of dissent to the fore. One of Cleaver's most damaging proclamations was the "pussy power" thesis, which limited female activism to an ability to sexually manipulate men. The tragic implications of this were many. Cleaver's ideas sowed dissension in the ranks and belied the growing presence of women in the Party. His sensationalist ranting both obscured the central role women played in the growth and expansion of the Party into black communities and made their lives much more difficult on a daily basis. Erika Huggins later remembered, "Women in the Party just hated his guts quietly, and stayed out of his way." Matthews, "No One Ever Asks," 242.

234. Cleaver, "The Following Is an Address by Eldridge Cleaver," 8.

235. Kelley, "Slangin' Rocks . . . Palestinian Style"; Franklin, "Jackanapes," 553–60; Ogbar, *Black Power*.

236. Hilliard and Lewis, *This Side of Glory*, 200–201.

237. U.C. Berkeley Library Social Activism Sound Recording Project, transcript, 11.

238. Seale, *Seize the Time*, 337.

239. Hilliard and Lewis, *This Side of Glory*, 201.

240. Seale interview by Williams; Austin, *Up Against the Wall*, 40–43, 102.

241. Alkebulan, "Role of Ideology," 104.

242. Churchill and Wall, *Agents of Repression*, 77.

243. Alkebulan, *Survival Pending Revolution*; Spencer, "Repression breeds Resistance," 190; Newton, *Revolutionary Suicide*, 328–31; Matthews, "No One Ever Asks," 242.

CHAPTER 6

1. Although Eldridge Cleaver did not flee into exile until November 24, 1968, his legal troubles and imminent prosecution for parole violations meant that his influence in Party leadership receded significantly by the fall of 1968.

2. *BPN*, November 2, 1968, 7; *BPN*, November 16, 1968, 14; *BPN*, December 21, 1968, 15; *BPN*, October 16, 1976, H; Alkebulan, *Survival Pending Revolution*, 31. There is some discrepancy about the timing and location of the first free breakfast program. In the November 2, 1968, *Black Panther*, a call for volunteers for a free breakfast program at Concord Baptist Church in Berkeley appeared. However, subsequent articles identified St. Augustine's Church and a local

community center in West Oakland at Forty-second and Grove as the location of the first free breakfast program.

3. Matthews, "No One Ever Asks," 157–61.

4. Newton, *Revolutionary Suicide*, 116–18.

5. Seale, *Lonely Rage*, 177; Robnett, *How Long, How Long*. Robnett's work has provided a model for considering the important role of women as "bridge leadership" who used their interpersonal relationships and social networks to create the infrastructure for social movements. Further inquiry is needed into this dynamic not only in civil rights organizations, but in Black nationalist/Power/radical groups.

6. Spencer, "Repression Breeds Resistance," 246. See, for example, Pearson, *Shadow of the Panther*; Hopkins, "Deradicalization of the Black Panther Party"; Holder, "History of the Black Panther Party"; Newton, *Bitter Grain*; Draper, *Revolutionary Black Nationalism*.

7. This chapter draws on the insightful and original research of Paul Alkebulan. See Alkebulan, "Role of Ideology" and *Survival Pending Revolution*, 27–45.

8. For an important discussion about political and economic strategies of southern migrants, see Gregory, *Southern Diaspora*; Williams, *Politics of Public Housing*; Orleck, *Storming Caesar's Palace*; Kornbluh, *Battle for Welfare Rights*; Moore, *To Place Our Deeds*; Rodriguez, *Repositioning North American Migration History*.

9. The term COINTELPRO refers to an initiative within the FBI targeting "Black Nationalist Hate Groups" begun in August 1967. Included within its purview were more traditional civil rights organizations as well as Black nationalist/Power/radical groups such as the Southern Christian Leadership Conference, Student Nonviolent Coordinating Committee, the Nation of Islam, and Revolutionary Action Movement. The Black Panther Party was added to this list in the fall of 1968. Grady-Willis, "Black Panther Party," 366; Churchill and Vander Wall, *Agents of Repression*; O'Reilly, *Racial Matters*; Hine, "Black Professionals and Race Consciousness"; Alkebulan, *Survival Pending Revolution*, 31.

10. *BPN*, November 22, 1969, 2; Salamunovich, "Party and the People," 52–53.

11. Salamunovich, "Party and the People," 52; *California Voice*, January 2, 1970.

12. For an example of the Panthers' devastating critique of Wilkins and the NAACP, see *BPN*, July 20, 1967, 7, 19.

13. Salamunovich, "Party and the People," 53; Jones and Hancock, "Preliminary Investigation"; *New York Times*, May 14, 1970; Wilkins and Clark, *Search and Destroy*.

14. Grady-Willis, "Black Panther Party," 372–73.

15. Heath, *Off the Pigs*, 84.

16. *BPN*, November 16, 1968, 15; Alkebulan, *Survival Pending Revolution*, 30; Spencer, "Repression Breeds Resistance," 44, 126; *BPN*, November 2, 1968, 7; *BPN*, November 3, December 21, 1968, April 27, 1969.

17. *BPN*, December 21, 1968; Alkebulan, *Survival Pending Revolution*, 27–33; Abron, "Serving the People," 178.

18. Neil, "Black Panther Party and Father Neil," printed transcript, 2 –3.

19. Newton, "On the Relevance of the Black Church," 66; Spencer, "Repression Breeds Resistance," 279.

20. Frazier, *Negro Church in America*.

21. Alkebulan, "Survival Pending Revolution," 8.

22. Alkebulan, "Role of Ideology," 9, 43.

23. Abron, "Serving the People," 183; Levine, *School Lunch Politics*, 139–40.

24. *New York Times*, January 5, 1971. While Reagan's proposal was ultimately vetoed by the California legislature, his rhetoric provides a context for the Black Panther Party's survival programs and electoral campaigns from 1968 through 1973. Burbank, "Governor Reagan and California Welfare Reform," 278–89.

25. *Oakland Tribune*, September 5, 1970.

26. Under the direction of Donald Rumsfeld, President Nixon dismantled the Office of Economic Opportunity, which was finally closed altogether under President Ford in 1972. Similarly, Governor Reagan emerged as a right-wing critic of Nixon's Family Allotment Act. See especially the column by Kevin P. Phillips, "The Welfare Crunch," *Washington Post*, May 8, 1971; *New York Times*, January 5, February 27, March 7 and 14, August 15, 1971, January 29, 1972; *Christian Science Monitor*, March 5, 1971; *Oakland Tribune* September 30, 1970, September 26, 1971; Lemann, "The Quiet Man: Dick Cheney's Discreet Rise to Unprecedented Power," *New Yorker*, May 7, 2001.

27. For examples of *BPN*'s coverage of social policy, housing, and welfare rights, see April 18 and 25, July 11, August 1 and 8, 1970, February 20 and 27, May 15, September 19, 1971; see also Matthews, "No One Ever Asks," 386. For a larger context, see Nadasen, *Welfare Warriors*; Williams, *Politics of Public Housing*; Orleck, *Storming Caesar's Palace*.

28. Woodard, *Nation within a Nation*; Brown, *Fighting for Us*.

29. Njeri, *My Life with the Black Panther Party*, 11.

30. Matthews, "No One Ever Asks," 303.

31. Ibid., 234–35; Seale, *Lonely Rage*, 177; Spencer, "Engendering the Black Freedom Struggle."

32. Matthews, "No One Ever Asks," 389n128; Brown, *Taste of Power*, 304.

33. Many of the women who joined the Party in other parts of the country and relocated to Oakland came from middle-class families or had attended college prior to joining the Party. Kathleen Cleaver typified this group. In fact, an internal skills survey conducted in 1973 revealed higher rates of college attendance among female Party members in comparison to their male counterparts. Historian Tracye Matthews has documented how the FBI tried to take advantage of this potential social division. Further research on the intersection between class and gender dynamics for both male and female members of the BPP is needed. Matthews, "No One Ever Asks," 217–18, 297n31; Posey and Rahman interview; Alkebulan, *Survival Pending Revolution*, 98, 151n1; Spencer, "Repression Breeds Resistance," 302.

34. "Oakland: A Base of Operations" was a series of articles published in the *BPN* from 1972 to 1973 in preparation for the BPP's mayoral and city council campaign. See chapter 7.

35. Huggins interview, 7; Brown, "Servants of the People," 24.

36. Huggins interview, 9.

37. For a summary of this conflict and COINTELPRO's central role in producing it, see Austin, *Up Against the Wall*, 225–40.

38. In contrast to Gail Sheehy's account in *Panthermania*, Brown draws on a 1992 interview with Ericka Huggins to argue that, upon returning to her in-laws in New Haven, Huggins did not intend to set up a Panther chapter, but she relented after many residents approached her about establishing a local chapter. Brown, "Servants of the People," 40–41; Sheehy, *Panthermania*.

39. U.C. Berkeley Library Social Activism Sound Recording Project, transcript, 14; Williams, *Black Politics/White Power*, 156–69; Brown, "Servants of the People."

40. Cleaver, "Cleaver Speaks"; Cleaver, "Message to Sister Ericka Huggins of the Black

Panther Party," 98; Brown, "Servants of the People," 54; Matthews, "No One Ever Asks," 108, 232–45, 338, 353; *BPN*, July 5, 1969, reprinted in Foner, *Black Panthers Speak*, 98–99.

41. Huggins interview, 1.

42. Ibid., 3.

43. Given the origins of the BPP at Merritt College and the longevity of its longest-running survival program—the Oakland Community School (1971–82)—it is striking that the Panther educational initiatives are one of the least studied and documented aspects of the Black Panther Party's history. This historiographical gap partially reflects a gender bias in early Panther scholarship that gave insufficient attention to so-called reformist community programs that had the greatest female involvement. The preoccupation with the period from 1966 to 1968, armed self-defense, and the more sensationalist aspects of the Party's history have obscured this very important dimension of BPP activism and of women's agency within the Party. Recently, this has begun to change. See Williamson, "Community Control with a Black Nationalist Twist," 137–57; Perlstein, "Minds Stayed on Freedom," 33–66; Peck, "Educate to Liberate."

44. Newton, *Revolutionary Suicide*, 117; Seale, *Seize the Time*, 20, 141.

45. Newton, *Revolutionary Suicide*, 19–28.

46. Peck, "Educate to Liberate."

47. Brown, "Servants of the People," 46.

48. Corbin, "Oakland Black Panther Schools," 12–13.

49. *BPN*, February 7, 1970; Matthews, "No One Ever Asks," 299n41; Huggins interview, 4.

50. Alkebulan, "Role of Ideology," 46.

51. *BPN*, August 2, 1969, 14.

52. Ibid.; Corbin, "Oakland Black Panther Schools," 14; *BPN*, February 7, 1970, 7.

53. *BPN*, August 2 and 9, 1969.

54. Abron, "Serving the People," 185; Heath, *Off the Pigs*, 107, 115; *BPN*, July 5, 1969; *BPN*, August 2, 1969, 1; *BPN*, August 9, 1969, 19.

55. Spencer, "Repression Breeds Resistance," 172–73; Corbin, "Oakland Black Panther Schools," 2, 14.

56. Corbin, "Oakland Black Panther Schools," 2, 14; Williamson, "Community Control with a Black Nationalist Twist"; Alkebulan, *Survival Pending Revolution*, 38–45.

57. Corbin, "Oakland Black Panther Schools," 10; Seale, *Seize the Time*, 417.

58. For a contrary view of Panther pedagogy, see Perlstein, "Minds Stayed on Freedom."

59. *BPN*, February 7, 1970, 7.

60. Huggins interview, 13.

61. The Panther school went through a succession of name and location changes that reflected current events and shifts in Party emphasis. Initially, the school memorialized Sam Napier, the circulation manager of the *Black Panther* newspaper, who was allegedly murdered by Cleaver's dissident faction. After relocating to 29th Avenue in the Fruitvale District, the Samuel Napier Intercommunal Institute changed its name to the Huey P. Newton Intercommunal Youth Institute, later shortened to the Intercommunal Youth Institute. Corbin, "Oakland Black Panther Schools," 2; *BPN*, October 7, 1972; Huggins interview, 2.

62. Huggins interview, 13.

63. Corbin, "Oakland Black Panther Schools," 20; Huggins interview, 3.

64. Corbin, "Oakland Black Panther Schools," 15–20; Hilliard and Lewis, *This Side of Glory*, 325–26; Alkebulan, "Role of Ideology," 74.

65. Alkebulan, "Role of Ideology," 46.

66. Boone interview; Posey and Rahman interview.

67. Williamson, "Community Control with a Black Nationalist Twists," 146; Peck, "Educate to Liberate," 213n43.

68. Huggins interview.

69. Ibid., 16.

70. Ibid., 4.

71. Corbin, "Oakland Black Panther Schools," 17.

72. Ibid., 38.

73. Abron, "Serving the People," 183; Newton, "The Defection of Eldridge Cleaver," in Newton, *Revolutionary Suicide*, 328–31.

74. Churchill and Vander Wall, *Agents of Repression*, 77.

75. Spencer, "Repression Breeds Resistance," 193–94.

76. Ibid., 189–90; Rhodes, *Framing the Panthers*, 114; Foner, *Black Panthers Speak*, 121.

77. Spencer, "Repression Breeds Resistance," 161; "Supplementary Detailed Reports—Staff Reports on Intelligence Activities and the Rights of Americans," 188, folder "FBI Files," box 6, HPN.

78. Newton, "War Against the Panthers," 108–9n120; FBI Memo to SACs in 27 Field Offices from Director, May 15, 1969, reprinted in Huey Newton, "War Against the Panthers," 108–9n120, as cited in Matthews, "No One Ever Asks," 199n130.

79. Memo to SAC, San Francisco, from Director, FBI, May 27, 1969, as cited in Matthews, "No One Ever Asks," 199–200.

80. Abron, "Raising the Consciousness of the People," 348.

81. Abron, "Serving the People," 183; Church Committee Report, 22–23; Memo to SAC, San Francisco, from Director, FBI, May 28, 1969, as cited in Matthews, "No One Ever Asks," 200n132.

82. Similarly, the San Jose Liberation School's battles with residents and local school board forced it to move three different times before finding a permanent home in the city's Our Lady of Guadalupe Church. *BPN*, August 2, 1969, 12–19.

83. Memo to SAC, San Francisco, from Director, FBI, June 16, 1970; Senate, Final Report, 200, citing Memorandum to FBI Headquarters from San Francisco Field Office, October 21, 1970, both as cited in Matthews, "No One Ever Asks," 200n134.

84. While Eldridge Cleaver encouraged this provocative style, the newspaper continued publishing articles with a similar tone in the months and years after his exile. See, for example, Newton's speech following the murder of Jonathan Jackson in *BPN*, August 21, 1970; Holder, "History of the Black Panther Party," 325.

85. Holder, "History of the Black Panther Party," 285–307.

86. Matthews, "No One Ever Asks," 174.

87. Spencer, "Repression Breeds Resistance," 197–259, esp. 247.

88. Holder, "History of the Black Panther Party," 269.

89. Murch, "When the Panther Travels"; Umoja "Black Liberation Army," 229; Holder, "History of the Black Panther Party," 259–60.

90. *BPN*, January 23, 1971.

91. Olsen, *Last Man Standing*, 18–27, 37–52.

92. Umoja, "Black Liberation Army," 228. The actual origin of the underground is a highly contested issue in Panther scholarship. More research is needed. For a contrary view,

see Olsen, *Last Man Standing*, 69–76; Austin, *Up Against the Wall*; Faraj, "Unearthing the Underground."

93. Holder, "History of the Black Panther Party," 250–318.

94. Olsen, *Last Man Standing*, 73. There is evidence that Huey Newton authorized the initial creation of the underground. Needless to say, much more research is needed on the history of the Panthers' clandestine activism.

95. Spencer, "Repression Breeds Resistance," 243–44; LeBlanc-Ernest, "Most Qualified Person to Handle the Job," 316, 337n57.

96. Spencer, "Repression Breeds Resistance," 244–54.

97. Ibid., 247.

98. Brown, *Taste of Power*, 320; Jennings, "Why I Joined the Black Panther Party," 267.

99. *BPN*, January 23, 1971, 6.

100. Hilliard, *Huey*, 194.

101. Despite their failed alliance, SNCC provided the BPP with an effective grassroots matrix for community outreach and institution building. Carson, *In Struggle*; Payne, *I've Got the Light of Freedom*.

102. Carson, *In Struggle*, 80; Perlstein, "SNCC and the Creation of the Mississippi Freedom Schools," 297–324; Alkebulan, *Survival Pending Revolution*.

103. Hilliard, *Huey*, 190; Newton, "Speech Delivered at Boston College," 20–38; Alkebulan, *Survival Pending Revolution*, 23; Spencer, "Repression Breeds Resistance," 236.

104. Spencer, "Repression Breeds Resistance"; Alkebulan, *Survival Pending Revolution*.

105. Newton, "On the Defection of Eldridge Cleaver," in in Newton, *To Die for the People*, 44–53; Alkebulan, "Role of Ideology," 38.

CHAPTER 7

1. *Oakland Tribune*, May 14, 1972; Brown, *Taste of Power*, 323.

2. *San Francisco Examiner*, March 18, 1972; *San Francisco Chronicle*, March 18, 1972, "Seale Expects to Win East Bay Mayor's Race," box 45, HPN; DeLeon, "Showdown in Oakland"; Mason, "Shift to the Middle"; Brown, *Taste of Power*, 323–24; Seale, *Lonely Rage*, 225; Spencer, "Repression Breeds Resistance," 326.

3. See, for example, Roy Wilkins, "Black Panthers Swap Violence for the Ballot Box," *Los Angeles Times*, October 2, 1972.

4. Mason, "Shift to the Middle," 80.

5. Alkebulan, *Survival Pending Revolution*, 119.

6. This inconsistency, in fact, became a point of contention in the Oakland election after Bobby Seale gave a strident and controversial speech at Yale University in November 1972. *San Francisco Examiner*, November 12, 1972.

7. Alkebulan, "Role of Ideology," iii–v, 91–96; Spencer, "Repression Breeds Resistance," 309–40; Alkebulan, *Survival Pending Revolution*, 60–64, 117–19; *San Francisco Examiner*, November 12, 1972.

8. Quoted by Singh in "Black Panthers and the 'Undeveloped Country,'" 69–70. Hilliard and Lewis, *This Side of Glory*, 319.

9. Brown, *Taste of Power*, 311–27.

10. Ibid., 304.

11. Spencer, "Repression Breeds Resistance," 264.

12. Ibid.

13. Altshuler, *Community Control*, 13–15.

14. Spencer, "Repression Breeds Resistance," 264.

15. Parliament, *Chocolate City*; Self, *American Babylon*, 211.

16. Marable, *Race, Reform and Rebellion*, 123.

17. Thornton, *Double Trouble*, 147–53; Spencer, "Repression Breeds Resistance," 310–12.

18. Woodard, *Nation within a Nation*, 202.

19. Marable, *Race, Reform and Rebellion*, 121.

20. Ibid., 121–23; Woodard, *Nation within a Nation*, 202–3; Diggs, Hatcher, and Baraka, "Steering Committee—National Black Political Convention," series 2, box 11, "National Black Political Convention," HPN.

21. For reprint, see *BPN*, April 29, 1972; additional coverage in *BPN*, April 15, 1972; Spencer, "Repression Breeds Resistance," 312.

22. "National Black Political Agenda," series 2, box 11, folder 12, "National Black Political Convention," HPN.

23. Woodard, *Nation within a Nation*, 207.

24. Letter to Don Hopkins and Ronald Dellums, May 5, 1972, letter from Lloyd Barbee to Richard Hatcher, Charles Diggs, Imamu Amiri Baraka, April 21, 1972, letter from Ronald Dellums to Huey Newton, June 12, 1972, "Black Political Convention—Sacramento—April 30, 1972, List of Delegates," series 2, folder 12, "National Black Political Convention," HPN.

25. Hilliard interview.

26. Spencer, "Repression Breeds Resistance," 309.

27. Hayes, *Power Structure*, 14.

28. Knowland was also a notorious antilabor politician. In his tenure in office he helped sponsor the Taft-Hartley Act and a "right to work" initiative that abolished the closed-shop union agreements; Hayes, *Power Structure*, 15.

29. Hayes, *Power Structure*, 19–23.

30. *Oakland Tribune*, January 7, 1973.

31. Crouchett, Bunch, and Winnacker, *Visions Toward Tomorrow*, 55–56; Self, *American Babylon*, 77–87.

32. Ibid., 45; Self, *American Babylon*, 77–87.

33. Lemke, "Afro-Americans in Berkeley," 62; Hopkins, "Development of Black Political Organization in Berkeley," 107–12.

34. Hopkins, "Development of Black Political Organization in Berkeley," 110–11. Excerpts reprinted from the *Oakland Post*.

35. Rodriguez, "From Personal Politics to Party Politics," 21; Rhomberg, *No There There*, 83. For more extensive discussion of brokerage in black politics in the East Bay, see Ware, *Breakdown of Democratic Party Organization*, 55.

36. Hopkins, "Development of Black Political Organization," 110–11.

37. Ibid., 108.

38. Ibid.; Thompson, *Double Trouble*, 150; Dellums, *Lying Down with the Lions*, 55.

39. Crouchett, Bunch, and Winnacker, *Visions Toward Tomorrow*, 55–56.

40. Lemke, "Afro-Americans in Berkeley," 62; Art Goldberg, "Organizing an Earthquake," unlabeled article, series 2, box 45, HPN.

41. Spencer, "Repression Breeds Resistance," 309–28; Alkebulan, *Survival Pending Revolution*.

42. Spencer, "Repression Breeds Resistance," 312; Rodriguez, "From Personal Politics to Party Politics."

43. Spencer, "Repression Breeds Resistance," 309–19; Sultan Ahmad interview, 1; Seale, *Lonely Rage*, 224–25.

44. Roy Wilkins to the *New York Post*, February 26, 1972, "The New Panthers," series 2, box 45, HPN.

45. Lloyd A. Barbee to Richard Hatcher, Charles Diggs, and Imamu Baraka, April 21, 1972, series 2, box 11, folder 12, "National Black Political Convention," HPN; Brown, *Taste of Power*, 32; Alkebulan, "Role of Ideology," 92–93; Spencer, "Repression Breeds Resistance," 314.

46. Spencer, "Repression Breeds Resistance," 314–15; *BPN*, May 13, 1972.

47. Brown, *Taste of Power*, 321; Wellman, *Union Makes Us Strong*; Oden, "Power Shift."

48. Spencer, "Repression Breeds Resistance," 314–18.

49. C.O.A, *Liberated Reporter*, May 16, 1972, HPN.

50. Alkebulan, *Survival Pending Revolution*, 118.

51. Throughout much of the Party's history, Huey Newton and Bobby Seale did not agree on the utility of electoral politics. Seale had always been much more receptive to this approach, and in November 1968 he discussed it as an essential component in the Party's survival programs. By contrast, as late as April 1971, Newton wrote emphatically, "We will never run for political office, but we will endorse and support those candidates who are acting in the true interest of the people." Within less than a year, the BPP made an abrupt about-face and began preparing its municipal campaign. Newton, "On the Defection of Eldridge Cleaver," in Newton, *To Die for the People*, 50.

52. *BPN*, August 12, 1972, Supplement, D; *BPN*, August 19, 1972, Supplement, A; Spencer, "Repression Breeds Resistance," 319–20; *Oakland Tribune*, August 2, 16, 18, and 24, 1972. For a more extensive history of the West Oakland Planning Committee and its central role in black struggles for inclusion, see Self, *American Babylon*, 243–46, 250–51; Rhomberg, *No There There*, 145–72; Kramer, *Participation of the Poor*; May, "Struggle for Authority."

53. *BPN*, July 29, 1972.

54. *BPN*, July 29, August 5, 1972. The "Oakland: A Base of Operations" series ran every week in a supplement to the newspaper from July 29, 1972, to April 7, 1973, with a total of thirty-seven different reports.

55. Matthews, "No One Ever Asks," 295n31, 363; Newton, *Revolutionary Suicide*, 298–99; Brown, *Taste of Power*, 251, 277, 281; Alkebulan, *Survival Pending Revolution*, 117–18; McCutchen, *We Were Free for a While*.

56. Sultan Ahmad interview, 9; *New York Times*, September 8, 2008; Rice, "Black Radicalism on Chicago's West Side."

57. Sultan Ahmad interview, 3.

58. Ibid., 9–10.

59. Self, *American Babylon*, 64–65; "Cobb, Seale, Brooks Highlight Political Meet," *California Voice*, December 7, 1972, HPN (possibly mislabeled).

60. Sultan Ahmad interview; Rhomberg, *No There There*, 2, 69–70; Ware, *Breakdown of Democratic Party Organization*, 51–59; *Oakland Tribune*, February 7, 1973; *California Voice*, February 8, 1973.

61. Sultan Ahmad interview, 8; McCutchen, *We Were Free for a While*, 143.

62. Sultan Ahmad interview, 5; Self, *American Babylon*, 305–6.

63. Sultan Ahmad interview, 13.

64. Ibid., 18, 21.

65. Brown, *Taste of Power*, 324–25.

66. Salamunovich, "Party and the People," 30.

67. The Panthers had a particularly bitter relationship with the *Oakland Post* that dated back to the late sixties. In the summer of 1968, the newspapers' offices were firebombed, and the July 17, 1968, issue insinuated that the BPP was involved. Like the Party's rapprochement with Roy Wilkins during the aftermath of Fred Hampton's shooting, relations between Tom Berkeley and the Panthers improved during Huey Newton's murder trial, and the *Oakland Post*'s publisher demanded that the court guarantee due process. However, after this crisis passed the antagonism continued. The conflict between Berkeley and the BPP was not universal, and other members of the local black press had closer ties with the Party, including the publisher of the *San Francisco Sun-Reporter*, Carleton Goodlett. *Oakland Post*, April 3, June 12, 1968; Salamunovich, "Party and the People," 25, 27, 30.

68. Sultan Ahmad interview, 14–15; Salamunovich, "Party and the People," 30; Brown, *Taste of Power*, 331.

69. *BPN*, August 9, 1971, Supplement, A–E.

70. *BPN*, June 14, 1969, 3; Salamunovich, "Party and the People," 30.

71. Salamunovich, "Party and the People," 32.

72. Ibid., 34; *BPN*, September 25, 1971, October 16, 1971, August 9, 1971, Supplement.

73. Salamunovich, "Party and the People," 33.

74. Ibid., 75; *Oakland Post*, September 9, 1971.

75. Roy Wilkins to the *New York Post*, HPN.

76. *BPN*, January 22, 1972, Supplement, B; *California Voice*, September 23, August 19, 1971; Salamunovich, "Party and the People," 36.

77. Salamunovich, "Party and the People," 32–36, 50; *BPN*, January 22, 1972, Supplement; *California Voice*, January 20 and 27, 1972; *Oakland Post*, December 17, 1972, April 11, 1973.

78. Salamunovich, "Party and the People," 49; Mason, "Shift to the Middle," 82.

79. Brown, *Taste of Power*, 324.

80. Roy Wilkins, "Black Panthers Swap Violence for the Ballot Box."

81. Newton, "The Women's Liberation and Gay Liberation Movements," 152.

82. Alkebulan, *Survival Pending Revolution*, 119; "Cesar Chavez, Dominga 15 De Abril," "Bobby Seale Calls upon Oakland City Council to Become First City in California to Provide Bilingual (English/Spanish) Ballots for Local Elections," "Come Meet Bobby Seale and Elaine Brown Support Gay Rights for Oakland," Alice B. Toklas Democratic Club flyer, BPP campaign ephemera, series II, subseries 7, box 45, folder 19, HPN; "Gays Will Back Bobby and Elaine," *Berkeley Barb*, April 6–12, 1973, 10; *BPN*, March 3, 1973; Newton, *To Die for the People*, 152–55; Spencer, "Repression Breeds Resistance," 211–14, 223–24, 330–31.

83. *Merritt Reporter*, January 19, 1973, HPN.

84. "Mills Student in City Council Race," *Mills Stream*, October 26, 1972, HPN.

85. Spencer, "Repression Breeds Resistance," 331–32; Black Panther Party, *CoEvolution Quarterly*, 32.

86. *Grassroots*, December 20, 1972.

87. BPP campaign ephemera, series II, subseries 7, box 45, folder 19, HPN.

88. Ibid.; *Oakland Tribune*, February 7, 1973.

89. *Oakland Tribune*, February 7, January 18, 1973.

90. *Montclarion*, March 28, 1973.

91. *California Voice*, March 15, 1973.

92. Goldberg, "Organizing an Earthquake," HPN.

93. *California Voice*, March 15, 1973.

94. *Oakland Tribune*, April 1, 1975.

95. *Montclarion*, April 5, 1975.

96. *Oakland Tribune*, April 18, 1973.

97. *Sun-Reporter*, n.d., HPN.

98. *Oakland Tribune*, May 16, 1973.

99. Self, *American Babylon*, 308.

100. Ibid., 298–316.

101. Arguably, this tendency had always existed in the BPP's aggressive stance against other Black radical groups that it attempted to eliminate or absorb, like the Afro-American Association and the Black Panther Party of Northern California. Pointer and Allen interviews.

102. *Peralta Community College Bulletin* 5 (February 26, 1968): 1; Dupree and McAllister, "A Campus Where Black Power Won."

103. *Oakland Tribune*, November 11, 1970; Dupree and McAllister, "A Campus Where Black Power Won."

104. Russell interview; Alkebulan, *Survival Pending Revolution*, 86–94; Alkebulan, "Role of Ideology," 65–71.

105. Russell interview, 10–25; Alkebulan, *Survival Pending Revolution*, 86–94; Alkebulan, "Role of Ideology," 65–71.

106. "Merritt Stays," *Lumpen: Revolutionary Student News Service*, Merritt Black Student Union, November 17, 1970, 3; Alkebulan, "Role of Ideology," 65–78; *CoEvolution Quarterly*, 32.

107. Russell interview, 21; *Oakland Tribune*, January 5, February 1 and 2, March 16, 1971.

108. Russell interview, 23; *Oakland Tribune*, November 11, 1970, February 2, 1971.

109. Russell interview, 21; *Oakland Tribune*, March 20, April 17, 1971, January 28, 1972.

110. Russell interview, 25.

111. Ibid.; *Oakland Tribune*, March 20, April 17, 1971.

112. McCutchen, *We Were Free for a While*, 141–42.

113. Pointer interview, 33–36.

114. Alkebulan, "Role of Ideology," 96–97; Pointer interview, 32–34; McCutchen, *We Were Free for a While*, 142. McCutchen stresses pointedly in his autobiography that this took place while Bobby Seale was out of town.

115. For a discussion of the problems of state absorption of radical black freedom movements in the late sixties and early seventies, see Crosby, *Little Taste of Freedom*; Jeffries, *Bloody Lowndes*; Reed, *Stirrings in the Jug*; Self, *American Babylon*, 311; Alkebulan, *Survival Pending Revolution*.

116. Self, *American Babylon*, 309–10; Brown, *Taste of Power*, 362.

117. Brown, *Taste of Power*, 321, 329–30, 333, 353; Austin, *Up Against the Wall*, 330.

118. Brown, "Elaine Brown,", 175–76; Brown, *Taste of Power*.

119. Brown, *Taste of Power*, 324–25; Sultan Ahmad interview, 19–21, 31–32; Austin, *Up Against the Wall*; Alkebulan, *Survival Pending Revolution*, 96.

120. Spencer, "Repression Breeds Resistance," 348.

121. Ibid., 349.

122. Brown, *Taste of Power*, 350–52.

123. Ibid., 333; Perkins, *Autobiography as Activism*. A number of Panthers and movement

scholars have criticized Brown's autobiography for its sensationalism and self-serving revisionism. However, details about the Party's involvement in illegal activity and use of corporal punishment have been confirmed in recent publications and oral history interviews conducted by a variety of former Panthers and scholars. See, for example, Alkebulan, *Survival Pending Revolution*; Austin, *Up Against the Wall*; Williams, *Black Politics/White Power*; Spencer, "Repression Breeds Resistance."

124. Newton, *To Die For the People*, 112–47; Brown, *Taste of Power*, 333–34; Murch, "Urban Promise of Black Power."

125. Sultan Ahmad interview, 26.

126. Spencer, "Repression Breeds Resistance," 356; Seale, *Lonely Rage*, 228–38; Brown, *Taste of Power*, 328, 333 336; Seale interview by Williams, 9–10.

127. Brown, *Taste of Power*, 347–53.

128. Seale interview by Williams, 9.

129. Spencer, "Repression Breeds Resistance," 352.

130. Holder, "History of the Black Panther Party," 268.

131. Posey and Rahman interview.

132. Hilliard, *Huey*, 187.

133. Alkebulan, *Survival Pending Revolution*, 124–25; Leblanc-Ernest, "Most Qualified Person to Handle the Job," 324–25.

134. Sultan Ahmad interview, 8; Brown, *Taste of Power*, 277.

135. Seale, *Lonely Rage*, 224.

136. Seale interview by Williams; Alkebulan, *Survival Pending Revolution*, 117; Seale, *Lonely Rage*, 228–29.

137. Brown, *Taste of Power*, 323, 334.

138. Alkebulan, *Survival Pending Revolution*, 118.

139. *San Francisco Examiner*, March 18, 1972.

140. Woodard, *Nation within a Nation*.

141. Mason, "Shift to the Middle," 82.

142. Many rank and file members were angered over the Party's failure to sufficiently aid Party members who had been jailed. Posey and Rahman interview.

CONCLUSION

1. For a contrary view, see Cha-Jua and Lang, "'Long Movement' as Vampire"; Matusow, *Unraveling of America*; Gitlin, *Sixties*.

2. Here I am referring to the Afro-American Association once it expanded its base at Merritt College and began to forge ties with the broader African American community of Oakland. Hine, "Black Professionals and Race Consciousness."

3. More longitudinal research is needed to understand the continuities between southern and northern black resistance. Rolinson, *Grassroots Garveyism*; Williams and Pointer interviews; Newton, *Revolutionary Suicide*; Hilliard and Lewis, *This Side of Glory*.

4. Self, *American Babylon*.

5. Self, *American Babylon*; Niyasha interview, 42.

6. Newton, *Revolutionary Suicide*.

7. See chapter 6 for a more complete historiographical discussion of this literature.

8. Painter, "Soul Murder and Slavery," 125–46.

9. Self, *American Babylon*; Rhomberg, *No There There*.

10. Bureau of the Census, *Population by Age, Race, and Sex in Oakland, Calif., by Census Tracts: 1940*; Bureau of the Census, *1950 Population Census*; Department of Labor, "Data from Census Bureau Estimates for Oakland, California."

11. Brenda Byes interview, 10.

12. See, for example, Pointer, Bazille, Allen, Johnson, and Boone interviews; Newton, *Revolutionary Suicide*; Seale, *Seize the Time*; Marvin X, *Somethin' Proper*.

13. Suri, *Power and Protest*.

14. Holder, "History of the Black Panther Party," 330.

15. Matthews, "No One Ever Asks," 135.

16. Alkebulan, *Survival Pending Revolution*.

17. Campbell, "Panthers and Local History," 99. A number of recent works have been published documenting Panther local chapters. See, for example, Williams and Lazerow, *Liberated Territories*; Jeffries, *Black Power in the Belly of the Beast*; Jeffries, *Comrades*.

18. "Transcript from 40th Anniversary," Black Panther Party reunion, October 2006.

19. In addition to the scholarly works cited above, Billy X's (formerly Billy Jennings) organization, It's About Time, has played a crucial role in preserving both the material culture and the oral memory of the Black Panther Party. For an overview of the group's activities, see its website, <http://www.itsabouttimebpp.com>.

20. Pearson, *Shadow of the Panther*.

21. Cleaver, "How TV Wrecked the Black Panthers."

22. Williams, "From Oakland to Omaha," 1–31.

BIBLIOGRAPHY

MANUSCRIPT SOURCES

Bancroft Library, University of California, Berkeley
  National Association for the Advancement of Colored People, West Coast Region
    Records
  Social Protest Collection
Department of Special Collections, Stanford University, Palo Alto, Calif.
  Dr. Huey P. Newton Foundation Papers
Ford Foundation Archives, New York, N.Y.
Harlan Hatcher Graduate Library, University of Michigan, Ann Arbor
  Joseph A. Labadie Collection
Institute for Governmental Studies, University of California, Berkeley
King Papers Project, Martin Luther King Research and Educational Institute, Stanford
    University, Palo Alto, Calif.
Merritt College Archives, Merritt College, Oakland, Calif.
National Archives, San Bruno, Calif.
  Records of the Committee of Fair Employment Practices, 1941–46
Oakland History Room, Main Public Library, Oakland, Calif.
H. K. Yuen Social Movement Archive, University of California, Berkeley

INTERVIEWS

Interviews are by the author and privately held unless otherwise noted. Some interviewees
requested that pseudonyms be used to protect their privacy.

Muhammad Ahmad (Max Stanford), October 16, 2007, Philadelphia, Pa.
Sultan Ahmad (Herman Smith), August 29, 2008, and September 4, 2008, telephone
    interview.
Ernest Allen, July 3, 2001, Berkeley, Calif.
Richard Aoki, July 15, 2001, Berkeley, Calif.
Walter Bachemin, June 28, 1998, Oakland, Calif., Oakland Oral History Project.
Leo Bazille, February 19, 2001, telephone interview.
Billy X, August 20, 2001, Sacramento, Calif.
J. Herman Blake, February 21, 2001, telephone interview.
Freddie Boone, August 8, 2003, Hayward, Calif.
Bertha Byes, August 5, 2003, Oakland, Calif.
Brenda Byes, August 8, 2003, Berkeley, Calif.

Eldridge and Kathleen Cleaver, interview by Clayborne Carson, April 29, 1980, King Papers Project, Stanford University.

Kathleen Cleaver, interview by Clayborne Carson, April 29, 1980, King Papers Project, Stanford University.

Margot Dashiell, March 12, 2002, Berkeley, Calif.

Maurice Dawson, July 7, 2002, Oakland, Calif.

Emory Douglas, March 7, 2002, San Francisco, Calif.

Eddie Ellis, October 23, 2007, New York, N.Y.

Jimmy Garrett, November 5, 2007, telephone interview.

Else Gianini, July 9, 1998, Oakland, Calif., Oakland Oral History Project.

Elihu Harris, August 3, 2008, Oakland, Calif.

Edith Hill, interview by Nadine Wilmot, September 24, 1998, Oakland, Calif., Oakland Oral History Project.

David Hilliard, August 16, 2003, Oakland, Calif.

Donald Hopkins, interview by Lisa Rubens, September 29, 2000, Regional Oral History Office, University of California, Berkeley.

Ericka Huggins, January 8, 2001, Oakland, Calif.

Raymond Johnson (pseudonym), March 3, 2001, Oakland, Calif.

Aubrey Labrie, October 18, 2007, Oakland, Calif.

Mary Lewis, November 24, 2001, Oakland, Calif.

Bill Love, March 9, 2001, Oakland, Calif.

Sister Makinya, May 5, 2005, Oakland, Calif.

Khalid al-Mansour (Donald Warden), July 22, 2002, telephone interview.

Michael Mills, July 16, 2008, Oakland, Calif.

Melvin Newton, March 3, 2001, Oakland, Calif.

Kilu Nyasha, April 24, 2007, Oakland, Calif.

Alex Papillon, September 17, 2002, Berkeley, Calif.

Fritz Pointer, December 14, 2001, Novato, Calif.

Shirley Posey (formerly Shirley Hewitt) and Mahjeeda Rahman, April 22, 2007, Oakland, Calif.

Cedric Robinson, March 8, 2002, Berkeley, Calif.

Virginia Rose, interview by Teron McGrew, March 28, 1998, Oakland Oral History Project.

Andre Russell, October 19, 2007, Berkeley, Calif.

Bobby Seale, telephone interview by Yohuru Williams, January 2, 1996.

Bill Somerville, May 17, 2001, Oakland, Calif.

Hadwick Alvin Thompson, April 18, 1998, Oakland, Calif., Oakland Oral History Project.

John Thornton (pseudonym), March 3, 2001, Oakland, Calif.

Richard Vanucci, June 17, 2001, Oakland, Calif., Oakland Oral History Project.

Eve Wallenstein, March 20, 2001, Oakland, Calif.

Earl Watkins, October 22, 1998, Berkeley, Calif., Oakland Oral History Project.

Anne Williams, March 19, 2007, Oakland, Calif.

Ted Wilson, August 7, 2007, South Orange, N.J.

Chuck Wollenberg, December 4, 2002, Berkeley, Calif.

GOVERNMENT DOCUMENTS

California Department of Transportation. *West Oakland—A Place to Start From: Research Design and Treatment Plan: Cypress I-880 Replacement Project.* Vol. I, *Historical Archaeology.* Oakland, Calif.: CALTRANS, 1994.

Committee of Fair Employment Practices. *Final Report.* Institute for Governmental Studies, University of California, Berkeley, 1946.

Counterintelligence Program, Black Nationalist—Hate Groups, Racial Intelligence. J. Edgar Hoover memo, August 25, 1967. Reprinted in Brian Glick, *The War at Home: Covert Action Against U.S. Activists and What We Can Do About It.* Boston: South End Press, 1989, 77.

Counterintelligence Program, Black Nationalist—Hate Groups, Racial Intelligence. J. Edgar Hoover memo, March 4, 1968. Reprinted in Brian Glick, *The War at Home: Covert Action Against U.S. Activists and What We Can Do About It.* Boston: South End Press, 1989, 78.

Dellums, C. L., and California Fair Employment Practices Commission. *Report on Oakland Schools: An Investigation under Section 1421 of the California Labor Code of the Oakland Unified School District 1962–1963.* Oakland, Calif.: OUSD, June 16, 1964.

Moynihan, Daniel Patrick. *The Negro Family: The Case for National Action.* Washington, D.C.: Office of Planning and Research, U.S. Department of Labor, 1965.

Redevelopment Agency of the City of Oakland. *Information Bulletin,* no. 1, March 13, 1958.

Scranton, William W., et al. *The Report of the President's Commission on Campus Unrest* (September 1970). Washington, D.C.: U.S. Government Printing Office, 1970.

U.S. Bureau of Labor Statistics. *Monthly Labor Review.* March 1965.

U.S. Bureau of the Census. *Population by Age, Race, and Sex in Oakland, Calif. by Census Tracts.* Washington, D.C., 1940.

U.S. Bureau of the Census. *1950 Population Census, Statistics for Census Tracks, Map San Francisco—Oakland, California and Adjacent Areas by Census Tracks.* Washington, D.C.

U.S. Department of Labor. "Data from Census Bureau Estimates for Oakland, California." 1980 Census, Run No. 831120. Washington, D.C.

U.S. Senate. Church Committee Report. *Final Report of the Select Committee to Study Governmental Operations with Respect to Intelligence Activities.* Book III, 22–23. Washington, D.C.: U.S. Government Printing Office, 1976. <http://www.aarclibrary.org/publib/contents/church/contents_church_reports_book3.htm>.

PERIODICALS

Berkeley Barb
Black Panther
California Voice
Christian Science Monitor
CoEvolution Quarterly
Daily Californian
Detroit Free Press
Detroit News
East Bay Express
Ebony
Flatlands

Grassroots
Jet
Liberated Reporter
Liberator
Los Angeles Times
The Lumpen: Revolutionary
   Student News Service
Merritt Reporter
Mills Stream
Montclarion
Movement

Muhammad Speaks

New Republic

Newsweek

New Yorker

New York Post

New York Review of Books

New York Times

OAH Magazine

Oakland Post

Oakland Tribune

People's World

Peralta Colleges Bulletin

Ramparts

San Francisco Chronicle

San Francisco Examiner

San Mateo Times

Slate Newsletter

Spider Magazine

Sun Reporter

Time

Wall Street Journal

Washington Post

BOOKS AND PAMPHLETS

Abbott, Carl. *The New Urban America: Growth and Politics in Sunbelt Cities*. Chapel Hill: University of North Carolina Press, 1981.

Ahmad, Muhammad. *We Will Return in the Whirlwind: Black Radical Organizations, 1960–1975*. Chicago: Charles H. Kerr, 2007.

Alkebulan, Paul. *Survival Pending Revolution: The History of the Black Panther Party*. Tuscaloosa: University of Alabama Press, 2007.

Allen, Robert L. *Black Awakening in Capitalist America: An Analytic History*. Garden City, N.Y.: Doubleday, 1969.

———. "Dialectics of Black Power." *Guardian* pamphlet, 1968.

Almaguer, Tomás. *Racial Fault Lines: The Historical Origins of White Supremacy in California*. Berkeley: University of California Press, 1994.

Altshuler, Alan A. *Community Control: The Black Demand for Participation in Large American Cities*. New York: Pegasus, 1970.

Anderson, James. *The Education of Blacks in the South, 1860–1935*. Chapel Hill: University of North Carolina Press, 1988.

Angelou, Maya. *I Know Why the Caged Bird Sings*. New York: Bantam, 1993.

Anthony, Earl. *Picking Up the Gun; A Report on the Black Panthers*. New York: Dial Press, 1970.

Archibald, Katherine. *Wartime Shipyard: A Study in Social Disunity*. Berkeley: University of California Press, 1944.

Armstrong, Gregory. *The Dragon Has Come*. New York: Harper and Row, 1974.

Austin, Curtis. *Up Against the Wall: Violence in the Making and Unmaking of the Black Panther Party*. Fayetteville: University of Arkansas Press, 2006.

Austin, Joe, and Michael Willard. *Generations of Youth: Youth Cultures and History in Twentieth-Century America*. New York: New York University Press, 1998.

Bakunin, Mikhail. *Catechism of the Revolutionist*. Stirling: Published jointly by Violette Nozieres Press and A.K. Press, 1989.

Baldwin, James. *The Fire Next Time*. New York: Vintage International, 1991.

Barlow, William, and Peter Shapiro. *An End to Silence: The San Francisco State College Student Movement in the 60s*. New York: Pegasus, 1971.

Baruch, Ruth-Marion, and Pirkle Jones. *Black Panthers 1968*. Los Angeles: Greybull Press, 2002.

Bazaar, Mona. *Free Huey: Or the Sky's the Limit.* Oakland, Calif.: M. Bazaar, 1968.

Bernard, Richard M. *Snowbelt Cities: Metropolitan Politics in the Northeast and Midwest since World War II.* Bloomington: Indiana University Press, 1990.

Bernard, Richard M., and Bradley Robert Rice. *Sunbelt Cities: Politics and Growth since World War II.* Austin: University of Texas Press, 1983.

Biondi, Martha. *To Stand and Fight: The Struggle for Civil Rights in Postwar New York City.* Cambridge, Mass.: Harvard University Press, 2003.

Bluestone, Barry, and Bennett Harrison. *The Deindustrialization of America: Plant Closings, Community Abandonment, and the Dismantling of Basic Industry.* New York: Basic Books, 1982.

Boyle, Kevin. *The UAW and the Heyday of American Liberalism 1945–1968.* Ithaca, N.Y.: Cornell University Press, 1995.

Bracey, John H., August Meier, and Elliott Rudwick, eds. *Black Workers and Organized Labor.* Belmont, Calif.: Wadsworth, 1971.

Bradford, Amory. *Oakland Is Not for Burning.* New York: D. McKay, 1968.

Branch, Taylor. *Parting the Waters: America in the King Years, 1954–1963.* New York: Simon and Schuster, 1988.

Brazeal, Brailsford Reese. *The Brotherhood of Sleeping Car Porters; Its Origin and Development.* New York: Harper and Brothers, 1946.

Breitman, George, ed. *Malcolm X Speaks: Selected Speeches and Statements.* New York: Grove Press, 1965.

Brilliant, Mark. *Color Lines: Civil Rights Struggles on America's "Racial Frontier," 1945–1975.* New York: Oxford University Press, forthcoming.

Brinkley, Alan. *The End of Reform: New Deal Liberalism in Recession and War.* New York: Vintage Books, 1996.

Brossman, Sidney W., and Myron Roberts. *The California Community Colleges.* Palo Alto, Calif.: Field Educational Publications, 1973.

Broussard, Albert S. *Black San Francisco: The Struggle for Racial Equality in the West, 1900–1954.* Lawrence: University Press of Kansas, 1993.

Brown, Elaine. *A Taste of Power: A Black Woman's Story.* New York: Anchor Books, 1994.

Brown, Scott. *Fighting for Us: Maulana Karenga, the US Organization and Black Cultural Nationalism.* New York: New York University Press, 2003.

Browning, Rufus, Dale Rogers Marshall, and David H. Tabb. *Protest Is Not Enough: The Struggle of Blacks and Hispanics for Equality in Urban Politics.* Berkeley: University of California Press, 1984.

Bush, Rod. *The New Black Vote: Politics and Power in Four American Cities.* San Francisco: Synthesis Publications, 1984.

Carmichael, Stokely, and Ekwueme Thelwell. *Ready for Revolution: The Life and Struggle of Stokely Carmichael (Kwame Ture).* New York: Scribner, 2005.

———. *Stokely Speaks: Black Power to Pan-Africanism.* New York: Random House, 1971.

Carr, James. *Bad: The Autobiography of James Carr.* Oakland, Calif.: AK Press, 2002.

Carson, Clayborne. *The Eyes on the Prize: Civil Rights Reader: Documents, Speeches, and Firsthand Accounts from the Black Freedom Struggle, 1954–1990.* New York: Penguin, 1991.

———. *In Struggle: SNCC and the Black Awakening of the 1960s.* Cambridge, Mass.: Harvard University Press, 1981.

Castells, Manuel. *The City and the Grassroots: A Cross-Cultural Theory of Urban Social Movements*. Berkeley: University of California Press, 1983.

Cayton, Horace. *Black Metropolis: A Study of Negro Life in a Northern City*. 1945. Reprint. Chicago: University of Chicago Press, 1993.

Churchill, Ward, and Jim Vander Wall. *Agents of Repression: The FBI's Secret War against the Black Panther Party and the American Indian Movement*. Boston: South End Press, 1988.

Clark, Steve, ed. *Malcolm X, February 1965: The Final Speeches*. New York: Pathfinder, 1992.

Clarke, John Henrik, ed. *Malcolm X: The Man and His Times*. New York: African World Press, 1991.

Cleaver, Eldridge. *The Black Man's Stake in Vietnam*. San Francisco: The Black Panther Party, 1970.

———. *On the Ideology of the Black Panther Party*. San Francisco: Black Panther Party, 1970.

———. *Post-Prison Writings and Speeches*. New York: Random House, 1969.

———. *Soul on Fire*. Waco, Tex.: Word Books, 1978.

———. *Soul on Ice*. 1968. Reprint. New York: Laurel/Dell, 1992.

Cleaver, Eldridge, and Kathleen Cleaver. *Target Zero: A Life in Writing*. New York: Palgrave Macmillan, 2006.

Cleaver, Kathleen, and George Katsiaficas, eds. *Liberation, Imagination, and the Black Panther Party: A New Look at the Panthers and Their Legacy*. New York: Routledge, 2001.

Coletta, Paolo E., and K. Jack Bauer. *United States Navy and Marine Corps Bases, Domestic*. Westport, Conn.: Greenwood Press, 1985.

Council for Democracy. *The Negro and Defense, a Test of Democracy*. New York: Council for Democracy, 1941.

Countryman, Matthew. *Up South: Civil Rights and Black Power in Philadelphia*. Philadelphia: University of Philadelphia Press, 2006.

Crosby, Emilye. *A Little Taste of Freedom: The Black Freedom Struggle in Claiborne County, Mississippi*. Chapel Hill: University of North Carolina Press, 2005.

Crouchett, Lawrence P. *William Byron Rumford, the Life and Public Services of a California Legislator: A Biography*. El Cerrito, Calif.: Downey Place, 1984.

Crouchett, Lawrence P., Lonnie G. Bunch, and Martha Kendall Winnacker. *Visions Toward Tomorrow: The History of the East Bay Afro-American Community, 1852–1977*. Oakland, Calif.: Northern California Center for Afro-American History and Life, 1989.

Crouchett, Lorraine Jacobs. *Delilah Leontium Beasley: Oakland's Crusading Journalist*. El Cerrito, Calif.: Downey Place, 1990.

Cruse, Harold. *The Crisis of the Negro Intellectual*. New York: Quill, 1984.

———. *Rebellion or Revolution*. New York: William Morrow, 1968.

Cummins, Eric. *The Rise and Fall of California's Radical Prison Movement*. Stanford, Calif.: Stanford University Press, 1994.

Cwiklik, Robert. *A. Philip Randolph and the Labor Movement*. Brookfield, Conn.: Millbrook Press, 1993.

Dahl, Robert Alan. *Who Governs? Democracy and Power in an American City*. New Haven, Conn.: Yale University Press, 1961.

D'Angelo, Raymond, ed. *The American Civil Rights Movement: Readings and Interpretations*. New York: McGraw-Hill, 2001.

Daniels, Douglas Henry. *Pioneer Urbanites: A Social and Cultural History of Black San Francisco*. Berkeley: University of California Press, 1990.

Davis, Angela Yvonne. *Angela Davis—An Autobiography*. New York: International Publishers, 1988.

De Graaf, Lawrence B., Kevin Mulroy, and Quintard Taylor, eds. *Seeking El Dorado: African Americans in California*. Seattle: University of Washington Press, 2001.

De Jong, Greta. *A Different Day: African American Struggles for Justice in Rural Louisiana*. Chapel Hill: University of North Carolina Press, 2002.

De La Cova, Antonio Rafael. *The Moncada Attack: Birth of the Cuban Revolution*. Columbia: University of South Carolina Press, 2007.

DeLeon, David, ed. *Leaders from the Sixties: A Biographical Sourcebook of American Activism*. London: Greenwood Press, 1994.

Dellums, Ronald V., and H. Lee Halterman. *Lying Down with the Lions: A Public Life from the Streets of Oakland to the Halls of Power*. Boston: Beacon Press, 2000.

Douglas, Emory. *Black Panther: The Revolutionary Art of Emory Douglas*. New York: Rizzoli, 2007.

Douglass, John Aubrey. *The California Idea and American Higher Education: 1850 to the 1960 Master Plan*. Stanford, Calif.: Stanford University Press, 2000.

Draper, Theodore. *Revolutionary Black Nationalism*. London: Secker and Warburg, 1971.

Du Bois, W. E. B. *The Souls of Black Folk*. New York: Penguin Books, 1989.

Dudziak, Mary L. *Cold War Civil Rights: Race and the Image of American Democracy*. Princeton, N.J.: Princeton University Press, 2000.

Elbaum, Max. *Revolution in the Air: Sixties Radicals Turn to Lenin, Mao and Che*. London: Verso, 2002.

Erikson, Erik H., and Huey P. Newton. *In Search of Common Ground; Conversations with Erik H. Erikson and Huey P. Newton*. New York: Norton, 1973.

Eymann, Marcia A., and Charles Wollenberg, eds. *What's Going On?: California and the Vietnam Era*. Berkeley: University of California Press, 2004.

Fairclough, Adam. *Race and Democracy: The Civil Rights Struggle in Louisiana, 1915–1972*. Athens: University of Georgia Press, 1995.

Fanon, Frantz. *Black Skin, White Masks*. New York: Grove Press, 1967.

———. *The Wretched of the Earth*. New York: Grove Press, 1968.

Farmer, James. *Lay Bare the Heart: An Autobiography of the Civil Rights Movement*. New York: Arbor House, 1998.

Farred, Grant. *What's My Name: Black Vernacular Intellectuals*. Minneapolis: University of Minnesota Press, 2003.

Fergus, Devin. *Liberalism, Black Power, and the Making of American Politics, 1965–1980*. Athens: University of Georgia Press, 2009.

Flamming, Douglas. *Bound for Freedom: Black Los Angeles in Jim Crow America*. Berkeley: University of California Press, 2006.

Foner, Philip Sheldon. *Organized Labor and the Black Worker, 1619–1981*. New York: International Publishers, 1982.

———, ed. *The Black Panthers Speak*. Philadelphia: Lippincott, 1970.

Forman, James. *The Making of Black Revolutionaries: A Personal Account*. New York: Macmillan, 1972.

Frazier, E. Franklin. *Black Bourgeoisie*. Glencoe, Ill.: Falcon's Wing Press, 1957.

———. *The Negro Church in America*. New York: Schocken Books, 1964.

Freeman, Jo. *At Berkeley in the '60s: The Education of an Activist, 1961–1965*. Bloomington: Indiana University Press, 2004.

Gabaccia, Donna R. *Militants and Migrants: Rural Sicilians Become American Workers*. New Brunswick. N.J.: Rutgers University Press, 1988.

Gaines, Kevin. *Uplifting the Race: Black Leadership, Politics, and Culture in the Twentieth Century*. Chapel Hill: University of North Carolina Press, 1996.

Gardell, Mattia. *In the Name of Elijah Muhammad: Louis Farrakhan and the Nation of Islam*. Durham. N.C.: Duke University Press, 1996.

Gilbert, James. *A Cycle of Outrage: America's Reaction to the Juvenile Delinquent in the 1950s*. New York: Oxford University Press, 1986.

Gilman, Nils. *Mandarins of the Future: Modernization Theory in Cold War America*. Baltimore, Md.: Johns Hopkins University Press, 2003.

Gilmore, Glenda. *Defying Dixie: The Radical Roots of Civil Rights, 1919–1950*. New York: W. W. Norton, 2008.

Gilmore, Ruth Wilson. *Golden Gulag: Prisons, Surplus, Crisis, and Opposition in Globalizing California*. Berkeley: University of California Press, 2007.

Ginwright, Shawn A. *Black in School: Afrocentric Reform, Urban Reform and the Promise of Hip-Hop Culture*. New York: Teachers College Press, 2004.

Gitlin, Todd. *The Sixties: Years of Hope, Days of Rage*. New York: Bantam Books, 1993.

Gordon, David M., Richard Edwards, and Michael Reich. *Segmented Work, Divided Workers: The Historical Transformation of Labor in the United States*. New York: Cambridge University Press, 1982.

Gottschaulk, Marie. *From the Gallows to the Prisons*. London: Cambridge University Press, 2006.

Green, Laurie B. *Battling the Plantation Mentality: Memphis and the Black Freedom Struggle*. Chapel Hill: University of North Carolina Press, 2007.

Gregory, James. *The Southern Diaspora: How the Great Migrations of Black and White Southerners Transformed America*. Chapel Hill: University of North Carolina Press, 2005.

Grillo, Evelio. *Black Cuban, Black American: A Memoir*. Houston, Tex.: Arte Publico Press, 2000.

Grillo, Evelio, Harriet Nathan, and Stanley Scott. *Experiment and Change in Berkeley: Essays on City Politics, 1950–1975*. Berkeley: Institute of Governmental Studies, University of California, 1978.

Grossman, James R. *Land of Hope: Chicago, Black Southerners, and the Great Migration*. Chicago: University of Chicago Press, 1989.

Guevara, Ernesto "Che." *Guerrilla Warfare*. New York: Vintage Books, 1961.

Hahn, Stephen. *A Nation under Our Feet: Black Political Struggles in the Rural South from Slavery to the Great Migration*. Cambridge, Mass.: Harvard University Press, 2003.

Haley, Alex, and Malcolm X. *The Autobiography of Malcolm X*. New York: Ballantine Books, 1964.

Hall, Simon. *Peace and Freedom: The Civil Rights and Antiwar Movements of the 1960s*. Philadelphia: University of Pennsylvania Press, 2005.

Hampton, Henry, and Steve Fayer. *Voices of Freedom: An Oral History of the Civil Rights Movement from the 1950s through the 1980s.* New York: Bantam Books, 1991.

Hanna, William John, and Judith Lynne Hanna, eds. *University Students and African Politics.* New York: Africana, 1975.

Harris, William, H. *The Harder We Run: Black Workers since the Civil War.* New York: Oxford University Press, 1982.

———. *Keeping the Faith: A. Philip Randolph, Milton P. Webster, and the Brotherhood of Sleeping Car Porters, 1925–1937.* Chicago: University of Illinois Press, 1977.

Harvey, David. *The Condition of Postmodernity: An Inquiry into the Origins of Cultural Change.* Cambridge: Blackwell, 1990.

———. *Social Justice and the City.* London: Edward Arnold, 1973.

Hayes, Edward C. *Power Structure and Urban Policy: Who Rules in Oakland?* New York: McGraw-Hill, 1971.

Haywood, Harry. *Negro Liberation.* Chicago: Liberator Press, 1976.

Heath, G. Louis. *Off the Pigs!: The History and Literature of the Black Panther Party.* Metuchen, N.J.: Scarecrow Press, 1976.

Herskovits, Melville J. *The Myth of the Negro Past.* Boston: Beacon Press, 1941.

Hill, Lance. *The Deacons for Defense: Armed Resistance and the Civil Rights Movement.* Chapel Hill: University of North Carolina Press, 2004.

Hilliard, David. *Huey: Spirit of the Panther.* New York: Thunder's Mouth Press, 2006.

Hilliard, David, and Cole Lewis. *This Side of Glory: The Autobiography of David Hilliard and the Story of the Black Panther Party.* Boston: Little Brown, 1993.

Himes, Chester. *If He Hollers Let Him Go.* New York: Thunder's Mouth Press, 1945.

———. *My Life of Absurdity: The Autobiography of Chester Himes.* Vol. II. Garden City, N.Y.: Doubleday, 1976.

———. *The Quality of Hurt.* Vol. I. Garden City, N.Y.: Doubleday, 1972.

Hirsch, Arnold R. *Making the Second Ghetto: Race and Housing in Chicago, 1940–1960.* New York: Cambridge University Press, 1983.

Ho, Fred, and Bill V. Mullen, eds. *Afro Asia: Revolutionary Political and Cultural Connections between African Americans and Asian Americans.* Durham, N.C.: Duke University Press, 2008.

Hobsbawm, Eric. *Primitive Rebels: Studies in Archaic Forms of Social Movement in the 19th and 20th Centuries.* New York: W. W. Norton, 1959.

Horne, Gerald. *Communist Front?: The Civil Rights Congress, 1946–1956.* Rutherford, N.J.: Fairleigh Dickinson University Press, 1988.

———. *Fire This Time: The Watts Uprising and the 1960s.* New York: Da Capo Press, 1997.

Howard, Elbert. *Panther on the Prowl.* Oakland, Calif.: BCP Digital Printing, 2002.

Hughes, Langston. *Fight for Freedom: The Story of the NAACP.* New York: Norton, 1962.

Hunter, Floyd. *Housing Discrimination in Oakland, California; A Study Prepared for the Oakland Mayor's Committee on Full Opportunity and the Council of Social Planning, Alameda County.* Berkeley, Calif.: Floyd Hunter Co., 1964.

Huntington, Samuel. *The Crisis of Democracy: Report on the Governability of Democracies to the Trilateral Commission.* New York: New York University Press, 1975.

Irvin, Dona L. *The Unsung Heart of Black America: A Middle-Class Church at Midcentury.* Columbia: University of Missouri Press, 1992.

Jackson, George. *Soledad Brother: The Prison Letters of George Jackson*. New York: Bantam Books, 1972.

Jackson, Kenneth T. *Crabgrass Frontier: The Suburbanization of the United States*. New York: Oxford University Press, 1985.

Jackson, Walter A. *Gunnar Myrdal and America's Conscience: Social Engineering and Racial Liberalism*. Chapel Hill: University of North Carolina Press, 1990.

Jacqz, Jane W. *African Students at U.S. Universities*. New York: African American Institute, 1967.

Jeffries, Hasan Kwame. *Bloody Lowndes: Civil Rights and Black Power in Alabama's Black Belt*. New York: New York University Press, 2009.

Jeffries, Judson. *Huey Newton: The Radical Theorist*. Jackson: University Press of Mississippi, 2002.

———, ed. *Black Power in the Belly of the Beast*. Urbana: University of Illinois Press, 2006.

Johnson, Charles, S. *The Negro War Worker: A Local Self Survey*. San Francisco: Julius Rosenwald Fund and the American Missionary Association, 1944.

Johnson, Daniel M. and Rex R. Campbell. *Black Migration in America: A Social Demographic History*. Durham, N.C.: Duke University Press, 1981.

Johnson, Marilynn, S. *The Second Gold Rush: Oakland and the East Bay in World War II*. Berkeley: University of California, Press, 1993.

Jones, Charles E. *The Black Panther Party (Reconsidered)*. Baltimore, Md.: Black Classic Press, 1998.

Jones, Jaqueline. *The Dispossessed: America's Underclasses from the Civil War to the Present*. New York: Basic Books, 1992.

Jones, LeRoi, and Larry Neal, eds. *Black Fire: An Anthology of Afro-American Writing*. New York: William Morrow, 1968.

Joseph, Peniel E. *Waiting 'til the Midnight Hour: A Narrative History of Black Power in America*. New York: Henry Holt, 2006.

———, ed. *The Black Power Movement: Rethinking the Civil Rights–Black Power Era*. New York: Routledge, 2006.

Journal of African American History. Special issue. "New Black Power Studies: National, International, and Transnational Perspectives" 92, no. 4 (Fall 2007).

Kaskins, Jim. *Power to the People: The Rise and Fall of the Black Panther Party*. New York: Simon & Schuster, 1997.

Keating, Edward. *Free Huey!* New York: Dell, 1970.

Kelley, Robin D. G. *Freedom Dreams: The Black Radical Imagination*. Boston: Beacon Press, 2002.

Kerr, Clark. *The Gold and the Blue: A Personal Memoir of the University of California*. Vol. 2, *Political Turmoil*. Berkeley: University of California Press, 2003.

———. *The Uses of the University*. Cambridge, Mass.: Harvard University Press, 1963.

Kirby, Jack Temple. *Rural Worlds Lost: The American South 1920–1960*. Baton Rouge: Louisiana State University Press, 1987.

Kirby, John B. *Black Americans in the Roosevelt Era: Liberalism and Race*. Knoxville: University of Tennessee Press, 1980.

Kirp, David. *Just Schools: The Idea of Racial Equality in American Education*. Berkeley: University of California Press, 1982.

Kiser, Clyde Vernon. *Sea Island to City: A Study of St. Helena Islanders in Harlem and Other Urban Centers*. New York: Columbia University Press, 1969.

Kornbluh, Felicia. *The Battle for Welfare Rights: Politics and Poverty in Modern America.* Philadelphia: University of Pennsylvania Press, 2007.

Kramer, Ralph M. *Participation of the Poor: Comparative Community Case Studies in the War on Poverty.* Englewood Cliffs, N.J.: Prentice-Hall, 1969.

Kusmer, Kenneth L. *A Ghetto Takes Shape: Black Cleveland, 1870–1930.* Urbana: University of Illinois Press, 1978.

Lane, Frederic C. *Ships for Victory: A History of Shipbuilding under the U.S. Maritime Commission in World War II.* Baltimore, Md.: Johns Hopkins University Press, 2001.

Lawson, Steven F. *Running for Freedom: Civil Rights and Black Politics in American since 1941.* Philadelphia: Temple University Press, 1991.

Lazerow, Jama, and Yohuru Williams. *In Search of the Black Panther Party: New Perspectives on a Revolutionary Movement.* Durham, N.C.: Duke University Press, 2006.

———. *Liberated Territories: Untold Local Perspectives on the Black Panther Party.* Durham, N.C.: Duke University Press, 2008.

Lemann, Nicholas. *The Promised Land: The Great Black Migration and How It Changed America.* New York: Vintage Books, 1992.

Lemelle, Sidney J., and Robin D. G. Kelley. *Imagining Home: Class, Culture, and Nationalism in the African Diaspora.* New York: Verso, 1994.

Lemke, Gretchen. *Afro-Americans in Berkeley, 1859–1987.* Oakland, Calif.: East Bay Negro Historical Society, 1987.

Lemke-Santangelo, Gretchen. *Abiding Courage: African American Migrant Women and the East Bay Community.* Chapel Hill: University of North Carolina Press, 1996.

Lester, Julius. *Revolutionary Notes.* New York: Grove Press, 1969.

Levine, Susan. *School Lunch Politics: The Surprising History of America's Favorite Welfare Program.* Princeton, N.J.: Princeton University Press, 2008.

Lincoln, C. Eric. *Black Muslims in America.* Trenton, N.J.: Africa World Press, 1994.

Lotchin, Roger W. *The Bad City in the Good War: San Francisco, Los Angeles, Oakland, and San Diego.* Bloomington: Indiana University Press, 2003.

———. *Fortress California, 1910–1961: From Warfare to Welfare.* Chicago: University of Illinois Press, 1992.

Luker, Ralph E. *Historical Dictionary of the Civil Rights Movement.* Lanham, Md.: Scarecrow Press, 1997.

Major, Reginald. *A Panther Is a Black Cat.* New York: William Morrow, 1971.

Mann, Eric. *Comrade George.* New York: Harper and Row, 1972.

Mansour, Khalid al-. *Black Americans at the Crossroads—Where Do We Go from Here.* Washington, D.C.: First African Press, 1991.

Mao Tse-tung. *Quotations From Chairman Mao (The Little Red Book).* Austin: University of Texas at Austin, Humanities Research Center, 1976.

Marable, Manning. *Race, Reform, and Rebellion: The Second Reconstruction in Black America, 1945–1990.* Basingstoke: Macmillan, 1991.

Marine, Gene. *The Black Panthers.* New York: New American Library, 1969.

———. *The Vanguard.* Boston: Beacon Press, 1970.

Marvin X. *Somethin' Proper: The Life and Times of a North American African Poet.* Castro Valley, Calif.: Blackbird Publishing, 1998.

Massey, Douglas S., and Nancy A. Denton. *American Apartheid: Segregation and the Making of the Underclass.* Cambridge, Mass.: Harvard University Press, 1993.

Matusow, Allen. *The Unraveling of America: A History of Liberalism in the 1960s.* New York: Harper, 1984.

May, Kirse Granat. *Golden State, Golden Youth: The California Image in Popular Culture, 1955–1966.* Chapel Hill: University of North Carolina Press, 2002.

McAdam, Doug. *Political Process and the Development of Black Insurgency, 1930–1970.* Chicago: University of Chicago Press, 1982.

McAdam, Doug, Sidney G. Tarrow, and Charles Tilly. *Dynamics of Contention.* Cambridge: Cambridge University Press, 2001.

McCormick, Richard Patrick. *The Black Student Protest Movement at Rutgers.* New Brunswick, N.J.: Rutgers University Press, 1990.

McCutchen, Steve D. *We Were Free for a While: Back to Back in the Black Panther Party.* Baltimore, Md.: Publish America, 2008.

McLennan, Rebecca M. *The Crisis of Imprisonment: Protest, Politics, and the Making of the American Penal State, 1776–1941.* New York: Cambridge University Press, 2008.

McWilliams, Carey. *California: The Great Exception.* Berkeley: University of California Press, 1949.

Meriwether, James Hunter. *Proudly We Can Be Africans: Black Americans and Africa, 1935–1961.* Chapel Hill: University of North Carolina Press, 2002.

Mitford, Jessica. *A Fine Old Conflict.* New York: Alfred A. Knopf, 1977.

Montgomery, Gayle B., and James W. Johnson. *One Step from the White House: The Rise and Fall of Senator William F. Knowland.* Berkeley: University of California Press, 1998.

Moore, Shirley Ann Wilson. *To Place Our Deeds: The African American Community in Richmond, California, 1910–1963.* Berkeley: University of California Press, 2000.

Morris, Gabrielle S. *Head of the Class: An Oral History of African-American Achievement in Higher Education and Beyond.* New York: Twayne, 1995.

Murray, Charles A. *Losing Ground: American Social Policy, 1950–1980.* New York: Basic Books, 1984.

Myrdal, Gunnar. *An American Dilemma: The Negro Problem and Modern Democracy.* New York: Harpers and Row, 1944.

Nadasen, Premilla. *Welfare Warriors: The Welfare Rights Movement in the United States.* New York: Routledge, 2005.

Nash, Gerald D. *The American West in the Twentieth Century: A Short History of an Urban Oasis.* Albuquerque: University of New Mexico Press, 1977.

———. *The American West Transformed.* Lincoln: University of Nebraska Press, 1985.

———. *World War II and the West: Reshaping the Economy.* Lincoln: University of Nebraska Press, 1990.

Newton, Huey P. *Revolutionary Suicide.* New York: Harcourt Brace Jovanovich, 1973.

———. *To Die for the People: The Writings of Huey P. Newton.* Edited by Toni Morrison. 1972. Reprint. Writers and Readers Publishing, 1995.

———. *War against the Panthers: A Study of Repression in America.* New York: Harlem River Press, 1996.

Newton, Michael. *Bitter Grain: The Story of the Black Panther Party.* Los Angeles: Holloway House, 1980.

Njeri, Akua (Deborah Johnson). *My Life with the Black Panther Party.* Oakland, Calif.: Burning Spear, 1991.

Nkrumah, Kwame. *Ghana: The Autobiography of Kwame Nkrumah.* New York: Nelson, 1957.

Ogbar, Jeffrey O. *Black Power: Radical Politics and African American Identity*. Baltimore, Md.: Johns Hopkins University Press, 2004.

Olsen, Jack. *Last Man Standing: The Tragedy and Triumph of Geronimo Pratt*. New York: Anchor Books, 2000.

O'Neill, William. *Coming Apart: An Informal History of America in the 1960s*. New York: Quadrangle Books, 1971.

O'Reilly, Kenneth. *Racial Matters: the FBI's Secret File on Black America, 1960–1972*. New York: Collier Macmillan, 1989.

Orleck, Annelise. *Storming Caesar's Palace: How Black Mothers Fought Their Own War on Poverty*. New York: Beacon Press, 2006.

Parenti, Christian. *Lockdown America: Police and Prisons in the Age of Crisis*. New York: Verso, 1999.

Patterson, James T. *Grand Expectations: The United States, 1945–1974*. New York: Oxford University Press, 1996.

Payne, Charles M. *I've Got the Light of Freedom: The Organizing Tradition and the Mississippi Freedom Struggle*. Berkeley: University of California Press, 1995.

Pearson, Hugh. *The Shadow of the Panther: Huey Newton and the Price of Black Power in America*. Reading, Penn.: Addison-Wesley, 1994.

Perata, David, D. *Those Pullman Blues: An Oral History of the African American Railroad Attendant*. New York: Twayne, 1996.

Perkins, Margo V. *Autobiography as Activism: Three Black Women of the Sixties*. Jackson: University Press of Mississippi, 2000.

Pitts, Dorothy W., and Sharon Taylor McKinney. *A Special Place for Special People: The Defremery Story*. Memphis, Tenn.: Better Communications, 1993.

Piven, Frances Fox, and Richard A. Cloward. *Poor People's Movements: Why They Succeed, How They Fail*. New York: Pantheon Books, 1977.

———. *Regulating the Poor: The Functions of Public Welfare*. New York: Vintage Books, 1993.

Plummer, Brenda Gayle. *Rising Wind: Black Americans and U.S. Foreign Affairs, 1935–1960*. Chapel Hill: University of North Carolina Press, 1996.

Prashad, Vijay. *Everybody Was Kung-Fu Fighting: Afro-Asian Connections and the Myth of Cultural Connections*. Boston: Beacon Press, 2001.

Raines, Howell. *My Soul Is Rested: Movement Days in the Deep South Remembered*. New York: Bantam Books, 1978.

Rawls, James J., and Walton Bean. *California: An Interpretive History*. 8th ed. New York: McGraw-Hill, 2003.

Record, C. Wilson. *Characteristics of Some Unemployed Negro Shipyard Workers in Oakland, California*. Berkeley: Institute of Governmental Studies, 1947.

Reed, Adolph. *Stirrings in the Jug: Black Politics in the Post- Segregation Era*. Minneapolis: University of Minnesota Press, 1999.

Reed, Merl E. *Seedtime for Modern Civil Rights: The President's Committee on Fair Employment Practice, 1941–1946*. Baton Rouge: Louisiana University Press, 1991.

Rhodes, Jane. *Framing the Black Panthers: The Spectacular Rise of a Black Power Icon*. New York: New Press, 2007.

Rhomberg, Chris. *No There There: Race, Class, and Political Community in Oakland*. Berkeley: University of California Press, 2004.

Ritterhouse, Jennifer. *Growing Up Jim Crow: How Black and White Southern Children Learned Race*. Chapel Hill: University of North Carolina Press, 2006.

Robnett, Belinda. *How Long, How Long: African American Women in the Struggle for Civil Rights*. New York: Oxford University Press, 2000.

Rodriguez, Marc S., ed. *Repositioning North American Migration History: New Directions in Modern Continental Migration, Citizenship, and Community*. Rochester, N.Y.: University of Rochester Press, 2004.

Rojas, Fabio. *From Black Power to Black Studies: How a Radical Social Movement Became an Academic Discipline*. Baltimore: Johns Hopkins University Press, 2007

Rolinson, Mary G. *Grassroots Garveyism: The Universal Negro Improvement Association in the Rural South, 1920–1927*. Chapel Hill: University of North Carolina Press, 2007.

Rooks, Noliwe M. *White Money/Black Power: The Surprising History of African American Studies and the Crisis of Race in Higher Education*. Boston: Beacon Press, 2007.

Rorabaugh, W. J. *Berkeley at War: The 1960s*. New York: Oxford University Press, 1989.

Rout, Kathleen. *Eldridge Cleaver*. Twayne's United States Authors Series 583. Boston: Twayne, 1991.

Ruchames, Louis. *Race, Jobs, & Politics: The Story of the FEPC*. New York: Columbia University Press, 1953.

Rural Organizing and Cultural Center. *Minds Stayed on Freedom: The Civil Rights Struggle in the Rural South—An Oral History*. Boulder, Colo.: Westview Press, 1991.

Sale, Kirkpatrick. *SDS*. New York: Random House, 1973.

Sales, William W., Jr. *From Civil Rights to Black Liberation: Malcolm X and the Organization of Afro-American Unity*. Boston: South End Press, 1994.

Salter, John R. *Jackson, Mississippi: An American Chronicle of Struggle and Schisms*. Hicksville, N.Y.: Exposition, 1979.

Sanchez, George. *Becoming Mexican American: Ethnicity, Culture and Identity in Chicano Los Angeles, 1900–1945*. New York: Oxford University Press, 1993.

Schiesl, Martin, ed. *Responsible Liberalism: Edmund G. "Pat" Brown and Reform Government in California 1958–1967*. Los Angeles: Edmund G. "Pat" Brown Institute of Public Affairs, 2003.

Schneider, Eric C. *Vampires, Dragons and Egyptian Kings: Youth Gangs in Postwar New York*. Princeton, N.J.: Princeton University Press, 1999.

Schuparra, Kurt. *The Triumph of the Right: The Rise of the California Conservative Movement, 1945–1955*. Armonk, N.Y.: M. E. Sharp, 1998.

Scott, Daryl Michael. *Contempt and Pity: Social Policy and the Image of the Damaged Black Psyche, 1880–1996*. Chapel Hill: University of North Carolina Press, 1997.

Seale, Bobby. *A Lonely Rage: The Autobiography of Bobby Seale*. New York: Times Books, 1978.

———. *Seize the Time: The Story of the Black Panther Party and Huey P. Newton*. New York: Random House, 1970.

Self, Robert. *American Babylon: Race and the Struggle for Postwar Oakland*. Princeton, N.J.: Princeton University Press, 2003.

Sellers, Cleveland, with Robert Terrell. *The River of No Return: The Autobiography of a Black Militant and the Life and Death of SNCC*. Jackson: University Press of Mississippi, 1990.

Shakur, Assata. *Assata: An Autobiography*. Westport, Conn.: L. Hill, 1987.

Shames, Stephen. *The Black Panthers: Photographs by Stephen Shames*. New York: Aperture, 2006.

Sheehy, Gail. *Panthermania: The Clash of Black against Black in One American City*. New York: Harper and Row, 1971.

Sides, Josh. *L.A. City Limits: African-American Los Angeles from the Great Depression to the Present*. Berkeley: University of California Press, 2003.

Simon, Jonathan. *Governing through Crime*. New York: Oxford University Press, 2007.

Singh, Nikhil P. *Black Is a Country: Race and the Unfinished Struggle for Democracy*. Cambridge, Mass.: Harvard University Press, 2004.

Skolnick, Jerome H. *The Politics of Protest: A Task Force Report Submitted to the National Commission on the Causes and Prevention of Violence*. New York: Simon and Schuster, 1969.

Smethurst, James Edward. *The Black Arts Movement: Literary Nationalism in the 1960s and 1970s*. Chapel Hill: University of North Carolina Press, 2005.

Smith, J. Alfred. *Thus Far by Faith: A Study of Historical Backgrounds and the First Fifty Years of the Allen Temple Baptist Church*. Oakland, Calif.: Color Art Press, 1973.

Smith, Jennifer B. *An International History of the Black Panther Party*. New York: Garland, 1999.

Smith, Jessie Carney, and Carrell Peterson Horton, eds. *Historical Statistics of Black America*. New York: Gale Research, 1995.

Sonenshein, Raphael. *Politics in Black and White: Race and Power in Los Angeles*. Princeton, N.J.: Princeton University Press, 1993.

Strain, Christopher. *Pure Fire: Self-Defense as Activism in the Civil Rights Era*. Athens: University of Georgia Press, 2005.

Sugarman, Tracy. *Stranger at the Gates: A Summer in Mississippi*. New York: Hill and Wang Publishers, 1966.

Sugrue, Thomas J. *The Origins of the Urban Crisis: Race and Inequality in Postwar Detroit*. Princeton, N.J.: Princeton University Press, 1996.

———. *Sweet Land of Liberty: The Forgotten Struggle for Civil Rights in the North*. New York: Random House, 2008.

Sullivan, Patricia. *Days of Hope: Race and Democracy in the New Deal Era*. Chapel Hill: University of North Carolina Press, 1996.

Suri, Jeremi. *Power and Protest: Global Revolution and the Rise of Détente*. Cambridge, Mass.: Harvard University Press, 2003.

Taylor, Quintard. *In Search of the Racial Frontier: African Americans in the American West, 1528–1990*. New York: Norton, 1998.

Theoharis, Jeanne, and Komozi Woodard, eds. *Freedom North: Black Freedom Struggles Outside the South, 1940–1980*. New York: Palgrave Macmillan, 2003.

———. *Groundwork: Local Black Freedom Movements in America*. New York: New York University Press, 2005.

Thompson, Phillip J., III. *Double Trouble: Black Mayors, Black Communities, and the Call for a Deep Democracy*. London: Oxford University Press, 2006.

Tolney, Stewart. *The Bottom Rung: African American Family Life on Southern Farms*. Chicago: University of Illinois Press, 1999.

Trotter, Joe. *The Great Migration in Historical Perspective: New Dimensions of Race, Class and Gender*. Bloomington: University of Indiana, 1991.

Tyson, Timothy B. *Blood Done Sign My Name: A True Story*. New York: Three Rivers Press, 2004.

———. *Radio Free Dixie: Robert F. Williams and the Roots of Black Power*. Chapel Hill: University of North Carolina Press, 1999.

Van Deburg, William L. *New Day in Babylon: The Black Power Movement and American Culture, 1965–1975*. Chicago: University of Chicago Press, 1992.

Van Peebles, Mario, Ula V. Taylor, and J. Tarika Lewis. *Panther: A Pictorial History of the Black Panthers and the Story Behind the Film*. New York: New Market Press, 1995.

Wacquant, Loïc. *Deadly Symbiosis: Race and the Rise of the Penal State*. Cambridge: Polity Press, 2008.

Walker, Samuel. *Popular Justice: A History of American Criminal Justice*. New York: Oxford University Press, 1998.

Walton, Sidney. *The Black Curriculum: Developing a Program in Afro-American Studies*. East Palo Alto, Calif.: Black Liberation, 1969.

Ware, Alan. *The Breakdown of Democratic Party Organization, 1940–1980*. Oxford, Eng.: Clarendon Press, 1985.

Watkins, William H., ed. *Black Protest Thought and Education*. New York: Peter Lang, 2005.

Weaver, Robert Clifton. *Negro Labor, A National Problem*. New York: Harcourt Brace, 1946.

Wellman, David. *The Union Makes Us Strong: Racial Unionism on the San Francisco Waterfront*. New York: Cambridge University Press, 1995.

Wendt, Simon. *The Spirit and the Shotgun: Armed Resistance and the Struggle for Civil Rights*. Gainesville: University Press of Florida, 2007.

Wilkins, Roy. *Search and Destroy: A Report by the Commission of Inquiry into the Black Panthers and the Police*. New York: Metropolitan Applied Research Center, 1973.

Williams, Heather Andrea. *Self-Taught: African American Education in Slavery and Freedom*. Chapel Hill: University of North Carolina Press, 2005.

Williams, Rhonda Y. *The Politics of Public Housing: Black Women's Struggles against Urban Inequality*. New York: Oxford University Press, 2004.

Williams, Robert F. *Negroes with Guns*. Detroit, Mich.: Wayne State University Press, 1998.

Williams, Yohuru. *Black Politics/White Power: Civil Rights, Black Power, and the Black Panthers in New Haven*. New York: Brandywine Press, 2000.

Wolfe, Tom. *Radical Chic & Mau-Mauing the Flak Catchers*. New York: Bantam Books, 1970.

Wollenberg, Charles. *All Deliberate Speed: Segregation and Exclusion in California Schools, 1855–1975*. Berkeley: University of California Press, 1976.

———. *Marinship at War: Shipbuilding and Social Change in Wartime Sausalito*. Berkeley: Western Heritage Press, 1990.

Woodard, Komozi. *A Nation within a Nation: Amiri Baraka (LeRoi Jones) & Black Power Politics*. Chapel Hill: University of North Carolina Press, 1999.

Woodruff, Nan Elizabeth. *American Congo: The African American Freedom Struggle in the Delta*. Cambridge, Mass.: Harvard University Press, 2003.

Wright, Gavin. *Old South, New South: Revolutions in the Southern Economy since the Civil War*. Baton Rouge: Louisiana State University Press, 1996.

Yee, Min S. *The Melancholy History of Soledad Prison: In Which a Utopian Scheme Turns Bedlam*. New York: Harper and Row, 1970.

ARTICLES AND ESSAYS

Abron, Jonina. "Raising the Consciousness of the People: The Black Panther Intercommunal News Service, 1967–1980." In Vol. 2 of *Voices from the Underground: Insider Histories of the*

Vietnam Era Underground Press, edited by Ken Wachsberger, 343–59. Tempe, Ariz.: Mica Press, 1993.

——. "Serving the People: The Survival Programs of the Black Panther Party." In *The Black Panther Party (Reconsidered)*, edited by Charles E. Jones, 172–92. Baltimore, Md.: Black Classic Press, 1998.

Avrich, Paul. "The Legacy of Bakunin." *Russian Review* 29, no. 2 (April 1970): 129–42.

"Back From Skid Row." *Time*, February 2, 1962. <http://www.time/magazine/article/0,9171,828966,00.html>.

Barber, David. "Leading the Vanguard: White New Leftists School the Panthers on Black Revolution." In *In Search of the Black Panther Party: New Perspectives on a Revolutionary Movement*, edited by Jama Lazerow and Yohuru Williams, 223–51. Durham, N.C.: Duke University Press, 2006.

Best, Wallace. "The South and the City: Black Southern Migrants, Storefront Churches, and the Rise of a Religious Diaspora." In *Repositioning North American Migration History: New Directions in Modern Continental Migration, Citizenship, and Community*, edited by Marc S. Rodriguez, 302–27. Rochester, N.Y.: University of Rochester Press, 2004.

Black Panther Party (Guest Editors). "Supplement to the Whole Earth Catalog." *CoEvolution Quarterly* 3 (September 23, 1974).

"Board Accepts Merritt Bid." *Peralta Colleges Bulletin*, January 10, 1969, 1–4.

Booker, Chris. "Lumpenization: A Critical Error of the Black Panther Party." In *The Black Panther Party (Reconsidered)*, edited by Charles E. Jones, 337–62. Baltimore, Md.: Black Classic Press, 1998.

Broussard, Albert S. "In Search of the Promised Land: African American Migration to San Francisco." In *Seeking El Dorado: African Americans in California*, edited by Lawrence B. De Graaf, Kevin Mulroy, and Quintard Taylor, 181–209. Seattle: University of Washington Press, 2001.

Brown, Angela Darlean. "Elaine Brown." In Vol. 1 of *Black Women in America: A Historical Encyclopedia*, edited by Darlene Clark Hine, Elsa Barkley Brown, and Rosalyn Terborg-Penn, 175–76. New York: Carlson Publishing, 1993.

——. "Kathleen Neal Cleaver." In Vol. 1 of *Black Women in America: A Historical Encyclopedia*, edited by Darlene Clark Hine, Elsa Barkley Brown, and Rosalyn Terborg-Penn, 252. Bloomington: Indiana University Press, 1993.

Brown, Scot. "The Politics of Culture: The US Organization and the Quest for Black Unity." In *Freedom North: Black Freedom Struggles outside the South, 1940–1980*, edited by Jeanne Theoharis and Komozi Woodard, 223–54. New York: Palgrave Macmillan, 2003.

Burbank, Garin. "Governor Reagan and California Welfare Reform." *California History* 70, no. 3 (1991): 278–89.

Butler, Kim. "Defining Diaspora, Refining a Discourse." *Diaspora* 10, no. 2 (Fall 2001): 189–219.

Campbell, James T. "The Panthers and Local History." In *In Search of the Black Panther Party: New Perspectives on a Revolutionary Movement*, edited by Jama Lazerow and Yohuru Williams, 97–103. Durham, N.C.: Duke University Press, 2006.

Carson, Clayborne. "Long, Hot California Summers: The Rise of Black Protest and Black Power." In *What's Going On?: California and the Vietnam Era*, edited by Marcia A. Eymann and Charles Wollenberg, 99–112. Berkeley: University of California Press, 2004.

Cha-Jua, Sundiata K., and Clarence Lang. "The 'Long Movement' as Vampire: Temporal and Spatial Fallacies in Recent Black Freedom Studies." *Journal of African American History* 92, no. 1 (2008): 265–88.

Clarke, John Henrik. "The New Afro-American Nationalism." *Freedomways*, Fall 1961, 285–95.

Cleague, Reverend Albert. "Myths about Malcolm X." In *Malcolm X: The Man and His Times*, edited by John Henrik Clarke, 13–26. New York: African World Press, 1991.

Cleaver, Eldridge. "Education and Revolution." *Black Scholar* 1, no. 1 (November 1969): 44–52.

———. "The Following Is an Address Given by Eldridge Cleaver at a Rally in His Honor Given a Few Days before He Was Scheduled to Return to Jail." *Ramparts*, December 14–28, 1968, 6–10.

———. "Message to Sister Ericka Huggins of the Black Panther Party." In *The Black Panthers Speak*, edited by Philip Sheldon Foner, 97–98. Philadelphia: Lippincott, 1970.

———. "My Father and Stokely Carmichael." *Ramparts*, April 1967, 12–13.

———. "On Lumpen Ideology." *Black Scholar* 4, no. 3 (November/December 1972): 2–10.

Cleaver, Kathleen. "How TV Wrecked the Black Panthers." *Channels*, November–December 1982, 98–99.

Cohen, Shalom, and Kokhavi Shemesh. "The Origin and Development of the Israeli Black Panther Movement." *Merip Reports* 49 (July 1976): 19–22

Davenport, Christian. "Reading the Voice of the Vanguard Party: A Content and Rhetorical Analysis of the Black Panther Party Intercommunal Newsletter from 1969–1973." In *The Black Panther Party (Reconsidered)*, edited by Charles Jones, 193–210. Baltimore, Md.: Black Classic Press, 1998.

De Graaf, Lawrence B. Review of Gerald Horne, *The Fire This Time: The Watts Uprising and the 1960s*. *Pacific Historical Review* 66, no. 1 (1997): 99.

De Graaf, Lawrence B., and Quintard Taylor. "Introduction." In *Seeking El Dorado: African Americans in California*, edited by Lawrence B. De Graaf, Kevin Mulroy, and Quintard Taylor, 3–69. Seattle: University of Washington Press, 2001.

DeLeon, David. "Eldridge Cleaver." In *Leaders from the Sixties: A Biographical Sourcebook of American Activism*, edited by David DeLeon, 66–71. London: Greenwood Press, 1994.

DeLeon, Robert. "Showdown in Oakland: Bobby Seale and Otho Green Battle to Become Mayor." *Jet*, April 12, 1973, 14–25.

Dirk, Annelieke. "Between Threat and Reality: The National Association for the Advancement of Colored People and the Emergence of Armed Self-Defense in Clarksdale and Natchez, Mississippi, 1960–1965," *Journal for the Study of Radicalism* 1 (2007): 71–98.

Doss, Erika. "'Revolutionary Art is a Tool for Liberation': Emory Douglas and Protest Aesthetics at the *Black Panther*." In *Liberation, Imagination, and the Black Panther Party: A New Look at the Panthers and Their Legacy*, edited by Kathleen Cleaver and George Katsiaficas, 175–87. New York: Routledge, 2001.

Douglas, Emory. "Art for People's Sake." *Black Panther*, October 21, 1972.

Douglass, John Aubrey. "Brokering the 1960 Master Plan: Pat Brown and the Promise of California Higher Education." In *Responsible Liberalism: Edmund G. "Pat" Brown and Reform Government in California 1958–1967*, edited by Martin Schiesl, 61–93. Los Angeles: Edmund G. "Pat" Brown Institute of Public Affairs, 2003.

Dupree, David, and Williams McAllister. "A Campus Where Black Power Won." *Wall Street Journal*, November 18, 1969.

Edwards, Brent. "The Uses of Diaspora." *Social Text* 19, no. 1 (Spring 2001): 45–73.

Epstein, Edward Jay. "The Black Panthers and the Police: A Pattern of Genocide." *New Yorker*, February 13, 1971, 45–63.

Etzioni-Halevy, Eva. "Protest Politics in the Israeli Democracy." *Political Science Quarterly* 90, no. 3 (Autumn 1975): 497–520.

Franklin, V. P. "Jackanapes: Reflections on the Legacy of the Black Panther Party for the Hip Hop Generation." *Journal of African American History* 92, no. 4 (Fall 2007): 553–60.

Garrow, David J. "Picking Up the Books: The New Historiography of the Black Panther Party." *Reviews in American History* 35 (2007): 650–70.

Garry, Charles R. "The Old Rules Do Not Apply: A Survey of the Persecution of the Black Panther Party." In *The Black Panthers Speak*, edited by Philip Sheldon Foner, 257–62. Philadelphia: Lippincott, 1970.

Gilbert, Mark. "Next Stop—Silicon Valley: The Cold War, Vietnam, and the Making of the California Economy." In *What's Going On?: California and the Vietnam Era*, edited by Marcia A. Eymann and Charles Wollenberg, 23–42. Berkeley: University of California Press, 2004.

Grady-Willis, Winston A. "The Black Panther Party: State Repression and Political Prisoners." In *The Black Panther Party (Reconsidered)*, edited by Charles Jones, 363–90. Baltimore, Md.: Black Classic Press, 1998.

Gregory, James. "The Southern Diaspora." In *Repositioning North American Migration History: New Directions in Modern Continental Migration, Citizenship, and Community*, edited by Marc S. Rodriguez, 54–97. Rochester, N.Y.: University of Rochester Press, 2004.

———. "The Southern Diaspora and the Urban Dispossessed: Demonstrating the Census Public Use Microdata Samples." *Journal of American History* 82, no. 1 (June 1995): 111–34.

Hall, Jacquelyn Dowd. "The Long Civil Rights Movement and the Political Uses of the Past." *Journal of American History* 91, no. 4 (March 2005): 1233–63.

Hanna, William John. "Students, Universities, and Political Outcomes." In *University Students and African Politics*, edited by William John Hanna and Judith Lynne Hanna, 1–22. New York: Africana, 1975.

Harris, William. "Federal Intervention in Union Discrimination: FEPC and the West Coast Shipyards during World War II." *Labor History* 22, no. 3 (1981): 325–47.

Hildebrand, Lee. "West Side Story." *East Bay Express*, September 28, 1979, 1–4.

Hinckle, Warren. "Metropoly." *Ramparts*, February 1966, 25–51.

Hine, Darlene Clark. "Black Professionals and Race Consciousness: Origins of the Civil Rights Movement, 1890–1950." *Journal of American History* 89, no. 4 (March 2003): 1279–94.

Hopkins, Donald. "Development of Black Political Organization in Berkeley since 1960." In *Experiment and Change in Berkeley: Essays on City Politics 1950–1975*, edited by Evelio Grillo, Harriet Nathan, and Stanley Scott. Berkeley: Institute of Governmental Studies, University of California, 1978.

Horne, Gerald. "Black Fire: 'Riot' and 'Revolt' in Los Angeles, 1965 and 1992." In *Seeking El Dorado: African Americans in California*, edited by Lawrence B. De Graaf, Kevin Mulroy, and Quintard Taylor, 377–404. Seattle: University of Washington Press, 2001.

Jeffries, Judson L., and Foley, Malcolm. "To Live and Die in L.A." In *Comrades: A Local History of the Black Panther Party*, edited by Judson L. Jeffries, 255–90. Bloomington: Indiana University Press, 2007.

Jennings, Regina. "Why I Joined the Black Panther Party: An Africana Womanist Reflection." In *The Black Panther Party (Reconsidered)*, edited by Charles E. Jones, 257–66. Baltimore, Md.: Black Classic Press, 1998.

Jones, Charles. "The Political Repression of the Black Panther Party 1966–1971." *Journal of Black Studies* 18, no. 4 (June 1988): 415–34.

Joseph, Peniel. " Black Studies, Student Activism, and the Black Power Movement." In *The Black Power Movement: Rethinking the Civil Rights–Black Power Era*, edited by Peniel Joseph, 251–79. New York: Routledge, 2006.

———. "Dashikis and Democracy: Black Studies, Student Activism, and the Black Power Movement." *Journal of African American History* 88, no. 2 (Spring 2003): 182–203.

Karmin, Monroe. "A Federal Study Finds Unrest Among Negroes Rising in Many Cities." *Wall Street Journal*, January 5, 1966.

———. "Jobs vs. Training: Many Negroes Prefer Former, Government Stresses Latter." *Wall Street Journal*, February 16, 1966.

Katz, Michael B. "The Urban 'Underclass' as a Metaphor of Social Transformation: Reframing the Underclass Debate." In *The "Underclass" Debate: Views from History*, edited by Michael B. Katz, 3–26. Princeton, N.J.: Princeton University Press, 1993.

Kelley, Robin D. G. "Slangin' Rocks . . . Palestinian Style." In *Police Brutality*, edited by Jill Nelson, 21–59. New York: W. W. Norton, 2000.

Kelley, Robin D. G., and Betsy Esch. "Black Like Mao: Red China and Black Revolution." *Souls* 1, no. 4 (Fall 1999): 6–41.

Lacy, Leslie Alexander. "African Responses to Malcolm X." In *Black Fire: An Anthology of Afro-American Writing*, edited by LeRoi Jones and Larry Neal, 19–38. New York: William Morrow, 1968.

LeBlanc-Ernest, Angela D. "The Most Qualified Person to Handle the Job." In *The Black Panther Party (Reconsidered)*, edited by Charles E. Jones, 305–36. Baltimore, Md.: Black Classic Press, 1998.

Lemann, Nicholas. "The Quiet Man: Dick Cheney's Discreet Rise to Unprecedented Power." *New Yorker*, May 7, 2001.

Lester, Julius. "SNCC and the Black Panthers." In *Revolutionary Notes*, 144–49. New York: Grove Press, 1969.

Lipset, Seymour Martin. Foreword to *University Students and African Politics*, edited by William John Hanna and Judith Lynne Hanna, v–vii. New York: Africana, 1975.

Lucas, Boby. "East Oakland Ghetto Blooms With Growth of Panther School," *Jet*, February 5, 1976, 19–25.

Lustig, Jeffrey. "The War at Home: California's Struggle to Stop the Vietnam War." In *What's Going On?: California and the Vietnam Era*, edited by Marcia A. Eymann and Charles Wollenberg, 59–82. Berkeley: University of California Press, 2004.

Mack, Carl. Foreword to *A Special Place for Special People: The Defremery Story*, by Dorothy W. Pitts and Sharon Taylor McKinney, i–iii. Memphis, Tenn.: Better Communications, 1993.

Maeda, Daryl J. "Black Panthers, Red Guards, and Chinamen: Constructing Asian American Identity through Performing Blackness, 1969–1972." *American Quarterly* 57, no. 4 (December 2005): 1079–1103.

Malcolm X. "The Ballot or the Bullet." In *Malcolm X Speaks*, edited by George Breitman, 23–44. New York: Pathfinder, 1989.

Marable, Manning. Foreword to *The New Black Vote: Politics and Power in Four American Cities*, by Rod Bush, 1-11. Seattle: Synthesis, 1984.

Martin, Waldo. "Shades of Brown: Black Freedom, White Supremacy, and the Law: Brown vs. Board of Education: A Brief History with Documents." In *The American Civil Rights Movement: Readings and Interpretations*, edited by Raymond D'Angelo, 230–53. Guilford, Conn.: McGraw-Hill, 2001.

Mason, B. J. "A Shift to the Middle: Chairman Bobby Seale Changes Black Panther Image to Fit the Times." *Ebony*, August 28, 1973, 80–87.

McKown, Robert E. "Kenya University Students and Politics." In *University Students and African Politics*, edited by William John Hanna and Judith Lynne Hanna. New York: Africana, 1975.

"Merritt Stays." In *The Lumpen: Revolutionary Student News Service*. Merritt Black Student Union, Merritt College, Oakland, Calif., November 17, 1970, 3.

Mosby, Donald. "Panthers Emerging Out of Ashes of Tragedy, Despair." *Muhammad Speaks*, March 16, 1973, 30.

Moses, Wilson J. "Segregation Nostalgia and Black Authenticity." *American Literary History* 17, no. 3 (Fall 2005): 621–42.

Murch, Donna. "The Campus and the Street: Race, Migration, and the Origins of the Black Panther Party in Oakland, CA." *Souls* 9, no. 4 (October 2007): 333–45.

Newton, Huey P. "The Defection of Eldridge Cleaver and Revolutionary Suicide." In *Revolutionary Suicide*, 328–31. New York: Harcourt Brace Jovanovich, 1973.

———. "On the Defection of Eldridge Cleaver from the Black Panther Party and the Defection of the Black Panther Party from the Black Community: April 17, 1971." In *To Die for the People: The Writings of Huey P. Newton*, edited by Toni Morrison, 44–53. 1972. Reprint. New York: Writers and Readers Publishing, 1995.

———. "On the Relevance of the Black Church." In *To Die for the People: The Writings of Huey P. Newton*, edited by Toni Morrison, 60–75. 1972. Reprint. New York: Writers and Readers Publishing, 1995.

———. "Speech Delivered at Boston College: November 18, 1970." In *To Die for the People: The Writings of Huey P. Newton*, edited by Toni Morrison, 20–38. 1972. Reprint. New York: Writers and Readers Publishing, 1995.

———. "The Women's Liberation and Gay Liberation Movements." In *To Die for the People: The Writings of Huey P. Newton*, edited by Toni Morrison, 152–55. 1972. Reprint. New York: Writers and Readers Publishing, 1995.

Orleck, Annelise. "I Decided I'd Marry the First Man Who Asked: Gendering Black Migration from Cotton Country to the Desert Southwest." In *Repositioning North American Migration History: New Directions in Modern Continental Migration, Citizenship, and Community*, edited by Marc S. Rodriguez, 352–87. Rochester: University of Rochester Press, 2004.

Patterson, Tiffany, and Robin D. G. Kelley. "Unfinished Migrations: Reflections on the African Diaspora and the Making of the Modern World." Special Issue on the Diaspora, *African Studies Review* 43, no. 1 (April 2000): 11–45.

Perlstein, Daniel. "Minds Stayed on Freedom: Politics and Pedagogy in the African-American Freedom Struggle." In *Black Protest Thought and Education*, edited by William H. Watkins, 33–66. New York: Peter Lang, 2005.

———. "SNCC and the Creation of the Mississippi Freedom Schools." *History of Education Quarterly* 30, no. 3 (Autumn 1990): 297–324.

Phillips, Kevin P. "The Welfare Crunch." *Washington Post*, May 8, 1971.

Polt, Harriet. "School Daze." *East Bay Express*, June 11, 1982.

Rauber, Paul. "The Case of the Languishing Landmark," *East Bay Express*, March 23, 1990, 12–20.

Rodriguez, Joseph A. "Rapid Transit and Community Power: West Oakland Residents Confront BART." *Antipode* 31, no. 2 (1999): 212–28.

Scheer, Robert. Introduction to *Post-Prison Writings and Speeches*, by Eldridge Cleaver, edited by Robert Scheer, vii–xxxiii. New York: Random House, 1969.

Singh, Nikhil Pal. "The Black Panthers and the 'Undeveloped Country' of the Left." In *The Black Panther Party (Reconsidered)*, edited by Charles E. Jones, 57–108. Baltimore, Md.: Black Classic Press, 1998.

Smith, Jessie Carney, and Carrell Peterson Horton. "Completion Levels: Percentage of High School and College 'Completers' (Aged 25 and Over) in Selected Cities, 1969." In *Historical Statistics of Black America*. Vol. 1, *Agriculture to Labor and Employment*, 530–31. New York: Gale Research, 1995.

"Special Report on Minority Group Relations Presented to the Trustees." *Peralta Colleges Bulletin*, January 12, 1968, 2–7.

Spencer, Robyn Ceanne. "Engendering the Black Freedom Struggle: Revolutionary Black Womanhood and the Black Panther Party in the Bay Area, California." *Journal of Women's History* 20, no. 1 (2008): 90–113.

Street, Emerson. "Nightstick Justice in Oakland." *New Republic*, February 20, 1950, 15–16.

Student Nonviolent Coordinating Committee of California. "Negroes Should Stop Fighting." *Movement*, September 1965.

———. "Oakland Is a Powder Keg." *Movement*, September 1965.

Taylor, Quintard. "The Civil Rights Movement in the American West: Black Protest in Seattle, 1960–1970." *Journal of Negro History* 80, no. 6 (1995): 1–14.

Theoharis, Jeanne. "Alabama on Avalon: Rethinking the Watts Uprising and the Character of Northern Black Protest." In *The Black Power Movement: Rethinking the Civil Rights–Black Power Era*, edited by Peniel Joseph, 27–54. New York: Routledge, 2006.

"This Course Is for Black Students Only." *Newsweek*, February 10, 1969, 58.

Thompson, Wayne. "City's War on People Problems." *Public Management* 46 (September 1965): 210–17.

Turner, Rex, and George McKee. "High School Planned to Serve Youths in a Low-Rent Community." *The Nation's Schools* 49, no. 6 (June 1952): 61–64.

Umezaki, Toru. "Breaking Through the Cane-Curtain: The Cuban Revolution and the Emergence of New York's Radical Youth, 1961–1965." *Japanese Journal of American Studies* 18 (2007): 187–207.

Umoja, Akinyele O. "The Ballot and the Bullet: A Comparative Organization in the Mississippi Freedom Movement." *Journal of Black Studies* 29 (1999): 558–78.

———. "1964: The Beginning of the End of Nonviolence in the Mississippi Freedom Movement." *Radical History Review* 85 (2003): 2010–26.

———. "Repression Breeds Resistance: The Black Liberation Army and the Radical Legacy of the Black Panther Party." *New Political Science* 21, no. 2 (1999): 131–56.

———. "'We Will Shoot Back': The Natchez Model and Paramilitary Organization in the Mississippi Freedom Movement." *Journal of Black Studies* 32 (2002): 271–94.

Warden, Donald. "The Black Negro." *Root and Branch: A Radical Quarterly,* 7, no. 1 (Winter 1962): 1–28.

White, John. Review of Ralph Luker, *Historical Dictionary of the Civil Rights Movement. Journal of American Studies* 32, no. 3 (December 1998): 529–30.

Wilkins, Roy. "Black Panthers Swap Violence for the Ballot Box." *Los Angeles Times,* October 2, 1972.

———. "The 'New' Panthers." *New York Post,* February 26, 1972.

Williams, Rhonda Y. "Exploring Babylon and Unveiling the 'Mother of Harlots.'" *American Quarterly* 57 (March 2005): 297–304.

Williams, Yohuru. "American Exported Black Nationalism: The Student Coordinating Committee, the Black Panther Party, and the Worldwide Freedom Struggle, 1967–1972." *Negro History Bulletin,* 60 (July–September 1997). <http://www.questia.com/googleScholar.qst?docId=5000495264>.

———. "The Black Panther Party: A Short Historiography for Teachers." *OAH Magazine of History* 22, no. 3 (July 2008). <http://www.oah.org/pubs/magazine/bpower/williams.html>.

———. "From Oakland to Omaha: Historicizing the Panthers." In *Liberated Territory: Untold Local Perspectives on the Black Panther Party,* edited by Yohuru Williams and Jama Lazerow, 1–32. Durham, N.C.: Duke University Press, 2008.

Williamson, Joy Ann. "Community Control with a Black Nationalist Twist." In *Black Protest Thought and Education,* edited by William H. Watkins, 137–58. New York: Peter Lang, 2005.

Wilson, Joel. "Invisible Cages: Racialized Politics and the Alliance between the Panthers and the Peace and Freedom Party." In *In Search of the Black Panther Party: New Perspectives on a Revolutionary Movement,* edited by Jama Lazerow and Yohuru Williams, 191–222. Durham, N.C.: Duke University Press, 2006.

Wollenberg, Charles. "California and the Vietnam War: Microcosm and Magnification." In *What's Going On?: California and the Vietnam Era,* edited by Marcia A. Eymann and Charles Wollenberg, 13–22. Berkeley: University of California Press, 2004.

ELECTRONIC SOURCES

Brown, H. Rap. "Free Huey Rally." U.C. Berkeley Library Social Activism Sound Recording Project: The Black Panther Party. Printed transcript, Pacifica Radio Archives, BB1708, February 1968. <http://www.lib.berkeley.edu/MRC/carmichael.html>.

Carmichael, Stokely. "Free Huey Rally." U.C. Berkeley Library Social Activism Sound Recording Project: The Black Panther Party. Printed transcript, Pacifica Radio Archives, BB1708, February 1968. <http://www.lib.berkeley.edu/MRC/carmichael.html>.

Cleaver, Eldridge. "The Fire Now." *Commonweal* 14 (June 1968). Reprinted in *Chickenbones: A Journal.* <http://www.nathanielturner.com/eldridgecleaverfirenow.htm>.

"Edwin Kelly—RIP." Message posted to *Allaboutjazz.com* forum, February 9, 2005. Archived at <http://forums.allaboutjazz.com/archive/index.php/t-8108.html>.

Eyes on the Prize. Transcript. <http://www.pbs.org/wgbh/amex/eyesontheprize/about?pt_203.html>.

Neil, Earl A. "Black Panther Party and Father Neil." *It's About Time: Black Panther Party Legacy and Alumni.* <http://www.itsabouttimebpp.com/Our_Stories/Chapter1/BPP_and_Father_Neil.html>.

Peters, Casey. "Peace and Freedom Party from 1967 to 1997." *Synthesis/Regeneration* 12 (Winter 1997). <http://www.greens.org/s-r/12/12-05.html>.

"The Pipes." *Answers.com.* <http://www.answers.com/topic/pipes?cat=entertainment>.

University of California, Berkeley, Library Social Activism Sound Recording Project: The Black Panther Party. Panel discussion of BPP and PFP alliance, Pacifica Radio Achives, BB1632, February 15, 1968. <http://www.lib.berkeley.edu/MRC/pacificapanthers.html>.

University of California, Berkeley, Library Social Activism Sound Recording Project: The Black Panther Party. Timeline transcript. <http://www.lib.berkeley.edu/MRC/pacificapanthers.html>.

AUDIO RECORDINGS

African American Association. *Burn, Baby, Burn.* Berkeley, Calif.: Music City, 1965.

Pacifica Radio Archives: A Living History. North Hollywood, Calif.

Parliament. *Chocolate City.* Casablanca Records 831, 1975.

Roach, Max. *Speak, Brother, Speak!* San Francisco: The Jazz Workshop, 1962.

Wonder, Stevie. "Living for the City." *Inner Visions.* Tamla Records, 1973.

FILMS AND VIDEOS

Peralta TV. *Merritt College: Home of the Black Panthers.* 2008

Sloan, Cle "Bone" (director). *Bastards of the Party.* New York: HBO Films, 2006.

Van Peebles, Mario (director). *Panther.* London: Gramercy & PolyGram Films, 1995.

UNPUBLISHED WORKS

Adams, Luther James. "'Way up North in Louisville': African-American Migration in Louisville, Kentucky, 1930–1970." Ph.D. diss., University of Pennsylvania, 2002.

Agee, Christopher Lowen-Engel. "The Streets of San Francisco: Blacks, Beats, Homosexuals, and the San Francisco Police Department, 1950–1968." Ph.D. diss., University of California, Berkeley, 2005.

Alkebulan, Paul. "The Role of Ideology in the Growth, Establishment, and Decline of the Black Panther Party: 1966 to 1982." Ph.D. diss., University of California, Berkeley, 2003.

———. "Survival Pending Revolution: Community Action in the Black Panther Party, 1969–1971." Unpublished seminar paper, University of California, Berkeley, Fall 2000.

Brenner, Johanna. "Public Higher Education in 'Post-Industrial Society': The Case of California." Ph.D. diss., University of California, Berkeley, 1979.

Brown, Angela Darlean. "Servants of the People: A History of Women in the Black Panther Party." A.B. thesis (Honors in Afro-American Studies), Harvard University, 1992.

Brown, Scot. "The US Organization: African-American Cultural Nationalism in the Era of Black Power, 1965 to the 1970s." Ph.D. diss., Cornell University, 1999.

Brown, William Henry. "Class Aspects of Residential Development and Choice in the Oakland Black Community." Ph.D. diss., University of California, Berkeley, 1970.

Bryson, Nicole. "San Francisco Race Riots." Undergraduate thesis, University of California, Berkeley, 1999.

City of Oakland Police Department. "History 1941–1955." Part 6. Unpublished report. Oakland History Room, Main Public Library, Oakland, Calif.

Community of Oakland. "Proposal to the Ford Foundation for a Program of Community Development with Special Reference to Assimilation of the Newcomer Population." June 1961, Ford Foundation Archives, New York, N.Y.

Corbin, Doug. "The Oakland Black Panther Schools: Its Evolution and Curriculum." Undergraduate thesis, University of California, Berkeley, 2004.

Crosby, Emilye. "The Calculus of Change." Unpublished article in possession of author, 2009.

Dellums, C. L. "International President of the Brotherhood of Sleeping Car Porters and Civil Rights Leader." Northern California Negro Political Series, Regional Oral History Office, Bancroft Library, University of California, Berkeley, 1973.

Faraj, Gaidi. "Unearthing the Underground: A Study of Radical Activism in the Black Panther Party and the Black Liberation Army." Ph.D. diss., University of California, Berkeley, 2007.

Ferriera, Jason. "All Power to the People: A Comparative History of Third World Radicalism in San Francisco, 1968–1974." Ph.D. diss., University of California, Berkeley, 2003.

Frazier, Robeson. "A Revolution Is Not a Dinner Party: Black Internationalism, Chinese Communism and the Post–World War II Black Freedom Struggle, 1949–1976." Ph.D. diss., University of California, Berkeley, 2009.

Hausler, Donald. "Blacks in Oakland." Unpublished manuscript, Oakland, California, 1980.

Holder, Kit Kim. "The History of the Black Panther Party 1966–1972: A Curriculum Tool for Afrikan American Studies." Ph.D. diss., University of Massachusetts at Amherst, 1990.

Hopkins, Charles William. "The Deradicalization of the Black Panther Party: 1967–1973." Ph.D. diss., University of North Carolina, 1979.

Jeffries, Hasan Kwame. "Freedom Politics: Transcending Civil Rights in Lowndes County, Alabama, 1965–2000." Ph.D. diss., Duke University, 2002.

Jones, Ron, and Mike Hancock. "Preliminary Investigation of the Relationship between the Black Panther Party and the Local Law Enforcement Agencies, January 31, 1970." Unpublished report.

Kraft, Horst P. R. "Oakland City College New Campus Planning and Development: A Report to the Faculty of the Graduate School of Business Administration." M.A. thesis, University of California, Berkeley, 1962.

Matthews, Tracye Ann. "No One Ever Asks What a Man's Role in the Revolution Is: Gender and Sexual Politics in the Black Panther Party, 1966–1971." Ph.D. diss., University of Michigan, 1998.

Maxell, John. "In Defense of Eldridge Cleaver." Undergraduate paper, University of California, Berkeley, 2003.

May, Judith. "Struggle for Authority: A Comparison of Four Social Change Programs in Oakland, California." Ph.D. diss., University of California, Berkeley, 1973.

McCarty, Heather Jane. "From Con-Boss to Gang Lord: The Transformation of Social Relations in California Prisons, 1943–1983." Ph.D. diss., University of California, Berkeley, 2004.

Mihailoff, Laura. "Protecting Our Children: A History of the California Youth Authority and Juvenile Justice, 1938–1968." Ph.D. diss., University of California, Berkeley, 2005.

Murch, Donna. "The Problem of the Occupational Color Line." Unpublished seminar paper, 1998.

———. "The Urban Promise of Black Power: African American Political Mobilization in Oakland and the East Bay, 1961–1977." Ph.D. diss., University of California, Berkeley, 2004.

———. "When the Panther Travels: Race, Migration, and Internal Diaspora in the History of the BPP, 1964–1972." Unpublished article, 2008.

Newton, Huey P. "War against the Panthers: A Study of Repression in America." Ph.D. diss., University of California, Santa Cruz, 1980.

Oden, Robert Stanley. "Power Shift: A Sociological Study of the Political Incorporation of People of Color in Oakland, California, 1966–1996." Ph.D. diss., University of California, Santa Cruz, 1999.

Peck, Craig. "Educate to Liberate: The Black Panther Party and Political Education." Ph.D. diss., Stanford University, 2001.

Research Staff of the School of Criminology, University of California, Berkeley. "Oakland City College Workshop on Cultural Diversity." 1964.

Rhomberg, Christopher. "Social Movements in a Fragmented Society: Ethnic, Class and Racial Mobilization in Oakland, California, 1920–1970." Ph.D. diss., University of California, Berkeley, 1997.

Rice, Jon. "Black Radicalism on Chicago's West Side: A History of the Illinois Black Panther Party." Ph.D. diss., Northern Illinois University, 1998.

Rodriguez, Joseph A. "From Personal Politics to Party Politics: The Development of Black Leadership in Oakland, California, 1900–1950." M.A. thesis, University of California, Santa Cruz, 1983.

Salamunovich, Jill. "The Party and the People: Relations between the Black Panthers and the Oakland Community." A.B. thesis, University of California, Berkeley, 2000.

Smethurst, James. "The Black Arts Movement." Unpublished manuscript on Black Power and Black Arts, 2003, in possession of author.

Spencer, Jonathan. "Caught in Crossfire: Marcus Foster and America's Urban Education Crisis, 1941–1973." Ph.D. diss., New York University, 2002.

Spencer, Robyn Ceanne. "Repression Breeds Resistance: The Rise and Fall of the Black Panther Party in Oakland, CA, 1966–1982." Ph.D. diss., Columbia University, 2001.

Tate, Will Dean. "The New Black Urban Elites." Ph.D. diss, University of California, Berkeley, 1974.

Thompson, Heather. "Attica." Manuscript in progress, 2008.

———. "Rethinking 1968, the Year That Shook the World." Roundtable Presentation, annual meeting of the Organization of American Historians, March 28, 2008.

"Transcript from 40th Anniversary," Black Panther Party reunion, October 2006, in possession of author.

Umoja, Akinyele O. "Eye for an Eye: The Role of Armed Resistance in the Mississippi Freedom Movement." Ph.D. diss., Emory University, 1997.

Veatch, Laurelyn Lovett. "African Students in the United States: Their Political Attitudes and the Influence of the US on These Attitudes." M.A. thesis, University of California, Berkeley, 1968.

Walker, Dick. "Industry Builds the City: Suburbanization of Manufacturing in the San Francisco Bay Area, 1850–1940." Department of Geography, University of California, Berkeley, 1998.

Wilkins, Fanon Che. "'In the Belly of the Beast': Black Power, Anti-Imperialism, and the African Liberation Solidarity Movement, 1968–1975." Ph.D. diss., New York University, 2001.

Willard, Michael Nevin. "Urbanization as Culture: Youth and Race in Postwar Los Angeles." Ph.D. diss., University of Minnesota, 2001.

Wilson, Joel. "'Free Huey': The Black Panther Party, the Peace and Freedom Party, and the Politics of Race in 1968." Ph.D. diss., University of California, Santa Cruz, 2002.

Wu, Ellen. "Race and Asian American Citizenship from World War II to the Movement," Ph.D. diss., University of Chicago, 2006.

INDEX

Abron, Jo Nina, 225

Acorn Housing, 47, 204

Africa, 52, 66, 75, 78, 80, 82–83, 85–86, 96, 111, 249 (n. 60), 250 (n. 95), 253 (n. 47)

African American population of Oakland and the East Bay, 2, 24; average age, 19, 59; backlash against, 59, 65, 230; concentration in West Oakland, 26; and deindustrialization, 37; origins, 19; politicization, 51, 197, 200; proximity to local universities, 8, 72; rapid growth, 4, 16, 30, 63, 232; and students, 80, 89, 105

African Americans: churches, 8–10, 17, 20, 23, 28–29, 39–40, 43, 45, 62, 84, 109, 121, 162–63, 169, 172–74, 180, 183, 185, 190, 199, 210, 212, 229–30; and civil rights, 4–5, 10, 17, 32–35, 39, 49–52, 68, 76–77, 81–82, 87–88, 99, 111, 119–20, 123–25, 137, 150, 163, 166–67, 170–72, 195, 234; criminalization and incarceration of, 64, 67–68, 134, 164–68, 229–33, 263 (nn. 225, 226, 228) (*see also* Associated Agencies of Oakland; California Youth Authority; Juvenile delinquency; Law enforcement; Police); and education, 7–11, 19–20, 24, 42, 48–58, 74–75, 91–93, 97–116, 135, 141, 154, 167, 178–83, 190, 217, 232–33, 235, 239 (n. 21); and electoral politics and local government, 4, 16–17, 39, 41, 48, 51, 59–62, 67, 134, 138, 191–222, 226–28, 258 (n. 142) (*see also* Black Panther Party: and election campaigns); and housing discrimination, 50, 230; and job discrimination, 31–37, 55, 67

Afro-American Association, 5, 7–9; and BPP, 126, 133, 135, 137, 160, 166, 201, 210,

214, 229, 232, 234, 238 (n. 9), 273 (n. 101); and Black Power, 72–73, 239–40 (n. 25); concept of blackness, 85–86; and electoral politics, 198–200, 210, 214, 239 (n. 20); expansion beyond Berkeley, 88–90, 93–96; founding, 71–85; ideology, 86–87; and Merritt College, 97, 105–11, 116; and street speaking, 7, 72, 89–92, 106, 108, 111, 133, 206, 233

Ahmad, Muhammad. *See* Stanford, Max

Ahmad, Sultan. *See* Smith, Herman

Allen, Ernest, 90, 95, 105, 111–12

American Federation of Labor (AFL), 33, 35

Anticommunism, 175–76. *See also* Marxism

Antiwar activism, 122, 136, 156, 159, 160, 161, 184

Aoki, Richard, 132, 139

Armed self-defense, 237–38 (n. 3); and BPP, 133–34, 148, 150–51, 167, 169, 183, 187, 267 (n. 43); and campus activism, 8, 109, 127; and RAM, 144; and southern origins, 6, 9, 44, 120–21, 137, 229, 240 (n. 28)

Asian Americans, 203

Associated Agencies of Oakland (AA), 59–64

Avakian, Bob, 156

Axelrod, Beverly, 144

Baldwin, James, 85

Baraka, Amiri, 195

Bazille, Leo, 8, 111–12

Berkeley, Calif., 2, 5, 14, 24–26, 34, 37, 44, 51, 76, 93, 126, 132, 146, 156, 160, 162, 172–73, 179, 198–99, 201, 203, 208, 210, 212, 214, 217

Berkeley, Tom, 102, 209–10, 272 (n. 67)

Beth Eden Baptist Church, 23

Black House, 212

Black Liberation Army (BLA), 187

Black nationalism, 72, 85, 87, 99, 111, 196, 237
(n. 3). *See also* Afro-American Association; Malcolm X; Nation of Islam

Black Panther, 10, 146, 154–55, 162, 171, 175,
178, 184–86, 188–89, 196, 203–4, 209,
259–60 (n. 169), 267 (n. 61)

Black Panther Party (BPP): and Afro-
American Association, 72–73, 94, 97, 160;
and antiwar movement, 153, 160; art of
(*see* Douglas, Emory); and black student
movement, 5, 126–27, 141–43, 154–60, 167,
212–13, 215–20, 234; breakfast and food
programs, 10, 171–72, 174–75, 179–80,
184, 185, 201, 264 (n. 2); Central Committee, 152, 157, 179, 185–86, 188, 203–4,
217, 222–23, 226, 234, 259 (n. 163); and
coalition politics, 138, 149, 152–53, 156–61,
192, 202–3, 211, 221, 260 (nn. 178, 185), 261
(n. 195); and colleges and universities, 142,
160, 212, 234; decline and fall, 221–28; and
election campaigns, 158–59, 191–228; and
incarceration, 9, 67, 121, 134, 149, 151–53,
165–68, 177–78, 185, 187–89, 224, 230–32,
261 (n. 191), 263 (nn. 225–27), 264 (n. 233);
internationalism of, 5, 154–55, 157, 183,
186, 188, 192–94, 202, 238 (n. 11); liberation schools, 177, 180–81, 268 (n. 82) (*see
also* Oakland Community School); and
lumpen proletariat, 67–68, 126, 133–34,
137, 141, 145, 159, 211, 217, 223, 229, 234,
261 (n. 194); and Malcolm X, 116, 126–27,
130–32, 142, 145, 165, 186, 255 (n. 46);
March on Sacramento, 6, 137, 145–48,
151, 167, 191, 234; and media, 94, 147–49,
151, 154–55, 168, 170, 184, 191, 203, 206–7,
233–35; and military veterans, 139–41;
name change, 259 (n. 154); and Nation of
Islam, 127–31, 133, 143, 166, 209; newspaper
(see *Black Panther*); Oakland Community
School, 178, 181–83, 225, 230, 267 (n. 43);
and police patrols, 7, 9, 131–36, 144, 148,
166, 169, 172, 178, 181, 183, 185, 198, 206, 233
(*see also* Armed self-defense); and political education, 10, 135, 148, 154, 169, 178–80,

190, 203–5, 223, 233, 235; and poverty programs, 127, 137, 172, 194, 198, 203, 235; rank
and file, 6, 35, 145, 155, 162, 168, 174, 176,
179, 187–88, 190, 194, 218, 221–24, 226, 228,
235, 274 (n. 142); recruitment, 132–42, 151,
155, 234; regional differences, 151, 186–87,
234–35; rivals, 5, 121, 125–27, 142–44, 187,
257 (n. 115), 273 (n. 101); and SNCC, 120,
123–25, 143, 155–60, 205, 255 (n. 28), 257
(n. 114), 260–61 (nn. 184–86), 269 (n. 101);
and southern origins, 5–7, 120–21, 123–25,
229, 237 (n. 3); split in, 165, 184–90; state
repression of, 144, 151, 160, 164, 166,
169–71, 174, 178, 189–90, 224, 231–32 (*see
also* COINTELPRO; Law enforcement);
survival programs, 64, 148, 174–76, 178,
183–84, 189, 191, 200, 204, 208–10, 214,
220, 230, 271 (n. 51); Ten Point Program,
127–30, 158, 169; and women, 10, 148, 169,
172, 176–78, 185, 188, 190, 192, 201, 211, 248
(n. 29), 264 (n. 233), 265 (n. 5), 266 (n. 33)

Black Panther Party for Self Defense
(BPPSD), 5, 68, 73, 97, 100, 119, 121, 127, 131,
137, 144, 147, 259 (n. 154)

Black Panther Party of Northern California
(BPPNC), 5, 142–43, 219

Black Power movement: in Bay Area and
California, 9, 72, 97, 119, 159–60, 218, 229,
235, 237 (n. 3), 250 (n. 86), 261 (n. 195);
origins, 3–6, 8. *See also* Afro-American
Association; Black Panther Party; Black
radicalism

Black radicalism, 3–11, 76, 99, 101, 122, 157,
166, 197, 210, 229, 234, 238 (nn. 5, 6), 239
(n. 21)

Black Student Alliance (BSA), 212, 222

Black student movement, 73, 126, 228, 234.
See also Afro-American Association;
Black Panther Party; Black students;
Merritt College

Black students: college, 71–75, 79–85, 89,
96–99, 101–16, 160, 212, 215–20, 228, 238
(n. 9), 248 (n. 49); grades K-12, 5, 48–58,
146, 178–83; unions (BSUs), 99, 212–13,
220, 228. *See also* Education

Black Studies, 8, 73, 85, 87, 98–101, 103–4, 108,

111–16, 119, 141, 167, 179, 180, 216, 220, 232–33, 239–40 (nn. 17, 19, 21, 25), 253 (n. 60)

Blake, J. Herman, 76, 83

Bradford, Amory, 125

Breakfast programs. *See* Black Panther Party: breakfast and food programs

Brotherhood of Sleeping Car Porters (BSCP), 17, 22, 26, 31–33, 198. *See also* Dellums, C. L.

Brown, Elaine: childhood, 221; election campaign, 195, 201–2, 206–8, 211–15; entry into BPP, 222; exchange with Alice Walker, 263 (n. 22); as head of BPP, 221–28; and Panther schools, 182

Brown, H. Rap, 156

Brown, James, 93

Brown, Willie, 192

Building and carpentry trades, 20, 101

California: community colleges, 7–8, 103, 166, 212–13, 239 (n. 17), 240 (n. 25); and defense industries, 7, 15–16, 44, 31, 229–30; higher education, 5, 7–8, 74, 97–100, 103, 114, 229, 233, 239 (nn. 17, 21); as most populous state, 74

California Fair Employment Practice Commission (CAFEPC), 52, 55–57

California Master Plan for Higher Education, 7–8, 74, 97–98, 105, 232, 239 (n. 17)

California Voice, 27, 208

California Youth Authority (CYA), 42, 46, 48, 58–60, 64–67, 134, 145, 165, 219, 230, 234, 247 (nn. 102, 114)

Carceral state, 4, 67, 153, 165, 167, 169, 227, 229–33, 263 (nn. 225, 228)

Carmichael, Stokely (Kwame Ture), 123, 143, 156–60, 219, 260 (n. 185), 261 (n. 187)

Carter, Alprentice "Bunchy," 162, 177, 187, 222, 262 (n. 209)

Carter, Glen, 162

Castlemont High School, 54, 125, 163

Castro, Fidel, 76, 83, 234

Chicago, Ill., 41, 76, 85, 142, 162, 167, 170–72, 179, 184, 195, 217, 235

Church Committee, 161, 167, 226

City council, Oakland, 59, 93, 111; and BPP, 9, 191, 194, 203, 214–15, 221; city-wide elections, 205

Civil rights, 4, 10, 17, 68, 237 (n. 3); in Berkeley, 34, 210; and BPP, 123–25, 149, 163, 166–67, 170–72, 190, 195, 210; and Black Power, 99–100, 119–20, 195; criticism of, 76–77, 81–82, 87–88, 92; in Oakland, 52, 31–37, 124–25; and police, 39; and schools, 49–58

Civil Rights Act of 1964, 120

Civil Rights Congress (CRC), 39

Clark, Ramsey, 171

Cleaver, Eldridge: early activism with BPP, 153–54, 158–60, 261 (n. 193); on gender and "pussy power," 178, 264 (n. 233); incarceration of, 66–68, 144–45, 232, 263 (nn. 226, 227), 264 (n. 231); journalist and writer, 147, 261 (n. 194); shoot out with police, 162–68; and split in BPP, 184, 186–89, 193

Cleaver, Kathleen (originally Kathleen Neal), 151–52, 157–58, 161–62, 176, 235, 266 (n. 33)

COINTELPRO, 161, 168, 170, 184, 189, 262 (n. 209), 265 (n. 9)

Cold War, 37, 42, 60, 73–74, 80, 171, 229, 233

Comfort, Mark, 124–25, 132, 145–47, 150–51

Communist Party, 151. *See also* Radicalism

Community alert patrol, 132

Congressional Black Caucus (CBC), 195

Congress of Industrial Organizations (CIO), 21, 249 (n. 66)

Congress of Racial Equality (CORE), 94, 106, 124

Cordonices Village, 44

Cuba, 9, 75, 82, 109–10, 234

Culture of poverty, 66

Deacons for Defense, 120, 225 (n. 46)

Decolonization, 6, 73, 80, 95–96, 108, 130, 133, 249 (n. 60), 250 (n. 95)

DeFremery Park, 46, 191, 202; Recreation Center, 52, 61–63, 158, 245 (n. 52); renamed Bobby Hutton Park, 140, 165, 245 (n. 29)

Deindustrialization, 17, 37–38, 66–67, 131, 229

Dellums, C. L., 22, 26–27, 31–37, 55, 57, 198

Dellums, Ronald, 62–63, 93, 95, 102, 156, 160, 195–96, 199, 202, 208, 210, 221, 239 (n. 20)

Democratic Party, 123, 195, 208, 215, 222

Douglas, Emory, 65–66, 136, 138, 144, 147, 150, 152–56, 166, 219

Dowell, Denzil, 145

Downs Memorial Church, 93, 106, 172–73

East Bay Democratic Club, 198

East Oakland, 25, 46, 57–58, 105, 124–25, 151, 163, 182–83, 201, 205

Economic Development Administration, 125

Education, 7–11, 19–20, 24, 42, 48–58, 74–75, 91–93, 97–116, 135, 141, 154, 167, 178–83, 190, 217, 232–33, 235, 239 (nn. 17, 21). *See also* Black students

Eggleston, Lennair, 132

Employment discrimination, 31–37, 55, 67

Everett, Ronald. *See* Karenga, Maulana

Fair Employment Practices Commission (FEPC), 31, 33. *See also* California Fair Employment Practice Commission

Fanon, Frantz, 133–34

Federal Bureau of Investigation (FBI), 58, 144, 160–62, 166–68, 171, 184–88, 265 (n. 9), 266 (n. 33)

Ford Foundation, 40, 64, 125, 171

Forman, James, 260 (n. 185)

Frazier, E. Franklin, 78, 86–87, 173, 250 (n. 68)

Free Breakfast for Children Program. *See* Black Panther Party: breakfast and food programs

Freedom of Information Act (FOIA), 161

Freeman, Jo, 75

Freeman, Kenneth, 142

Free Speech Movement, 72, 75, 136, 160, 247 (n. 2)

Frey, John, 148–49, 168, 172

Garry, Charles, 211

Garvey, Marcus, 82, 84, 86, 186

Gary convention. *See* National Black Political Convention

Great Society, 10, 64, 113, 121, 174–75

Grillo, Evelio, 42, 59, 244 (n. 1)

Grove Street College, 97, 212, 216–19. *See also* Merritt College

Guevara, Che, 255 (n. 46)

Hampton, Fred, 7, 167, 170–71, 175

Harris, Elihu, 1, 95

Herskovits, Melville, 86–87, 250 (n. 95)

Hewitt, Ray "Masai," 140, 223

Hewitt, Shirley, 224

Higher education. *See* Education

Hilliard, David, 7, 142, 148, 166, 184–85, 193, 231, 264 (n. 231)

Hilliard, June, 132

Ho Chi Minh, 234

Hoover, J. Edgar, 58, 160–61, 168, 183–86, 226

Hopkins, Donald, 71–72, 79, 89, 95, 196, 198–99, 210

Houlihan, John, 125

Housing discrimination, 50, 230

Howard, Elbert "Big Man," 139, 167, 219

Howard University, 75, 78, 80

Huggins, Ericka, 176–79, 181–82, 203, 225, 266, 278, 294

Hulett, John, 120, 123

Hutton, Robert (Lil' Bobby), 137, 147, 164–66, 168, 170, 189, 202, 245 (n. 29)

Intercommunalism, 192–94, 234

Intercommunal Youth Institute (IYI), 178–82, 222, 267 (n. 61). *See also* Oakland Community School

Internal colonization thesis, 133

Jackman, Marvin (Marvin X), 112

Jackson, George, 193, 232, 263 (n. 226)

Jackson, Jesse, 192, 195

Jennings, Bill (Billy X), 275

Ji Jaga. *See* Pratt, Geronimo

Jim Crow, 9, 31, 53, 75, 120, 230–31

Joblessness, 67, 202. *See also* Unemployment

Johnson, Charles, 15, 20, 33, 50, 53, 87

Johnson, Deborah (Akua Njeri), 175

Johnson, Lyndon, 121, 150

Jones, Leroi. *See* Baraka, Amiri

Jonesboro, La., 120
Juvenile delinquency, 42, 48–50, 58–68, 165,
263 (nn. 226, 227)

Kaiser Hospital, 149
Kaiser shipyards, 16, 27, 32–36, 51, 115
Karenga, Maulana, 72, 94–95, 239–40 (n. 25)
Kerr, Clark, 73–74
Key System, 34–35
King, Coretta Scott, 192, 195
King, Martin Luther, Jr., 82, 93, 109, 163–64,
172, 228, 262 (n. 216)
Knowland, Joseph, 51, 197, 204, 258 (n. 142)
Knowland, William F. (Bill), 27, 51, 125, 197,
204, 255 (n. 31), 258 (n. 142), 270 (n. 28)

Labor movement. *See* African Americans:
and job discrimination; American Federation of Labor; Congress of Industrial
Organizations; Organized labor
Laney College, 100–101, 141, 212–13
Latinos, 182, 203, 211
Law enforcement: attempts to desegregate,
39; conflict with BPP, 9–10, 121, 133–34,
139, 144–49, 153, 160–72, 184–90, 192, 197,
218, 245 (n. 29), 247 (n. 112), 258 (n. 142),
259 (n. 159), 262 (n. 215), 263 (nn. 225, 226);
criminalization of black youth, 9, 42,
58–68; East Bay, 64–65; harassment of
African Americans, 7, 9, 38–40, 47, 64,
120, 133–34, 125, 153; local and federal, 58,
161, 184. *See also* Black Panther Party;
Federal Bureau of Investigation;
Oakland Police Department; Police;
Police brutality
Liberalism, 7, 75, 93, 232–33
Liberation schools. *See* Black Panther Party:
liberation schools
Little Red Book, 132, 142, 270 (n. 77)
Los Angeles, Calif., 8, 16–17, 24, 38, 49, 51,
66, 67, 72, 99, 120–21, 142, 162, 176, 177, 187,
204, 214, 221–23, 228, 235, 237 (n. 3), 244
(n. 27), 255 (n. 24), 263 (n. 225)
Louisiana, 21, 26–29, 42–43, 45, 53, 55, 103,
109, 120, 151, 187, 229, 232, 255 (n. 46)
Love, Bill, 102

Lowndes County (Ala.) Freedom Organiza-
tion (LCFO), 120–21, 123–24
Lumpen proletariat. *See* Black Panther
Party: and lumpen proletariat
Lumumba, Patrice, 76

Machel, Samora, 193, 234
Malcolm X, 4, 82, 116, 249 (n. 66); and Afro-
American Association, 71, 73, 76, 83–84,
92, 94, 106, 116; and BPP, 130–31, 165, 186
Mansour, Khalid al-. *See* Warden, Donald
Maoism, 6
Mao Tse-tung, 132, 142
Marxism, 8, 79, 106, 109, 134–35, 157–58, 183
Master Plan. *See* California Master Plan for
Higher Education
Maximum feasible participation, 113, 174
McClymonds High School, 49, 52–58, 94,
245 (n. 52)
McKinney, Gene, 148
Media, 29, 75, 77, 94–96, 99, 123, 156, 184. *See
also* Black Panther Party: and media
Men of Tomorrow, 198
Merritt College, 97–116; and Afro-American
Association, 91, 97, 105–11, 116; and BPP,
100–101, 119, 126–27, 132, 135, 137, 142–43,
166–67, 216–21, 228, 232, 235; and Black
Studies, 111–16, 239–40 (n. 25); importance of, 8–9, 100. *See also* Black students
Mexican Americans, 46, 50, 159, 192, 211
Migrants. *See* Migration
Migration (southern), 10–11; backlash
against, 30–31, 38, 40, 42, 48–51, 59, 137,
139, 230–31; chain, 4, 16, 43–44; and
churches, 24, 28–29, 46; and criminalization, 38, 64; and education, 24, 56–58,
75, 97–99, 102–6, 160, 179, 216, 229, 235;
and electoral politics, 194, 205, 207–8,
226–27; and escaping segregation, 24; and
gender, 45–47; Great Migration, 16; and
juvenile delinquency, 42, 48–50, 58–68,
165, 263 (nn. 226, 227); links to BPP and
Black Power, 3–11, 72, 121, 137, 164, 169,
237 (n. 3), 238 (n. 6); and "Living for the
City," 3–4, 230; and mechanization of agriculture, 16–19; and militancy, 4, 68, 121;

negative images of, 11; and newcomers vs. oldtimers, 30–31, 130, 238 (n. 7); "political migration," 176, 204; postwar, 15–16, 40, 41, 44, 240 (n. 4); push and pull factors in, 17; rural-urban, 20, 44, 241 (n. 29); and scholarship, 11; wartime, 15–21, 25–37, 41, 44–45; of whites, 121; and youth, 4–11, 41–68, 103, 121, 193, 216

Miranda, Douglas, 217–18

Muhammad, Elijah, 71, 81, 84

Mulford Act, 148

NAACP. *See* National Association for the Advancement of Colored People

Napier, Sam, 155, 267 (n. 61)

National Association for the Advancement of Colored People (NAACP), 17, 22, 34–35, 49, 51, 106, 150, 152, 198; support for BPP, 171; U.C. Berkeley student chapter, 71, 76–77, 80, 82–83, 89, 93–94

National Black Political Convention, 192, 195–96

National Committee to Combat Fascism (NCCF), 217

Nation of Islam, 62, 73, 81–83, 85, 90, 106, 120, 127, 130–31, 133, 143, 166, 249 (n. 66), 265 (n. 9)

Neil, Father Earl, 163, 172–73, 210

New Left, 6, 144, 159–61. *See also* Black Panther Party; Peace and Freedom Party

New Orleans, La., 20, 59, 151, 187

Newton, Huey: ambivalence about March on Sacramento, 147–48; and Afro-American Association, 72, 93, 95, 248–49 (n. 45); childhood, 45, 47–48, 55, 104, 179, 233; conflict with "Grove Street" activists, 218–20; decline of, 221–26, 228; founding of BPP, 5, 119, 131–36, 143–44, 234; and "Free Huey" campaign, 160–61; incarceration of, 67, 125–26, 162, 166–68, 176, 187, 232, 263 (n. 226), 264 (n. 231); as intellectual, 92, 119–20, 134–36, 192–94; and Merritt College, 8, 103, 109, 112, 116, 218–20; outreach to women, gays and lesbians, 192, 211; shoot out with John Frey, 148–49,

168, 172; on state repression, 184; turn to survival programs, 183–89, 233, 271 (n. 51)

Newton, Walter, 21, 45

Nichols, Bishop Roy, 83, 93, 94

Nixon, Richard, 171, 174, 184–85, 266 (n. 26)

Njeri, Akua. *See* Johnson, Deborah

Nkrumah, Kwame, 95

Oakland Army Base, 122

Oakland City College. *See* Merritt College

Oakland Community School, 178, 181–83, 225, 267 (n. 43)

Oakland Police Department, 38–39, 60, 64, 121, 134, 136, 140, 148, 163–64, 218. *See also* Law enforcement

Oakland Post, 102, 198, 208, 210, 272 (n. 67)

Oakland Recreation Department, 61–64

Oakland Technical High School, 163

Oakland Tribune, 27, 86, 89, 124, 197, 220, 258 (n. 142)

Office of Economic Opportunity (OEO), 40, 266 (n. 26)

Organized labor, 35, 37. *See also* American Federation of Labor; Brotherhood of Sleeping Car Porters; Building and carpentry trades; Congress of Industrial Organizations

Panthers. *See* Black Panther Party

Peace and Freedom Party, 157

Pentecostals, 7, 9, 28, 96, 109

People's Revolutionary Constitutional Convention, 175

Piedmont, Calif., 146

Pittman, Tarea Hall, 198

Pointer, Fritz, 28–29, 45–46, 48, 66, 219–20

Police, 3–4, 6–7, 9, 16, 27, 38–40, 41, 47–48, 59–60, 64–66, 68, 119, 124–27, 130–50, 153, 160–72, 183–85, 187, 190, 192, 194, 214, 217–18, 226–27, 230, 232–33, 235, 254 (n. 13), 259 (n. 159), 262 (n. 215). *See also* Law enforcement; Oakland Police Department

Police brutality, 38, 119, 121, 126, 130–34, 146, 149, 162, 211, 213, 227

Port of Oakland, 202, 214

Poverty, 10, 11, 17, 37, 40, 42, 49, 66–67, 92, 95, 103–5, 120, 122, 170, 172, 174–76, 202, 206

Poverty programs, 62, 127, 137, 194, 198, 203, 209, 235, 254 (n. 1)

Pratt, Geronimo (Ji Jaga), 7, 140, 187–88, 240 (n. 28)

Preston School of Industry, 48, 65

Public housing, 25–26, 32, 44, 46–47, 95, 185

Pullman porters, 22–23, 30, 37. *See also* Brotherhood of Sleeping Car Porters

Racial segregation. *See* Segregation

Radicalism, 122, 135, 153, 157, 202. *See also* Black Panther Party; Black Power movement; Black radicalism

Ramparts, 122, 144, 147, 166, 176

Randolph, A. Philip, 35

Reading, John, 198, 214–15

Reagan, Ronald, 147, 174, 261 (n. 193), 266 (n. 26)

Red Book. See *Little Red Book*

Republican Party, 27, 51, 52, 61–62, 146, 174, 197–200, 205, 210, 214, 258 (n. 142)

Restrictive covenants, 23, 31

Revolutionary Action Movement (RAM), 5, 126–27, 135, 143–44, 187, 239 (n. 21), 257 (n. 115), 265 (n. 9)

Richmond, Calif., 26, 29, 32, 36–37, 39, 51, 73, 90–91, 115, 132, 145–46, 151, 172, 179, 185, 198, 241 (n. 29)

Riots. *See* Urban rebellions

Roach, Max, 90

Robinson, Cedric, 82–83, 95

Rose, Joshua, 30

Rumford, William Byron, 34, 61, 63, 198–99

Rumsfeld, Donald, 266 (n. 26)

Rush, Bobby, 7, 204

Russell, Andre, 139–40, 216–18

St. Augustine's Episcopal Church, 163, 172–73, 191, 210, 264 (n. 2)

San Francisco, Calif., 22, 31, 33, 37, 43, 51, 62, 66, 72–73, 81, 90–91, 112, 134, 144, 149, 151, 155, 160, 179–80, 185–86, 192

San Francisco State University, 8, 72, 86, 88, 90, 100–101, 105, 115, 141, 239 (n. 17), 240 (n. 25)

San Jose, Calif., 104, 268 (n. 82)

San Leandro, Calif., 47

Seale, Artie, 162

Seale, Bobby: and Afro-American Association, 95; arrest and incarceration of, 162, 166–68, 177, 263 (n. 226); childhood, 44–45, 233; departure from BPP, 222–25; founding of BPP, 7, 119–20, 124–33, 255 (n. 28); on intercommunalism, 194; leads March on Sacramento, 147; media portrayal of, 191–92; and Merritt College, 8, 106, 111–12, 125–27, 142–43, 219–20, 273 (n. 114); military service of, 139, 167; and National Black Political Convention, 195–96; political campaigns, 158, 191–92, 200–202, 206–15, 219, 226–28, 271 (n. 51); and survival programs, 10, 171–72, 174, 180, 200

Seale, John, 140, 203

Segregation: 30, 39, 43, 75, 78–79, 81, 87–88, 92, 121, 226; housing, 24–25, 28; school, 49–58, 67

Self-determination, 95, 169, 192, 234

Shabazz, Betty, 142–44

Smith, Herman (Sultan Ahmad), 203–6

Smith, Norvel, 24, 216, 218

Soul Students Advisory Council (SSAC), 5, 112, 126, 130, 135, 139, 143

Southern Christian Leadership Conference (SCLC), 152, 195

Southern culture, 31

Southern diaspora, 7, 16, 27, 29, 40, 72, 97, 176, 190, 231, 235

Southern migration. *See* Migration

Stanford, Max (Muhammad Ahmad), 144

Student Committee for Travel to Cuba (SCTC), 9, 109–10

Students for a Democratic Society (SDS), 124, 188

Student Nonviolent Coordinating Committee (SNCC), 119, 151–52, 156–60, 205, 255 (n. 28), 257 (n. 114), 260 (nn. 184, 185), 261 (n. 186), 265 (n. 9), 269 (n. 101)

Suburbanization, 17, 112, 148, 214
Sun Ra, 182

Telegraph Avenue, 79
Ten Point Program. *See* Black Panther Party:
   Ten Point Program
Till, Emmett, 4
Ture, Kwame. *See* Carmichael, Stokely

Unemployment, 17, 37–38, 40, 42, 67, 119, 122,
   131, 206. *See also* Joblessness
United Front Against Fascism Conference,
   161
United Nations, 76
University of California at Berkeley: and
   African students, 80, 82–83, 96; and BPP,
   159; Black Power conference, 124; and
   campus radicalism, 71–75, 83, 100–101;
   growth in student body, 74; importance
   for Black Power and Black Studies, 9; and
   national defense, 122, 229; and Malcolm
   X, 71, 73, 76, 83–84, 106, 119; proximity
   to black neighborhoods, 8. *See also* Afro-
   American Association; Black student
   movement; Black students; Kerr, Clark
University of California at Los Angeles, 177,
   187, 222, 262 (n. 209)
University of California system, 75, 98,
   113–14, 116. *See also* California Master Plan
   for Higher Education
Urban League, 61, 94, 171
Urban rebellions, 72, 144, 153, 164, 167. *See
   also* Watts
Urban renewal, 203
US organization, 72, 142–43, 177, 239 (n. 25),
   257 (n. 113), 262 (n. 209)

Veterans, 84, 100, 111, 139–40, 257 (n. 100)
Vietnam War, 122, 153, 203

Warden, Donald (Khalid al-Mansour): and
   Black Studies, 108, 111, 116; childhood,
   77–78; conflict with Newton and BPP,
   248–49 (n. 45), 257 (n. 114); and "Dignity

Clothes," 107; experience at Howard,
   78; founding of Afro-American Association, 71–72, 75–90, 93–94, 96; organizing
   economically marginal, 90, 95, 133, 146;
   outreach to celebrities, 93, 251 (n. 126);
   street speaking, 90–92; view of economic
   uplift, 108
War on Poverty, 122
Watts (Los Angeles), 5, 66, 255 (n. 24); Black
   Panther Political Party of, 121; rebellion,
   5, 9, 72–73, 92, 94, 119, 121–22, 132, 167, 237
   (n. 3)
Watts, Daniel, 248 (n. 27)
Weather Underground Organization
   (Weathermen), 188
Welfare, 10, 59, 62–63, 122, 172, 174–76, 189–
   90, 195, 209, 233, 266 (n. 26)
Welfare rights, 170, 175, 201, 266 (n. 27)
West Oakland: and black public sphere, 90;
   decline of, 122, 203–4; mosque, 81, 83, 130;
   political significance of, 198, 202; schools,
   53–54; settlement of, 21–30, 43, 58; signifi-
   cance for Afro-American Association,
   94–95; and youth culture, 45–47, 61–62
West Oakland Church of God, 28–29, 46
West Oakland Planning Committee, 203,
   221, 271 (n. 52)
Wilkins, Roy, 57, 76, 82, 171, 201, 210, 272
   (n. 67)
Williams, Anne, 8–9, 42–43, 45, 108–11
Williams, Landon, 131, 140, 174
Williams, Robert, F., 73, 76, 82–83, 89–90,
   110, 140, 144
Wilson, Lionel, 27, 162, 215, 221, 227
Women, 81, 95, 109, 148, 221; in campus and
   youth culture, 45, 79, 109; in migrant
   community, 19, 27–28, 53, 61–62; in war
   effort, 19; white, 38, 84, 161. *See also* Black
   Panther Party: and women
Wonder, Stevie, 3, 230
World War II, 4–5, 15, 17, 21, 24–37, 40–41,
   44, 50, 58, 65, 68, 82, 139, 198, 232, 241
   (n. 29)